THE WAR DIARY OF
THE MASTER OF BELHAVEN
1914—1918

THE WAR DIARY OF
THE MASTER OF BELHAVEN
1914—1918

WITH FRONTISPIECE AND MAPS

LONDON
JOHN MURRAY, ALBEMARLE STREET, W.
1924

FIRST EDITION . . *October,* 1924
Reprinted . . *December,* 1924

PREFACE

THE writer of these notes, Lieut.-Col. the Hon. Ralph Gerard Alexander Hamilton, Master of Belhaven, was the only son of the 10th Lord Belhaven and Stenton. He was born on 22nd February, 1883, and educated at Eton and Sandhurst.

He served throughout the war in France and Flanders, and was on leave when the German offensive started on 21st March, but hurriedly returned, and was killed during the defence of the Avre, near Amiens, whilst commanding the 106th Brigade of the Royal Field Artillery, on Easter Sunday, 31st March, 1918, and was buried in the village cemetery at Rouvrel, near Castel.

This diary was constantly written up, day and night, as opportunity offered, and often under great difficulties, and was periodically sent home for typing and preservation.

The maps are drawn from sketches made by himself.

He was twice mentioned in despatches, twice recommended for the D.S.O., and received the Croix de Guerre—avec palme.

LIEUT.-COLONEL THE HON. R. G. A. HAMILTON, MASTER
OF BELHAVEN, 1918 .   . *Photogravure Frontispiece*

LIST OF MAPS

viii LIST OF MAPS

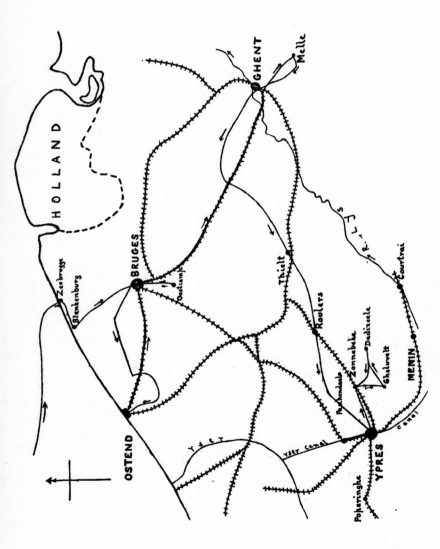

ROUTE OF THE 7ᵀᴴ DIVISION, OCT. 1914.

THE WAR DIARY OF
THE MASTER OF BELHAVEN

WHEN war was declared I was in command of the Essex Horse Artillery, and remained with them all August and September. When I found that there was no chance of my battery going on active service, I hunted round to see in what possible capacity I could get out to the Front. I at last discovered that officers with a knowledge of French and German were being taken as interpreters, and with great difficulty I persuaded the War Office to accept me in this capacity.

At the end of September I was informed that I had been appointed interpreter with the 7th Division, then being formed, and was ordered to report myself immediately at Lyndhurst, near Southampton.

On arriving there, being a gunner, I was posted to the 22nd Field Artillery Brigade, commanded by Colonel Fasson.

On Sunday, the 4th October, we suddenly received orders to embark. The division marched to Southampton in ship-loads, but there was considerable confusion and my ship carried Headquarters 22nd Field Artillery, Headquarters 22nd Infantry Brigade, a Signal company, and half a battalion, besides various odds and ends.

We marched out from Lyndhurst at midnight on the 4th–5th and embarked at daylight on Monday, the 6th October. We sailed at 9 o'clock in the morning, without any knowledge of where we were going.

Our first orders were to call at the south side of the Isle of Wight, near Ventnor, after which we steered a course which we thought would bring us to Bordeaux. Great excitement prevailed on board all day as to where we were going, and we followed the course of the ship with our compasses and maps.

During the afternoon the ship suddenly turned about and headed straight up Channel. We now knew our destination could not be Bordeaux or St. Nazaire, and we felt sure it must be either Havre or Boulogne. Our astonishment can be imagined when late in the afternoon we again altered our course and headed north-west in the direction of England.

Soon after dark we came opposite the lights of a large town, which the captain informed us was Folkestone, and eventually came to anchor outside the harbour of Dover. Here we were met by an Admiralty tug, which told us to remain outside the harbour all night, at the same time giving us the cheering news that there were several German submarines in the neighbourhood.

The whole of the 6th we spent moored against the outside mole of Dover Harbour and we were unable to communicate with the shore.

Meanwhile, large numbers of other troopships arrived, and by the evening the whole division was concentrated in Dover Harbour.

As soon as it was dark we left the harbour and proceeded, with all lights out, in a northerly direction. It was a very strange sight to see this fleet of troopships steaming through the night, one behind the other, each with a torpedo destroyer on our northern side. The captain still did not know where we were going. We knew, however, that the British mine-field extended across the Channel and that we must be passing through it.

We spent another cold and very uncomfortable night on the deck of our boat, which, I may say, was a cattle-boat usually running between Canada and Liverpool. I believe these cattle-boats pride themselves on never washing their decks, and certainly it must have been many years since ours had indulged in such a luxury.

At dawn the next morning, the 7th, we found ourselves anchored off a low-lying coast and were told that we had arrived at Zeebrugge. None of us had ever heard of this place before, but we soon found it on the maps and discovered that we were on the Belgian-Dutch frontier. Zeebrugge has a very large mole extending half a mile into the sea, and there was room for five large transports to lie alongside at once.

We commenced landing about ten o'clock and quickly got our horses on shore. We then received orders to rendezvous—marching independently—at Oostcamp, a small village some five miles south of Bruges.

We arrived there, after a march of about twenty miles, just after dark. This march was one of the most extraordinary experiences I have ever had. The wretched Belgians, who for weeks had expected to be overrun by the Germans and treated in the usual Teuton manner, went absolutely mad at seeing the British troops. Passing through Blankenberg, we were fairly mobbed, and it was with the greatest difficulty that we forced our horses through the crowd, who pressed cigars, apples, and Belgian flags on us in thousands.

This continued all the way, and by the time we had passed through the streets of Bruges we looked more like a Bank Holiday crowd than soldiers. Every gun and waggon was decorated with large Belgian flags ; most of the men had given away their badges and numerals, and all were wearing flowers and ribbons of the Belgian colours. I shall never forget seeing Colonel Fasson riding at the head of his brigade, clutching an enormous apple in one hand, whilst the Belgian girls were stuffing cigars into his pockets.

My horse—whom I call Bucephalus, because of his carthorse-like appearance—was completely upset, and, the streets being very slippery, I expected him to come down at every moment.

By the time we reached Bruges it was dark, and, there being no staff officers or guides to show us the way to Oostcamp, I went on ahead of the column, with a small party, to find the way.

It was then, to my horror, that I discovered that neither French nor German was of the slightest use, as the language of the country was Flamande—a horrible mixture of bad Dutch and worse German.

We eventually arrived at Oostcamp and were told to go into billets. Our headquarters were in a large château belonging to Count ————. We were most hospitably received, and sat down to an excellent dinner with our hosts. The owner and his wife had fled to Paris, but the château was being used by his brother and sister-in-law, Count and Countess Henri ————. These latter had escaped from their own estate, which was near Liége, with the greatest difficulty, as the Germans entered their park from the other side. They had heard that the Germans had looted and burnt everything, but they were very pleased to have got away safely themselves. Their small boy, aged about twelve, told me with pride that he had been in the Belgian trenches whilst the Germans were bombarding them, and I am not at all sure that he had not been firing a rifle himself.

We expected to be given the next day to collect the rest of the brigade and get straight before advancing. We heard that the Germans were some thirty miles off, and that there was a line of Belgian outposts between us and them.

At 4 o'clock in the morning, 8th October, I was awakened by the adjutant, who came into my room and told me that orders had been received that we were to retire immediately, and, if possible, reach Ostend before night, no explanation of this manœuvre being given.

We started before dawn and, marching all day, we reached the canal three miles south-east of Ostend by 5 o'clock in the evening. The infantry took up an outpost line on the canal, on the line Oudebrugge-Zandvoorde-brugge-Plassehendaele, covering Ostend.

Early the next morning we marched into Ostend, and there received orders to entrain for a destination unknown. There are three stations at Ostend, and there were a large number of trains collected in the town; but the work of entraining a complete division, with all its horses, guns, transport, etc., was quite beyond the capacity of the

Belgian railway authorities. No progress was made all day. Although there were plenty of trains, they were all mixed up in an inextricable mass in the various sidings, the Belgian station-masters running up and down the platform like rabbits.

It was not until late in the afternoon, when Sir Percy Girouard took over the entire arrangement of the train services, that there appeared any chance of our ever getting away. My brigade entrained from the main station in the middle of the town, and when the train arrived for the guns and wagons the station-master told us that we could start loading. It had not apparently struck the idiot that it was impossible to entrain guns and wagons off a platform unless ramps were prepared.

With great difficulty we managed to get hold of a Belgian company of Engineers and tried to show them how to make a ramp at the end of the platform so that we could run our guns and wagons on to the train from the end. When it was explained to them what was wanted they appeared to understand, and, after a considerable time, they produced two baulks of wood, about forty feet long and strong enough to bear many elephants. They had dragged these up from the docks. With enormous difficulty, and after great delay, they made a magnificent ramp at the end of the platform. There was then a space of about a yard between the last truck and the end of the ramp. On the train being backed to close up this yard, it gave the gentlest possible tap to the end of the ramp, which promptly collapsed on to the ground.

Our patience being now exhausted, we bundled the whole of the Belgians out of the station and took charge of matters ourselves. It was not long before the ramp was re-erected and properly secured, and the entraining proceeded rapidly. About three in the morning we got off in train loads carrying a battery each.

Early the following morning, the 10th, we stopped at a station and found that, after all our tribulations—forced marches, etc.—we had arrived back again at Bruges, the place that we had left so hurriedly forty-eight hours before. Here we found thousands of British sailors and marines who had escaped from Antwerp; but we were told that some four thousand British marines had been cut off and that we were to go on at once and try to relieve them. Our train, therefore, proceeded and took us on to Ghent.

On arriving at the station, we were met by a Staff Officer, who told us to get out of the train as quickly as we could, as the Germans were attacking the town on the far side.

It did not take us long to detrain, and we at once posted off through the streets and out of Ghent in the direction of Melle. We could hear the guns firing quite close. The 22nd Brigade took up a position at Melle, covering the crossings of the Scheldt and facing east. However, except for desultory firing on the part of the Belgian artillery, nothing exciting happened that day.

At nightfall we withdrew a mile and billeted ourselves in a deserted château. I went on ahead to arrange about accommodation for the brigade headquarters, and found the château in darkness and all the doors locked. I was certain, however, that it was occupied, as I had seen a light in one of the windows as I rode up the drive. After hammering on the door for a long time, a window was opened upstairs and a servant put out his head and asked what we wanted. I explained that a party of British officers wished to pass the night in the château. The man was very uncivil, and said that he was not going to open the door for English or French or Belgians. I then addressed him in somewhat violent German, which he understood, and told him that, far from being French, British, or Belgians, we were the advance guard of the German Uhlans. This frightened him thoroughly, and he made great haste to open the door and place everything at our disposal. Our servants installed themselves in the kitchen, and soon a quite decent dinner was ready.

We had just finished dinner and were settling down for the night, when a terrific rifle fire broke out from the trenches immediately in front of us. This was our first experience of heavy firing, and most alarming it was in the darkness. The firing appeared to roll up and down the lines, sometimes dying down to a solitary shot, at other times being a continuous roar.

Gone were our visions of a comfortable night. Food baskets were packed up, horses saddled, and the brigade stood to arms. It was a very cold night, though fine, and we passed the remainder of the hours of darkness sleeping alongside the road with our horses' bridles through our arms.

In the morning we discovered that what had happened was as follows : The Germans had attacked the French sailors, who were on our left, more with the intention of finding out where they were than with any idea of assaulting, and had without difficulty been driven back. The French pursued the Germans with the bayonet and advanced some hundreds of yards in front of their position. Unfortunately, in returning to their trenches they did not return quite the way they came, and retired at an angle which brought them across the front of the Warwickshire Regiment, who were our left. This regiment, hearing advancing troops on them in the darkness, naturally assumed that they were Germans, and opened fire on them. The French sailors, who by this time had apparently lost all sense of direction, imagined that they were being attacked by Germans. Hence the terrific battle which disturbed our night's rest. Before the mistake was discovered many thousands of rounds must have been expended on both sides, and I regret to add that the total casualties were one man of the Warwickshires, who was slightly wounded in the foot.

Before dawn next morning (the 11th) we returned to our positions, and no sooner had we occupied them than two batteries of Belgian artillery trotted up on our flank and immediately started firing. We inquired of the Belgian officers what they were firing at, and were told " nothing." This struck us as peculiar, and, on asking the reason, we were told : " We always fire in the early morning and late in the evening just to let the Germans know we are there " !

All that day we remained in our positions, expecting to be attacked. We had no idea what force was in front of us, but it was variously estimated as being a few battalions of the German advance guard or several Army Corps. As a matter of fact, I believe that there were practically no Germans at all near us.

In the course of the morning we captured three prisoners, who were brought before me to be examined. I ascertained that they were men of the Landwehr, and that they belonged to a division which had just arrived from Antwerp. They had been lost in a wood during the previous night attack, and were very willing to tell me all they knew, but this did not amount to much. The quartermaster-sergeant of the brigade brought me a document which had been given to him that morning by a Belgian soldier. It was carefully sewn up in waterproof cloth and had been found in the lining of a German's tunic. It was very badly written, but, with the assistance of another interpreter, we managed to decipher it. It turned out to be a long and rambling account of an episode that happened in 1746, to the effect that a certain German count, having lost his temper with his servant, ordered him to be beheaded. The executioner duly tried to cut off his head, but the sword refused to cut. This surprised the Herr Graf, and he asked the culprit how it was that he was immune from the sword. The man replied that if the count would spare his life he would tell him his secret, which consisted of a number of cabalistic words. The count, being much interested, spared the man's life and ordered many copies of this formula to be written out and distributed among his people. Evidently the unfortunate German soldier of 1914 had hoped that the carrying of this talisman would protect him also.

That evening I believe there was a conference between General Rawlinson, General Capper, the Belgian Commander, and the French Admiral, who was in supreme command of this expedition. Our movements so far had not inspired any of us with great confidence, and it was decided that, Antwerp having fallen and the greater majority of our sailors and marines having safely got back to us, it would be better to withdraw as quickly as possible.

It must be remembered that our one division, with its allies—the Belgians and the "Marins français," who had never been on land before—was in a most precarious position, being practically in the heart of the enemy's country and without any supports nearer than the coast. We knew that the Germans were north, east, and south of us, and that they held the country from Ghent to Lille. A German advance from the direction of Courtrai or Roulers would have driven us back on the sea, and if this had been pressed in strength we should either have been driven into the sea or over the Dutch frontier.

It was decided that the Belgians and French should go first and that the 7th Division should cover their retirement. We took over their trenches in the afternoon of the 12th, and as soon as it was dark the whole division retired through Ghent.

The people of Ghent, who had received us with such joy as their saviours the previous day, were quite at a loss to understand why we were going back into the town, and it was most pathetic the way in which the townspeople anxiously asked us whether we thought there was any danger of the Germans arriving. It was very difficult to know how to answer them. We could not say there was no danger, and had we told them the truth—that the Germans would occupy the town within an hour of our leaving it—it would immediately have caused a panic, and the population fleeing from Ghent would have blocked the roads for us. As a matter of fact, the Germans entered the east side of the town as we left the west.

I shall never forget that night march. The column, which was of interminable length, was led by a staff officer in a motor. No smoking was allowed and no talking, as we knew the Germans must be close to us. On the other hand, the motor that was leading us could go only at a foot's pace and made enough noise to be heard ten

2

miles off. The men had been in the trenches all day, and had stood to arms the whole of the night before. They were, therefore, thoroughly tired before starting, and were marched without halting—except for five minutes at a time—from 7 in the evening until 7 o'clock the next morning.

Soon after daylight (13th October) we reached the village of Hansbeke, and were told to go into billets there. The village was already half full of French sailors, but we managed to cram in somehow. We were given only some four or five hours' rest and continued our retreat to Thielt, via Bellem, Aeltre, and Ruysselede. At Aeltre I saw my brother-in-law, Cochrane, for the first time since leaving England. He was in charge of the Scots Guards' transport, and seemed very cheerful.

All that day we heard alarming rumours that the Germans had forced the bridges of the canal at Nevele and Deyenze, which were on our left flank. The confusion at Thielt was something indescribable. The 7th Division, which had been marched on two different roads with the Belgians and French, all converged on Thielt, and it took us some two or three hours to get through the market square.

Our billets here were the worst that we had during the time I was out. We were in a horrible little dirty slum, and our headquarters was a small tobacconist's shop.

After a very uncomfortable night, we marched early the next morning (the 14th October) and in heavy rain proceeded to Roulers. This being a large town, we found much better accommodation, my headquarters being in a club. Here I was able to buy some eggs, chocolate, etc., and we sat down to a very comfortable dinner.

The next day (the 15th) we continued our retreat, and early in the afternoon reached Ypres. I went on ahead with my trumpeter to see about billeting, and was just in time to see two German officers, whose aeroplane had been brought down by our naval guns, brought into the town in a motor. The car was blocked in the street close to me,

Ypres
15th Oct.
1914

and I had an opportunity of seeing how the Belgians treat their captured prisoners. The two German officers were sitting in the back of a motor and in front of them was standing a French corporal. The latter was mad with excitement and was frantically waving an automatic pistol, which he was pointing at the heads of the unfortunate German officers and also continually waving round his head. He was screaming with excitement, like an irritated monkey at the Zoo. The street being thickly crowded with guns, transport, and troops, and his finger on the trigger, I expected every second that he would kill someone. A large crowd immediately collected round the car, and I thought at every moment that the German officers would be pulled to pieces. One " brave Belge " leaped on to the step of the motor and caught hold of one of the German officers by the collar and proceeded to shake him like a rat. This was more than my horse, Bucephalus, could stand.

That night we were billeted on a prosperous, bourgeois family who could not do enough for us. They gave us an excellent dinner with wines of every description, and, better than all, a hot bath—the first I had had since leaving Lyndhurst.

The next morning (the 16th) we started out in a south-western direction, and we imagined that we were to continue our retreat. However, we halted in a field a mile south of Ypres station, and remained there the whole day.

We now heard that it had been decided to take up a position round Ypres and protect it at all costs. Personally, I had a very agitated morning, as my trumpeter reported to me just before starting that his horse had disappeared. We hunted up and down the place, but could not find it. The loss was the more serious, as the horse carried everything Wellingham possessed, and also most of my maps and papers. However, later on in the morning Wellingham arrived with the horse, which he said he had found a man in another regiment calmly riding. This is a form of looting with which I have no patience, and had I been able to get the name of the man I would have exerted every effort to make matters extremely unpleasant for him. However, all's well that ends well, and I hoped that the fright he had had would make Wellingham very chary of leaving anything about in future.

In the evening we marched through Ypres again, and went into billets in an abandoned tobacco factory a mile north-east of the town. We had a strong force of Franch infantry round us, but, being a Territorial force, they did not inspire us with any very great confidence. There is no doubt that the French are a gallant race and fight magnificently. They have, however, a rather disconcerting habit of changing their dispositions in the night, without warning the troops on their flank.

Late that night we received orders that the 22nd Infantry Brigade, supported by the 22nd Field Artillery Brigade, would take the village of Zonnebeke by assault before dawn. We now felt that we were really in for it. Hitherto we had marched from the extreme north to the extreme south of Belgium—to say nothing of various circles in the middle—and scarcely a shot had been fired. Little did we know that this little town of Zonnebeke, which we now heard of for the first time, would be the centre of one of the greatest battles in history.

Other brigades on our right received similar orders to take villages occupied by the German advance guard, at the same time.

We paraded at 8 a.m. (17th October) and in dead silence marched off down the Ypres-Zonnebeke road. No smoking and no talking were allowed, of course. It was rather weird, and, at the same time, a very anxious time keeping touch from front to rear of the column.

After going about a mile, we passed the barricades which had been our advance post the evening before. These barricades are always formed at night out of two of the poplars that line all the roads. They are cut down and allowed to fall across the road.

With great difficulty, in the pitch dark, the column

negotiated the obstacle. A military policeman stood by
the barricade and warned all vehicles to keep well over
to the right, there being a space of about six feet between
the end of the barricade and the ditch on the right. It
was then necessary to turn at right-angles to the left, cross
the road and pass the second barrier which projected from
the right, thus forming a very sharp letter S.

We now knew that at any moment we might get in
contact with the enemy, and in front of us there was
nothing but three miles of road before we should reach the
German outpost line. The Germans, however, being well
served, as usual, by their spies, knew of our attack, and
the Uhlans who were holding Zonnebeke evacuated it
on the approach of our infantry.

As dawn began to break, we found ourselves close to
Zonnebeke and news was passed down the column that
the village had been occupied without opposition. The
artillery halted at the level-crossing south of the village,
whilst the infantry proceeded to take up a position on a
line from Zonnebeke station in the direction of south-
east. We had the new Cavalry Division, which included
the Household Cavalry Brigade, on our left. They were,
I believe, at this time at St. Julien, and were responsible
for the ground between there and Zonnebeke.

Fortunately, as it turned out, General Capper decided to
at once entrench a position covering Zonnebeke and Ghele-
vult. The 22nd Infantry Brigade held the part in front
of Zonnebeke, their centre being the cross-roads half a
mile east of Zonnebeke. This decision to entrench turned
out, as will appear later, to be our salvation.

We billeted in Zonnebeke that night. The town was
full of its inhabitants ; shops were open and life going on
in a normal manner. Little did the townspeople imagine
that twenty-four hours later they would be flying for their
lives, with shells bursting all round them.

That night the General Staff planned an elaborate
attack on Menin. This was drawn up as an attack in
three phases, times being allotted to each. It was all
very elaborate and beautifully thought out, and would

no doubt have gone off successfully if the enemy had not interfered.

The 22nd Brigade was to march east and take Dadizeele. Another brigade, moving down the Ypres-Menin road, was to capture Gheluwe ; and a third brigade, passing through Zandvoorde, was on their right. In the third phase of the attack, all were to change front, half right, and concentrate in an attack on Menin, which it was confidently expected would be taken with little opposition. The 22nd Field Artillery Brigade, with which I was, rendezvoused at Veldhoek, at which point the Divisional Headquarters were situated.

We spent the whole morning (18th October) there, and I, becoming bored with nothing to do, rode over to Headquarters to see Sir Frederick Ponsonby, who was acting as Chief Interpreter to the Division. I told him that I was bored with so little to do, and he arranged for me to be attached to the Provost-Marshal. I found the duties of helping this officer less interesting than I had expected. They consisted in rounding up stragglers and hearing complaints from local inhabitants. To show what impossible people the Belgians civilians are, the following incident is a good example :

A young man of military age arrived at Headquarters in the course of the morning, and calmly presented us with a bill for more than 7,000 francs, which he claimed for damage done by the British troops in entrenching themselves in front of Zonnebeke. I carefully inquired whether he accused the troops of having done wanton damage or looting, but he frankly admitted that the damage had only been caused by digging trenches for the defence of the position, and it struck us that a demand for compensation for digging entrenchments was about the limit. The gentleman retired without his 7,000 francs, and with a very good idea of our exact opinion of him.

It was now about 2 o'clock in the afternoon. Reports had been coming in from all the brigades that everything was progressing favourably, according to time-table, and it was nearly time for the wheel southwards and for the combined attack on Menin. At this moment heavy gun-fire broke out on our left, in the direction of Moorslede and Rolleghemcappelle. This being the flank on which my own brigade was operating, I thought it was my duty to return to them and see what was happening. With some difficulty, I found the batteries who were occupying positions in the immediate neighbourhood of Dadizeele. I had scarcely reached them when the disconcerting news arrived that we were being attacked in tremendous force on our left flank, where the cavalry were, and immediately afterwards we heard that the cavalry had been driven in and our flank was exposed. Colonel Fasson, who had been forward with General Lawford, commanding 22nd Infantry Brigade, to reconnoitre, returned to the batteries and ordered them to limber up and move as quickly as possible through Dadizeele to Strooiboomhoek. Before we could reach this place the German attack had developed and our infantry were being driven back through these places. I thought that the guns would inevitably be cut off. I remained behind to bring on the brigade-staff and telephone cart, and as we were passing through Dadizeele I asked an infantry officer how near the Germans were At that moment firing broke out at the far end of the village, and my friend told me that the Germans were then entering the village some three hundred yards away. The infantry fought magnificently and disputed every inch of the ground, but were fairly overwhelmed by numbers. Their stand, however, enabled us to get the guns away.

At Strooiboomhoek it was obvious that if the guns could do anything it would only be as single batteries. There would be no time or possible opportunity of going into action as a brigade. This being so, Colonel Fasson asked me to take the Brigade Staff back to Zonnebeke, a difficult and complicated road which they would never have found by themselves. I did so, and we duly arrived at Zonnebeke just before dark. The roads were horribly blocked by the whole civil population of the district, who were flying before the Germans. It was an extraordinary sight to see them—farmers with their carts, containing the women and children with all their movable goods piled up inside, people on bicycles, cattle being driven along the road, horses, donkeys, carts drawn by dogs, and even an old woman of eighty being trundled along in a wheelbarrow by her husband of the same age. Panic had got hold of these people, and it was only with the greatest difficulty that the troops were able to move on the roads with them.

At Zonnebeke I found the Household Cavalry Brigade and met Lord Frederick Blackwood, whom I had not seen since we were at Rawal-Pindi eight years ago. The cavalry appeared to have been very roughly handled in the action on our left.

In the course of the evening the batteries arrived, and, passing through Zonnebeke, went into billets a mile or so on the Ypres side. Headquarters, however, remained in the village.

All that night the population of the country streamed through the town, and by next morning (19th October) the streets were fairly clear. Our infantry, after falling back, took up the entrenched line which they had providentially prepared two days before.

At daylight the guns also took up positions immediately in the rear of the infantry brigade. From that moment the battle of Ypres began.

All that day we were bombarded by the Germans, but so far they confined their attention to the trenches and did not drop shells in the town. Also, they had evidently not yet got up their heavy guns, as we were only under shrapnel fire. The German infantry did not make any attempt to assault.

I spent most of the morning with Bolster, who commanded the 106th Battery, in his dug-out immediately in the rear of the infantry trenches. He was killed two days later. We were on the crest of a small rise, and thirty or forty yards in front of us, on the forward slope, was the line of our infantry trenches, at that point held by the South Staffordshire regiment. We had an excellent

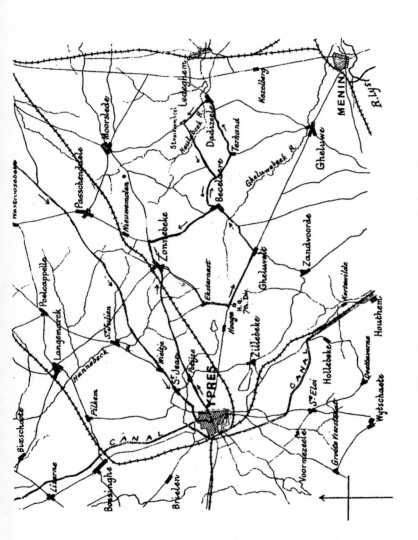

THE YPRES SALIENT, OCT. 1914.

view of the country to our front, which much resembled
Essex or Suffolk, being greatly enclosed and with many
hedges and small woods.

Standing in the trench, with nothing but my eyes showing, I watched, with Bolster, the enemy's infantry trickling
over the skyline. They came into view at 3,400 yards,
but as they were in very open order and came on in short
rushes, they did not present much of a target for artillery ;
and, owing to the farms, woods, and hedges, we could only
see them here and there as they crossed open patches.
This ridge they were crossing was under fire of our guns,
and whenever we saw enough of them bunched together,
we let off a few rounds at them. I shall never forget
seeing some thirty or forty Germans running across a
green field which was divided in two by a wire fence
probably barbed, as I noticed that on reaching the wire
fence they all concentrated and ran through a gate in it.
Our lines of fire were already laid out, and from the map
we were able to get the range to a yard. The next time
we saw a party crossing the field and making for the gate
Bolster ordered a round of gun-fire. At this short range
(2,800 yards) with my Zeiss glasses I could almost see the
faces of the Germans, it being a gloriously fine, sunny day.

Just before they reached the gate, he gave the order to
fire. The guns, which were hidden behind us, loosed off
and we heard the shells whining away. As the Germans
clustered in the gate, a shell from No. 1 gun burst
immediately in front of them. The whole lot at once
lay down, and at first I thought that they were taking
cover until our fire stopped. However, I watched them
for some hours, and not one of them moved again. I
counted fifteen in a circle of some twenty yards diameter.

By now a good many of the German infantry had crossed
the ridge, not only immediately in front of us, but all
along the front. Owing to their being so close, and the
fact that our guns were behind the crest of our hill, we
were unable to reach them. We continued, however,
to pour shrapnel on their supports as they crossed the
skyline, doing considerable damage.

At one time I was leaning against the wall of a little house, some twenty yards from Bolster, who was in his hole, and I pointed out to him that the enemy were bunching behind a certain clump of bushes. My head was eight or nine feet higher than his, and he could not see them. He, therefore, asked me to range the battery for him, and so one of the ambitions of my life was realised in that I ranged a battery of guns in action. Measuring off the angle between the place at which we were then firing, and the place where I had seen the Germans bunching, with the graticules of my glasses, I gave the necessary switch of some five degrees, and ordered a round of battery fire. The ground sloped away from left to right. The range on the left was about right, but the right section were short. This was owing to the angle-of-sight being different for the two flanks of the battery. However, as I did not wish to upset the battery angle-of-sight, I increased the range in the right section by 50 yards, and then ordered a round of gun-fire. This was completely successful, two shells bursting in the clump of bushes in which I had seen the Germans collecting. I think that some twenty or thirty of them must have been in these bushes, and when the shells burst I saw only two or three run out. One ran away altogether ; the other two, after staggering a few yards, collapsed. The remainder, I think, must have been knocked out at once. Meanwhile, the German infantry, who were now too close and too much in the hollow below us for our guns to reach, were coming on, and we soon saw their scouts emerge from a pheasant cover not 200 yards in front of us. As the guns were only 200 yards behind us, this was getting uncomfortably close for artillery. However, we did not feel any anxiety, as our own infantry were well dug in between us and them. As soon as these German scouts appeared our infantry opened fire on them at 200 yards, and the wretched Germans, who evidently did not know of the existence of this branch, began to fall thickly. They at once retired into their pheasant cover, and, being reinforced in considerable strength, opened fire on us.

Things were now very lively, and Bolster could neither leave his observation hole, nor could I leave the wall against which I had flattened myself. At the same time, the German field artillery discovered the position of our trenches and the shrapnel began to arrive. Every time one put one's head out it was immediately saluted with half a dozen bullets, which made a noise like very loud and angry mosquitoes as they passed. I stopped at this place for some time, but in a lull of the firing I managed to run back to the gun-line.

In the course of the afternoon General Lawford asked me to take a message to the colonel of the Staffordshires in his trench. With some difficulty I got there, crawling the last 20 yards, perfectly flat. I found that the Staffordshires Headquarters had made themselves extremely comfortable in a very big bomb-proof, which one approached by going down several steps. The colonel told me that his pioneer sergeant was a coal-miner, and I at once recognised the pitman's work by the way in which the roof of the bomb-proof had been "propped." I had tea with them down there, and a cigarette, and was quite sorry to leave these comfortable and perfectly safe quarters for the perilous journey of returning to Zonnebeke. I had, of course, left Bucephalus with the wagon-line, some half a mile in the rear. I found I had chosen a bad moment to return, as the enemy were searching the ground in the rear of the trenches in the hope of getting our guns. They were firing their shells in pairs at the same elevation, the second shell always falling some thirty yards to the left of the first.

I had scarcely left the Staffordshires' bomb-proof when a shrapnel burst just behind me and on my right, the bullets striking the ground some ten yards to my right. Ten seconds later the second shell of the pair arrived, and burst 10 or 20 yards to my left. Had I been 10 yards more to the right or more to the left, one or other would have got me.

I had the same luck all the way back, many shrapnel bursting all round, but none touching me.

That night we again stayed in Zonnebeke, the guns being withdrawn at dusk.

All the next day (20th October) the Germans continued to shell our trenches. The loss among the infantry was very heavy, but the guns, being well concealed, and not having been located by the hostile aeroplanes, scarcely suffered at all. As usual, the batteries were withdrawn at nightfall and went into billets round Frezenberg, some two miles west of Zonnebeke. Our headquarters were in a dirty little inn on the cross-roads in Frezenberg. We occupied our old positions before dawn (21st October), and the battle continued.

The Germans had, however, been very heavily reinforced and the attack was much heavier.

About midday, the enemy began to bombard the town itself for some hours, but only with shrapnel. This did not do very much damage, but was very alarming, as the bullets from the shrapnel and the pieces of the shells flew about the streets like hail. They were firing in bursts —that is to say, six shells arriving at a time. The air was thick·with the flying lead, fragments of steel, slates from the roofs, glass and bricks. The noise was appalling : one could hardly hear oneself speak. One really wondered how anything could live in such an inferno, the more so as the main street of Zonnebeke was a prolongation of the German line of fire, and rifle-bullets were continuously whining down the street.

There is something peculiarly disconcerting in the smack of a rifle-bullet striking a brick wall close to one's head. A sharp thud and a small cloud of red dust are all that can be heard and seen. Unlike shell fire, one does not realise the presence of a rifle-bullet until after it has passed. In the case of a shell, you can hear it coming for a long time—probably two or three seconds before it reaches one—and after a time one can tell with fair accuracy where it will go ; though, of course, it is impossible to tell at what point of its flight it will burst.

In the open, when a shrapnel bursts there is the sudden and violent tearing noise peculiar to these shells, a puff of white smoke, and nothing else. But in a town or on a road, in addition to the foregoing, there is also the violent patter of the bullets striking the ground. As a shrapnel, to be effective, must burst fairly close to the ground, shells which explode 100 feet or so in the air are comparatively harmless. Fortunately for us, a very large proportion of the German shrapnel burst too high ; in fact, I hardly saw any burst on percussion, except in the cases where they struck the roofs of houses.

About 3 o'clock in the afternoon the " Black Marias " (high-explosive shells) started. Zonnebeke has a church standing in a small " place," with a very high steeple, and evidently the German gunners, knowing that our head-quarters were in the centre of the town, were using the church steeple as a target. This bombardment in the streets of a town by high-explosive shells was, I think, the most alarming part of the whole experience. Everything in the town shook when one of these shells burst. The whole ground appeared to tremble as in an earthquake, even when the explosion was 100 yards away.

About 5 o'clock news came down that Major Malony, who commanded the 104th Battery, in action near the level crossing, had been seriously wounded. He was observing from the infantry trenches some 800 yards in front of his guns and at the foot of the windmill by Zonnebeke Station. The medical officer at once went off to try and find a motor ambulance, and I rode up to the station. The fire was so hot in the street that I decided to leave Bucephalus under a large porch, and I continued my way to the windmill on foot, keeping close in to the walls of the houses on the side from which the shells were coming. So long as the houses in the street were continuous, they afforded me complete protection from shrapnel or rifle-bullets, and I was only hit by bricks and mortar from the walls of the houses ; but, as I neared the outskirts of the town, the houses became detached one from another, and then it was very unpleasant having to cross the spaces between them. The shrapnel was bursting at intervals of ten or fifteen seconds, and it was impossible to judge when they would come. However, I found that by waiting until a shell had just burst, I usually had time to run like a hare to the next house. The rifle-bullets, of course, could not be legislated for at all.

I eventually reached the windmill close to Malony's observation post. Here I found a young officer of, I think, the Queen's, who was sheltering under the mound of the windmill with some twenty men. He told me that he and his men were all that were left of a company of 250. He also told me that Malony had been dragged out of his trench and was lying behind a cottage on the other side of the road. On reaching this, I found that he had already been moved back towards his battery. I could see him being carried on a stretcher. He was now under cover from rifle-fire and it was much better to let them continue across the 800 yards intervening between where he was hit and the battery, than to take him all the way round through the streets of the town, which were being heavily shelled.

I therefore started back down the street towards where I had left my horse, and was met by the motor ambulance which the doctor had sent up. I stopped it, made the man turn round and got in beside him, telling him to drop me when we passed my horse. The motor was a Daimler with the well-known curved scuttle-dash. I sat on the floor and stuck my head well under cover of the dash. I thought that if I was going to be hit I might as well avoid getting it in the head.

In spite of the shells bursting in front and behind us, the ambulance was not hit, and the driver certainly exceeded the speed limit.

I found Bucephalus happily munching some hay, and remounted him. I sent the ambulance on to the level-crossing.

By this time the Germans had got the range of the church very accurately, and the open " place " which I had to cross was thick with white smoke from bursting shrapnel. I never expected to cross it alive. The street was paved with round cobbles and covered with slimy mud

—a place, under ordinary circumstances, I should have hesitated to ride along at a walk. However, on this occasion we negotiated it, including a right-angle corner, at as fast a gallop as poor old Bucephalus was capable of, and regained the cover of the narrow streets untouched.

I found the ambulance at the level-crossing, and took it up to the farm, where we were joined by the medical officer. Malony had just arrived at the farm and was lying on some straw in the kitchen, with several other wounded men. At first I thought he was dead, the bullet having struck him at the side of the head and apparently had passed through the brain. He had been looking through his director when hit. He was breathing very heavily and the doctor thought he was in a very bad way. I was, however, able to tell him that only an hour or two before, Malony had told me that he had a bad attack of asthma, and this probably accounted for the breathing.

We got him into the motor ambulance, and sent him off to Ypres. The doctor and I trotted along the road leading from the farm to the main road, immediately behind the ambulance.

It was now just dark. The wagon-line of Malony's battery was in a field beside us. The battery had not been shelled all day, but suddenly a single shrapnel burst 20 feet above our heads in the darkness. It must have been a chance shot. The ambulance put on speed and the doctor and I galloped after it. At the time we had no idea that the shell had done any damage. However, the next morning we heard that it had flattened out two complete teams.

Our infantry were all this time being subjected to appalling fire both by shrapnel and " Black Marias," the trenches in many parts being completely blown in, and the men in them buried alive. They dug out as many as they could, but when the cover was gone the survivors were exposed to view, and as nothing can live under fire unless entrenched, I fear that many of the men were buried alive.

By nightfall it was obvious to General Lawford that our position was becoming untenable, and it was decided to withdraw as soon as it was dark.

By this time we had no supports, the supports and reserves having long ago been sent up into the trenches. Even the General's own headquarter guard had gone up, too. The only men available were some belonging to a company of the R.E. These hastily threw up a little shelter trench at the level crossing, and if the worst came to the worst we hoped to be able to hold the crossing until the remains of the infantry got through.

Unfortunately, we had no position prepared in rear, and it seemed quite likely that we should have no chance of digging in at a fresh place. The same thing had been happening on our right, and the other brigades were compelled to withdraw also. The remains of the brigades evacuated their trenches and retired in the course of the night in good order and without confusion, though most of the baggage was lost.

At dawn the next morning (22nd October) we took up a position extending roughly from the level-crossing west of Zonnebeke to the V of Veldhoek. This line, unfortunately, passed through a thick wood, and it was in this wood that on succeeding days our losses were most heavy.

The previous afternoon we had been much bothered by spies, who adopted every possible sort of trick to communicate with the enemy. At one time it was noticed that the arms of a certain windmill were turning in a most erratic manner. The windmill was deserted, the sails furled, and there was no one in it. It was, therefore, quite clear that someone was playing with it ; and by the time we reached the windmill the spies had got away. We blew it up next day.

We also suspected that the Germans had adopted their usual trick, when evacuating a town, of leaving men behind, concealed usually in the cellars of the houses, with a telephone.

General Lawford instructed me to go with the provost-sergeant and search the house for spies. This was as unpleasant a task as one could well hope to perform.

By now the eastern part of the town, where I was searching, was being subjected to a heavy and continuous shrapnel fire. The street was also enfiladed by rifle fire. All the doors had been locked by their owners before leaving the town, and I think that this part of Belgium must make a peculiarly strong form of locks and bolts. I never would have believed it would have been so difficult to break in doors. However, at last we found a forge, and in it a large bar of iron, so heavy that it was as much as two men could do to carry it. Our task now became quite easy. The sergeant and I would take up our positions, revolver in hand, on each side of the door, whilst two men charged across the street with the heavy bar of iron. One blow was almost invariably enough. The bar and its carriers would collapse on the pavement, whilst the sergeant and I rushed in.

We searched dozens of houses in this manner, but found them all empty. However, we came to one house where, on rushing in, we were met by a man in plain clothes with a rifle, who immediately fired and shot the provost-sergeant practically through the heart. He did not live many minutes, but our assailant did not survive to see the result of his treachery.

By now the roofs of the houses were coming in, and I withdrew my search-party to brigade headquarters and reported to General Lawford that I did not consider it possible to continue a house-to-house search until the fire moderated. He approved of my action and ordered the search to be discontinued.

The enemy captured Zonnebeke immediately after we left, but fortunately did not press their attack.

The next morning (23rd October) the guns took up positions in the neighbourhood of Eksternest, with our infantry just in front. I reported myself again at Divisional Headquarters, and had some of the most interesting work which I did out there.

A good many German prisoners were being captured in

3

the woods, and it became my duty to interrogate them. The majority of these were men of the Landwehr who had recently been called up for service—a very respectable class who much regretted the atrocities which their armies had committed. I made a short précis about each one, and handed it in to the General Staff. The following is an example of the sort of information I got from them:

"German prisoner brought in to 7th Division Head-quarters, 2nd October, 1914, at 8.30 a.m.

"August Hoffmann, Landwehr Pionier Co., No. 21, 18th Army Corps.

"Called to the colours on the 6th August, at Mainz.

"Has generally been well fed.

"Present at siege of Antwerp. Marched from Antwerp to here in 6 days.

"Has only seen two of the large howitzers.

"His Pioneer Company was attached First Marinen Corps at Antwerp, and is now with 54th Division (Land-wehr). In his Division is the 24th infantry regiment.

"Have Saxon cavalry with them.

"Was captured by Scots Fusiliers in the dark, being part of a patrol which walked into our outposts.

"They no longer received reinforcements from Germany. After heavy loss, two or more companies are joined up into one.

"His company was at Mainz till 27th September."

These reports are of great use as showing us what Divisions and Army Corps are in front of us. I found most of the prisoners quite willing to give any information in their power, and was able to check their veracity by comparing statements of different prisoners, examined separately. One and all appeared to be overjoyed at having been captured, and, so far as I can make out, there is no enthusiasm in the German ranks over this war.

The battle continued without incident, except alternate retirements and advances, over 200 yards for the next two days.

Headquarters was in a large château on the Menin road, which fortunately, having only just been built, was not marked on any of the maps. The Germans evidently knew that our Headquarters were in a château in this neighbourhood, and they systematically shelled all the other châteaux around which were marked on the map. For all this, a certain number of stray shells struck our château.

On one occasion, a group of officers—of whom I was one—was standing on the wide steps in front of the door when a shell arrived, bursting just in front, and practically cut in two a chauffeur of a car standing at the door.

In the evening an officer, who has since been killed, galloped into headquarters and told General Capper that a certain regiment were leaving their trenches and retiring. General Capper looked round and, seeing me, ordered me to mount at once and at all costs rally this regiment and take them back to their trenches.

Bucephalus and I started on our mission, and soon reached the neighbourhood of the trenches, which were on the far side of a pheasant cover. The report was quite unfounded. There was no sign of the regiment leaving their trenches, and I think the officer who brought the news must have been misled by seeing some bearer parties bringing away wounded men. To make sure, I went along the position behind the wood to see what had happened farther to the left, and I was returning at a gallop when a shell burst practically on me. The next thing I remember was finding myself lying on the ground with my horse on top of me. I was quite certain at first that we were both dead. However, in a few seconds the pain in my side and leg made me realise that we were still alive. Bucephalus, having recovered from his fright, was good enough to get off me, and I picked myself up, to find that neither of us had been touched at all by the shell. I think the shell must either have burst under his nose or else under my feet. In any case, the whole of the contents of the shell had gone forward, and we had only received the concussion.

I remounted with some difficulty, and, my mission being completed, returned to Headquarters. I thought then that I had merely bruised myself, and that I would be all right in a few hours.

Before dark I returned to the 22nd R.F.A. Brigade Headquarters in time for dinner, but as we were about to sit down, a message came through from General Capper to General Lawford, inquiring where the French were who had been supposed to come up on our left and take the place of some of our troops who were being withdrawn. We replied that nothing had so far been heard of the French, and instructions were then sent that I should go out and find the French, and make what General Capper calls the " liaison."

I at once started off with Wellingham, in pitch darkness, to try and find the French. I must admit I did not feel very happy over this job, as no one could tell me where the French were, and I knew that our own positions only extended some half a mile to our left ; and, moreover, the German lines were not above 600 or 800 yards in front.

Before starting I studied the map until I had committed this part to memory, as I knew that it would be unsafe to strike a match or use my electric torch, once I was near the trenches. The night was pitch dark and I dropped my reins on Bucephalus's neck, trusting to him to find the track. The road I had to follow was a narrow track between high hedges, and about a hundred yards in rear of our own infantry trenches, which at this point were held by the Queen's.

When I had gone a quarter of a mile I was challenged in a stage whisper, and it proved to be a picket of the Queen's. The sentry informed me that he was the extreme left of his regiment, and could give me no information whatever of what there was beyond.

We were now some 800 yards from the outskirts of Zonnebeke, where the houses in front of us were burning. I could clearly see with the naked eye the silhouettes of the German soldiers passing in front of the flames. I told Wellingham, my trumpeter, to keep 30 yards behind me, as I expected at every moment to walk into a German patrol, and if I did so I wanted him to be able to get back to Headquarters with the news.

After proceeding another 400 yards, to my intense relief we came to an arch under a railway, and I knew that I was still on the right road. In the shelter of the arch I ventured to examine my map with the electric torch, and made out that I must be within 200 yards of the main Ypres-Zonnebeke road.

We duly reached the cross-roads, where I suddenly found myself surrounded by men, and my bridle was seized. At first I thought I was captured by the Germans, but immediately discovered, to my intense relief, that I had struck the French. I was at once taken to the colonel of the regiment, who was delighted to see me as he did not know whether the British were on his right, and he did not dare advance to the line he wished to occupy until he knew exactly where our extreme left rested, as otherwise in the darkness the English and French might have fired on each other.

I asked the colonel to remain where he was until I returned to our own lines and found the colonel of the Queen's. With some difficulty I did so, and brought Colonel Coles of the Queen's back with me. I introduced the two colonels to each other and interpreted for them. They settled exactly where their flanks should meet and the " liaison " was successfully made.

After reporting by telephone to Headquarters what I had done, I was very glad to get my dinner, better late than never.

Next morning (27th October) I was so stiff, and in such pain, I could hardly get on my horse, and, on being examined by the brigade doctor, was informed that I had seriously injured myself inside.

I rode at a walk to the nearest dressing-station, and handed over my horses to the 1st line transport, which was parked near there. I was fortunately able to get a lift in a Belgian officer's motor into Ypres, and Wellingham brought on my kit later. On arrival at Ypres, I found that the British hospital was already full, and that they were starting another one in the Rue de Lille. I accordingly made my way there, and found it was being run by the 22nd Field Ambulance, under an excellent doctor. I was one of the first patients to arrive, but within four hours they had taken in over 300 wounded.

There was only one surgeon and, I think, one assistant, besides a few orderlies, and many of the wounded had to wait on stretchers in the courtyard.

The sights here were too terrible to describe, and the operating-room soon resembled a shambles. The building was evidently a Catholic school, and some of the nuns were still there and tried to help. But the poor creatures could talk no English, and were much in the way, although they meant well. One old nun kept bringing in small parties of the well-to-do citizens of the town. At first I thought they had come to try and help, but eventually we came to the conclusion that the good nuns were charging sixpence at the door, for people to come and look " at the beasts " ! After this we protested, and had no more visitors.

I was in the officers' ward. We had no very dangerous cases, but several were pretty badly wounded.

Next morning (Sunday) we were told that we were to be shipped off to England immediately. We were hurried off to the station in motor ambulances, but did not get a train till late in the evening. There were several wounded Germans with us. One wretched boy of about seventeen was shockingly wounded, and was lying on a stretcher in the waiting-room. A large crowd of Belgians was standing round, jeering at him. I made them a short speech, in which I conveyed to them my exact opinion of them. They seemed surprised.

As soon as the brave Belgian crowd had been disposed of some of our own men came up, and as I went away I saw them giving the German boy cigarettes and soup.

We eventually got off, and after a fourteen-hour journey at never more than five miles an hour, we reached Boulogne. We were at once transferred to a large hospital ship, well fitted up and with crowds of doctors, nurses, etc., but not before I had had café-au-lait in the well-remembered buffet on the pier. How different from the last time I had been there, whilst waiting for my motor to be landed !

After a rather rough voyage, we reached Southampton. We had a narrow escape, as a Belgian refugee ship was blown up by a German submarine just off Boulogne, that afternoon.

We were landed at 10 o'clock the next morning, and were put into a hospital train which was alongside the ship, and in two hours were in London. Here we were met by motors and sent to different nursing-homes, whilst the men went to hospitals. I went to Mrs. Rupert Beckett's house in Grosvenor Street, and was examined by Sir William Bennett. Two days later I went before a medical board at the War Office and was allowed to go to my own house.

The above account has been written from memory immediately after my return, as officers were not allowed to keep diaries.

I hope to be well enough to return to the Front in two or three weeks.

The battle of Ypres is still going on, and I hear that the 7th Division has been withdrawn from the firing-line to " refit," having lost the appalling total of 70 per cent. This means that out of some 14,000 fighting men we have lost over 10,000 in little more than a week's fighting, in one division alone.

I was gazetted to the 2nd Life Guards on the 9th December, and joined them at Windsor, where I remained with them until the 6th of January. On Christmas Day I got orders to be ready to start for France at any moment.

6TH JANUARY, 1915

I obtained leave for a few days pending embarkation and am at St. James's Terrace. I got a wire from Windsor at lunch time to-day, ordering me to start immediately for the Front. Usually one has to go by Southampton and Havre, which means hanging about the Base for an indefinite time. However, on this occasion I am able to go by Folkestone and Boulogne, which will enable me to join the regiment at Hazebrouck direct, where they were in reserve. I left Charing Cross at 4.30 p.m., and on arrival at Folkestone was told there was no boat crossing to-night. I went to the Pavilion Hotel for the night, and rang up Captain Hann, whom I had served with in India. The 3rd Hussars, Reserve Regt., is at Shorncliffe now, and I was glad of the opportunity of seeing Hann again. He dined with me, and gave me all news of the regiment.

7TH JANUARY

We sailed at 10.30 a.m., and had the worst crossing I have ever known. At Boulogne I got a train up-country which started at 3 in the afternoon, and arrived at Hazebrouck at 7 o'clock. By that time it was quite dark, and no one was able to tell me where the 2nd were. With some difficulty I found the Headquarters of the 3rd Cavalry Division, and introduced myself to the staff there. They told me the regiment is at Staple, but said this was some way out, and that I had better stay with them for the night. I dined with the " Q " staff, and they have given me a room here.

I met a chaplain called Hamilton-Boyd, who is the senior chaplain of the 3rd Cavalry Division, and was interested to hear that it was he who buried young Petersen at Zillebeke.

8TH JANUARY

After breakfast I found a supply lorry which was taking rations to the Regiment. I got a lift on this, and was jolted the four miles out to Staple. The Headquarters of the 2nd are in the village, and the squadrons are distributed amongst the various farms around.

I lunched with Colonel Ferguson, who posted me to " D " Squadron, which is commanded by Malcolm Lyon. An orderly was sent to the Squadron to fetch horses and a cart for my kit.

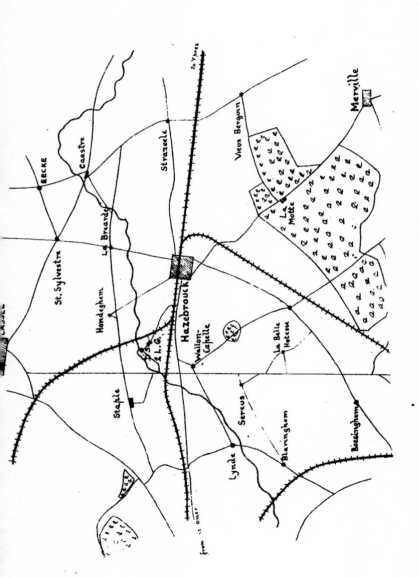

HAZEBROUCK, JAN. 1915.

" D " Squadron has a collection of farms a couple of miles from Staple, headquarters being in the largest of these, and possibly the least dirty. Lyon and I share the Headquarters farm, the other officers having another one not far off.

I have got a good servant, a young man belonging to the 2nd, who will, I think, look after me fairly well. Three horses have been applied for for me, but have not yet arrived, but I have borrowed a good one to go on with. —France is getting quite civilised, yesterday's *Daily Mail* and *Times* being brought round to the farms by an enterprising French boy, a halfpenny paper costing two-pence.

It is a great relief to be in a part of the country where they speak French, as the Flemish of Belgium was beyond me altogether. So far as I can see, we are likely to stay here for some time.

9TH JANUARY

To-day we had a regimental field-day, but as the country is half under water, and we are not allowed to go off the roads, it was not very interesting. We did a reconnaissance to St. Omer, but it is odious trotting on the *pavé* roads.

The country round here is much the same as Belgium, perfectly flat, with a few woods dotted about.

I have seldom known such a wet day, and but for my new water-proof should have been wet to the skin.

10TH JANUARY

I took the squadron to Church Parade, but it was an odious walk, two miles there and two miles back in liquid mud. I don't think anybody enjoyed it much.

After lunch I rode into Hazebrouck and got a few things I wanted there. Hazebrouck is the only town near us, and is a typical little country place, very few shops, and what there are very bad.

The country here is extraordinarily quiet and peaceful ; there is nothing at all to show there is a war going on ; except for the absence of able-bodied men, life seems to be going on much as usual. They are cutting the hedges along the roads and working steadily in the fields. One thing strikes one, and that is there are no soldiers to be seen training, as there are in England.

11TH JANUARY

Still raining, and I have a bad cold. This morning we had a squadron parade and did some dismounted action; but, as I said before, it is not very realistic as we cannot go off the roads, and one has to imagine the whole thing.

" Stables " are carried out under difficulties. Each troop has a little farm of its own, and, by dint of using every scrap of space, all the horses have been got under cover. After being accustomed to ordinary English or Indian stables where one has the horses in rows, it is very strange having them like this, where you get two horses in a farm loose box, half a dozen in a barn, half a dozen in an open shed with tarpaulins round the sides, and probably one or two in the pig-sties. The mud is awful, and one has to wear gum-boots most of the time.

12TH JANUARY

Another squadron parade, more for the sake of exercise than anything else.

In the afternoon we had the Finals of the Brigade Football competition, which was won by my squadron.

I have sorted out my kit and arranged it so that I can pack up and move at a moment's notice. I find that everyone has a pack-horse for his kit, which makes one independent of transport. Theoretically this is an excellent arrangement, but, as I know from my experience in India, carrying heavy weights on a pack-horse is not

always as easy as it sounds. To begin with, the load has
to be divided into two parts of exactly equal weight, and
also has to be strapped on with the greatest care. Otherwise, as soon as the horse starts to trot the saddle turns
round, or pieces fall off. If one is not very careful, the
pack-horse is apt to get a sore back.

On active service one usually has to harness up and
move off before daybreak, and I am afraid the system of
carrying the things on pack-horses will be very troublesome, if we have much moving. The arrangement is
that the officer rides one of his chargers, his groom rides
his own troop-horse in the ranks, and one's first servant
rides one's other horse and leads the pack-horse.

The weather here is perfectly awful ; it never stops
raining, one can hardly get along the roads, and, as for the
fields, one sinks in it up to the knees. Fortunately my
field-boots have been so soaked in oil that nothing can get
through them.

I have not seen the other squadrons yet, as the regiment
is so scattered about the country.

13TH JANUARY

We have heard heavy firing to the east for the last
twenty-four hours. There is a rumour that the Germans
have broken through at Ypres, but I do not believe it—
all the same, something is evidently happening. I don't
think the cavalry will be sent into the trenches again,
as we are too valuable to be used up like that, now that
there are plenty of infantry.

A German spy was caught here yesterday ; he had
his German uniform on under an English greatcoat.
Two others were caught about five miles off. The poor
devils will probably be shot.

14TH JANUARY

This afternoon I rode into Hazebrouck with the other
squadron officers to see a demonstration of bomb-throwing.
It was a most dangerous amusement. We left our horses

on the road and waded through 18 inches of liquid mud
to a part of the field where some dummy trenches had been
dug. An engineer officer, who was in charge of the proceedings, showed us all the various types of bombs in use,
and explained their mechanism. The two favourites
seem to be the " Hair-brush " bomb and the " Jam-pot."
The former consists of a piece of wood the shape of a hair-
brush, to each side of which a half-pound slab of gun-
cotton is firmly tied. Six-inch wire nails are fastened all
round the gun-cotton, and with a detonator and short
length of fuse the thing is complete. When it goes off the
nails fly in every direction, and must cause horrible wounds.

The " Jam-pot " bomb consists of an ordinary jam-tin
filled with broken bits of iron, and containing a small slab
of gun-cotton. The fuse is lighted with a match or cigarette
and then flung as far as possible. The fuses are cut
into lengths of 2 or 8 inches, which are cut so as to burn
sufficiently long to give one time to throw the thing. I
certainly hope I shall not have to use them.

We were invited to throw some of them to see how it
worked. There was nearly a bad accident, as one idiot,
after lighting his fuse, was so petrified with terror that
he forgot to throw it. Everybody yelled at him to
fling it away, and threw themselves in the mud. The
wretched man completely lost his head and eventually
flung it in the wrong direction. It had hardly left his
hand before it exploded, but by some miracle no one was
hurt.

We were also shown a prehistoric trench-mortar which
consisted of a 8-ft. length of iron drain-pipe of about
6-in. diameter. One end is closed, except for a small hole
through which the fuse is inserted. A small bag of black
powder is dropped in first, and then a jam-tin bomb is put
in on top of it with a piece of flannel tied round to act as
a driving band. This primitive weapon has no sights or
means of elevating. The range is determined by the angle
at which the pipe is stuck up in the air, and the amount of
powder put in. I should think it is as dangerous, if not
more so, to the people who use it as to the enemy.

It was bitterly cold, with a strong wind blowing, and raining hard; so my cold has not been improved.

15TH JANUARY

Another regimental field day; rather more interesting this time, as we did a strategic reconnaissance in the direction of Merville. We started out at 9 and did not get back till after 5, having covered over thirty miles.

16TH JANUARY

This morning we did a little judging distance; after being accustomed to shooting at ranges from 8,000 to 5,000 yards in the artillery, it seemed quite funny to be estimating ranges under 1,000 yards.

In the afternoon we had another football match, " B " Squadron beating the Leicestershire Yeomanry. We all motored over to Hondegem in the regimental car; for once it was fine, but a bitterly cold wind.

We are really quite comfortable in our farm, which is typical of most in this country. It is built round four sides of a yard, the centre of which is occupied by a huge manure heap. Dozens of cows and pigs roam about loose, and the smell reminds me of Canton; but as Lyon was in West Africa, we are very careful about boiling the milk, and never touch water, always drinking cocoa, tea, coffee, or claret.

17TH JANUARY (SUNDAY)

I had a horrid job this morning. I took the squadron to have a bath in the brewery. This is a dreadful ceremony, and much resented by most of the men. Huge tubs in which beer is made during the week are filled with hot water and used as baths. Never will I drink beer in France again.

18TH JANUARY

This morning we rode out five miles to see a line of trenches which is being dug under the superintendence of the R.E. This is a reserve line of which several are being dug at various distances behind the front, in case we should be driven out of our present positions. We can still hear heavy gun-fire ; it sounds nearer to-day, but this is probably caused by the change in the wind. There is thick sleet blowing with half a hurricane, and my hands and feet were so cold I could hardly sit on my horse. Unless something a little more lively turns up, I think I am going to be very bored. So far as one can see, there is little chance of the cavalry moving for some time. They say that in the spring, when all the New Army are here, we are going to break through the German lines at all costs. If this comes off the French and British cavalry divisions are to be flung through the gap to harry the retiring Germans; it ought to be exciting work—but first catch your sparrow before you salt him. From what I saw of the Germans in Belgium, I think it will take us all our time to break their line.

19TH JANUARY

A regimental day. The 7th Brigade—which consists of the 1st and 2nd Life Guards and Leicestershire Yeomanry—carried out an entrenching scheme under General Kavanagh. We dismounted as many men as possible, and armed with picks and shovels, which had followed us in a motor-lorry—we proceeded to dig ourselves in across some ploughed fields. The picks were quite unnecessary——buckets would have been much more useful. The surface is wet, but as soon as you scrape the ground a pool is formed at once. We can still hear firing in the direction of Ypres.

I see there has been a Zeppelin raid in England, so I have written to G. and advised her to see that our fire insurance policies cover this risk. It. would be rather sickening to lose everything in the house if a bomb should fall on it.

The weather has suddenly taken a turn for the better, and we have even seen a watery sun. The cultivation of the country is going on busily, all the work being done by old men and boys, helped by the women. This harvest is going to be very important, as, if it is good, the Germans will be able to keep the war up longer.

20TH JANUARY

We have had another brigade day, and have been trotting up and down the roads till 4 o'clock this afternoon. It is good exercise for men and horses, but will not give the officers brain fever. After dinner we all played *chemin de fer*—a horrid game, at which I lost £15.

21ST JANUARY

It has poured all day ; we have been able to do nothing except have an inspection of rifles and swords. The three horses which had been applied for for me from the base have arrived. I would not be seen dead on any of them—they are the most horrible weedy little brutes I have ever seen. I do not know whether they are classed as mounted infantry cobs, but to send them as cavalry officers' chargers was nothing less than an impertinence. The man who bought them for the army ought to be shot for dishonesty if he paid more than £10 apiece for them.

22ND JANUARY

Actually a fine day. It is freezing hard, but quite cheerful with the sun shining. This morning we had a little excitement as a German aeroplane came over our heads ; I believe it dropped a bomb in Hazebrouck. It was a new pattern to me and different to the Taubes which I saw at Ypres.

23RD JANUARY

A glorious day, with bright sun. We took advantage of the weather and had a brigade field day. The roads were very slippery, and it was difficult to keep one's horse from falling. We were out all day digging trenches beyond Hondegem.

I asked G. to send me out some peppermint bull's-eyes. When I got back I found two enormous parcels waiting for me, each of which contained at least 5 lb. of these things. We shall probably all be sick.

24TH JANUARY

Leave has started and Lyon is going to Paris to-night. Mrs. Lyon joins him there. When it is my turn, I think we must do the same.

25TH JANUARY

Fine, but very cold. The whole regiment practised a dismounted attack through a thick wood. We had to advance across a ploughed field and then force our way up a steep hill through dense undergrowth, finally doing a bayonet charge at the top. I lost a spur, and was so out of breath that, if there had been any Germans at the top, they could have knocked me on the head like a rabbit.

26TH JANUARY

This morning Colonel Ferguson inspected the horses of the squadron. We have a few of the old London black horses left, but the majority are strange-looking beasts for a cavalry regiment.

News has just arrived that the regiment is to go into the trenches for ten days, starting next Sunday, and, of all places, to Zillebeke ! This is the place where the regiment was so badly cut up on 5th November.

27TH JANUARY

The Prince of Wales and Sir John French inspected the regiment dismounted at Staple this morning. Sir John made a speech in which he thanked the regiment for their gallant behaviour during the Ypres fighting.

We expect to start for Zillebeke on Monday.

28TH JANUARY

General Kavanagh inspected the horses this morning. It was fine, but bitterly cold, so we kept the horses rugged up in the stables until he came round. All the same, they did not look their best.

We have now got definite orders for the move. The horses are to be left here in charge of a small party, whilst as many men as possible go by motor-bus to Ypres. The trenches we are taking over are said to be only 80 yards from the German lines, and, as there is a full moon, we should have a lively time.

29TH JANUARY

Another fine day. I rode into Hazebrouck and bought two large bottles of iodine for use in the trenches; we have been warned that enteric is raging round Ypres. From all one hears it looks as though we might expect a big attack next week.

31ST JANUARY

My mother has sent another huge bottle of iodine. However, one cannot have too much. It is useful for both men and horses. There is a lot of tetanus in this highly fertilised country, and one ought to dab on a little iodine the moment one scrapes one's hand. It is the same thing with the horses; they are always knocking bits off themselves, and iodine is quite the best thing to dry a wound up—sore backs included.

Apparently my letters arrive in England very erratically, at least those that go by post. Fortunately a good many men are going on leave, and we get our letters taken to England by them. The men leave here at 4 a.m., and get to London in time for lunch the same day. So we are not so very far off. Three hours by train to Boulogne, two hours to get across to Folkestone, and two more to London. As we are only two miles from the station here, it makes it eight hours from door to door, or the same thing as London to Wishaw.

4

We have had an alarm to-day. Packed our kit, saddled up, and turned out in ten minutes. I believe the fighting at La Bassée has been rather serious. It is said that a battalion of the Scots Guards has been wiped out. It may only be a rumour.

The story is that a German deserter came into the lines and said that a tremendous assault was just going to take place. We rushed all the supports and reserves into the firing trench, and immediately afterwards the Germans exploded mines under the trench and blew most of the battalion into the air. It may or may not be true; we get the wildest rumours here.

To-day is the Kaiser's *geburtstag*. What a difference from last year, when I dined with the White Dragoons at Darmstadt! I fancy very few of them are left now, as I heard they were cut to pieces by the French when the latter got close to Strasbourg in the first days of the war.

Our unofficial post is really very quick. One of the men has just brought me a letter from G. which was written this morning.

I am getting quite accustomed to farm life, and no longer mind falling over pigs.

The people in this part of the world have a most ingenious method of churning the butter. The churn itself is inside the house, and is connected by a shaft passing through the wall to an enormous wheel 8 or 9 feet high, which stands against the outside of the house. For two hours every morning they turn a large dog loose into a little enclosure round the wheel. He gets on to the inside of the wheel and runs forward. As the wheel is very well balanced it revolves under his feet in the same way as one sees white mice in a cage. The funny thing is that the dog seems to enjoy it; it is the only exercise the poor brute gets.

2ND FEBRUARY

A cold, wet hurricane. Lyon came back from Paris last night, where he seems to have enjoyed himself very much. Unfortunately he had to be recalled a day before his leave was up, as the regiment was going to the trenches. This morning the men paraded in full kit to be inspected. Of course, they leave their spurs and swords behind and wrap up in mufflers and woolly gloves, with rifles and bayonets. They would never be taken for cavalrymen. Let us hope the trenches will be deep enough or their heads will certainly stick up over the top.

Each squadron is leaving one officer behind to look after the horses. I expect I shall be very dull for the next ten days all alone.

3RD FEBRUARY

The regiment went off in motor-buses from Staple this morning. They will motor as far as Ypres, and then have to walk out to the trenches, which I gather are some three miles east of the town. Who would ever have thought, in the old days, that the Life Guards would go into action by motor-bus ?

This evening I dined with Butler of the 1st Life Guards, who has a farm a few hundred yards from here. He had an exciting time at the beginning of the war, as he was wounded during the retreat from Mons and taken prisoner by the Germans. They seem to have treated him very well, and he was released when we recaptured the place.

4TH FEBRUARY

Being left in charge of 160 horses with only 80 men is not pure joy, as all the horses have to be exercised every day and " stables " have to be carried on as usual. The only way I can do it is by taking them out in three parties.

We have had a little excitement of our own to-day, as the German aeroplanes have been over. They dropped several bombs on Hazebrouck, evidently hoping to hit the railway station. In this they failed, and only succeeded in dropping their bombs in the streets around. Except that one woman was killed, no damage was done. She was standing close to where a bomb fell, and I believe there was very little left of her. The effect of these bombs is very slight. They break windows within about a hundred yards and smash anything they actually hit, but their effect is very local.

5TH FEBRUARY

The usual trouble over exercising this morning. However, I have got the thing organised now, and shall be able to get the horses out for half an hour's walk and trot every morning. We have had no news from the regiment yet. The Blues are said to have lost some men yesterday.

Butler dines with me to-night.

6TH FEBRUARY

A lovely day, with warm sun. I was on a Field-General Court Martial this morning; Sir F. Carden, 1st Life Guards, President.

The regiment was attacked last night, but I do not think we had many casualties. Apparently there is very little shelling, as the two lines are only 25 yards apart; but there is a good deal of bombing and trench-mortaring. They are to be relieved on Monday night and go into billets in Ypres. The inhabitants of the town are beginning to return, although the place is still a bit more or less bombarded.

The casualties of the Blues were one killed and nine wounded by bombs.

8TH FEBRUARY

Torrie came round this morning; he is in command of the regiment, whilst Colonel Ferguson is at Ypres. He says we may have to take the horses up to the regiment. I hope this is not so. It is twenty miles, and would be an awful job with so few men. It is all very well for one man to lead three horses across country in the open, but to get along the *pavé* roads with columns of motor-buses passing will be difficult. However, we will manage it somehow.

9TH FEBRUARY

The regiment has come out of the trenches and gone into billets in Ypres.

I lunched at Headquarters with Torrie and Sinclair. It is bitterly cold and blowing hard.

A periscope has arrived from G., which will be invaluable the next time we go to the trenches.

Several trains have passed here to-day full of Turcos and Algerian Cavalry going north. They are very picturesque with their sky-blue tunics, red breeches and high red turbans.

10TH FEBRUARY

A motor cyclist has come back from the trenches ; he says we have had one killed and three wounded. If we have no more casualties we shall have been lucky.

I am getting very bored all by myself here, with no one to talk to. There is nothing to do but take the horses out in the morning and see them cleaned afterwards.

They have put us on bully-beef to-day for a change, but after the tough meat we usually get, it does not much matter. I drink cocoa for breakfast and lunch, and red wine of the country at 1.75, a large bottle for dinner, with ration rum as a liqueur.

11TH FEBRUARY

To-day I have been quite busy as I had to go round the ten farms occupied by the squadron and pay the weekly bills for forage, etc. It is rather a business, as I have to make out all the bills myself in triplicate, and argue it all out with the farmers' wives. Their husbands are all away fighting, but they know exactly how many centimes there are in a franc. In fact, they are as bad as natives at bargaining.

Most of the people round here are very willing to help us, but some of them are brutes. They are not really French but Flemish, though most of them speak French fairly well.

The regiment is coming back to-morrow, for which I am thankful, as I am bored to death by myself. I am hoping to get a week's leave soon. It will be a great joy to get back to my own house after living in this pig-sty. The filth and dirt of these farms is indescribable, and, as for the people themselves—one has to pass on the windward side of them.

Sir Morgan Crofton got back from the trenches to-day. He says we have had no more casualties, but the 1st had eleven killed and nine wounded yesterday by a shell in Ypres.

12TH FEBRUARY

I took as many men as I could spare this morning to Staple for a promulgation of court-martial parade. A man got three months' hard labour for striking an N.C.O.

The regiment is expected back by bus at 10 o'clock to-night.

13TH FEBRUARY

The regiment got back at 4 a.m. this morning. On the whole, they seem to have had quite a good time. They were very lucky, as the Germans did not attack whilst they were in the trenches, and the total casualties only amounted to one killed and three wounded. Curiously enough, they were relieved by the 3rd Hussars. Whilst they were in rest billets in Ypres they were in the Rue de Lille, where I was in hospital in October.

One night the town was bombarded by a German armoured train. Fortunately none of our houses were hit, though shells fell in the street outside. A house occupied by the 1st was hit, seven men being killed and nine wounded. The Leicestershire Yeomanry, who are in our brigade, also had some casualties, including an officer killed.

Lyon has brought back some souvenirs that he got in Ypres, including about sixty very nice old blue tiles.

15TH FEBRUARY

The squadron did some musketry this morning, rather different to the ordinary course on a rifle-range. We put up tin cans against the railway embankment and shot at them from 50 yards off.

I have taken over a new horse ; he is eighteen hands,

and coal black. He is very heavy, but quite a fine beast, and certainly up to my weight.

Great excitement during "stables" this morning. A monoplane came down near our farm. We all thought it was a German, so went off to it prepared to capture the occupants, but were much disappointed to find it was an English one after all. Shrove Tuesday, but no pancakes !

19TH FEBRUARY

Had a long regimental field-day, doing a reconnaissance at the Forêt de Nieppe, covering about 80 miles. It was very difficult going through the woods, as we had to cross dykes full of water.

Leave has been stopped, as they say the Channel is full of submarines.

20TH FEBRUARY

There is a rumour that the regiment is going back to the trenches. Three officers and 93 men per squadron must always be ready to start at a moment's notice.

21ST FEBRUARY

No news yet of when we go to the trenches. I rather doubt if we shall go for some time.

Two more aeroplanes came over to-day, one of which looked very much like a Taube. I do not know if they dropped anything.

22ND FEBRUARY

My birthday—what a cheerful place to spend it in ! We had a long scheme this morning ; supposed to seize a bridge and hold it till the infantry came up.

The newest rumour is that America has declared war on Germany. Also that a German submarine has been caught filling up with petrol in Cornwall !

23RD FEBRUARY

All leave has been stopped. This is a great disappointment, as I expected to get mine this week. Fenwick

Palmer has rejoined from sick leave. Shelly and twenty-three men from the squadron have gone to look after the horses of the 9th Lancers whilst they are in the trenches.

I do not think I shall be able to stand the dullness of this life much longer. I always did dislike watching horses being groomed for hours on end, even in India. It requires absolutely no intelligence or initiative. So far as I can see there is no chance of cavalry being used as such for months, if at all.

We know the Germans have prepared line after line of trenches back to the Rhine, and when we do force them back out of their present position, they will only fall back on another one. I really think I shall have to try and get a staff job, or something a little more interesting.

To-day's rumour is that Italy has also declared war on Germany.

24TH FEBRUARY

A horrible day, heavy snow and sleet. This morning we had a horse inspection by the principal veterinary officer.

Rumours are coming in thick and fast. To-day we hear, first, that all the cavalry are going back to England, and, second, that we are going to Dixmude to take over the Belgian trenches.

25TH FEBRUARY

A new system of trenches is being dug a few miles east of this place. Lyon and Fenwick Palmer have taken a working party of thirty-three men there to-day, and it will be my turn to-morrow. To-day's rumour is that the cavalry are going to Syria.

26TH FEBRUARY

I have spent to-day with a working party continuing the trenches that were begun yesterday. We rode out to La Belle Hôtesse, about 5 miles, and started digging there. It was very cold, but I kept myself warm by digging hard. We are not making real trenches, as the ground is too wet, but breastworks—that is to say, we first build up a wall of hurdles and then fill it up outside with earth. It is all being done under the superintendence of R.E. officers, and I think will make a good line.

No letters to-day. I hope the Germans have not submarined the mail-boat.

Last night one of " B " Squadron's farms was burnt down. I went to see it this morning, a most extraordinary sight. Twenty cows were burnt to a cinder, and one could hardly recognise what was left of them. The wonder is that more of these tumbledown farms are not burnt, with so many men sleeping in the barns. It is dark by 5 o'clock and the only light the men have is candles, a most dangerous form of illumination in the straw.

I heard the Germans tried to torpedo the leave boat yesterday, missing it by 7 yards.

They have asked for officers to volunteer for duty with the Foot Guard battalions. I have not volunteered. I am an artilleryman and cavalryman, and have no desire to become an infantryman as well.

27TH FEBRUARY

Fine but very cold. We have sent another party under Lyon and Palmer to continue the digging.

To-day's rumour is that we are going to Mesopotamia at once. Apparently the only place we are not going to so far is Honolulu.

I have collected all the rumours of the last week and find that we are to go to the following places : Dixmude in Belgium, back to England, Syria or Palestine to march on Constantinople, Salonika to attack Hungary, Alsace to advance up the Rhine Valley with the French cavalry, and Italy to join in the attack on Trieste. As a matter of fact, it is a thousand to one that we stay where we are.

This morning I saw the Warwickshire Horse Artillery ; they are the only Territorial R.H.A. who have got out so far. I had hoped to bring out my own battery at the same time as them. I don't fancy they have been in action much.

28TH FEBRUARY

Another day's hard digging at La Belle Hôtesse.

1ST MARCH

We can hear heavy firing from the direction of Ypres, but have not heard anything yet.

This afternoon I rode into Hazebrouck, and got a very nice lace handkerchief for G. as a wedding-day present.

This morning was extraordinarily fine with bright sun, but at 3 o'clock it suddenly became so dark we had to light the lamp, then heavy thunder with hail and a double-barrelled hurricane. Half an hour later the sun was shining again.

I see we are sending a mounted division to the Dardanelles. I wish I could get a staff job with them. There may be a chance of some cavalry work there.

No letters to-day, so I suppose the mail boat has been stopped again. The papers are very uncertain. Sometimes we get the morning papers at 4 o'clock on the day of issue, and sometimes they are more than twenty-four hours late.

2ND MARCH

I took the squadron out for exercise this morning. My chestnut mare is very lame, so I must rely on "Sambo" and my other chestnut.

3RD MARCH

Apparently we are not going back to the trenches after all. G. wants to come out here, but I am afraid it is quite impossible, as nobody is allowed to land unless they are working for the Red Cross.

4TH MARCH

A fine warm day. Got quite warm riding this morning. My Kodak has arrived, and I hope to get some interesting snapshots.

The whole of the Cavalry Corps are now out of the

trenches, and have been relieved by infantry, so I suppose it will not be our turn again for some time.

5TH MARCH

Shelly came back to-day from looking after the 9th Lancers' horses. I don't think I ever was so bored before. I have now been eight weeks in this dirty little farm.

6TH MARCH

We had a court-martial parade at Staple this morning. A long list of offences for which men can be shot was read out—apparently it is very easy to get shot on active service.

8TH MARCH

Veterinary inspection this morning. Heavy firing from the direction of Ypres again. I wonder what it is about.

I have sent home a roll of Kodak films to be developed, but I am very doubtful if they get past the Censor.

9TH MARCH

Cold but fine. We have had a revolver competition for officers and corporals-of-horse.

We have just had orders to-night for the regiment to be ready to start for the front at 6 o'clock to-morrow morning, in full marching order. We do not know what has happened, but presume the Germans are attacking.

10TH MARCH

Reveille at 5 o'clock this morning. We stood to arms all day, but have not moved. There is a great battle going on near La Bassée. We are attacking with forty-eight battalions. Let us hope we shall break through. We expect to start at any moment.

At 10 o'clock this morning who should walk into the farm but Lord Dundonald and Hugh O'Neill. He was very cheerful and looked very well. I wonder what he has come out for. Evidently not to pay a visit to the regiment, as he only stayed five minutes, and went on in a motor to the front to see the fighting.

11TH MARCH

Reveille at 4 a.m., the whole brigade marched off at 4.45 in the dark and went to La Motte via Hazebrouck.

We spent the day hidden in a wood. Gun firing is now very heavy, and we expect to go forward at once.

I was sent on with Gale and Wilson to arrange for billeting the regiment. To-night we are in a little inn one mile north of Merville.

The battle is still going on. I hear we have taken 1,500 yards of trenches and a thousand prisoners. If the infantry can get on a bit farther the cavalry ought to be able to get through.

Cunningham has rejoined the squadron to-day from sick leave, which makes us over establishment, as he is one of the original officers of the squadron; he will probably relieve me, in which case I may go back to Windsor to the reserve regiment.

12TH MARCH

Reveille at 4 a.m.; we have remained at this place all day, expecting orders to move every moment.

The Greys and 12th Lancers have gone forward mounted. Things are beginning to get exciting.

18TH MARCH

Up at 4 o'clock again. Tremendous bombardment going on. I have never heard anything like it. Four hundred German prisoners have been brought into Merville and put on board barges on the canal.

I spoke to some of the German officers, who seemed quite relieved to have been captured. They say that our bombardment was tremendous. At 5 o'clock we got the depressing news that the attack had definitely failed, and is to be abandoned. We have taken over 2,000 prisoners, but it is said that our losses are about 8,000.

The ambulances have been going past in a continuous procession all day.

As soon as it was dark all the cavalry started back to their permanent billets. We had a most tedious march in the dark back to our farm at Staple, arriving in the early hours of the morning.

14TH MARCH

It is as I thought: now that Cunningham has come back I am going to the reserve regiment at Windsor until I am wanted again.

Now that our great attack is over, probably there will be nothing doing for the cavalry for many months again. This being so, I am not sorry to get back to England, where I shall have a better chance of getting an interesting staff job. Out here I can do nothing, as I never see anybody.

At 5 o'clock we again heard very heavy firing, this time from the direction of Ypres. It lasted for about half an hour, and was heavier than anything we have heard so far. All the windows of the farm rattled, although we are more than twenty miles from where it is taking place.

15TH MARCH

At 8 o'clock I got orders to report to the D.A.G. at Rouen, so I borrowed a car from Divisional Headquarters, and took my servant and kit to the station at Hazebrouck. I got a train at 8 o'clock and started down-country. So far as I can see, we may be days getting to the Base. It is now late at night and we have not got half-way there yet.

16TH MARCH—ROUEN, HÔTEL D'ANGLETERRE

I travelled down-country with Captain Ponsonby of the 8rd Dragoon Guards, with whom I have made great friends.

We reported ourselves to the D.A.G. here, and got orders to sail for England to-morrow. We had an excellent dinner at the big café, and had a look at the cathedral, which is magnificent.

17TH MARCH

Margaret Hamilton lunched with me at the hotel; she is running one of the big officers' hospitals here.

At 3 o'clock we embarked on the s.s. *King Edward*, which is one of the Clyde excursion steamers. It is most uncomfortable, as there are no cabins of any sort on her. Fortunately I have my fur bag with me, and am sleeping on deck.

18TH MARCH

We reached Southampton at 7 o'clock this morning, but could not land till 10.

I got home in time for lunch, and telephoned to Windsor, asking for a few days' leave. I wonder how long I shall be at home this time.

ALDERSHOT, 30TH AUGUST, 1915

The last day in England. We start to-night for Southampton *en route* for the Front. For the last three days I have been gradually clearing up and getting ready for the move, so that now there is little left to be done. Grizel came down to say good-bye on Saturday (28th), and to-day my mother came over from Bagshot. We motored into Aldershot town to get a few last things from the stores there for the mess. The 24th Division has been going now for some days, and we are almost the last to start. We have no idea where we are to concentrate; all that we know is that we land at Havre. One rumour is that we go to the Argonne, but that seems very unlikely; it is more probable that we shall prolong the present British line near Arras. However, we shall soon know now. I have complete confidence in my battery, and feel sure we shall be able to give a good account of ourselves.

H.M.T. "AUSTRALIND," 31ST AUGUST, 1915

We paraded at 3.30 a.m. and marched to Farnborough station. There we proceeded in two trains to Southamp-

ton. The landing went off without a hitch and we were
ready long before the train was due to start. I took
Shepard in my train with exactly half the battery, giving
the other half to Harvey. Kenny went over to Havre a
week ago to make arrangements for our arrival.

On reaching Southampton I was disgusted to find
that not only was my battery not all going on the same
ship, but that we were to be still further split up, so
as to be on three ships. I therefore sent Shepard with
twenty men and forty horses off with the embarkation
staff officer, and hoped for the best. I have given him the
sergeant-major, so hope they will be all right. I have not
heard of Harvey at all. On my boat are the whole of
our B Battery, half the Ammunition Column, under
Potter, and details of the Royal Sussex Regiment (6th
Battalion), with three officers. I am " O.C. Troops,"
which entails a lot of work. I have been solemnly given
a key-word to the cipher of the day, by which the naval
escort communicates orders to us ; one would think it
would be simpler to have given it to the captain of the
ship. This boat, the *Australind*, has just come back from
the Dardanelles—she was in the landing when we had
such casualties, and was hit all over.

All lights have to be out after dark and no noise allowed.
I have had a practice in falling in at alarm posts and
handing out life-belts. We are very comfortable and
well fed, which is lucky, as the mess-cart has gone with
the other part of the battery. I have two parties of forty
men told off for the bows and the stern in case of attack
by submarines. However, they say it is very unlikely.

HAVRE, 1ST SEPTEMBER, 1915

One ship anchored off the harbour about 4 a.m. and was
berthed at 7. Disembarkation commenced at once, and
by 9.30 all my guns and horses, etc., were on shore. Shepard,
with his party, turned up, having come over in a fast
paddle-boat ; and Harvey reported that his half of the
battery were disembarking at another dock.

Having obtained a guide, we marched off to the rest camp, some two miles. I was given my orders for entraining, and find that we are to leave the Gare des Marchandises at midnight, but still no orders of where we go. The newest rumour is Le Touquet, the bathing-place. If so, it probably means going on to Ypres again. I would rather go to a new place for a change. Kenny, who is still doing Railway Transport Officer, came to see me and said he was being overworked. This rest camp is a horrible place, especially as it has rained all day, and the place is a sea of sticky mud. I think France keeps a peculiar brand of mud of its own ; at least the only mud that I know that can compare with this camp is that of Flanders last winter. This is a huge camp of all sorts of units passing through on their way up-country. Some stay two or three days, others only a few hours. We passed some German prisoners on the way from the Docks, who had evidently just arrived from the Front. They looked much cleaner than the ones I saw at the battle of Neuve Chapelle. I am to take part of the Ammunition Column on my train, so we shall be a large party.

MARLES, 3RD SEPTEMBER, 1915

On the night of the 1st September we paraded at 11 p.m. and marched to the Havre Goods Station, where we entrained. As we have four wagons of the Ammunition Column, it made an enormous train of. fifty trucks, being over 400 yards long. I was not told my destination, but was told that on arrival at Abbeville I should be told where to detrain. We had an old-fashioned 1st-class carriage, but were very comfortable. We had a fearful job in getting the Ammunition Column mules on to the train. However, we got it over punctually to the time laid down. We stopped at a junction not far from Amiens for about half an hour in the early morning. Water was ready for the horses and we at once watered and fed. Two men travelled in each truck with eight horses. They had a proportion of hay and corn with them. At the halt hot coffee was provided for all the men, with a dash of brandy in it. The officers had the large motor luncheon box with them and fared remarkably well. We stopped again at 2 p.m. for forty minutes at Abbeville, and I was there told by the Railway Transport Officer that our destination was Montreuil. After passing Etaples we reached Montreuil at 4.30 p.m., and there I was told that we were to go on to Maresquel, some half-hour further. On arrival we found the General—Sir Godfrey Thomas— and his Staff Captain, Major Roberts. The detrainment went off very well, and by 6.30 p.m. the battery was ready to march off. We reached our billets at midnight, after a trying march in pitch darkness. The road was very difficult to find, as it was cross-country, with narrow lanes full of sharp turns.

On arrival at Marles I found that no billets had been arranged, and, after getting the battery into a large field, I started off with my electric lamp to find farms that would do. As the whole brigade had to get into the one small village, it was not an easy matter ; but eventually I got them all under cover in barns.

It rained hard all the time, from our arrival at the station, and I doubt if the men will ever forget their first night on active service.

This morning, on going down to the lines, I was horrified to find that the field that I had camped in was so close to the river that, after a night's heavy rain, the place had become a bog. Some of the heavy baggage wagons had sunk half-way to the axles. With great difficulty I found new billets, and in the afternoon marched out to the other side of the village and camped on some high ground. It took twelve horses to move the heavy wagons. The officers are very comfortable, in a large farm. We have two rooms : one the kitchen, where I sleep on the floor, and we have our meals ; the other a small bedroom where Kenny, Harvey and Shepard sleep. I am told that we shall probably stay here about five days before going into action.

MARLES, 4TH SEPTEMBER, 1915

To-day we spent in squaring up camp and billets. It began by a few gleams of sunshine, but quickly started raining again. The gun-park is on a stubble field, so that the guns sink in, and we have to get drag-ropes to move them.

Thanks to my having got the village school for a dining-room, the men are far better off than any other battery. In spite of wet clothes, etc., they are very cheerful. As for officers, we are in the lap of luxury. I sleep on the stone floor of the kitchen, but in my fur bag I am as happy as possible.

In the afternoon we had a great conference—all the B.C.s and the Supply Officers. They all want to invent new ways of drawing supplies and making local purchases. I tried to persuade them to stick to the way it has been done in other divisions since the beginning of the war.

MARLES, 6TH SEPTEMBER, 1915

The result of the supply officer's funny little ways with his wagons is that yesterday (Sunday) I only received half my forage, which gave me the trouble of riding ten miles to see about it. In the afternoon Kenny and I rode to Montreuil to church there. Last time I was there, I was motoring through on my way to Darmstadt, and the time before when G. and I slept the night there on our way to Paris, in the big Napier. Now it is full of British troops.

At the bridge just before entering the town were an English and French sentry, side by side, with fixed bayonets, one in khaki and the other in pale blue—a curious contrast.

To-day I took the battery out for a little exercise ; it is ideal ground for artillery—small hills and valleys, with plenty of good roads. It was very hot in the sun, and the horses seemed to feel it, as they are out of condition after the long voyage and train journey.

At midday, all battery commanders met our new Army Corps Commander, General Haking, who has just been appointed to command the new XIth Corps. He was very nice and cheerful, and told us that the great push will come very soon now and that we shall be in it. Apparently we are to be in reserve for the great attack, and shall be flung through the gap when the German line is broken. It looks as if we should have great chances of distinguishing ourselves.

MARLES, 7TH SEPTEMBER, 1915

To-day we had a divisional field-day for the benefit of our new Corps Commander. Very hot ; it took a lot out of the horses, as this part of the country is nothing but steep hills and valleys. I cannot say it was the least instructive to anyone, except possibly the Staff.

At last I have got hold of the Field Cashier, and was able to pay the battery, also got an advance of frs. 200 for Imprest Account. By paying on a system, I was able to get through the battery in just under the hour—which is fairly quick work with 140 men, each signing his name.

MARLES, 8TH SEPTEMBER, 1915

Another really hot day. Went round the village and paid for the straw and vegetables, etc., that we had bought. In the afternoon the Requisitioning Officer turned up, and with great difficulty was persuaded to pay for my purchases. As usual, they try to cut one down as much as possible. If one is not very careful it means paying half the things out of one's own pocket. The Veterinary Officer came round the horses. He is a youth who has just joined the Army Veterinary Corps for the war. I don't think either he or his sergeant knows a horse from a cow. Fortunately, there are others in the battery who do.

At 9 p.m. it was reported to me that a secret telephone wire had been found leading out of the village. We searched, but could not find the end of it. I suspect that it is an old English wire left behind after some unit had been practising with it. The German spies' wires that I saw near Ypres were much more carefully laid, and could not have been found so easily. On my way home I found

some of my men with a lighted candle in the billets. I
have placed the N.C.O. in charge under arrest; he ought
to be drowned. The 2nd Life Guards had two billets
burnt down that way last winter.

MARLES, 9TH SEPTEMBER, 1915

Another glorious hot day. I took out my battery
staff and worked out some prismatic compass problems
with them. How quickly one gets out of the way of the
various formulæ if one does not practise them every day!
We had a practice alarm this afternoon. It took me
exactly one hour to turn out and get clear of my lines—
not so bad, as it was quite unexpected and we had to pack
the baggage-wagon. The brigade marched out a couple
of miles and then went home to tea. At 10 p.m. I got
orders to march at 8 a.m. to-morrow morning, to go up
to the trenches. So we have packed everything up and
have arranged to be called at 4 a.m. It will take us three
days to march the forty-odd miles to the firing line, so it
won't be long now before we are in the middle of it. We
are to be attached to the Indian Division. I wonder if
I have forgotten all my Hindustani?

At 6 o'clock this morning, I got an urgent message to
send my baggage-wagon into the A.S.C. Depot at Neu-
ville, some four miles off. Now I have to send a team of
horses at 4 a.m. to get it back. The manners and customs
of these people are beyond the intelligence of ordinary
mortals. I only wish I could meet the man responsible
for the muddle, alone on a dark night. He, at any rate,
would make no more muddles.

LAIRES, 10TH SEPTEMBER, 1915

To-day we have done some twenty-five miles and reached
this place, just before dark. My baggage-wagons arrived
only half an hour before we started, and were drawn
by my own horses, the A.S.C. having failed to send
theirs in time. We marched via Beaurainville-Royon-
Créquy-Fruges and Lugy to Laires. Some terrible hills

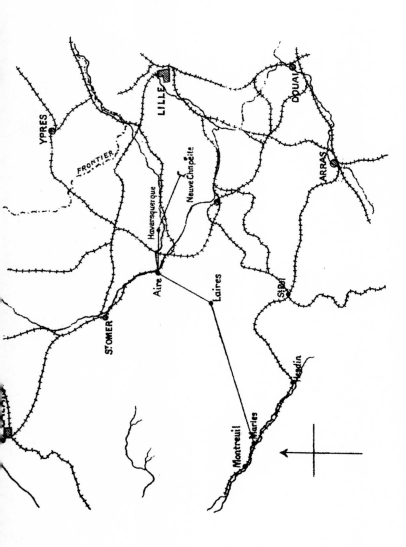

LAIRES-DOUAI-YPRES, SEPT. 1915.

and only one halt of four minutes in over four hours ! It is cruel and has knocked up several of my horses. One cannot hope to keep horses fit at this rate. To-morrow we continue our march towards the firing-line, starting 1 p.m.

Aire, 11th September, 1915

A short march of about ten miles ; we started after lunch and did it comfortably by 5 o'clock. The usual muddle about the luggage-wagon. When we got to the starting point, I was told to abandon it and that it would be brought on by the A.S.C.

Haversquerque, 12th September, 1915

Another short march of some ten miles. Very fine old church; I should think mostly dating from fifteenth century, with a good many additions. Last night we all slept in the gun park, as the billets allotted to us by the French townspeople were too bad to occupy. A fine night, and I was very comfortable in my bivouac tent.

In Action before Neuve Chapelle, 13th September, 1915

Rode over in the morning with Birch of our D 108, to report to Colonel Maxwell, commanding the Artillery Brigade we are attached to. He was very kind and showed me my position, etc. Brought the battery up after dark, having carefully reconnoitred the ground with Harvey and the four No. 1's. Dined with the 88rd Battery Major (Vaughan), after which we all went out to meet the battery. Coming off the road was not an easy job at all, as it was quite dark, and there were two bridges to cross, only 9 feet wide, over deep ditches. However, they all got across without any hitch. The 88rd had partly prepared gun-pits, which we took over and completed. They are like miniature forts, very deep and roomy inside, with splendid underground chambers for the men and ammunition. They are roofed over with corrugated iron, covered with earth, then a layer of bricks and, finally, more earth

[margin note: Neuve Chapelle 13 Sept -17 Sept.]

on top of that. The roof is supported on iron girders and railway irons, resting on huge walls of sandbags. The men eat and sleep with the guns and are warm and comfortable. The officers have a small farm just in front of the battery; it has been badly knocked about by the German artillery, but is still better than nothing. By 7 a.m. I thought we had done enough, so stopped work for an hour's sleep. Everyone very tired after fifteen-mile march and twenty-six hours' continuous hard work.

IN ACTION BEFORE NEUVE CHAPELLE, 14TH SEPTEMBER, 1915

At 10 a.m. I went to the Observing Station of the 83rd Battery, which they are kind enough to let me use. I think to-day has been the most interesting day of my life. Our Observing Station is in the remains of a house close to the church in the middle of the famous village of Neuve Chapelle. For the first half-mile or so Vaughan and I walked along the paths in the open, after which we took to the communicating trenches that go up to the front from a mile in rear. There are narrow trenches about 6 or 8 feet deep. The bottom of the trench has wood boards, with a space between to let the water through. Every 6 feet or so there is a pit to catch the water. The boards are covered with wire netting, to prevent one slipping in wet weather.

On arrival at Neuve Chapelle village, Vaughan took me up to his Observation Post, which is in the roof of a ruined house close to the church. The place looks as if it would fall down if you touched it. From the top floor one can see the German trenches about 400 yards in front quite well. One has to use a periscope, as it is not safe to put one's head up. We share a long barn near the centre of my zone, and get all the guns on to that, so that now I can switch off on to any other point required.

NEUVE CHAPELLE, 15TH SEPTEMBER, 1915

To-day Kenny is in the O.P. and Harvey in the Battery. I went down there in the morning and shelled the German lines all day. I cannot see the left of my zone from the house, so went on into the firing-trench of the Manchesters. From there, with a periscope, I could see the German trenches very plainly some 200 yards in front. I had great fun dropping shell after shell into their communicating trenches. It annoyed them so much that they turned on a battery of 6-in. howitzers to stop me. They evidently had not located my battery, but mistook me for another battery about 300 yards to my right. They suddenly bombarded this unfortunate battery with about a dozen high explosives, and made an awful mess of it. Two wagons of ammunition set on fire. They had the range to a yard, and dropped all their shells right into the middle of the guns. Later on they tried to get me with " pip-squeaks " (field-guns), but got nothing nearer than 200 yards in front. In the evening I shelled a large barn behind their lines that may have been used as an Observation Station., After putting a lot of percussion shells into it, it caught fire and burnt merrily. After dark it made a fine glare.

Visited by the local general, who seemed very pleased with everything. Sat up till midnight working out angles and ranges on the large-scale map 1/10,000. This is indeed a scientific war. To think that the guns are in holes in the ground two miles away and yet that I can hit anything I like, getting within 25 yards every time. I must say I am having the time of my life—this is quite the most interesting experience I have ever had.

Neuve Chapelle, 16th September, 1915

Visited by the colonel this morning. Harvey in the trenches, Kenny in the battery. In view of yesterday's bombardment, I have strengthened my gun-pits with more earth and bricks. After lunch I went down to the Observing Post. I established a new Observation Post in the front trench of the Manchesters. From here, I have a splendid view of the whole of the German trenches, only 300 yards away, also of the whole front of the Bois du Biez. I got into communication with the company officer in charge of the front trench. He told me that they had been much worried by a minenwerfer, or bomb-throwing trench gun. He pointed out the house it was in, and I at once turned my Right Section on to it. I got my range very soon, and then gave it two rounds of section fire at fifteen seconds. Every shell went into the house and burst inside. The house collapsed and caught fire. I don't think that the Hun will use it again. The shooting was perfect, every shell going exactly where it was wanted. The infantry officers were delighted. I have run out my telephone wires to the front trench and have an officer there night and day. Our trenches here are simply a wall of sandbags, open to the rear. It was rather nervous work, as my shells were passing over my head only a few feet above. The range was 3,000 yards, so the angle of descent is not great. The telephones are working well, and from my headquarters I am always in communication with my observing officer in the trenches, with my battery, and with Brigade Headquarters. Via the latter, I can speak to any other battery along the front. In the trenches all observation is done through a periscope, and I find that the best sort is a plain stick with two long mirrors. No shells reached the battery to-day, and so far I have had no casualties.

NEUVE CHAPELLE, 17TH SEPTEMBER, 1915

Another glorious day, but very hot. Still in action at the same place. To-day I went down to the infantry trenches and had a consultation with the local company commander. He pointed out a small object near the edge of the Bois du Biez, and close behind the German trenches. It looked like a very large periscope about 6 feet high and 2 feet wide, with a window near the top. It was very hard to make out as it was in deep shadow and half behind a tree. The infantry said that it had a door in the back that was sometimes open and sometimes shut. I decided to take it on. After two shots I got quite close, but found it very difficult to get a direct hit on it. Shot after shot burst just short or just over or just right or left. Eventually,

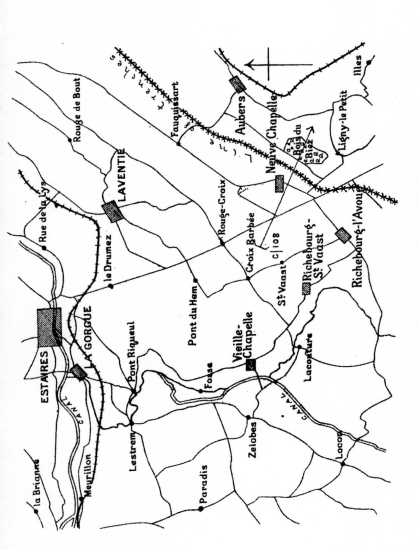

NEUVE CHAPELLE, SEPT. 1915.

after using a lot of shells, I got one that burst immediately in front of the thing, and it disappeared in a cloud of dust, smoke, and branches of trees. The infantry gave a great cheer; it pleased them immensely, and made them feel that their own guns could and would help them. I believe this to be one of the most important duties of a battery commander in war time.

At 6 o'clock I received orders to come out of action and rendezvous at Fosse. I sent Kenny back to the wagon line (six miles off) and he brought up the horses and transport at 9 p.m. We got away without difficulty, and the Hun fortunately did not shell us whilst the horses were on the position. We had a tragedy to-day. Poor "Little Willy," the battery monkey, was killed by one of our guns. He got loose and ran out in front of a gun.

NŒUX-LES-MINES, 18TH SEPTEMBER, 1915

We marched all last night, the 17/18, and reached this place at dawn. Our wagon line is about a mile to the west of the town. We have now reached a mining district exactly like Wishaw. Large byngs, pit-heads, and usual " rows " of miners' cottages. It seems very strange to be fighting in such country.

As soon as I had had breakfast I took my trumpeter and rode over to the headquarters of the Group we now come under—(3rd Heavy Brigade, Colonel Poole). He showed me on the map where the battery positions would be, after which I rode back to the battery. No sooner had I arrived than I got a message from the colonel that he wanted all battery commanders to ride out with him and reconnoitre the positions. So I bolted a piece of bully-beef and put a couple of biscuits in my pocket and started off again, back to Noyelles-les-Vermelles. There we met Colonel Poole, who took us on to Grenay. My battery position is in a piece of waste ground in the middle of the town, as it were, between the Glasgow Iron and Steel Works and the Stinton Works at Wishaw. I have taken over the gun-pits of I. Battery, R.H.A. They are beautifully made, each gun being in a small fort of its own.

Besides the gun-pits there are good pits for the section commanders and the telephonists ; these are connected with the gun-pits by speaking-tubes, so that one battery can be fought entirely underground, without a single head showing.

From the gun positions we walked on partly down the communicating trenches to the Observing Stations. These are about a mile and a half to the front, and just in rear of the infantry trenches. My O.P. is in a row of little houses, locally known as " Artillery Mansions." It is a mean little street, like Craigneuk. I go into the house, which was once an estaminet, and then down into the cellar, which is well sand-bagged on top in case the house is brought down. From the cellar there is a low tunnel which leads under a tiny garden at the back and comes up in a small outhouse. Through a small hole in the wall I can see our trenches, and those of the Germans, to the outskirts of the town of St. Pierre. My zone includes all this town and a large byng on the right, with a pit-head at the end. After examining the position, etc., I rode back to the battery, some six miles more. Had a short dinner and then brought the guns up into action. I arranged to drive into the position soon after dark. Everything worked smoothly and by 11 p.m. I had the guns in their pits with the whole of the ammunition in the dug-outs beside them (704 rounds in the battery). As soon as Kenny had taken away the limbers and empty wagons, we started building up the parados or sandbag walls behind the gunpits. I also had the roofs much strengthened with additional sandbags, broken bricks, and iron rails. The newest idea is that earth is no good as a protection against high explosive shells of large size, and one must have something hard, like iron or brick that will detonate the fuse *before* it penetrates inside the dug-out. I got to bed at 2 a.m., after being on the go, without shutting my eyes, for forty-three hours, having ridden about forty miles.

GRENAY, 19TH SEPTEMBER, 1915

Spent the morning laying out my lines of fire by the map and prismatic compass. I chose a church spire in St.

Pierre that I could see well. After measuring the range and angles very carefully I went down to my Observation Post and commenced firing. The very first shot burst within 2 degrees of my target, which pleased me greatly, as it proved that my calculations were all right. After that, I " registered " various things on the near side of St. Pierre. Then I searched all the likely places that I could see for German Artillery Observation Posts, and fired shrapnel through the windows. I don't know if I hit anyone, but at any rate it must have been very unhealthy in these places.

GRENAY, 20TH SEPTEMBER, 1915

A tragic day. I went down to my Observation Post in the morning, with Shephard, and amused myself shelling the pit-head on my right, and also the German trenches just in front of it. I was in the middle of ranging on another large factory when I was rung up on the telephone and told that the colonel had just been killed. The Huns have been shelling Bde. H.Q. for the last two days, as there is a fresh battery of 75's quite close. They have been dropping " Jack Johnsons " on the road in front of Bde. H.Q.'s door every few minutes. The colonel had been standing in the door when one burst just in front of him. It did not touch him, but killed one and wounded another infantryman who was passing. The colonel ran out to get in the wounded man. At that moment another shell landed close to him and killed him instantly. He was carried into the house at once, but was quite dead. He had been hit in the right forearm and also in the head. Poor old man ! It was very sporting of him to have come out at his age—over sixty. Everyone was devoted to him and we shall feel his loss greatly. As soon as I heard the news I started back to Bde. H.Q., Harvey advising me to come along the communicating trench as far as possible. This I did, till I got some 400 yards from Bde. H.Q., after which I had to come along the street. I had just reached the Bde. H.Q. and was stopping in front of the door, when a Jack Johnson burst right alongside of me. It seem to me to burst at my feet. I was flung down in the road, but not touched. I had an awful fright, as I thought I was stone blind, as I could see nothing at all; but in a few seconds I could distinguish things near me. I then realised that it was only the black smoke from the explosion. It is marvellous that I was not hit, as the whole air whistled with fragments of shells, bricks, glass, and stones. When I got inside the house I found Colonel Poole, who commands our Group. He gave me certain very important and detailed orders that I must not write down yet. The poor old colonel was lying on the floor of a room near the door. The whole place was swimming in blood, and several wounded and dying men in the cellar. Colonel Poole was very nice and sympathetic. Fortunately he left the house between the arrival of two shells.

After I had made various arrangements with the adjutant, as to sending for an officer from the Column, etc., I started to go over to C Battery. I had not got 30 yards from Bde. H.Q. when another shell burst just behind me. I flattened myself against a wall, and again was not touched.

I had a meeting of officers at 7 p.m. and gave them their orders for to-morrow. I have decided to move H.Q. some four hundred yards, so as to be away from the place they always shell. We got hold of a Church of England padre and buried the colonel in a quiet little garden behind this house. We could not bury him till 9 o'clock at night, as the shelling was too heavy; then we brought him over here on a stretcher and by moonlight, and with a hurricane lamp, we buried him. It was very simple but very impressive.

I slept at the new Bde. H.Q., but it was not till 3 a.m. that we got settled in. All the telephones had to be shifted, then we had to prop up the girders of the cellar we are using and sandbag the floor above. Also we have put many tons of bricks on to the sandbags, in the hope of detonating shells before they penetrate into the cellar. It should keep out anything up to 6-in. howitzers; of course, 6-in. or over would go through like paper. Still, it is all we can do and we feel comparatively safe for the present.

GRENAY, 21ST SEPTEMBER, 1915

To-day is the first day of the great bombardment. And what a bombardment it is ! There must be hundreds and hundreds of French and English guns all concentrated at this one spot. We have an almost unlimited allowance of ammunition and are letting it off at a tremendous rate. I have spent most of the day in my cellar, with my adjutant, surrounded with maps and telephones. Every few minutes I get an order from Group H.Q. to say that such-and-such an area is being shelled by German batteries in the direction of Loos or St. Pierre. I then look up on my coloured tracings which of my batteries can best deal with the particular area and then phone to them to turn their fire on to the place. Since dawn this morning the noise has been appalling. Field-guns, howitzers, large and small, big naval guns, " mothers," and even " grandmothers," are all joining in. The poor Hun must be having a rotten time. By evening his fire had distinctly slackened off. I think we must be fairly drowning him with shells. At last we are beginning to get our own back. So far during this war the German has always had the vast superiority of fire ; now, for the first time, he is hopelessly out-numbered in guns and shells. After dark the fire was not so continuous, but it is still being kept up fairly heavily, with bursts of intense gun fire every half-hour or so. The French 75 batteries on our right and left seem to keep at it the whole time.

I have been at the telephone all day except for meals. It is very dull down in my dark wine-cellar, with only one small hole up into the air, whilst all the battery commanders are in their Observing Posts, watching the fun. However, my place is at the end of the telephone and my work is of the greatest importance, as from here I direct and control the fire of all the batteries. By dark this evening the batteries had fired over 50 rounds per gun. Late in the evening I had a message from our Group Commander to say that we were keeping down the hostile fire, and that he was pleased with the work of the brigade.

About 10.30 at night I got a message from Harvey, who is now in command of my battery, to say that the Germans were firing down the Grenay-Loos road with machine-guns. We could hear it quite distinctly back here. I at once turned A and C Batteries on to this road and the market square in the centre of Loos. This stopped the machine-guns at once.

" And so to bed " in my horrid cellar.

GRENAY, 22ND SEPTEMBER, 1915

I woke early this morning to hear the great bombardment continuing. The volume of fire is simply appalling. The whole earth is trembling, and this house shakes the whole time with the concussion of the guns firing. There are French 75 batteries right and left of us and a 6-in. howitzer battery immediately behind our house. As I was writing this, I saw Colonel Pereira, who was my company commander in the Grenadiers, so ran out to speak to him. He is commanding a pioneer battalion along our front.

Our bombardment has continued all day and now, after dark, is still being kept up by intermittent bursts of fire, especially by the French batteries around us.

At 10 p.m. I again heard machine-gun fire in the direction of St. Pierre, so I went out myself and arranged for a brigade salvo to be fired on my whistle, to be immediately followed by a round of gun-fire. I had all guns laid on the square in front of the church in St. Pierre. The batteries all fired at exactly the same second, and if the German convoys were passing through the town then, which it is practically certain they would be, the result must have been serious to them. If, as I suspect, the square was packed with men and wagons, with food and ammunition for the trenches, we must have caused horrible slaughter. It is a horrible thing to have to do, but war is a horrid thing and the more we kill the sooner it will be over. After all, they have done this sort of thing to us. What is more, it pleases our own infantry to know that our guns are always ready to help them, night and day.

It is a glorious moonlight night, and I could see the reflection in the sky of the bursting shells.

Our forward observing officers report that the whole of St. Pierre and Loos is blotted out in smoke, whilst parts of the towns are in flames. I also hear that our heavy guns have been playing havoc with their infantry trenches.

This afternoon they fired one 12-in. shell, which fell near here, but so far they have not repeated it.

Perhaps they will try again in the middle of the night. We have been firing a great deal of our new high-explosive shells to-day.

GRENAY, 23RD SEPTEMBER, 1915

Our batteries did not open fire very early to-day, as there was a mist. The Hun, on the other hand, shelled us from 8 to 9, with 8-in. shells. He fired about twenty shots, which all fell at exactly the same spot—100 yards in rear of D Battery and 300 yards from my H.Q. We were all shaving at the time, and I expected to cut myself every shot, as the whole house rocked with the concussion. Pieces of shell struck our house, but, fortunately, did not come through the windows. I appealed to Group H.Q. for help, and they at once turned some of our very heavy howitzers on to them. It stopped the Germans at once, and so far (11 a.m.) we have had no more shells near us. The general bombardment is going on merrily again and, as usual, the place is rocking and shuddering with the noise. Our aeroplanes are going to take photos of the enemy's positions between 12.30 and 1 p.m., so we have to stop firing, or else they would see nothing for smoke.

4 p.m. The roar of the guns has increased greatly, and is now simply appalling. The French batteries never seem to stop. I have been watching one gun and found that it was firing continuously at the rate of 1 round every 3 seconds, or 20 rounds per minute per gun. They seem to keep it up for about a minute at a time, then they

all run back to their dug-outs, which are some way from the guns. The extraordinary thing about the French batteries is that they do not dig in the guns at all ; in fact, they stand out in the open without any protection at all. We, on the other hand, make small forts over each of our guns that will keep out anything under a 6-in. shell.

This afternoon I have been plastering St. Pierre and Loos with shrapnel, by " search and sweep," i.e. each gun in the batteries fires nine shots and three different ranges and three different angles. I am glad I am not there.

7 p.m. Things have quietened down again now.

8 p.m. The most extraordinary phenomenon is happening. There is a loud wailing in the air, just like the wind in the trees, only louder. It also somewhat reminds me of jackals in the East, or a dog howling. It has been going on for some time now. It is the weirdest and most mournful thing I ever heard, following on the day's bombardment. If one was superstitious, which I am, one would say it was the spirits of the killed, wailing in the air. The true explanation more probably is that the wind has got up and that it is whistling through our broken roof.

Last thing before going to bed in my cellar, I ordered all batteries to sweep the main streets of Loos and St. Pierre with shrapnel. It is a brutal thing to do, but will certainly cause the Germans considerable losses in their supply columns, and, besides that, the moral effect on their infantry in the trenches should be great, if their food fails to arrive.

GRENAY, 24TH SEPTEMBER, 1915

A letter from G. and some tobacco : both very welcome.

The Hun did not give us our usual reveille of Jack Johnsons to-day. Can it be that he has withdrawn his heavy guns in anticipation of shortly having to retire ?

3.45 p.m. The fun is waxing fast and furious. We are increasing our fire : every half-hour I get orders to plaster poor Loos or St. Pierre. I have taken to " search and sweep " 18 rounds per gun with two batteries at a time. I should think we must be doing a lot of damage. The Hun has been quiet all the morning, but now he has started on our trenches and observing-stations with big stuff, since my violent efforts to retaliate on his vulnerable spots.

The adjutant of the battery group to which we belong has been round to-day and says they are very pleased with this brigade, which is distinctly gratifying. I am going over to dine with them to-night to get my final instructions for to-morrow. Our own R.A. general, Sir Godfrey Thomas, and Roberts, his staff captain, came round this afternoon, so I suppose we shall soon join up with our own division.

I rode over to Noyelles, after dark, to dine with Colonel Poole, who commands the group of counter-batteries. Had a most enjoyable dinner—whisky, white wine, port, and Benedictine. They do themselves well, which is sensible. On my road there, I took a wrong turning and found myself in the middle of a battery, which started firing just as I passed. The flash of the guns lit up the whole street and the noise was deafening. " Wuzzy," my first charger, nearly had a fit, but was very good. After the first shot he hardly minded it at all.

On my return I had a conference with the battery commanders, and gave them detailed instructions for to-morrow. The assault takes place at 0 hours 00 minutes o'clock. We " lift " our fire further and further on, at certain times from 0 to 00. Only *I* have known hitherto what 0–00 was. Now I have told the B.C.s. The orders are somewhat complicated, and I shall be very much relieved when it is all over.

Besides taking on the German batteries, we have to put up a " barrage " of fire across two of their important communication trenches. This I have entrusted to Birch (D Batt.) as the one I think who will do it best. I have sent Govan, who is one of the best subalterns in the brigade, on with the infantry. He takes three tele-phonists with him, who will lay out a wire as they go.

6

His duty is to keep me informed how far our infantry get on, so that we may not fire on them.

GRENAY, 25TH SEPTEMBER, 1915

11 *a.m.* The great assault has taken place. So far as we can tell at present, it has been completely successful. It was timed to take place at 4.50 a.m., but at the last moment was put off till 5.50, as the wind was not right. We used our new guns for the first time, but I cannot make out yet if it was a great success or not. Loos is taken, and so is Hulluch, on our left. So far, about 200 German prisoners have been marched through Grenay. They say we have not lost heavily, but some hundreds of our wounded have already gone through. Only the worst cases go in the ambulances; the remainder walk back about a couple of miles to the field ambulance in Les Brebis. Most of them are only hit in the hand and look quite cheerful. They say that the Germans made hardly any resistance in the first trenches, being quite taken by surprise by our gas. My Forward Observing Officer (Govan) has done very well indeed. He went on with the telephone, in company with the infantry, and has kept me informed all the time of how far our people had got. He has now telephoned from Loos that the enemy are on the run, and that our infantry are pressing on in pursuit. He is going on with them.

Everything went on well until about 3 p.m., when a heavy German counter-attack developed on Loos, from behind St. Pierre. As soon as I got the news from Group H.Q. I turned three batteries on to it, and all our heavy batteries got on to them too. The attack was soon stopped, and we were not driven back beyond the eastern side of Loos.

At 5 p.m. I got orders to report immediately to G.O.C. 24th Div. Art. at Vermelles. On getting there, I found Sir Godfrey Thomas and Hannay, the Bde. Major, who handed me my orders. I was to report to G.O.C. 72nd Inf. Bde. (General Mitford), to whom my brigade is attached. With some difficulty I found him, and he told

me that he was then advancing to the attack, his objective
being Vendin le Vieil. He requested me to follow and
support him at once. I told him that my batteries were
then still in action, five miles away, with the horses and
limbers another five miles off ; and that consequently,
by the time I had ridden back to the batteries and sent
for the horses, got them up to the guns and trekked over
to Vermelles, it would be long after dark. I, therefore,
asked that a representative of the Inf. Bde. might meet
me at the rendezvous, Le Rutoire, to guide me to where
the Inf. Bde. had gone. This General Mitford declined
to do, saying that when I got to the rendezvous anyone
would be able to direct me on. I went back to the brigade
in Grenay and collected them as quickly as possible ; but
it was not until 9 p.m. that I was able to march with
H.Q., C and D Batteries. A Battery horses not having
come up, I had to leave them to follow on. We picked
up B Battery on the way, at a point I had previously
arranged.

The march to Vermelles was a nightmare, as the road
was blocked with at least three rows of traffic—artillery,
ammunition columns, infantry cook-carts, and ambulances ;
also by a stream of wounded who were finding their own
way back from the advanced Field Dressing Stations to
the field ambulances in rear. Eventually we reached
Vermelles at 11 p.m., and I reported to Div. H.Q., but
could get no information as to where the 72nd Brigade
were. I therefore left the batteries in the street of
Vermelles, which was not being shelled very heavily, and
took on the battery commanders to hunt for the 72nd
Brigade, and, if possible, choose positions in the dark.

On reaching Le Rutoire, we were told that the 72nd
Brigade had gone on into the plain beyond the trenches.
There is an enormous plain of waste clay land, without
roads or cultivation, and without a house for miles.
We wandered about in the dark for three hours, being
shelled all the time by heavy guns. It was an absolute
nightmare: everyone we asked said something different;
that the brigade was just in front, that it was two

miles to the right, that it was a mile to the left, and so on. Eventually we got out beyond, not only our own trenches, but beyond the German trenches, too. All this in the dark, and having to cross dozens of trenches by slippery wooden planks.

At last I came to the conclusion that it was an impossible task to find General Mitford that night, and that, moreover, he was so far to the front that it would be impossible to get the batteries across the muddy plain before daylight, let alone dig them in. I therefore returned to Vermelles, and woke up Sir Godfrey Thomas, who then told me to come into action close to Le Rutoire. This we did, using our old line of support trenches. The guns are just behind the trenches, and the men can jump down into them, if heavily shelled. The headquarters established themselves in an old and filthy dug-out some 20 yards from the right flank of the brigade.

LE RUTOIRE, 26TH SEPTEMBER, 1915

A Battery joined up in the morning, and took up a position 100 yards in rear of the brigade. I could get no information beyond that I was to barrage some German communication trenches, whilst the 72nd and 71st Brigades attacked Hill 70. We heard nothing more till about 11 a.m., when I got an urgent telephone message from my F.O.O. that the attack had failed, and that our men were falling back fast all along the line. Soon after, he reported that a major of a Highland regiment had told him to get out of it at once, and that he was coming in with his instruments and telephonists.

Soon after this, we saw the infantry streaming back over the near sky-line, some 2,000 yards in front of us, whilst a number of batteries which were in action near Lone Tree limbered up and were coming back as quickly as possible. Still I had had no orders from Div. H.Q., so I took the responsibility of turning the batteries on to the slopes of Hill 70. If the Germans were really coming down then to the assault, it should have just caught them nicely. At the same time I sent back for the horses of the whole brigade, so that if the worst came to the worst we might have had a chance of getting the guns away. I then sent for battery commanders, and told them if the horses did not arrive before the infantry had retired through us, that they were to continue firing at the Germans until the latter got to within 400 yards, when they were to destroy their guns and remove the sights, after which they could get away as best they could. Fortunately, at the last moment fresh infantry were moved forward and the remainder rallied, and the German advance was stopped.

The afternoon was fairly quiet. They put a few Jack Johnsons near us, but did no harm. We now come under the left group. The artillery of the whole XI Corps has been lumped together under General Wardrop, the C.R.A. of the Guards Division. As far as I can make out, the 24th and 21st Divisions have been very badly hit, and will have to be withdrawn to refit, but I suppose we shall be left in action.

All the afternoon I tried to get orders and information from the front, but was unable to do so. I therefore dared not fire any more.

LE RUTOIRE, 27TH SEPTEMBER, 1915

Nothing happened in the morning. The batteries continued to improve their gun-pits. At lunch time I was sent for to Group H.Q., and told that the Guards were going to assault the Chalk Pit and Hill 70. My batteries were ordered to barrage a road on their left. I personally was to go at once to the H.Q. of the 1st Guards Brigade, and remain with General Feilding during the attack. I worked out the zones for the various batteries, and gave them their orders to keep up a steady fire from 3 to 5 p.m.

I had an awful time trying to get up to where General Feilding was. I had to walk about a mile up our own communicating trench and came to our old fire trenches, the ones we had been in till two days ago. After that it was necessary to get out into the open and pass through our wire into the neutral zone. Crossing the space of some

400 yards before reaching the German trenches was simply
Hell incarnate. It was being swept continuously by the
German heavy guns and also with shrapnel, to say nothing
of rifle-bullets which were coming over the crest. This
ground presented a terrible sight, the dead lying about
everywhere—principally our own men who had been killed
in the assault two days before. Besides these were
hundreds of rifles and the kits of the wounded. The
latter had already been brought in. Needless to say, I
lost no time in getting across, and was much relieved when
I dropped safely down into the German front-line trench.
With great difficulty, I made my way along this, as it
was very narrow, and packed with Coldstream Guards,
who were waiting to do the assault. Eventually I found
General Feilding with his Staff Captain, Lord Gort, and
reported that my batteries were barraging the road on
his left.

It was now 3 p.m., and suddenly our shells began to
come over my head in a continuous stream from the four
batteries. The shooting was distinctly good, the great
majority of the shells falling near the road or bursting over
it. The assault was timed to take place at 4 p.m., and a
few minutes before the hour our people on the left sent up
clouds of white smoke—a harmless smoke that gave off
dense white clouds. The wind was blowing from us to
the Huns, and the smoke made a complete screen between
our assault and the people on the left. The result was
that the assault was completely hidden from the German
sight. The smoke screens are very successful, and the
infantry were delighted with them.

Precisely at the hour, the officers leaped up on to the
parapet, immediately followed by the men—this was the
2nd Bn. Irish Guards. There was a shout of " They
are off ! " and the assault commenced. Almost at once
they were lost to sight in the valley in front of us, and, so
far as we could see, they had very few casualties to start
with. The Germans now began to fire fast, with shrapnel
and rifle. Our look-out place in the rear parapet of the
German trench became unhealthy, and we were all so

excited in watching the assault that we continued looking
out. We had a Coldstream machine-gun about ten yards
on our right, which was firing over the heads of the assaulting troops. Suddenly a shrapnel burst just on our right,
and the machine-gun stopped a few moments later. Someone reported that it had just caught the gun crew, and
killed and wounded the lot, except the actual man who
was working the gun, who was not touched.

After a time some of our wounded began to crawl and
stagger back. They said that they had got through the
wood, but had been taken in flank by machine-guns, and
the assault had been brought to a stop. This turned out
to be true, and the brigade had to be content with entrenching themselves on the road at the foot of the hill
they had hoped to take. General Feilding went on to
see what was happening, but told me to remain in the
German trench by my telephone. Whilst I was waiting
for him to come back, I had a look round and was astounded
to see what a palatial place it was. I was specially struck
by the officers' quarters. One of them must have been
quite 20 feet under ground, a long, sloping passage leading
down to it. The soil is hard chalk a few feet below the
surface. A room had been cut out underground some
15 feet by 12 feet; the floor was boarded, and so were
the walls. There were two iron bedsteads, a large table,
chairs, and a large looking-glass. The walls were decorated
with pictures, and, in fact, there was every luxury. The
place was dry and warm; dozens of empty bottles were
lying about; also cigar-boxes—but alas! neither wine
nor cigars were left. I got a copy of the *Kolnische Zeitung*,
three days old, which afforded much amusement when I
got back to my dug-out. Also a roll of maps of the district.
These were very rough and disappointing.

The walk back was a nightmare. It was about two
miles in the dark,- partly in the communicating trench
and partly across the open ; as it was raining, the clay soil
had become exactly like vaseline, and for every step one
took forward one slipped back 6 inches—added to which I
kept falling into shell-holes in the dark.

Le Rutoire, 28th September, 1915

Spent a very uncomfortable night in our dug-out in the trench, near the guns. Soon after daylight they started shelling us from the direction of Hulluch. The shelling was done entirely by a 6-in. or 8-in. battery with high explosives. However, no damage was done during the morning, although these big shells were falling all among the guns.

At lunch-time I was told that the Guards were going to attack again, and that I was to support them with two batteries, and keep the other two batteries in hand, ready to turn on to anything required. I detailed A and B to fire. No sooner had we begun our bombardment than the Hun got on to us seriously with 8-in. shells. He started on A Battery, which was some 50 yards behind my H.Q. dug-out, where I was. Edmond, the C.O., went on firing steadily all through it, till he was hit by a large piece of a shell in the side, which went right through his lungs. The doctor gave him two hours to live. Immediately after, Caldwell was killed by a shell landing on his dug-out, and at the same time Jennings was wounded in some forty places —I hope, however, not dangerously. No officer was now left in A Battery, and the sergeant-major withdrew the men some 300 yards into a trench. As soon as the shelling stopped they came back to the guns, and I went across to them. They had one man besides the officers killed, and about fifteen wounded.

Meanwhile, B Battery was firing away hard, and as soon as I saw that A was out of action I turned on C to deal with the same target. Almost immediately the Germans switched on to B and C, and shelled them hard, about a shell every ten seconds. They got a direct hit on one of the C guns, smashing it to pieces and killing most of the men round it. Suddenly they stopped sending these huge Jack Johnsons into us, and gave us Woolly Bears instead. These are 4·2 howitzers which burst their shells in the air, just over one's head. They were firing gas-shells, which fill the air with some horrible fumes of ammonia and

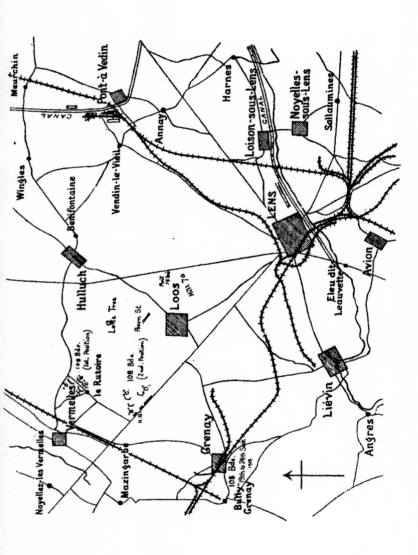

LOOS, SEPT. 1915.

sulphur. One shakes, cannot speak, and the eyes smart and pour tears. It was impossible to keep the batteries in action, and I reluctantly had to go over to Group H.Q. and say that the brigade had been silenced for the time. I could hardly speak with shaking.

Things quieted down about 6 p.m., and we were able to take stock of what was left, collect the dead, and see what the damage was. I was greatly relieved to find that there was much less damage than I expected. A Battery had lost all its officers except one, who was with the wagon line, and a good many gunners. As the brigade was already short-handed in officers, owing to the colonel being killed, and Kenny and Potter being sick, I decided to break up A Battery for the present. I am sending two of their guns to C Battery, who have had one gun smashed to-day, and one gun each to B and D. This gives me three 5-gun batteries, which in many ways will be easier to handle.

Late at night we buried the killed in a common grave at the farm, with dozens of men who have died after being brought in wounded. It was a mournful business, in pouring rain and standing in 6 in. of liquid mud. We put Caldwell alongside his men at one end of the grave. It rained hard all night and the water dripped through the roof of our H.Q. dug-out, making us all very wet and uncomfortable. I have decided to move to our positions at dawn—half a mile the other side of the farm. I cannot move at night as it is imperative that all the batteries should be ready to help the infantry in case of a counter-attack to-night.

LE RUTOIRE, 29TH SEPTEMBER, 1915

At dawn I rode off with battery commanders to find a new position. It was impossible to do so in the dark as one could not see the lie of the ground. On the other hand, it is almost suicide to drive guns into the open by daylight, in full view of Fosse 8, where the Huns have an observing post. B Battery moved first, and got their horses away safely before the morning mist had cleared off enough for the Hun to see him. C Battery had to wait at the old position till B were ready to fire from the new one. The result was that just as they were moving off, the Germans opened fire with heavy shell. Fortunately, no one was hit, and they came into action in the new place. Within half an hour the German heavy guns had got the range to a yard, and they dropped sixty huge Black Marias right into the battery in thirty minutes, exactly one every half-minute. I was standing with Cammell, in B Battery, all the time. We were about 300 yards to the right of C. I watched Harvey through my glasses. He was standing in the open, apparently taking no notice of the shells which were falling all round him. At last he called his men away, and they all sauntered over towards us, sitting down and eating when they got a couple of hundred yards from the guns. I was watching the shells bursting, when a large piece of steel hit me on the leg above the knee, and knocked me flying. Fortunately, it had me with the flat side, so that my leg was only bruised and not cut at all. However, I have been very stiff all day on that leg.

I expected to find all the guns had been knocked out, but to my surprise found that only one gun and one limber had been damaged. That now makes two of C Battery's guns out of action, leaving them with one section of their own and one section of A.

About 2 o'clock I was sent for to go to Le Rutoire. On arrival there, I found the Prince of Wales, who had come to visit the Guards Division, which are here. It was an awful risk, as whilst he was there they were shelling the farm hard, just over our heads, with bricks and mortar falling all round. General Feilding was with him. I warned them that I had just come along the road and that it was being heavily shelled. They waited till the burst was over, and then went on. Within a quarter of an hour of the Prince going, the Germans really started shelling the farm in earnest with 8-in. shells, dropping them in regularly, one after another, into the buildings. They really ought not to have let him come to such a place, but I believe he is always trying to get into the front trenches.

I was first told that we were to be relieved to-night, but later a report came down that the field batteries were to move up to-night on to the ridge, to cut wire. This is right out in the open, and in full view of the Observation Post on Fosse 8 and the German balloon. If it is true, it is simply murder. A fearful afternoon.

We have got our H.Q. into a ruined estaminet on the Loos-Vermelles road. As they say, the worst billet is better than the best bivouac, certainly in this wet clay.

At 8 p.m., just as I was having dinner, a message came that I must go at once to 1st Guards Brigade H.Q., and sleep the night there, in case of a counter-attack. I rode over there and arranged to stay with our group H.Q., which is close to 1st Guards Brigade H.Q., and where there was more room. I had my horses in the farm, and also young Shepard, who could have taken messages, if necessary, for me.

Le Rutoire, 30th September, 1915

A miserable night. I lay on the bare floor of the dugout, which was hard wood ; no blanket or pillow—only my cloak. My feet were sopping wet from running about in the liquid mud, and it was a cold night. Slept till about 3 a.m., when I was so cold I could not sleep any more. To my surprise, I had no cold when I woke.

Returned to my own H.Q. for breakfast. Had a quiet day. Both the Hun and we seem to be resting after our late effort. Both sides send occasional shells over just to show that they are still there. In the afternoon there was a rumour that we were going to be withdrawn to join our 24th Division, but at tea-time I got a message from a certain Colonel Cartwright to say that we were now attached to his group. I believe he commands the left group of the XI Corps Artillery.

Later. I have just seen Colonel Cartwright, who tells me that the Guards Division are being withdrawn to-night and replaced by the 24th Division. All the rest of the 24th Divisional Artillery are going away except my poor brigade, which has been more knocked about than any of the others. I think we are to be attached to the 35th Infantry Brigade. The confusion at H.Q. is awful; no wonder we cannot defeat the highly-trained German General Staff. To think that this brigade in the last ten days has belonged to the 24th, 47th, 24th (second time) Guards, and 12th Divisions! It would be laughable if it were not so damnably serious.

Thank Heaven we are not connected to anyone by 'phone to-night! Our late masters have gone away, and the new not come. I hope for a good night!

Le Rutoire, 1st October, 1915

The nights are now very cold—almost frosty. I am glad I had my fur bag last night.

4 *p.m.* So far, to-day has been a peaceful day. There seems to be a lull in the battle. Both sides are no doubt preparing for a fresh effort. The Hun has dropped a few " crumps " about the country, just to show he is still there. At the present moment I don't know what infantry brigade I am supposed to be supporting, so we are enjoying a holiday for the moment.

Later. I am told off to support the 36th Infantry Brigade, 12th Division. I have spent five hours in going round the whole of the front of the 36th Brigade, mile after mile in the trenches, being shelled more or less all the time.

At one point I got to within 100 yards of Hulluch, and was then only 15 yards from the nearest Germans. We were in a trench leading from Hulluch to the old German trenches. We had a sandbag wall across the trench; then there was a space of 15 yards, and then came the German sandbag wall. Needless to say, I did not look long, as it was not a healthy spot. Fortunately, they did not throw over any bombs whilst I was there. I visited the colonels of all the four battalions, and got as much information as I could about the position of the advanced trenches. The trenches we now occupy are the late German second line. The dugouts are really wonderful—subterranean passages with rooms 20 feet or more underground. I should think they would keep out a 12-in. shell. I examined the new wire that the Germans are putting up in the night, as I shall probably be told off to destroy it to-morrow. It will be a difficult job, as on my left, near Hulluch, it is only 50 yards in front of our own trenches. I am supposed to have a battery connected by telephone to each infantry brigade, but as I have no more wire this is impossible, the more so as we are now reduced to three batteries. However, I must have an officer with each colonel, and if they cannot get their wires there they must send orderlies back to the telephone—a most unsatisfactory method, but one cannot make bricks without straw.

I hear that I have to barrage the Hulluch-Loos Road again to-night. This is a job I hate, as it is impossible to know where the infantry patrols are. They tell me that they are holding a certain line, and then they send out scouts and covering parties well to the front. If my shells hit them they squeal that they are being hit by their own artillery. There does not seem to be much co-operation between the infantry and the artillery staffs. They seem to leave it to the regimental officers to arrange between themselves. This would be all right if they then left the artillery brigade commander alone, but they don't. The artillery staff order me to fire on certain spots, quite irrespective of whether I have found out from the infantry that their covering parties will be out.

To-night, instead of barraging the road I shall fire into Hulluch. It will probably annoy the Germans much more and will ensure not hitting our own people.

LE RUTOIRE, 3RD OCTOBER, 1915

Barraged again all last night; hope we annoyed the Hun. But I refused to fire on the road, as I knew from the infantry that they would have covering parties out, practically to the road. Was sent out to group H.Q. at 8 a.m., waited three-quarters of an hour and, as no one turned up, came back again. Have just had orders to cut wire in front of Hulluch.

One section of D having been withdrawn last night, we are only 2½ batteries. Started them off at midday. At

2 o'clock we were told to stop firing and that we were going into reserve to-night. Shall be very glad to have a chance of reorganising the batteries properly. Also, it will be a blessing for everyone to get out of the zone of fire for a bit. .

Yesterday, whilst going round the trenches, I suddenly came across Kit Tower and General Wing, to whom he is A.D.C. I had not seen him for a long time. I talked to them for some time and then went on ; a few minutes later both were killed by a shell. How very extraordinary that, after not seeing him for so long, I should then be the last person to see him alive !

5 p.m. Orders have just arrived that we are to come out of action to-night and join our own 24th Division at Watou. This appears to be close to Ypres and in Belgium. Heaven only knows why they have gone up there ! We march via Bethune, Locon, Les Lobes, Merville to Vieux Berquin, where we halt for the night. We go into billets there, and I am praying for a comfortable house and a peaceful night. What a blessing it will be to have one night away from this continual roar of the guns. After three weeks of it, never ceasing night or day, one longs for a few hours' quiet. From there our route is via Caestre, Steenvoorde, and on to Watou. After Merville I shall be in country that I know, as it is not far from Hazebrouck, where I spent the winter with the Second Life Guards. I have issued my march orders and there is nothing more to do here. At present (7 p.m.) there is a tremendous " strafe " going on to the north-west of Hulluch. I expect the Hun is making a counter-attack on Hohenzollern, which I believe we took yesterday. D Battery have been heavily shelled this afternoon, some thirty or forty 6-in. shells having been put right into their line. Only one limber has been smashed, and no men hurt, as they were withdrawn to a flank when the shelling began. A gun in the next emplacement has been smashed altogether. This is one of the section of another brigade, which relieved a section of D last night.

At 8 p.m. the batteries started to withdraw ; the guns

were dragged out of the pits and the horses came up for them. Suddenly, at 8.15 p.m., a terrific fire broke out on our left. Machine-guns and rifles, guns large and small ! I at once got orders to stand fast and to be prepared to assist the infantry. I at once had the guns of the brigade faced round in the direction of the attack, and lines laid out by magnetic bearings. Fortunately, the firing died down and we got orders to carry out the move.

VIEUX BERCQUIN, 4TH OCTOBER, 1915

The batteries were withdrawn successfully late last night, and went back to the wagon-lines. I did not move H.Q., as we were fairly comfortable where we were.

At 5 p.m. the brigade concentrated one mile to the west of Vermelles. Horrible confusion was caused by 20 batteries and 4 ammunition columns being ordered to march on the same road at the same time. However, eventually we got started and marched some seventeen miles to this place, via Bethune and Merville. We are now close to Hazebrouck. We are billeted in a very nice little village, which is quiet—and, oh, what a relief to be away from the roar of our guns and the vile scream of the shells ! Fancy being able to go to sleep without wondering whether one would be woken by an 8-in. shell bursting in one's house ! Hannay, the Brigade Major, met us in his car and was very polite, saying that we had done very well. Our losses in action this week have been : officers, 3 killed and 1 wounded ; N.C.O.s and men, 6 killed and 20 wounded and 1 missing.

WATOU, BELGIUM, 5TH OCTOBER, 1915

A cold and damp morning. At 10 o'clock we marched and came via Caestre and Steenvoorde. We crossed the Belgian frontier at 3 p.m. and reached this place. I am depressed beyond words at being back in this vile country : I hate the Belgians and Belgium. We are billeted in a filthy farm, full of squealing children, and dirty beyond words. It is like all the farms in Flanders, only a little

worse. We were met by our new Colonel, Bt. Lieut.-
Col. Walthall, D.S.O., and I handed over the command
to him, rejoining my own battery. I have had great luck
in commanding a brigade right through what is practically
the biggest battle we have fought yet. It is an experience
that any battery commander would have given his
eyes for.

I am not altogether sorry to get back to my own battery
—at any rate, I shall be decently fed again. The H.Q.
messing arrangements are quite vile.

WATOU, 6TH OCTOBER, 1915

The usual depressing Belgian weather: mud and dirt
everywhere. The people of the farm are, of course, pro-
German. I have no doubt they would betray us if they
got half a chance. I have warned everyone that they
must now consider themselves as in a hostile country.

This afternoon the brigade was inspected by Major-
General Capper, who has now succeeded Sir John Ramsay
in the command of the 24th Division. We waited in
a field for two hours, and then marched past in column
of route. It is hardly the sort of resting the men had
looked forward to. I hear that a new officer is being
posted to me to-day, vice Kenny, who is going home, as
his wound is too bad for him to go on any longer. The
horses are not looking well. I should think that the drivers
did nothing at all in the wagon-line all the time we were
fighting.

This farm has more flies to the square inch than any
other place I have yet met; it is also dirtier and the
children more noisy. Altogether, a more offensive place
could not have been found for a rest camp in all Europe.

WATOU, 7TH OCTOBER, 1915

Deacon arrived last night, and I have posted him to
the right section. We are suffering from a plague of flies
here: they are an absolute pest. Fortunately, we have
a good supply of fly-papers, and these become black with
flies as soon as they are put up. It is horribly insanitary,

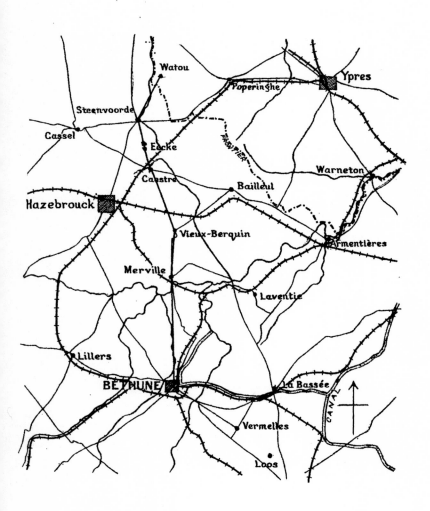

YPRES − BETHUNE, OCT. 1915.

as all the flies come straight off the enormous manure-heap
that fills the yard of every Flemish farm. It is almost
sarcastic to call such a filthy place a " rest camp." However, we are away from the incessant roar of the guns
for a time, which is certainly a blessing. Kenny is off
home to-day for a much-needed rest. I doubt if he will
be fit for any more service this campaign.

Rode round the country in the morning to see if I could
find a better farm, but found everything occupied near
here.

In the afternoon the colonel had a meeting of B.C.s,
and explained the latest methods of trench warfare.
Apparently the 24th Division is going to relieve the 17th
Division at Wytschaete.

Rode home in the dark—very cold. Orders to move
to-night ; B goes into action to-morrow night. We should
have, but we have only two guns in action, for the moment.

BOESCHEPE, 8TH OCTOBER, 1915

After a lot of trouble with our landlord—who, like all
Belgian-Flemish farmers, is hostile to the English—we
moved off and marched south into France at Abeele. We
have got distinctly better billets this time, except there
seems to be no means of making a fire in our room, and it
is horribly cold on the stone floor. Have sent into the
nearest village to try and get some coal.

BOESCHEPE, 9TH OCTOBER, 1915

A quiet and peaceful day. I have had the drivers on
harness-cleaning all day, and the harness is now once more
looking a little like what it ought to be. Lazy devils !
All the time the gunners were fighting, the drivers must
have lain in the mud, doing nothing. The horses also
were in a disgraceful state. Four officers are not enough
for a battery ; it means that one cannot be spared to look
after the wagon-line.

Autumn is now coming on : the days are getting short,
and it is much colder.

7

BOESCHEPE, 10TH OCTOBER, 1915

Sunday. I like our new colonel very much ; he inspires me with great confidence. To-day he told me that he thought I should very likely get a brigade of my own. I wonder ! Still no news of when we go up to the trenches, but I should think soon. Everyone says that it is a very quiet part of the line here.

This afternoon we had a great football match between C and D batteries, which ended in a draw.

BOESCHEPE, 11TH OCTOBER, 1915

Did nothing but lazing and exercise. Lovely day with bright sun. Wrote a lot of letters and wrote up my Standing Orders Book. I think I have got everything squared up now, as far as possible. Hear my fourth gun has arrived at railhead. Now when I get some sights I shall be ready to go into action again.

BOESCHEPE, 12TH OCTOBER, 1915

Same as yesterday. The latest rumour is that two brigades of artillery from this division will be in the line at a time. That will mean six weeks' fighting at a time, followed by three weeks' rest. A bad arrangement, as no one wants to rest for three weeks on end, and six weeks is too long to fight.

BOESCHEPE, 13TH OCTOBER, 1915

Last night Reninghelst, our divisional H.Q., was badly " strafed " by a long-range gun. It is about three miles from here, and we wondered what it was.

BOESCHEPE, 15TH OCTOBER, 1915

Heavy white mist all the morning. C played A at football this afternoon, and won. The men are very keen on it : it keeps them amused and in good condition. D are sending one gun into action to-night.

BOESCHEPE, 16TH OCTOBER, 1915

At 12 o'clock I suddenly got orders to reconnoitre part of the Ypres salient, near Zillebeke, with a view of finding

battery positions. I took Harvey and we got off as soon
as possible. The road was in a fearful state, and we had
to walk most of the way. It took us 2½ hours to get to
Dickebusch, where B Battery is now in action. On
arrival at the cross-roads, one mile on the Ypres side of the
road, we were stopped by a military policeman, and told
that it was not safe to go any farther. We therefore
left our horses with the trumpeter and went on on foot
as far as Voormezeele. Here we found a dead horse
that had been killed by shrapnel shortly before.

Before we could get to the area that I had to examine
it was necessary to get across the canal. We had the
greatest difficulty in finding out where the bridges were,
as, although we were close to the infantry trenches, there
was no one to be found. Eventually, an R.E. subaltern
put us on the right path, and we continued our pilgrimage
past a lot of Belgian batteries, which were firing. The latter
frightened me far more than Huns, as it was impossible
to know where they were, and they kept going off close
to us. At the best, I expected to have the drums of my
ears broken, as they were firing straight at us and not
more than a hundred yards off. I at once put a pair
of ear-protectors in my ears, which deaden the concussion
almost entirely ; on the other hand, they are very dangerous, as they prevent one from hearing the approach of
the enemy's shells, and so having time to throw oneself
down. However, I thought I would risk the Hun shells,
as there were not many about.

When we reached the bank of the canal a sentry told
us that it was not safe to cross the bridge, so we had to
go through a narrow tunnel in the bank, and then across
a footbridge under the real bridge ; the same on the other
side. Having now reached our area, and having about
an hour and a half of daylight left, we felt that there was
no use in aimlessly wandering over a space some 2,000
yards long by 1,000 wide. Seeing a battery in the grounds
of a château, we turned and found the officer in charge.
He turned out to be a subaltern with a section of 6
howitzers, who had been round there for months and knew

all the district. He assured me that there were no suitable battery positions between there and Ypres, and volunteered to take me to a place near there where he thought I might find what I wanted. This was a small clump of trees in the grounds of the château. I did not care for the place much—it would have meant everyone living in dug-outs. I also suspected that it was in view of the Wytschaete Ridge, but could not tell for certain, as there was too much mist.

I called on another 18-pr. battery there, and got much the same information.

We had a long walk back to the road where we had left the horses, and on the way met Reynolds, who married Doris Petersen. Rather an extraordinary coincidence, as at the moment we were within sight of the church of Zillebeke, where poor young Petersen is buried. I was looking at it through my glasses when Reynolds came up. He took me off to his billet and gave us tea. They do themselves extremely well on every possible luxury from Cherkley Court—roast ducks, fresh butter, kippers, combined with electric bells ! If we are going to be neighbours in the salient we arranged to go to Zillebeke on the 6th November—the anniversary of the day Peter was killed. We had a long and tedious ride home in the dark, arriving back at 8.30 in time for dinner.

BOESCHEPE, 17TH OCTOBER, 1915

Sunday. Made my report to the colonel on yesterday's reconnaissance. In the afternoon, Shepard, Gliddon, and I rode over to the Monastery at Mont-des-Cats, and home by Abeele, a round of about ten miles.

BOESCHEPE, 21ST OCTOBER, 1915

Still very busy doing nothing. I hear we are likely to go into action in the course of the next few days, near Zillebeke.

My new giant protractor has arrived from Negretti and Zambra. It is just what I wanted, and will be invaluable, as I hear we are going to do counter-battery work again.

I am delighted to hear it, as there is no anxiety attached to this game. A bad shot does not matter, beyond the waste of a round ; whereas a shot that falls a few yards short of the German trenches may hit our own.

To-day I sent Harvey into Ypres to get three cartloads of bricks to make a floor for my winter stables. He says that there is not a house left standing now. I must go there one day and see.

The colonel is dining with us to-night. I have sent Shepard to Bailleul for whisky.

BOESCHEPE, 22ND OCTOBER, 1915

Rode to the lines of the 106th Brigade R.F.A., as I was President of Court of Inquiry. Took the wrong turning coming out of Reninghelst, with the result that I went five miles out of my way. Court of Inquiry was on two horses who had dropped dead on the road fatigue at Poperinghe yesterday. We came to the conclusion that the fault lay in only having a pair of horses to drag heavy carts full of slag on the vile Belgian roads. Personally, I send teams of six on these fatigues.

As I had to meet the colonel and reconnoitre gun positions in the afternoon, it was not worth going back to my lines ; so I rode on to the cross-roads beyond Dickebusch and off-saddled there for a couple of hours, till he arrived. Fortunately, I was able to buy a copy of yesterday's *Daily Mail* on the road (for the modest sum of 2d.) which helped to pass the time. The colonel, Harvey, and Nosworthy turned up at half-past three, and we left our horses and hunted round for a position. We have chosen one in a hedge, well away from any other battery, and with the remains of a farm close in rear.

A long and very cold ride home in the dark. It is really a great nuisance having the wagon-lines eight or nine miles behind the position.

DICKEBUSCH, 23RD OCTOBER, 1915

Made all arrangements to bring the men up to the position in the afternoon, and managed to get quite a lot of timber out of the C.R.E. and a couple of thousand sand-bags to go on with. I was President of a Field General Court Martial at Reninghelst, at 10 o'clock, which was a great bore, as there was so much to do. However, the excellent Harvey had everything ready to start by the time I came back.

We had lunch and got under way at 8 o'clock. I bor-rowed five G.S. wagons from the ammunition column, and with my own baggage-wagon we looked quite like a convoy of the Army Service Corps.

We halted in Dickebusch and loaded up the timber from the R.E. store there. Leaving Harvey to bring on the wagons when loaded, I rode on with the officers and sergeants to the cross-roads, where one has to dismount ; then, leaving the horses, we walked on a mile or so to the position. I first laid out the direction the gun-pits are to face—150° right of Magnetic North.

The wagons arrived in due course, after one being upset in a shell-hole, and started work on the gun-pits about 9 o'clock. It was a splendid full moon, and we worked on to 4 a.m., with half an hour for hot tea at midnight.

DICKEBUSCH, 24TH OCTOBER, 1915

After the night's work, everyone slept on till midday : just woke up to feed, and then slept on till dark, when we started work again. I am making four small forts, of tremendous strength, to hold the guns. I can see it will take many nights' work to complete.

It came on to rain in the middle of the night, which made everything very uncomfortable. It is also bitterly cold. I live in my gum-boots.

DICKEBUSCH, 25TH OCTOBER, 1915

A miserable night. I got to bed about 8 a.m., and woke up later to find the water dripping through the ruined roof and forming pools in which I was lying. Thank goodness I have my beloved fur sleeping-bag, which, being covered with waterproof material, kept me dry.

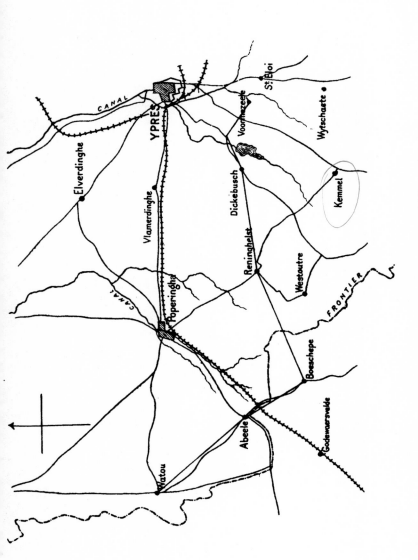

WEST OF YPRES, OCT. 1915.

As yesterday, we slept all day and started work as soon as it was dark. I forgot to say that we have to be very careful, as we are in full view of the German trenches, only 2,000 yards away.

DICKEBUSCH, 25TH OCTOBER, 1915

Same procedure as yesterday. We have got a fire going now in our room in the farm, so we can get a little warmer. I am building up a thick wall of sandbags and bricks round our mess-room, to try and keep out splinters, at any rate. The gun-pits are getting on : the walls are nearly finished and the uprights in.

DICKEBUSCH, 26TH OCTOBER, 1915

Bright moonlight last night, so we worked on till 4 a.m. There was a small bomb attack about 11 p.m., which caused a lot of rifle-fire. This afternoon the Hun amused himself shelling the road just behind the farm. He put quite a number within a hundred. yards of us, but did not actually hit the farm.

Harvey brought up the rations and more timber about 8 o'clock.

DICKEBUSCH, 27TH OCTOBER, 1915

Same procedure every day—or, rather, night. It is getting very monotonous and very tiring, working in the cold and wet from 5 p.m. to 4 a.m. We are finding great difficulty in building high walls with sandbags, as they are all different sizes ; also the ground is very unstable.

DICKEBUSCH, 28TH OCTOBER, 1915

As usual, we worked all night. It is an extraordinarily slow job. I have not yet calculated what the weight of the sandbags for a gun-pit is, but it must be quite stupendous.

This afternoon the colonel came round with the new General (Philpotts). He has come vice Sir Godfrey, who has gone home. It was really very sporting of the old gentleman to have come out at all, at his age : he is about sixty.   We shall all miss him; he was such a *sahib*.

It has poured with rain on and off all day, which is turning the ground into liquid mud.   It is a very serious matter, as the men are bound to leave deep tracks in the long grass leading up to the gun position.   These are horribly visible from the air, and give the position away worse than anything.   The only thing I can do is to march the men up and down for some distance *past* the gun position, so as to make the path continue on.   Then the aeroplanes may think it is only a short cut to the trenches in front.   For the last two nights there has been something very mysterious happening; sandbag walls that were very strongly built have fallen down in the early morning, after we have left work.   I can only think that there must be a spy about—probably a Belgian, so I shall mount an armed guard to-night.

DICKEBUSCH, 29TH OCTOBER, 1915

Another wet night.   I got to bed at 6 a.m. this morning. The moon is rising late now, which makes it very difficult to work.   We are getting on slowly but surely.   The walls are nearly finished, and the steps down into the tunnels are finished and roofed over with heavy timber.   Each gun-pit is connected with the next one by a subterranean passage, 6 feet deep,   The walls of the pits are built up 7 feet above the ground, and are made of from 10 rows of sandbags at the bottom to 3 at the top; over this there is a foot of earth at a slope of about 45 degrees, held up by low hurdles of osiers ; and over that heavy turfs, that will have to be picketed down and wired on.   I hope they will grow together and form one whole.   The roofs are supported by six pillars, 9 ft. × 6 ft., with three rafters across them of the same thickness.

Crossing these are eight 9-ft. railway irons, and on top of them the roof of 2-in. deal planks.   I shall put a layer of sandbags on that, and cover them with a foot to 18 in. of broken bricks, with earth and turfs on top, which will join up with the turf slopes of the walls.   This will be the same all round, except for the opening in front for the gun to fire out of ; and here it will be closed by a screen of .hop-pole frame, with painted sacking stretched over it. When the whole thing is finished these forts should be green mounds, like the tumuli on Salisbury Plain. They have been built in a hedge of large willow-trees, and I am transplanting large numbers of other similar trees to thicken the hedge and make it a belt, as wide as the gun-pits. What makes the more work is the fact that all the earth for the sandbags, etc., has to be carried for a long distance, so as not to make marks near the position itself. For the same reason, I have laid down a path of planks for the men to walk on. Before daylight these are removed and hidden and all the work hidden by branches and bushes planted in the fresh earth, and sandbags. Before leaving the place in the mornings I go round and make certain that there is nothing to be seen from above.

DICKEBUSCH, 30TH OCTOBER, 1915

Knocked off work at 6 a.m. this morning. The men are really wonderful. Night after night they work from dusk to dawn, and are still as cheerful as ever. I have two breaks of half an hour each at 10 p.m. and 2 a.m., and then breakfasts at 6 o'clock. After a week or so of this night life one gets accustomed to it, and I no longer feel tired by morning. In fact, this morning I went for a walk after the work was over. There is really something to show for all this labour now, and I think another three or four nights ought to about finish it. To-night I shall start tunnelling between the telephone pit and the guns. I dare not break the surface here, as it is 20 yards across the open fields, and it would be bound to show from above, as the long grass would get trampled down and muddied. I have several coal-miners in the battery, and it will be a simple matter for them to drive a gallery through the sandy subsoil.

DICKEBUSCH, 1ST NOVEMBER, 1915

We have been going on exactly the same every night. The work is not finished yet, but it grows, and I hope to be finished this week. To-day I had a visit from General Capper, commanding our division, and General Philpotts, the C.R.A. General Capper seemed much taken with my gun-pits and said they were the best he had seen. It is raining hard and the ground is turning into liquid mud, which makes the work doubly hard. Also, I am terrified of making muddy tracks through the long grass, which will give the show away. It is so dark to-night—as the moon does not rise till late—that it is impossible to start work yet. One of our supply wagons has broken down in a ditch and has had to be abandoned. Fortunately, it had already delivered the rations to us. It would have been a catastrophe if it had broken down farther back ! Our wagon line is nine miles back.

DICKEBUSCH, 2ND NOVEMBER, 1915

To-day being misty, it has been possible to do some work by daylight. The worst is now over, but there still remains a great deal to do. The guns came up last night, and we had a terrible job to get them into position. After all this rain, the ground is like butter, and it would have been impossible to bring the horses into the field. Accordingly, the guns were unlimbered on the road behind the farm and taken 300 yards across country by hand.

I laid a bridge of 9 × 3 planks across the ditch off the road, but, to my horror, the planks snapped in half the moment the weight of the gun came on to them. I certainly thought such heavy timber would have been strong enough. Fortunately, the ditch is only a couple of feet deep, but even so it took forty men on the drag-ropes and wheels to get it out. We laid planks all along the grass for the guns to run on, but in the dark I found it was impossible to keep the wheels on them ; and once they were off the planks and had sunk into the wet ground, it was impossible to get them on again. It became such a nuisance that I gave up the planks altogether and dragged the guns over the long grass by sheer strength. At some places they actually sank in till the axles touched the ground. We took each gun a different way to avoid making

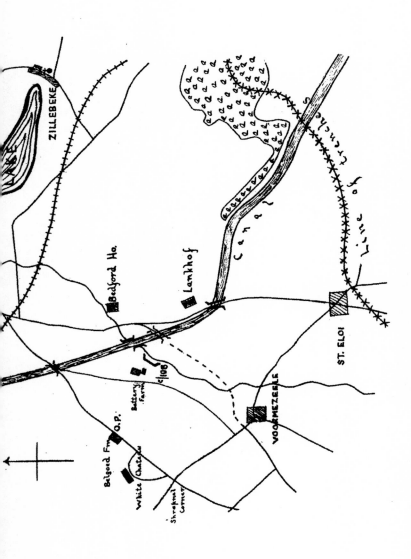

ZILLEBEKE – ST. ELOI, NOV. 1915.

the wheel-tracks more noticeable than could be helped,
and before dawn I had every yard of the wheel-ruts filled
with turf, so that, when daylight came, there was no trace
of ruts at all. Had they been visible to the Hun aeroplanes
the whole position would have been given away.

I am convinced that this place is only possible so long
as we are not spotted. We are so close up to the trenches
(only 2,000 yards) that if once we are located they will
destroy us in ten minutes with heavy shells.

DICKEBUSCH, 3RD NOVEMBER, 1915

To-day I have seen a wonderful but terrible sight. A
real aeroplane battle in the blue sky, just above my head.
About midday one of the new German fighting planes
came over, some 5,000 feet up. He was at once attacked
by three of our machines. For a quarter of an hour they
manœuvred over each other, circling round and round
just like birds. It was a fine day and with a bright sky,
and through my glasses I could see the heads of the airmen.
They were firing their machine-guns all the time and
seemed to be so close to each other that they almost
touched. Suddenly we saw the Hun turn over and begin
to fall. He came down in a small spiral, head down, and
falling at a terrific pace. But, even so, he seemed to take
hours to reach the ground.

As he got near the earth he seemed to be falling faster
and faster till, at the end, it looked as if he were falling
like a stone. He fell about a mile from here and crashed
on top of a dug-out, killing three of our infantry who were
inside. Of course the German airmen were killed instantly.
I imagine the pilot had been hit by the fire of our aeroplane's machine-guns. It looked just like a cock-pheasant
that is hit in the head. At one moment he was flying as
strongly and firmly as possible ; the next, he crumpled up
and came down like a " rocketer."

The colonel came round again and said how pleased
both the generals were with my position. It is a great
thing to be able to please a general. Apparently Capper
was delighted because I stopped him from walking outside

a hedge that was in view of the German trenches. I naturally was not going to let anyone give my position away.

DICKEBUSCH, 4TH NOVEMBER, 1915

General Philpotts came round to-day. Apparently this place has some fascination for generals ; they can't keep away from it ! He discovered what I have known all along—that we are not under cover from the ridge, so far as our flashes are concerned. There is no doubt that in the twilight and at night they will see our flashes quite well. I am having some large screens made up of 20-foot hop-poles, with wires crossing them and willows woven in between the wires. I only hope these will not be very conspicuous. As usual, the Hun has the top of the ridge and we are on the slope underneath. Also, under these circumstances, I think it is a great risk having the guns so close up, especially as we could have done our work just as well 600 yards farther back. However, the responsibility is not mine—the position was chosen for me. I am also not at all certain that we shall not be enfiladed from Wytschaete.

DICKEBUSCH, 5TH NOVEMBER, 1915

Nothing of interest to-day, except that there was another aeroplane fight, which ended in the Hun making off home as fast as he could leg it—or, I should say, wing it.

We were awakened this morning at 6 o'clock by a really quite respectable bombardment. Apparently the Hun began it, and we took it up with all our heavy batteries. For about an hour there was a most unholy noise, the big shells screaming over our heads, going both ways. They sound like express trains rushing through a station without stopping. They were going over in salvos of four continuously. Evidently there is no shortage of ammunition now.

DICKEBUSCH, 6TH NOVEMBER, 1915

It is just a year to-day since Peter Petersen was killed with the 2nd Life Guards. I determined to go over to

Zillebeke, to see if his grave was all right. His brother-in-law, Reynolds, wrote to say he would lunch with me and go together if he could get away. His Battery C/53 Brigade is in action not far off. However, as he did not turn up, I started off alone, after an early lunch. It is about two miles across country. Fortunately, it was a very misty day, and when I got over the ridge it was hardly possible to see the German trenches. I was, therefore, able to walk along the top of the railway embankment with a reasonable amount of safety from snipers. With the exception of a few stray bullets, I was not fired at at all. Had it been a clear day I should have had to keep down in the communicating trench all the way. As this was full of water, I was very glad it was not necessary.

I reached the place without difficulty, and at first could not find the grave, as it was not quite where I had been told. The south side of the church has been heavily shelled, and many of the Belgian tombs have been torn open and present a horrible sight. But the shelling seems to have come almost entirely from the S.E., and the N.E. has not been touched, as it is protected by the town. There is nothing left of the church except the western tower.

Poor Peter lies 27 feet out from the church, at right angles from the most western buttress of the wall, on the north side of the church. He is next to Lord Bernard Gordon-Lennox, who was also a brother officer of mine in the Grenadiers.

The grave is grown over with rough grass, but not disturbed in any way. Reynolds tells me he is replacing the existing wooden cross with a new and stronger one.

I made a sketch and plan of the place, and sent it to Mr. Petersen.

On my way back I called on D Battery and had a look at their position. It struck me as being excessively bad. They found it ready made, but I hope they will improve it a great deal before it is my turn to go in there. The roofs of the dug-outs are only resting on sandbags, which will probably collapse soon.

DICKEBUSCH, 7TH NOVEMBER, 1915

The colonel came round in the morning and said he was sure we were covered from view for our flashes. It does not convince me in the least; however, we can only wait and see, as Mr. Asquith says.

We had just started lunch when a terrific din started. I made certain that they were shelling the battery, and so ran down to the position at once, to take the men out of the gun-pits, as there was no object in getting them killed for nothing. However, I found that although the shells were falling within a hundred yards of my left flank, they were not coming any closer. At first I was certain that a Hun aeroplane had spotted us, and that they were shelling me. However, I soon saw that the shells were meant for the canal bridge, which is some 200 yards to my left. I therefore let the men go on with their dinners. Pieces of shell were fairly humming round, so I kept well under cover of the pits. Some of the shells pitched into the canal, sending up fountains of black mud and water 50 feet into the air. They sent over about forty shells in five minutes, and then stopped.

After lunch—which was cold by the time I got it—I went over to the bridge to see what damage had been done. Although the place was stiff with batteries, not a man was touched, the only damage being a number of telephone wires which were cut. They were mended within an hour—an expensive " hate " for the Hun, with nothing to show for it.

The colonel told me that I had been recommended for reward over the Loos affair, but I doubt if I get a D.S.O., and am not eligible for a Military Cross, being a field officer. The most I hope for is to be mentioned in despatches. However, it is always something to know that my name has been sent in.

DICKEBUSCH, 8TH NOVEMBER, 1915

This afternoon I determined to have a battle, but it turned out to be a fiasco. My only " director " was lost at Loos, and I failed to borrow one from any other battery, so I had to lay out my lines on Hollebeke Château by pure guess-work. I went over to my Observation Post, in fear and trembling, as it is always being shelled, and fired a few rounds. But I could not see any of them. After firing half a dozen shells I gave it up in disgust. It was the more impossible as three other batteries were firing at the same target, and it was impossible to distinguish between my shells and theirs. I shall try again to-morrow. I am also not quite certain which of two châteaux on the map is the one that I can see. If it is the other one, it is not surprising that I can't see the bursts.

DICKEBUSCH, 9TH NOVEMBER, 1915

I managed to borrow a " director " from A Battery this morning, so was able to lay out my lines properly.

Harvey went for a walk to the Bluff, which is close behind our first-line trenches. I wanted to see if I could use that part of the line for an Observation Post to shoot at Hollebeke Château, which I have chosen for my Zero Line. I always dislike wandering about near the front by myself in a new place, as one does not know what places are dangerous. I was looking for a place among some trees, and on getting to the edge of the wood found I was looking straight into the loopholes of the German trenches at not more than 500 yards' range. Needless to say, I retired hastily.

On our way to the Bluff we crossed a bridge over the Ypres Canal, and just before we got to the place on our way back the Germans started shelling it. They smashed one of the big overhead girders. Had we been a few minutes earlier they would have just caught us crossing it.

Directly after lunch I started my little battle. After yesterday's fiasco I was rather nervous as to whether I had got the right château on the map. But by some good fortune, the very first shell hit fairly in the middle. In fact, I got all four guns registered on the exact spot with 22 rounds. The château is on the edge of the wood, and if the shells go over too far they are lost to sight in the trees.

On the other hand, the château is not far in advance of our trenches, so one has to be very careful to get the range right. The map range is 3·400 yards and I hit it with an elevation of 3·100, so the guns are still shooting 300 yards long—the same as they were at Neuve Chapelle. Just as I was getting the last gun on the Germans began shelling my Observation Post—which was very unpleasant, as it is simply a few planks balanced on the rafters of a half-ruined house. It would only want a good shake for the whole roof to fall in. They burst one shrapnel just over the roof, which was hit by some of the pieces.

I had hardly got back to the battery when they put a shell close to that. It gave me a bit of a fright, as I thought they must have spotted us. But as no more came over, I think it was meant for some infantry who were going along a path just in front of the battery.

DICKEBUSCH, 10TH NOVEMBER, 1915

We have not fired to-day, but have been going on quietly finishing off the pits. There is little to be done now, except make the telephone pit and finish the drain. It has fallen in in places, owing to the horrible sticky clay, and its great depth—10 feet in places. I expect we shall have to revet most of it. My new officer, E. Bishop, arrived this afternoon—formerly an architect in Brussels. Shepard has retired to the Ammunition Column.

A good deal of noise on the part of the Hun, and some shells uncomfortably close.

DICKEBUSCH, 11TH NOVEMBER, 1915

At 8.30 a.m., just as we were starting breakfast, I was rung up by H.Q., and told that an aeroplane had gone up to observe for me. Hastily finished breakfast and worked out angles of sight, etc. Then waited, with all the telephonists ready, till 1 p.m. ; but nothing happened, and as I could not get any answer from H.Q., I imagine the wires were cut by shell-fire. The Hun has been very active to-day, and at last managed to hit our farm. Fortunately, the shell burst in the stable, which is the next room to where I was sitting at my maps. There is a wall of sandbags between the stable and my room, so nothing came through. The horses were not touched—by some miracle. I had lent my own horse to the sergt.-major to go to be interviewed by the general about getting a commission. The pieces of the shell all struck the place where my horse stands. He would have certainly been killed had he been in the stable. The men collected all the pieces, and I have been almost able to construct the shell again. It must have been a 15-pr. high explosive.

There has been a great deal of shelling to-day, and a good many shells have fallen near us, but I still do not think that they have located us. But I think they are searching. To-night there is a new moon, and I shall try and get the telephone pit done before dawn. It can only be done at night, as it is right out in the open.

DICKEBUSCH, 12TH NOVEMBER, 1915

A vile day. We worked the whole of last night in pouring rain, inky darkness, and a high wind. However, we managed to finish the telephone pit before daylight, and remove all traces of the work. The tunnel connects with the telephone pit, so that one can get there without going out into the open. We went to bed, meaning to have a late breakfast, but were awakened by a shell just missing the house and bursting just outside. Thinking it might be the beginning of a " strafe," we hastily got up and dressed—which latter operation consists in putting on one's gum-boots and tunic. Odd shells have been coming over all day, but no one has been hit. A Battery, who are on our right, have had two men killed and four wounded this afternoon. It is only a question of time before they get some of us, as this place is in full view of the German trenches. Various infantry parties keep moving along a path in front of our gun positions and draw fire. I doubt if the Hun has actually shot at us yet, but he is constantly potting at the infantry parties, and as he evidently has not got the correct range to the path most

8

of his shells come unpleasantly close to us. I had to throw myself down in the liquid mud this afternoon when one " pip-squeak " came extra near. As a matter of fact, one has not really got time to get down before they burst. The ones one hears coming are only the ones that are over. The short ones that hit you burst before one hears them. It is different with a crump (4·2 or 6 in.) ; they give plenty of warning—usually at least five seconds. There is to be a bombardment of the Hun trenches at 5.45 a.m. to-morrow morning by the division on our left, so we shall have to " stand to " in case we are wanted.

No papers have come to-night, so we shall have nothing to read.

DICKEBUSCH, 13TH NOVEMBER, 1915

Turned out at 5.30 a.m. Quite dark, pouring wet, a tremendous wind, and very cold. The expected bombardment did not come off ; I expect everyone was too busy baling out their trenches and gun-pits. The river has risen and overflowed the banks. The field in front of the guns is flooded to within 10 yards of pits. All my beautiful trenches have fallen in because the R.E. have not given me material to revet them. It will take days and days of hard work to get them clear again and, in the meanwhile, the trenches are rapidly filling with water.

We have no glass in the window of our farm, so, as the wind and rain are pouring in, we have been obliged to board up the window altogether and live by lamplight, even in the morning. Not very cheerful—but it is Flanders !

The general and the colonel came round this morning and paid me a visit. They were much amused to find us living by oil-lamp in the middle of the day.

As far as I can make out, we shall remain in action till about the end of the month, and then go back to the wagon line for a fortnight's rest.

There has been a good deal of shelling to-day by both sides, but nothing very close to us. The place is absolutely water-logged.

The new expanding iron has arrived for revetting my

trenches, so I shall experiment with it to-morrow ; but I fear it is too late to make much of a job of it now, as most of the trenches have already fallen in. It is very bad luck, after all the work that has been done.

Grizel has sent me a wonderful telescopic magnifying periscope. I must go down to the trenches and try it. Also my new fan-shaped protractor for the 1/20,000 map has come. The first one I had for the 1/10,000 map has been a great success.

DICKEBUSCH, 14TH NOVEMBER, 1915

A lovely day, so, like the proverbial Englishman, let us go out and kill something. Too bright to do much work at the position, as the air is humming with planes belonging to both sides.

When I had digested my lunch and finished a cigar, I decided to go over to the O.P. and have a little battle. After a little difficulty with the telephone, caused by Sergeant Meecham at one end ringing up No. 1 Unit, and the telephonist at the other end doing the same with No. 2 wire—we got started. I fired on Hollebeke Château, which is reported in the Corps Summary of Intelligence as being used as an artillery observation post. It has a nice white tower, which makes a beautiful dust when hit. After getting my lines exactly correct, with shrapnel, I turned on section salvos with high explosive. Made quite a good mess of it. Let us hope the Hun observers were there when we started.

I am more than anxious about my flashes. I am certain they can be seen from the ridge.

Later. The expected has happened—two large shells have landed a hundred yards behind the guns and two more only 20 yards short of A and B guns !

Now we are in for it. Harvey has gone back to the wagon line and been relieved by Deacon. The latter says he hopes we shall have some excitement. I have no doubt we shall get plenty before long.

To-night I shall see that everything is ready to turn out quickly in case they start shelling us in the night.

BOESCHEPE, 16TH NOVEMBER, 1915

Yesterday, the 15th November, is a date I shall not forget. For the second time in two months my poor battery has been put out of action! We had just finished breakfast and I had gone down to the guns when the first shell arrived. With a terrific howl through the air, it burst like a clap of thunder on the canal bank a hundred yards on our left and a hundred yards in rear. We waited anxiously to see whether it was Bedford House or us that they were after. The next shell would decide the matter. In two or three minutes it came, still a hundred yards behind, but in direct line with us and not fifty yards from the farm.

I waited for no more, but at once ordered all the men out of the gun-pits. I sent Bishop to lead the way and told the men to follow him, one by one, along the bank of the stream, keeping out of sight under the trees. Sergeant Aisthorpe and I brought up the rear, after seeing that everyone had gone.

We had hardly got clear of the battery when a third shell burst just behind A gun and hurried us up a bit. We halted about two hundred yards away and watched the shelling. It was at once obvious that it was going to be serious, as they were using very heavy stuff.

We were bombarded for days at Le Rutoire with 6-in. shells, but these were much bigger, and I put them down as being 8-in.

Huge columns of black earth were sent up higher than the tops of the tall poplars. There were also volumes of black smoke, and a terrific report.

They quickly got the exact range, and then shell after shell fell just among the guns. There were some trees in the hedge between us and the guns, so we could not see exactly where they were falling. The men were wonderfully cheerful, and had bets as to which gun was hit. This went on for an hour, during which time thirty shots had been fired. Then it stopped. After waiting a quarter of an hour to see if it was all over, I cautiously went back to the guns.

I was relieved to find that, although there were huge craters all round, and in between the guns, A, B, and C were not touched. When I got to D., however, I gasped. The first thing I saw was half a wheel sticking out through the doorway. At the same time I had a presentiment that there was more to come. I turned and started to go back, when I suddenly heard the ominous little bang, so faint that it is very hard to hear at all. Three seconds later I heard the shell coming—just a low murmur at first, gradually rising to a loud scream, just like an express train passing through a station without stopping. I flung myself down at the foot of A sub-section's pit and at the back of it. With a roar, it passed a few feet above my head and burst thirty yards away. The noise was horrible, and the ground shook like a person kicking a table. Huge pieces of turf fell in showers all round. As soon as the bits of shell and turf had stopped falling, I got up and ran for my life back to the stream where the others were.

Till half-past one they kept it up steadily, sometimes on the guns and sometimes on the farm. One shell landed right on the barn, which stands 20 yards from our farm. A huge column of bright red smoke and brick-dust went up 50 feet in the air. When it cleared away all one side of the house had disappeared, and the roof was completely wrecked.

After that they stopped for about half an hour, and I really thought they had finished. At the same time it was reported that the servants and cooks were missing. A signaller, called Carter, volunteered to go with me to the farm, and see if they were there, in which case I was certain they would all be dead. As a matter of fact, I was certain that no one could have been such a fool as to stop there during such a bombardment, and I expected to find that, like us, they had gone out into the fields to one side. In order to get to the farm it was necessary to cross a place a hundred yards wide that was in view of the German trenches. When I got to the gate of the farm, to my astonishment I saw a crowd of servants and cooks standing in the yard. I shouted to them to come out with me, when at that moment I heard the first note of a shell that was coming. I gave myself up for lost, as I was at the exact spot where the last half-dozen shells had fallen. I was certain that it was coming straight for us. I shouted to Carter, who was alongside of me, to lie down, and flattened myself against the ground. There was no cover of any sort near—right out in the open. I suppose that the shell took four or five seconds to arrive, but it seemed hours. At the end, I realised distinctly that it was nearer than any shell I had ever heard before.

The end of the world seemed to come. A roar—or, rather, crash—such as no words can describe, and to which nothing can be likened that in any way compares with the noise. The air seemed to hit me on the head like a blow with a sandbag, and there was immediately after the sound of a thousand lashes being swished through the air, as the great pieces of jagged shell, weighing anything up to forty or fifty pounds, flew in every direction. Then a pause, and the deluge of débris began—bricks, tiles, stones, bits of trees and large clods of earth and turf. These continued to fall for a long time, some having been blown into the air higher than others. Over all, an inky darkness that stank horribly of some bitter fumes.

When I got up I found I was standing on the brink of a crater, 10 feet deep and 20 feet wide. Had it struck 5 yards farther, there would have been nothing left of us all. Probably not even a boot or a bit the size of a cricket-ball.

I yelled to the servants to come on, and we raced away from the farm out into the open, but had not gone 50 yards before another shell struck the cook-house, sending it to heaven in a cloud of red smoke. We had just time to fall flat and let the pieces fly over us.

After that, I had decided not to go back till after dark, as it was obvious that they could see the ground all round the farm and guns, and that they were waiting to fire again any time they saw any signs of life. They evidently saw us all run out, as they followed us up with shrapnel and gas-shells.

All the afternoon they kept it up, the shells falling all round the battery and farm. They caught an unfortunate telephonist belonging to another battery, who was mending wires in the neighbourhood, taking his head clean off.

From A Battery's mess, I spoke to the colonel at H.Q. He told me that the general said it was useless to stay in that position, and that I should have to withdraw the following night.

At 5.45 p.m. the great bombardment that was arranged for some days ago began.

Every gun on our front started firing as hard as it could at the German roads and approaches. The whole place was lit up by the flashes of the guns and the noise was deafening. I had already got a headache from the shells that burst so near me and this row on top of it was very painful.

The Hun refused to be drawn out; except for a few " pip-squeaks " that passed well over our heads, he did not reply. Let us hope we did some damage. I was to have fired, too, but had not been able to get near the guns or to my maps to work out the angles.

As soon as it was sufficiently dark for them not to be able to see us from the ridge, Deacon and I walked over to our farm to see what damage had been done, and to get our coats. Luckily, they did not shell us, and we got there all right.

I left Deacon in the yard to listen for shells coming, as it would be better to be in the open than in the house if one burst near. I would rather risk being hit by a flying piece in the open than buried under the beams of a falling house.

I found the interior of the house untouched, and everything just as we had left it in the morning. I got out coats, and, after seeing that the horses were all right, we cleared out quickly and went back to Voormezeele, where I had left Bishop with the men. To my rage, I found three unspeakable Belgians looting in the yard. I cleared them out very quickly and called at their farm on the way and had out the " brigadier " in charge of the party.

At 5 o'clock our great bombardment started. Every gun in the Corps let fly, as hard as they could, principally at cross-roads and places that we know from deserters that the Germans use as refilling points. I imagine that we must have disturbed their ration parties pretty badly. I sincerely hope that some of our heavies got on to the battery that knocked me about so badly to-day. The din was appalling, as all the batteries were firing salvos. It lasted on and off for about an hour. When it was over, and it was quite dark, except for the moon, I took the men back to our position. The colonel had previously rung me up on the 'phone and told me that I should probably have to clear the next night.

The sight on arrival was really extraordinary. There was a bright moon, so that one could see like by day. The whole appearance of the place had changed. Everywhere were enormous holes where the 8-in. shells had fallen. I sent an N.C.O. round to count them. There were eighty just round the farm and guns, and that did not include a dozen or so that had not burst—" duds," as we call them—also a large number that had fallen near the canal, and in front of the stream. There must have been about 120 all together. The wonderful thing is that they did not hit the house itself. One had gone into the barn alongside the farm and blown half of it into the dust, and there were a dozen to twenty within 20 yards of the building. The field between the guns and the farm that had been a flat meadow was one series of huge craters, so that it was difficult to find a path across it. Each hole was about 20 feet across and 6 to 8 feet deep.

When I reached the guns I felt certain that there could be nothing left at all of them. " A " gun-pit looked fairly all right from the rear, except that it seemed lower and to cover much more ground ; but when I got round to the front I could hardly believe my eyes. Where the gun had been there was a crater 10 feet deep, and extending to 20 feet in front of the walls of the original gun-pit ; the roof and front wall had gone, and there was no sign of the gun. When I looked up there was the gun, high up in the air, and balanced on the side-wall ! One wheel we found in the field behind, and the other across a high hedge in another field. The steel shield of the gun was blown to pieces, and it looked like an aeroplane stuck up on the wall. All the trees round were hung with pieces of coats, water-proof sheets, and sandbags, and on the top of one of the tall poplars there was a cap. B and C gun-pits were not touched, although there were holes in the intervals between them and in front and behind them. D was completely wrecked, as I had seen during my short visit in the morning. Never have I seen such a scene of wreckage before ; even Le Rutoire was not so bad, as they had only used 6-in. shells there against us. The size and quantity of the holes were really terrifying. It was not very sporting of them to have used such enormous stuff against one poor little 18-pounder battery. What a time the German observing officer must have had !

The cooks soon got the fires going, and we all had our dinners. The men and officers were all starving and nearly dead with cold, as we had had to come away without coats or gloves, etc. Every moment I expected them to shell us again, as they might have guessed that we should go back after dark to recover our things. However, they did not. Sergeant Meecham managed to tap D Battery's telephone wire, so we were able to get into communication with H.Q. again.

During dinner the colonel rang me up and said that an order had come through from the general that we were to evacuate the position immediately. I telephoned to Harvey, who was at the wagon-lines ten miles away, and told him to bring up the limbers, wagons, and all spare men, as quickly as possible, as it was imperative that we should get out of sight behind the Ypres-Dickebusch road before dawn. The order reached Harvey at 10 o'clock, just as he was going to bed, and I can imagine his feelings on hearing that the battery was out of action, and that he had to come up at once. They must have turned out very quickly, as they reached us at 2 a.m.

Meanwhile, we had all been working like niggers, and

got out the two surviving guns. The moon lasted till about midnight and, as there was a hard frost, the ground was not so soft, which made it easier to get the horses down the field to the guns. We tried all we could to get the damaged guns away, but had to leave them for the time.

As soon as we had got the two remaining guns up on to the road, I sent them and the ammunition and G.S. wagons off home, as I did not want to keep the horses up there a moment longer than I could help, in case they started shelling again. I kept most of the men and two limbers and teams in the hope of getting the damaged guns away, after all.

We built a ramp of sandbags under the gun that was perched up on the sandbag wall and levelled off the parados, or back wall. Meanwhile, I had the wheels taken off a wagon and its limber, ready to put on the guns. The men worked like slaves till about 5 a.m., when I saw it would be impossible to get the work finished before dawn. I therefore left the guns covered up with branches to hide them from aircraft and mounted a guard over them. I was rather nervous about the guard, but I told them they must remain within sight, but well away from the position, in case of any more shelling.

We put the men into an empty G.S. wagon that I had kept back for the purpose. We had not gone a hundred yards when the wagon, in trying to avoid a shell-hole in the road, fell into the ditch. I spent an hour trying to get it out, but failed to move it. It was now beginning to get light, and as it would have been fatal to have been caught in the open with the men and horses, I had to leave the wagon also. I divided the men up into the second G.S. wagon, and made them walk alternatively with the party who were in the wagon. We just managed to get out of the danger zone by the time it was fully light.

After a tiring march of ten miles over vile Belgian roads, we reached our wagon-lines at 9 a.m. Everyone was pretty tired by then, especially those who had had to walk half the way on foot.

On arrival I was met by the cheerful news that the whole of my kit was lost. It was put on top of the G.S. wagon, and must have fallen off in the dark without being seen. This is, indeed, cheerful, as I am left with just what I stand up in ! My beloved fur sleeping-bag that I have had throughout the campaign, my blankets, pillow, waterproof and change of clothes, tobacco, cigars and, worst of all, every boot that I possess ! I have only the pair of half rubber boots that I was wearing at the time, and which are useless, except for paddling about in the mud. A cheerful prospect for the next week or two before I can get anything out from England. I have sent to the Provost-Marshal to ask him to tell his people to look out for it, but I have little hopes of ever hearing of it. Probably some vile Belgian will loot it, and either use or sell all the things.

After breakfast, the others went to bed, but, tired as I was, I was too upset at the loss of my kit to be able to sleep, so I spent the day pottering about the lines and writing up this diary.

Whilst we have been in action the drivers have been making stables for the winter. The mud is awful ; a foot deep where the horses are standing. The pattern is just an open, pent-roof shed, with hop-poles for supports and rafters, and thatched with straw. It will be very cold, but should keep the horses dry.

I have had a charming note from the colonel, saying that both General Capper and General Philpotts had sent me messages to say how sorry they were about the disaster, and that what a pity it was that so much hard work had been wasted.

To bed at 10 p.m., after being on the go for forty hours without shutting my eyes.

BOESCHEPE, 17TH NOVEMBER, 1915

I had an awful night, without any bedding and on a stone floor. I borrowed some blankets, but, as the room is full of draughts and it was freezing hard outside, I was bitterly cold.

Last night I sent Deacon and Bishop back to the gun
position to get the guns. They arrived back here at 5 a.m.,
having been completely successful, and bringing the two
damaged guns on four new wheels, the G.S. wagon that had
been abandoned in the ditch and various things, like the
pump. Fortunately they were not shelled, and it all
went fairly easily.

The colonel came over to see me this morning, and was
very sympathetic at the loss of two more guns. He said
it was an experiment putting them so far forward. If
it had come off, we should have been able to do very useful
work, being so close up to the trenches. He gave me the
startling news that the whole 24th Division is to be withdrawn from the Line next week, and goes into general
reserve near St. Omer—ostensibly for a rest. But what
I am wondering is : does it mean Servia ? I know some
Divisions have already gone from here.

BOESCHEPE, 18TH NOVEMBER, 1915

Another miserable night on an old door, and with
nothing but blankets. I have sent all over the country
about my valise, but cannot hear of it. I spent the whole
morning with my office clerk, going through papers that
have been accumulating all the time we have been in
action. The weather is vile ; hard frosts at night and an
icy rain all day.

The I.O.M. (Inspector of Ordnance Machinery) came
to-day to see the damaged guns. He has condemned the
gun-carriages as scrap-iron, but thinks that the guns
themselves may be worth saving. They are to go into
the Corps' workshops to-morrow. I have had visits from
every sort of people to condole over the disaster, and to
see the remains of the guns.

This evening, at 5 o'clock, we all went to Reninghelst
to attend a magic-lantern lecture by the Flying Corps.
They showed us slides of the trenches in front of Ypres,
from photos taken in aeroplanes. Some were very good
and interesting. I was immensely excited to see one of
Hollebeke Château, which I have been firing at so much.

The moment I saw the photo I understood why it was that I had had such difficulty in getting the exact range. The house stands on the top of a very narrow ridge, and the garden behind slopes down steeply into an ornamental lake, quite close to the house. Whenever one of my shells went just over the Château, it must have pitched into the lake and I did not see it. I wish they had sent me the photo before I started ranging, as it would have helped me a great deal.

On my way back I called in at the Provost-Marshal's office to ask if there was any news of my kit, when my joy can be imagined to hear that it was found and was in possession of the military police at Ouderdom. I at once sent the battery trap for it, and it arrived safely during dinner. Everything is complete, except my fleece-lined waterproof. The bedding is a little wet, as it must have fallen into some water; but what does that matter?

BOESCHEPE, 19TH NOVEMBER, 1915

I have sent the periscope home by a sergeant of the Ammunition Column, as it will be more likely to arrive safe than if sent by post. It is too high a magnification, and, consequently, too small a field of view. Very useful for infantry, but quite. useless for my work.

Have just had a wire from the Ordnance people that my two guns have arrived at railhead. This is, really, wonderfully quick. Apparently the 24th Division is to be relieved by the 3rd next week. We march out on the night of the 23/24th.

Have spent all day writing up arrears of official correspondence. There seems to be as much office work on service as in peace time. One beastly woman at Brighton is pestering me with a claim for a few shillings for washing supposed to have been done a year ago!

BOESCHEPE, 20TH NOVEMBER, 1915

Cold and nasty. General Philpotts rode over from Reninghelst on purpose to say how sorry he was that we had been smashed up. Very good of him. I was able to tell him that I have already got my two new guns, complete with all sights. It is really very wonderful. My poor old guns are now on their way to England.

BOESCHEPE, 21ST NOVEMBER, 1915

This morning a squadron of seventeen German aeroplanes raided Poperinghe and the towns round. They dropped some bombs at Abeele, which is close here. I could not think what the noise was. At first, I thought they must be shelling Reninghelst with their long gun, as they did once before. In the afternoon, I had a visit from the colonel of the brigade that is relieving us. Dined with the column.

BOESCHEPE, 22ND NOVEMBER, 1915

Rode six miles into Bailleul with Potter. There was a piano where we lunched, and for two hours Potter played all my pet things. The Barcarole, Triomphe March from Aida, Gounod's Ave Maria, etc. He plays quite beautifully, being practically a professional. I understand that he plays the organ in many of the big churches in London, and also at concert halls. It was a real day-out, and I enjoyed my holiday immensely. When I got back I found that our long-expected gramophone had come.

BOESCHEPE, 23RD NOVEMBER, 1915

Had a full marching order parade to see if we could get everything on the wagons—we have collected such a lot of stuff. It is wonderful how things grow. My water-cart has got a brother, so has the officers' mess-cart, and now a new G.S. wagon has turned up. I suppose they fell down out of the sky into my lines. He who asks no questions will be told no lies. My official eye has not seen them ! The whisky has come, so we are having a dinner party to-night—Miller and Webber. To bed at 1 a.m., after a cheerful evening.

BOESCHEPE, 24TH NOVEMBER, 1915

It is thawing to-day, which makes the place even more muddy and dirty than ever. We are not going to start now till the 25th. An advance party of the 109th Battery have arrived.

Had a battery gun drill this afternoon; found that everyone had got very slack. I shall fairly wake them all up when we get back to our new quarters. It seems that we shall be going very near the coast, in the direction of Calais. When we come back to the Line I sincerely hope it will not be Flanders. I hate the district with a hate beyond words.

STEENVOORDE, 25TH NOVEMBER, 1915

We were relieved by the 109th Battery at 3.30 p.m., and, after handing over various maps and trench stores, we started at once. We had not been on the road for an hour before it was dark and bitterly cold. I had to keep taking my feet out of the stirrups or they would have frozen.

We reached this place about 7 o'clock, having been frequently delayed by broken-down wagons of the Div. Amm. Col. They seem to be quite unable to keep on the road. I suppose their officers are quite incompetent; they mostly look it. We had an awful time getting into the field where we were to camp, as there was no road and we had to get over the ditch at the side of the road in pitch darkness, except for electric torches. We found no fire in the farm-house, and altogether had rather a miserable evening.

STEENVOORDE, 26TH NOVEMBER, 1915

The colonel came round this morning and said he would try and arrange for me to go on leave on the 10th December till the 18th. That would suit me very well.

We have had a dense snow-storm during stables, so thick that one could not see two hundred yards. It is bitterly cold.

ARNEKE, 27TH NOVEMBER, 1915

A march of about fourteen miles. A fine, sunny day, but very cold, as it is freezing hard. My fur coat, that I got out of Ordnance, kept me beautifully warm, except as to my fingers and feet. I must get a pair of wooden stirrups. I believe they are much the best for this weather.

There was horrible confusion in the market square of Steenvoorde when we all got to the rendezvous, as D Battery only left about a hundred yards between A and themselves for B and C to get into. As we each take up 400 yards of road, there was a mess !

We passed Cassel, a pretty, old-world town on the top of a hill, and were inspected by General Headlam, C.R.A. of the II Army. It is a true saying in the Army that, the bigger the inspecting officer, the more fatuous his criticisms. The only thing he could pick on to find fault with was the fact that all the nosebags were not tied to the saddle at quite the same height ! I have promised to " see that this does not occur again."

This is a pretty little village of well-to-do small villas. The people seem very hostile to the troops, door after door being shut in our faces when we asked for billets. I have got quarters in the house of a " petit rentier," a dear old couple who are doing all they can to make us comfortable. The old man was at Sedan in 1870, and was wounded there.

Apparently my leave for the 10th is all right. The Colonel goes on the 2nd, leaving me in command of the brigade again. After commanding it in a great battle, I don't think it will worry me much. We were able to buy a *Daily Mail* here, which gave me the latest news up to yesterday, which was a blessing, as there has been no mail to-day.

Harvey and Bishop are billeted in a château where they are being very well done. Sheets on the beds ! I am sure they will catch dreadful colds !

Moringhem, 28th November, 1915

A truly dreadful day. To begin with, it had been freezing hard all night after yesterday's thaw, and the road was one sheet of ice. The horses could not keep their feet, and fell every few yards. We did not make two miles an hour and the column got spread out over miles of road. The whole four artillery brigades of the division were marching together, with the 107th in front of us. It was a twenty-two-mile march, and in my whole life I have never felt such cold. The last five miles in the dusk were really terrible. There must have been twenty degrees of frost, and the road was along the crest of a high hill. In addition, there was a strong wind blowing from left to right that went through one like a knife. I walked nearly the whole way on foot, both to keep warm and also as my horse could hardly stand up on the icy surface. I was very thankful to have my fur-lined coat—the great collar, that came right up round my ears, just saved my life.

On arrival here we were horrified to find that this—our rest-camp for a month—is about the worst thing in billets we have struck since we came out. It is a tiny and poverty-stricken little village, where one can buy nothing. Even bread cannot be had. There is no water, except a cesspool in the farmyard, which is the colour of coffee. I wonder that the horses will touch it.

The men have got quite decent barns, so they are all right. Harvey and I have clean and Spartan rooms in the priest's house, but it is miserably cold. We hope to get a stove to-morrow ; meanwhile we are shivering in our cloaks, mufflers, and gloves. We have had our dinner with the priest, who has a small stove in his room. He is a cheery soul, and played marches on his harmonium. Very painful to listen to, but he meant it well. We retaliated with Wagner on our gramophone.

I have had to be very firm with the local inhabitants, who, as usual in this part of the world, resent having British troops billeted on them.

9

Montgomerie goes on leave to-night, and will be in London to-morrow in time for tea—lucky devil! My sergeant-major is also going. The cold depresses me; I would rather be in action again—if it was warm.

MORINGHEM, 29TH NOVEMBER, 1915

The leave boat did not run to-day, so the sergeant-major had to come back. He goes again to-morrow. They say more mines have got loose in the Channel. For the same reason, no mail to-day. We spent the day cleaning up and getting things straight. Still most ghastly cold.

MORINGHEM, 30TH NOVEMBER, 1915

It is exactly three months since we left England. What a lot has happened in that time! To-day I had an inspection of equipment. It is really appalling the amount of stuff the men lose. I won't put up with it any more, and they will have to pay for things in future. Every time we march they leave something behind. There is an idea throughout the Army that there is an unlimited supply of everything just behind the firing line, and that a man has only got to ask to be given anything he likes. They will be leaving a gun behind soon. Of course, the excuse always is that things were blown up in the gun-pits!

MORINGHEM, 1ST DECEMBER, 1915

The colonel came in last night and stayed and talked so late that I did not have my weekly bath! Oh for my own beloved bathroom at home. I have got neuralgia all down one side of my face, which is a nuisance. It is this damnable cold. I shall try ten grains of aspirin to-night. This place is quite impossible on account of the water, and we are to move the day after to-morrow.

I had a letter to-day from Malcolm Lyon. The 2nd Life Guards are at a place called Hucquelines, not far from Boulogne and only about ten miles from where we are going. My leave seems to be all right from the 11th to the 18th, if nothing unforeseen happens. The colonel has handed over to me, and starts at about 4 a.m. to-morrow. It is blowing a hurricane, which will not improve the horses.

MORINGHEM, 2ND DECEMBER, 1915

I took my ten grains of aspirin last night, and had a good sleep. My faceache seems better to-day, though I feel very heavy and stupid after the drug. The sun is trying to shine, so life does not seem quite so depressing as usual. In the afternoon we packed up and got ready for to-morrow's move. I shall be glad to get away from this place, which is depressing to a degree. I have never lived in such a poverty-stricken place. One can buy absolutely nothing locally. Even bread cannot be had nearer than St. Omer (6 miles).

ALQUINES, 3RD DECEMBER, 1915

The brigade started at 8.45 a.m. at quarter-hour intervals, the ammunition column leading.

Miller and his second-in-command are both leaving the brigade to-morrow. The former is going to the Flying Corps and the latter transferred to 107th Brigade.

Our new billets are a slight improvement on the last. We have plenty of good water and most of the horses can be got under cover. On the other hand, we are much scattered—B is three miles from H.Q. and the ammunition column a mile the other way. I took C Battery to their village and installed them there. After lunch, the adjutant called for me and we went round B, A, and D to see how they were getting on. I have sent my servants and kit to H.Q., and shall live there till the colonel comes back. Made myself quite at home at H.Q. They feed quite well, but it is not as cheerful as my own mess.

In the afternoon I rode round the batteries. On my way back from B I found one of A's men lying outside an estaminet, dead drunk and covered with blood. The women of the estaminet, who were in hysterics, said that one of our ammunition wagons had stopped there, and that the men had had a fight. I was naturally furious, and on my return placed the whole party under arrest.

ALQUINES, 4TH DECEMBER, 1915

Poured all day. In the morning I visited the ammunition column. They seem very comfortable. During lunch General Philpotts and Hannay called, and apparently were very worried to find that D Battery had not got their horses under cover. I promised to see about it myself. I spent the afternoon with Birch and the local Maire in going through every hole and corner in his area, and at last succeeded in getting the whole of the horses and men in.

On my return I was met by the cheering news that leave has been cut down to one individual per brigade per week, i.e. it will take 750 weeks, or fifteen years, to let every man go on leave once! This is hardly the reward one expects after Loos and Ypres. However, it is the usual way one must expect to be treated. I doubt now if I shall be able to get away.

ALQUINES, 5TH DECEMBER, 1915

Sunday. General Capper arrived on a surprise visit. He was very affable, and said he would inquire into our mails being so irregular. He was also much annoyed to find that we have to send sixteen miles for them and sixteen back.

When he had gone I rode over to C and B and found on my way back that General Philpotts had also come. It seems to pour generals now. They have nothing else to do, so they come running round to visit units. Having a clear conscience, it rather amuses me. General Philpotts seems to be quite satisfied with us, as he said he did not propose to come to us any more, as we were getting on all right, and he insinuated that he was not so pleased with other brigades. I spoke to him about my leave, and I still hope that it will be all right. At any rate, I have

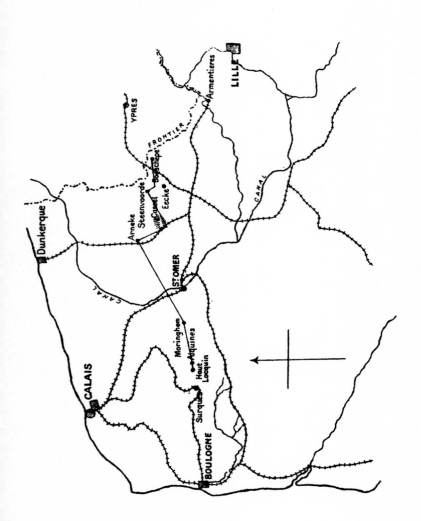

LILLE – CALAIS, DEC. 1915.

put in for it for the 11th. The colonel comes back on the evening of the 10th, so I shall be able to hand over to him. General Capper proposes to lecture to the officers of the brigade on the 10th, so I shall have to stay for that, as I cannot leave the brigade without a field officer when he comes. A letter from G., but no papers again.

ALQUINES, 6TH DECEMBER, 1915

Pouring with rain and blowing hard, but not at all cold. The wind is coming off the sea. In the morning I inspected D Battery's billets and horse-shelters. They are all under cover. In the afternoon I went round half A Battery. Hector, who is in charge of A whilst Montgomerie is on leave, is really an excellent officer—he and Harvey are quite fit to have batteries of their own. I have no doubt that if the war lasts much longer they will get promoted.

ALQUINES, 7TH DECEMBER, 1915

Much colder to-day, and I think the wind has changed. After lunch I rode over to C Battery and had a talk with Harvey. They seem to be getting on very well.

ALQUINES, 8TH DECEMBER, 1915

A fine day, for once in a way. In the morning, I thoroughly inspected C Battery, and could not find anything to complain of. After that I went on to Surques, where there is a narrow-gauge line to Boulogne. I find there is a train at 6.34 in the morning that gets to B. at 8.30. I think I shall go that way. Surques is only 8 miles from here, so it will be much better than going 15 miles by road to St. Omer and then having a four-hours' journey in the train via Calais. I called on B. on my way back. Tea with D. and also A.

ALQUINES, 9TH DECEMBER, 1915

I got a telegram at 11 p.m. last night to say that General Capper would be inspecting us this morning, so warned batteries first thing this morning to be ready. I waited in all the morning, but the general did not turn up till about 12 o'clock, when he passed my headquarters, going at a great rate towards C and B. To illustrate how generals' inspections are the same whether at home in peace-time or here within sound of gun : at breakfast the brigade major rang me up to say what things the generals were looking at and finding fault over with other brigades. I, of course, immediately passed it on to all battery commanders. As for his surprise visit to C and B yesterday, he had not got a hundred yards past here before the batteries had been notified that he was on his way to them —the field telephone has many advantages over mounted orderlies. Result : when the generals arrived they found everyone hard at work at exactly what they ought to have been doing, according to the programme of work that they had sent in for the week. As a matter of fact, I have no doubt whatever that they would have been working hard in any case, but it is as well to make sure in these matters. Awful idea if, at the moment the generals arrived, the officers had been trying a new gramophone record ! Otherwise a very dull day.

ALQUINES, 10TH DECEMBER, 1915

A wet but warm day, and very stormy. I am afraid I shall have a bad crossing to-morrow.

At 2.80 p.m. General Capper gave a lecture to the officers and N.C.O.s of the brigade. He is a fine speaker and gave a quite excellent address. He pointed out that we are fighting an enemy who is unscrupulous and cannot be treated with the courtesies of civilised warfare. The idea he emphasised was that, without descending to disgraceful methods, we must kill every armed German on every possible occasion.

After tea I went over to C Battery and installed myself there for the night, as the colonel is due back some time this evening. We had a very cheerful evening, with an excellent gramophone concert, thanks to a lot of new records lent us by D Battery. To bed at 11 p.m., but not to sleep. Am too excited at the prospect of getting home to-morrow. Have ordered my horses for 5.40 a.m. and the men's cart to take the remains of A Sub-section Gun.

1, ST. JAMES'S TERRACE

Home once more ! I was called at 4 a.m. and started for Surques railway station at a quarter to five. It was then quite dark, but I had taken the precaution to ride over the road by daylight. It is 4 miles to Surques, and I arrived in good time for the train, which was supposed to start at 6.30. It is a metre-gauge railway and exactly the same as the one by which I crossed the No-Tien-Ling Pass in Manchuria some years ago.

After endless stops, we reached Boulogne at 8.30. I at once went to the hotel at the docks and had breakfast. The boat sailed at 11 a.m. and I, fortunately, managed to secure a cabin, as the sea was rough. After a pretty bad passage, we reached Folkestone, and found a train of Pullman cars waiting. We got into Victoria Station at 4.30 p.m. and there I found my mother waiting for me with the carriage. I went to Lennox Gardens first and had tea there; after which I took a taxi home.

What a joy it is to be in one's own comfortable house again, after three months of the sort I have had ! My chief impression is one of colour. The carpets, curtains, chairs, etc., etc., all look so very bright and cheerful, after the horrible mud, filth, and nothing but khaki. An excellent dinner—with oysters and a white shirt and collar !

BOULOGNE, 18TH DECEMBER, 1915

My leave is over and I am back again in France. Six days is all too short, but well worth the long journey. I have had time to get new clothes and do many things that I have wanted. I left Victoria at 9.50 a.m. and did a non-stop run to within three miles of Folkestone, where they side-tracked us for four hours. Heaven only knows why. Fortunately, being a Pullman train, we were able to get a good lunch. We went on board at 4 p.m., some 300 officers and 1,000 men. After a very rough passage we reached Boulogne at 6.30. Being no trains up-country to-night, I have gone to the Louvre Hôtel for the night. Quite a good dinner, the hotel is full of officers returning to the Front. Spent a very pleasant evening with various people whose names I do not know.

ALQUINES, 19TH DECEMBER, 1915

I tried to borrow a car from the Red Cross to run me out to the brigade, but failed. So I sent a telegram through the signal people to say I wanted my horses and the mess-cart to meet me at Surques at 4.30 p.m. After lunch I took the metre-gauge train up-country and duly reached Surques at 6.30. To my intense relief I found my horses and the cart waiting and rode the 8 miles in time for tea. The gramophone records were a great success, and we have played Wagner, Piccini, Verdi, etc., till nearly midnight. We go up to the line again about the 29th, so we shall have Christmas here.

ALQUINES, 20TH DECEMBER, 1915

Had a small scheme this morning, brought the battery into action in very difficult ground. In the afternoon had tea with the colonel at H.Q.

ALQUINES, 21ST DECEMBER, 1915

Rained, so brigade field-day fixed for this morning was cancelled. Harvey has gone round the district buying pigs and turkeys for the Christmas dinner.

ALQUINES, 22ND DECEMBER, 1915

Rained as usual. Took the battery out this morning without the guns or wagons. Did a sort of "follow my leader " with them up and down all the worst banks and steep hills. Very good for their driving and riding. After-noon a lecture by the colonel on gunnery. Gramophone all the evening. Bought two pigs for the men's Christmas dinner.

ALQUINES, CHRISTMAS DAY, 1915

The men had their Christmas dinner in an estam et. We got them two pigs and two barrels of English beer. They also had cigarettes, sweets, and plum-puddings from the *Daily Chronicle*. I presented them with 3,000 cigar-ettes and cigars for the sergeants' mess. They had a glorious time, most of them being horribly drunk by 2 o'clock. However, fortunately, they behaved themselves and there was no crime. The poor devils have a dull time out here, and I am glad they should enjoy themselves for once.

ALQUINES, 27TH DECEMBER, 1915

We were supposed to go up into the line, starting to-morrow, but it has been cancelled at the last moment. It may mean we are going to the East instead. At any rate, that would be warmer.

ALQUINES, 28TH DECEMBER, 1915

The cat is out of the bag ! We go to Hooge, the worst spot in the whole line ! However, someone had got to go there, so we must just make the best of it. We start on Monday. To-day we had a brigade route march. A peculiarly dull form of amusement, and of no educational value to either officers or men.

ALQUINES, 29TH DECEMBER, 1915

It did not rain to-day ! Had a brigade battery staff scheme all the morning.

ALQUINES, 30TH DECEMBER, 1915

Another fine day ! Had the battery out taking up positions. Harvey has gone up to the trenches with a telephonist ; he will have a dull time till we arrive next week. Some new records have arrived that G. has sent, including two "Parsifal"; they are really magnificent. Gilmour is coming to dinner to hear them.

ALQUINES, 31ST DECEMBER, 1915

Fine, but very windy. Another brigade scheme day. The "meet" was at my headquarters. I had drinks ready, and tried to imagine it was a hunt breakfast! We are giving a big dinner-party of ten. Heaven knows how we shall manage for plates, etc. We are under orders to start for Ypres on Monday morning.

ALQUINES, 1ST JANUARY, 1916

Another New Year, and the war still going strong. I wonder where we shall be this time next year! Last night we gave a great dinner-party, all the battery commanders, Cammell, Birch, Montgomery, Wilkins, Condon, Lewis, and our four selves. We kept the gramophone going hard the whole time, and by midnight were quite ready to drink the health of the New Year, to the tune of " Auld Lang Syne." This morning we again got a telegram " all orders cancelled," so we are still waiting to know where we are to go to.

ALQUINES, 2ND JANUARY, 1916

We are still in the dark as to what has happened. But, as we still belong to the Vth Corps, I suppose we shall go to Hooge.

ALQUINES, 3RD JANUARY, 1916

We now hear that we move to Quelmes, between here and St. Omer, on the 6th, presumably *en route* for Ypres. Had the battery out to-day till lunch, doing a scheme, one section *v.* the other. These young New Army officers are quite good for trench warfare, but their ideas of open warfare are pitiable. God help us when we advance!

ALQUINES, 4TH JANUARY, 1916

We move to-morrow morning. Devoted the day to cleaning and packing up. Lunched with the colonel. He is going on ahead by motor, so I shall have to take charge of the brigade for the journey. The papers arrived to-day with the list of people mentioned in despatches. There are 8,000 names, of whom more than 600 are on the Staff.

QUELMES, 5TH JANUARY, 1916

We arrived here in time for lunch after a short march of 8 miles. There was a terrible hill of about 1 in 5 and a mile long. I fully expected the G.S. wagon to stick, as it was badly overloaded. We have taken over the other billets that the divisional ammunition column had. They must be a dirty lot ; I have never seen a place in a worse mess. The colonel has gone on up to Ypres to see the place, so I am in charge of the brigade.

QUELMES, 6TH JANUARY, 1916

We are very comfortable here—the officers have a room in the school, where I also sleep. The horses are in the gun-park, which is good enough for a short time. I have had a wire run out from the Brigade H.Q., so I can run the brigade and battery quite easily.

QUELMES, 7TH JANUARY, 1916

We leave here to-morrow. I have made out the orders for the march with great care.

NOORDPENE, 8TH JANUARY, 1916

Arrived here about 2.80 p.m. after a comfortable march of 15 miles. We passed through the outskirts of St. Omer, and then skirted the forest of Clairmarais, where all the wood for fuel comes from. The whole valley is under water. It must be a wet place at any time, as there are thousands of little canals, just like Holland. All the country produce is carried to the railways in small flat-bottomed boats. To-night we have a specially good billet in a large château, which belongs to a French officer. It is uninhabited, but a certain amount of furniture left. B and C Batteries shared it, and had a combined mess. We lived in a large dining-room, where the gramophone sounded very well.

STEENVOORDE, 9TH JANUARY, 1916

As we had a short march to-day, I had a late start. We passed Cassel again and had to go up the long and steep hill. It is really extraordinary that there should be no road round the town so as to avoid the hill. To-night we are in the same farm as we had coming out of action six weeks ago. The room with seven doors, all letting in draughts—and the horrible family who walked through the room from 4 a.m. onwards at one-minute intervals. It is one of the worst billets we have had out here.

POPERINGHE, 10TH JANUARY, 1916

The batteries marched here independently and went to their new wagon-lines. I marched off at 10 a.m. and crossed the Franco-Belgian frontier at midday. Once more I am back in this hateful country ! My wagon-lines are about a mile and a half from Poperinghe on the Ypres side. Never have I seen such a filthy place to camp. The battery who were here before me (D/80 of the 17th Division) must be quite the dirtiest lot in the Army. I do not complain of the mud, which is in many places up to the horses' girths, but of the filth and refuse left round the men's sleeping quarters. There is only a small farm with two rooms, so that it is quite impossible for the officers to live there. We have a big house in Poperinghe itself, close to the cathedral.

POPERINGHE, 11TH JANUARY, 1916

The colonel is commanding a group of batteries, and is in action the other side of Ypres. My battery not being

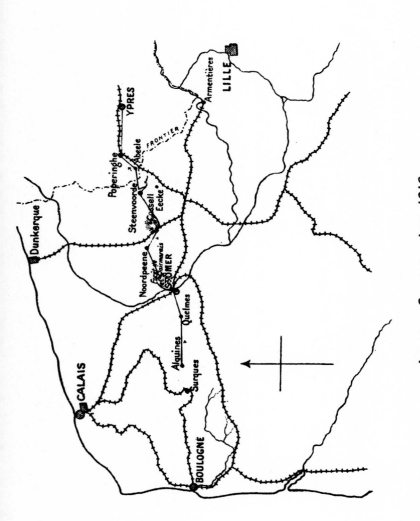

LILLE − CALAIS, JAN. 1916.

in action for the moment, I have taken over command of all the wagon-lines. It means a lot of work, principally writing, as all indents for materials for improving the horse-lines and also for the gun positions have to go through me. I have also to arrange for convoys to take the timber, etc., up to the guns.

POPERINGHE, 12TH JANUARY, 1916

The Huns have been trying to be nasty this morning : they put two shells close to my lines. I expect they were meant for the railway. It is impossible to do any work ; the only thing that can be done is to have constant fatigues, trying to cut roads through the mud ; but as I can get no bricks or timber from the R.E., I cannot get much improvement.

POPERINGHE, 13TH JANUARY, 1916

Harvey went on leave this morning, starting at the awful hour of 4 a.m. It really seems very unnecessary to send off the leave train at 4 a.m. in order that it should reach Boulogne at 10 a.m. ! Fortunately it has been fine since we arrived. When it really rains again, I tremble to think what a state the roads and my mud camp will be in.

POPERINGHE, 14TH JANUARY, 1916

It is like living in a town that is besieged. Nearly every window is broken, and many houses have great holes in their walls. We have not been bombarded since we arrived, but I hear they put 300 shells into the place one day last week.

POPERINGHE, 16TH JANUARY, 1916

Nothing new. I am still hard at work cleaning up the camp, but I cannot do much good till I can get some materials from the R.E. It is easier to get blood out of a stone than anything out of them. The gramophone is our

one great joy. Bishop plays it for hours every evening—
we can seldom tear ourselves away from it much before
midnight. We play principally Wagner, and have now
got most of the best-known parts. " Parsifal " is our
favourite. For light music, our usual ones are the four
" Indian Love Songs" and the " Rosary." During dinner
I suddenly got orders from Divisional Headquarters to
proceed to Bailleul to-morrow for a Senior Officers' course.
Apparently lectures on the co-operation of artillery with
the other arms. Rather short notice.

BAILLEUL, 17TH JANUARY, 1916

Handed over command of the battery to Bishop. I
also handed over the command of the wagon-lines
to Gilpin, who commands the ammunition column. I
sent Bath—my servant—in the mess-cart with my kit,
and followed on later with my horses. Fortunately I
happened to call at Divisional Headquarters in Reninghelst on my way, and was offered a motor to take me on.
The general also gave me lunch. He has not got such good
quarters as I have ! The house he occupies is principally
taken up by his office, and they have to mess in a small
wooden hut in the garden. I came on here after lunch
by motor with a captain of the East Surreys, who is in
our 72nd Brigade—a very nice fellow. We exchanged
experiences about Loos. Apparently it was even a worse
muddle than I ever realised. The Town Major allotted me
a billet—68 Rue d'Ypres—a small house, where they have
given me a tiny bedroom ; but it seems clean, which is the
main thing. The one advantage of Bailleul is that it
has a fine cathedral, with good music.

BAILLEUL, 18TH JANUARY, 1916

I tried the pub that was allotted to me for meals, but
it is so beastly that I have changed to the Hôtel Faucon,
which is a commercial hotel in the Grande Place. There
are also more amusing people there. Half my course go

to one and the other half to the other. There are two men here that I like—the East Surrey fellow and a man called Wormald in the K.R.R., who seems to be a London man. We had two lectures to-day—in the morning on Aeroplane Co-operation with Artillery, which was quite interesting, and in the afternoon on Guns in Support of Infantry. This course is not really for the purpose of teaching us anything, but to promote discussions and get ideas from Battery Commanders. It is also very useful, as it enables artillery and infantry officers to exchange views in a peaceful atmosphere, and get some insight into each other's needs and difficulties.

BAILLEUL, 19TH JANUARY, 1916

A lovely day. Two more lectures to-day; the first by Butler, a man I knew at Larkhill, on " flash spotting," quite interesting, but not much new ; the other by Colonel Coates, who commanded the next group of batteries to me on the right, at Loos. Went for a walk with Wormald and had tea at the Canadian tea-shop. Got a large packet of letters by my cyclist orderly, including a charming little edition of the *Imitation of Christ* from Sonia. During dinner an orderly arrived from Bishop with a letter to say that the wagon-line was being heavily shelled by 6-in. guns, and asking what to do. The poor devil of an orderly had walked all the way ! I at once went over to Canadian " Signals " and in less than a minute got through to 24 Divisional Artillery and got hold of Hannay, the brigade major. He promised to send a message on to the battery to tell them to take the horses out of the lines till it was over.

BAILLEUL, 20TH JANUARY, 1916

Two more lectures to-day. One by Colonel Walthall and the other by Colonel Pelham-Burn of the Gordons. I hear that very little damage was done yesterday— a few horses killed in the wagon-lines, but no men or guns damaged. Young Shepard was wounded yesterday—shell splinter in the foot. This is the one in D Battery.

BAILLEUL, 21ST JANUARY, 1916

Two more lectures, neither very good. To-day is the last day. I am beginning to get a little bored. There are only about three men on the course who are at all interesting, and we have about talked each other out.

POPERINGHE, 22ND JANUARY, 1916

Two lectures, one very good one by Colonel Poole, who was my group commander at Grenay, during the great bombardment. He was talking about counter-batteries, and, pointing to me, said : " I see one of my late brigade commanders who did excellent counter-battery work with his field-guns." After the lecture he asked why I had not got a brigade of my own yet, and said it was a " damned shame." However, I live in hopes. The division sent a car for me, and Wormald, Onslow, and I motored back. I went into the Town Major's office at Bailleul and found that individual to be none other than Cassilis. My late sergeant-major (Walker) has just got his commission, and dined with us.

POPERINGHE, 23RD JANUARY, 1916

An exciting night. It was a full moon and light as day. At midnight a Hun aeroplane came over and amused himself dropping bombs on the town. He dropped six or eight all round my house, and killed several people, besides making a beastly noise. I woke up at 1.30 to find another one doing the same thing. This morning I heard that a third visited us about 4 o'clock.

POPERINGHE, 24TH JANUARY, 1916

Spent the whole morning going through papers that had

come since I have been away. Three p.m. Harvey and I are just starting for Ypres. I am taking up a party with wagons to prepare a place for guns close up behind the trenches. It will be close to where Peter Petersen is buried, but nearer the Hun. I am not looking forward to it, as there is a full moon, and I think it quite possible that Fritz will see us ; at any rate, he is sure to hear us and will probably turn on his machine-guns. However, if the thing can be done, it will be a very good thing, as we shall be able to fire into the Hun trenches from behind ! In fact, we shall have the curious phenomenon of being between the Hun gun and his target, and both firing the same way !

POPERINGHE, 25TH JANUARY, 1916

Got back here safely with nothing worse than a bullet through my cap. It was a long and exhausting business. Starting at 2 p.m., we got to Ypres at 5 o'clock, having had to wait at Vlamertinghe for half an hour whilst the road beyond was being shelled. Just as we reached the Asylum, two hundred yards short of Ypres, they put two 4·2 high explosives alongside the road and about 80 yards from us. After that we had no more trouble till we got to Zillebeke. There I had to wait three hours till I could get trucks on the trench tramway. We transferred the timber, sandbags, tools, etc., to two trolleys, just like there are in the streets of Mombasa. It was very hard work pushing the trolley up-hill, the more so as the track was often a foot deep in water and mud. We were sniped all the time. It was too dark for the Germans to see us, but the bullets that missed our trenches came on past us. At times the air fairly buzzed with them. I chose a place near Maple Copse for the gun, in a hedge. We worked hard and soon made a light emplacement, with 9 × 8 timber, and sandbags. It is only meant to keep out bullets and shrapnel, not for big shells. At 4 a.m. I started back with Harvey and all the men except seven and Sergeant Hughes. We came back by a communicating

10

trench more than two miles long and very deep, which led past Zillebeke Lake. We entered Ypres by the Lille Gate, and found the G.S. wagon waiting at the Asylum, as I had ordered. I put the men into it and was just getting in myself when a motor came past. We stopped it and asked for a lift. Foolishly we assumed it was going on to Poperinghe; instead, we suddenly found ourselves at Ouderdom. Then we had to walk to Reninghelst (1 mile)—then got a lift in a passing G.S. wagon as far as our D Battery. We found them at morning stables, and I borrowed their mess-cart, which landed us home here at 7 a.m.! After breakfast I shaved and got on with my day's work. Curiously enough I did not feel at all tired, although I had been walking and carrying sandbags all night. Now at 9 p.m. I am simply rather sleepy, but do not feel the loss of a complete night's sleep at all.

POPERINGHE, 26TH JANUARY, 1916

Have made great preparations for taking the gun up to-night, also a wagon load of ammunition. All the harness has been covered in sacking, and the horses will wear sacks with a little bran on their feet. We cannot take the gun up by the tram-line, so shall have to drive right up to the place. I am taking Perry with me this time; it is his first experience of being under fire. I hope he will like it!

POPERINGHE, 27TH JANUARY, 1916

Got back here at 7 a.m. after an exciting night. We had a bad start, being shelled in Vlamertinghe. Left the Menin Gate at 10 p.m. and reached Zillebeke all right. There I halted and muffled the wheels. I left the wagon in Z., and went on with the gun and twenty dismounted men. As soon as we passed the church we started the long climb up Observatory Ridge; it is nearly a mile long and exposed the whole way. The night was very clear, and the flares showed up the horses and gun on the sky-line quite distinctly. I made the drivers lie flat on their horses' necks and led the lead horses by the bridle myself. The mud was awful at the sides of the road, and there was only just room on the *pavé* centre for the horses, so I had to plunge along in the mud beside them. I dared not stop for fear the gun should stick, or the Hun machine-guns get our range. When I found that it was not too impossible I sent Perry and half the men back to bring on the wagon. We got them all up to the position with the loss of only one man wounded (Sadler Hewett, who got a bullet in the chest). I found that Sergeant Hughes had got on with his emplacement and we put the gun in, dumping the ammunition. There were a lot of bullets going past all the time, but I am not sure if they actually saw us or not. My party helped Sergeant Hughes to fill sandbags, etc., till 3 a.m., when we started back. We got through Ypres without any trouble. I handed the wounded man over to a motor ambulance and we came home in the G.S. wagon that had been waiting for us all night. It was bitterly cold, and, as Perry and I were hot after walking 10 miles, we got up and drove ourselves, Perry in the centre and I in the lead, to the huge amusement of the men in the wagon.

POPERINGHE, 28TH JANUARY, 1916

Spent the whole day doing correspondence of sorts. It is really terrible the amount of writing that has to be done. The division is eternally asking for returns. One day last week I was actually asked, " How many rounds of ammunition have you ? " And, " Where do you carry it ? " My establishment is 704 rounds. I was very tempted to reply, " 703 in wagons and limbers, and 1 in my haversack." However, it seldom pays to be funny.

POPERINGHE, 29TH JANUARY, 1916

A dull day. I was President of a Field General Court-martial: two cases—one a simple drunk, the other very serious. I have sent Perry up to-night to see the zone of our new position. We shall send up one section on Monday night, and I take over command on Tuesday night.

YPRES, 31ST JANUARY, 1916

This evening I brought the Right Section of my battery into action at Ypres, relieving the Left Section of D Battery. They come under Birch's command until the relief is completed to-morrow night. We got up here without being shelled, and took over without any trouble. I am staying with Birch for the night. They do not do themselves as well as we do—in fact, they " pig " it. The officers' mess is actually in the Lille Gate, a most curious place. It must be about sixteenth century, and was evidently the old guard-room. It is a vaulted room, or rather three rooms, with no windows, except a few slits, looking out over the moat. The battery is just the other side of the moat. We get to it through a tunnel in the ramparts, and across a small wooden footbridge which is known as " Pip-squeak Bridge," as it is always being shelled by shrapnel. The mess is really more like a cellar than anything else. It is rather a nuisance having always to live by lamplight ; also it is bitterly cold by day, as we cannot have a fire for fear of the Hun seeing the smoke.

YPRES, 1ST FEBRUARY, 1916

To-night my other section came up, and we relieved the remainder of D Battery. Birch and his people went off to our late billets in Poperinghe, leaving me in command here. I have taken over all the maps, orders, etc. I have got Smith and Perry with me and Harvey in the wagon-line. Bishop is on leave till the end of the week. We have had quite a peaceful day.

YPRES, 2ND FEBRUARY, 1916

I was called at 5.30 a.m., and after a short breakfast

Smith and I, with two telephonists, started for the Observation Post. It was quite dark when we started, but beginning to get light by the time we got there. It is a bad O.P., as one cannot get in or leave it by daylight, being in full view of the Hun. I think I have spent one of the coldest days of my life. Imagine a hole in the mud some 10 feet long by 5 wide; sandbag walls and roof; no doors or windows, and half full of water. We first had to start by baling out the water. It was very misty, so that till about 11 o'clock I could see nothing. Eventually it became clear enough to distinguish the Hun trenches, and also our own facing them. I could see part of Hooge, and also just make out Stirling Castle, which was our old 7th Division H.Q. during the first battle of Ypres, in October 1914. At that time we held it, including Zonnebeke; now, alas! it is held by the Hun. Just before midday the fog lifted to some extent, and the Hun started bombarding our front-line trenches. He fairly deluged them with really big shells. It was a terrible sight, as it looked as if nothing could possibly live in such an inferno. As a matter of fact I heard afterwards that only four men were actually killed. The infantry at once 'phoned to all the batteries for help, and we immediately turned our guns on to the enemy's front-line trenches. It was very hard to distinguish my shells from all the others, as there was so much smoke and mud flying about. However, I knew about where to look, and saw the German trenches being pretty well knocked about. I could see the sandbags and pieces of wood jumping into the air when my shells burst in their trenches. In the afternoon the Hun fired some 4·2 and shrapnel on the right of my O.P., but a long way off. As soon as it was dark enough for me to leave my O.P., I went forward half a mile to call on the Rifle Brigade battalion who are holding the trenches that I am covering. I had tea with them, and they implored me to deal with a machine-gun that was worrying them. I said I would take it on there and then, so 'phoned back to the battery and gave it half a dozen high explosives, just to give it something to think about.

YPRES, 3RD FEBRUARY, 1916

I have got an awful cold and cough through spending yesterday in that icy cold O.P. after getting hot walking there. In the morning they put a few shrapnel over us. After lunch they really got to work and shelled the battery and this part of the town, but as they were only firing small shells (4·2 and 77 mm.) it did no harm. I stood in the gate and watched them hitting the houses a hundred yards off. Colonel Burne, who commands the Right Group in which we are, asked me to go over to H.Q. and see him, which I did. I got safely there without being shot at, but no sooner had I got inside than half a dozen shrapnel burst just outside the door, where I had been standing a minute before. At 11 o'clock at night they shelled the battery with shrapnel. I was in bed, but I have the 'phone beside my bed, and can talk to the officer who sleeps with the battery without getting up. Perry, who is with the battery to-night, reported where each shot fell. They kept it up till 1.30 a.m., but hit no one. In the course of the night the Rifle Brigade asked me to fire on the machine-gun that has been bothering them for some time.

YPRES, 4TH FEBRUARY, 1916

Have felt very ill all day with this violent cold and did not go out. A few shells over the battery. About 11 o'clock communication with the O.P. broke down and I could get no word from Smith, who is F.O.O. I heard from A Battery's O.P. that my O.P. was being heavily shelled. I felt very nervous about Smith and his party, as I was afraid they must have got a direct hit on their dug-out. However, they turned up all right after dark, just as I was sending out a search party. They had 150 high-explosive shells within 50 yards of them, but the O.P. was not hit. A really wonderful escape, as the Hun must have meant to get them. I never liked that O.P., and I shall abandon it now and try and get a better one. At 9 p.m. the infantry again asked me to strafe the machine-gun, so I gave it four rounds of H.E. (16 shells). Now at 11 p.m. they want me to take on another machine-gun, but as they do not say where he is, I have had to ask them to be more explicit. The Rifle Brigade have asked me to lunch with them to-morrow ; if I feel better I will go.

YPRES, 5TH FEBRUARY, 191€

I was rung up at 9.30 a.m. by H.Q. to say hat an aeroplane had gone up to register P6 for me. This is the crossroads at Westhoek, where we halted for lunch one day with the 22nd Brigade. I remember the place well ; it is funny that I should now be firing at it ! My first salvo was reported at " B–2 o'clock." That meant the line was nearly correct and I was 100 yards over. The next salvo was 50 yards over. And the next " O.K.," which means correct. My new instrument that I have had made for this work justified itself. I was much bothered by Hun aeroplanes that kept coming over. I am afraid they must have seen me firing, though I stopped firing several times. Still, it is bad luck on my aeroplane to keep him waiting while *he* is being shot at. All this afternoon I have been going for various machine-guns in the front trenches. The infantry have been observing for me and are simply delighted. I fire salvos, and " gun fire " immediately after. However, the Hun fairly lost his temper with me to-night, and has been bombarding me for the last two hours. Houses and walls have been falling about like a pack of cards, and of course my wires were cut as usual. No damage done except that I have got a headache from the noise. If I go on like this, I shall make the place too hot to hold me, as usual. The Flying Corps man who was observing for me came to tea and told me all about this morning's shoot. He was very pleased, and said our shells were bursting right over the target.

YPRES, 6TH FEBRUARY, 1916

Quiet night after 11 p.m. This morning they put about

250 4·2's into Ypres, near the Lille Gate. But we kept inside and no one was hit. The Rifle Brigade rang me up at 11 a.m. to say that the machine-gun we have been attending to lately got the " wind up " last night and did not dare fire as usual. They also thanked us for what we have done for them. Bishop arrived back from leave this evening and Harvey came up with the rations, so we were complete for tea for once. The colonel wants Smith to go back for a week's rest, so I am still left with only two officers, which is quite inadequate for the work.

YPRES, 7TH FEBRUARY, 1916

A fairly quiet day. The Hun has done very little shelling round us. He has had another " hate " on the railway, just outside the Lille Gate. I cannot imagine why he is so angry with that spot, as there is nothing there. To-night I had up 400 more rounds of H.E. just to go on with. My aeroplane said he was coming to observe again, but did not turn up. I studied the wretched map till nearly 1 a.m. to try and find a new observing post.

YPRES, 8TH FEBRUARY, 1916

The aeroplane arrived this morning, but after two salvos he went home again with engine trouble. At 11.80 a.m. an appeal came from the infantry for help, as their front lines are being heavily shelled. I retaliated with fifty rounds. I stayed in all the afternoon in case my aeroplane came back. At dinner the Wesleyan Chaplain of the 72 F Ambulance came in for shelter, as the road was being heavily shelled outside. We had a great Wagner concert after dinner till midnight. The Hun shelled the Lille Gate badly all the evening ; in fact, he hit it once, about 10 yards from my window. It shook the place ; in fact, the whole room rocked like an earthquake.

YPRES, 9TH FEBRUARY, 1916

My aeroplane came back at 10 a.m., and finished register-

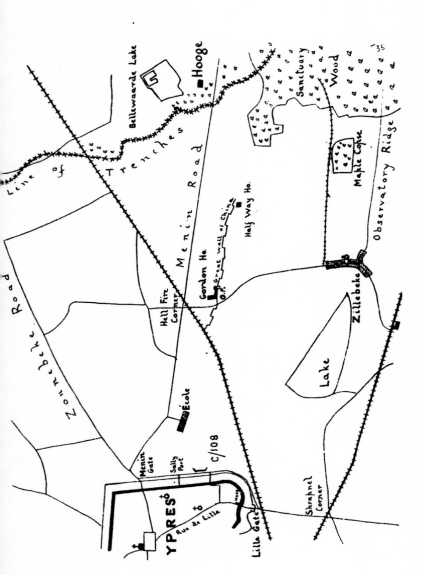

YPRES, FEB. 1916.

ing P.8. We got it in two shots. It is really absurdly easy. A little later a Hun 4·2 shelled the railway near here, so I gave twenty rounds of H.E. I was not sure which battery it was, but thought it might be my old friend of Westhoek, so, as I had registered the cross-roads close to him, I " searched " for him. As he stopped firing at once, I think I must have got uncomfortably close to him. This afternoon I took Perry to look for a new O.P., and found two excellent ones ; one in Gordon House and the other in the sandbag wall. We had a quiet walk down the railway and were not shot at at all, for once. The sandbag wall is a great wall of sandbags half a mile long, with traverses every few yards. It reminds one of the Great Wall of China at Shan-hai-kwan ! I am going to pull down one of the traverses and make it hollow inside, with just room for the observer and one telephonist. After that I went on and made the liaison with the Buffs, who are now in the trenches that I cover. The second-in-command is a Hamilton, a son of Lord Claud H. They do not seem such a good lot as the Rifle Brigade.

YPRES, 10TH FEBRUARY, 1916

A fairly quiet day. At 8 p.m. I took a large party to the new Observation Post to fortify it. We worked all night and made it fairly strong, but there is another night's work at least to finish. I have used an old cow-shed that has only three walls and no roof. I put in a roof of steel arches and covered that over with 8 feet of brick. Also the sides and front have been made 4 or 5 feet thick with rubble and sandbags. They shell the place a good deal, but I hope to make it proof against anything except a direct hit from a big shell.

YPRES, 11TH FEBRUARY, 1916

A bad day. All day long I have had frantic appeals

for help from the infantry, as their trenches were being
heavily bombarded. I replied with over 300 rounds of
H.E. The general came round in the afternoon and was
frantic to find how much ammunition I had used. However, it can't be helped. If the infantry want assistance,
I feel very strongly that they must have it. Just as we
were settling down to dinner Corporal Heathcote rushed
in to say that all our ammunition wagons that were coming up with more H.E. had been smashed up just outside.
I at once went out, and found that the Rue de Lille was
being plastered with shrapnel. I found my unfortunate
wagons and horses in a heap in the middle of the road.
The leading wagon had four horses killed or dying, the
next wagon three more ; one of the drivers of the first
wagon (Perryman) badly wounded, and the other two
missing. Besides mine, there were two infantry wagons
with their mules down, both infantry drivers killed and
lying in the middle of the road. One poor fellow had
the top of his head blown off. The road was blocked with
all these men and animals, and there was a procession of
transport waiting to pass. No one had made the slightest
effort to clear up the mess, although there were any number
of officers and men standing there. It was pitch dark,
raining and very cold, and the whole road wet with mud.
The first thing I had to do was to go round shooting all
the maimed animals. I shot four of my own and two
mules—not an easy job in the dark, with an electric torch,
and the poor brutes struggling. Next I got the dead men
to the side of the road. With the greatest difficulty we
" side-lifted " the wagons, so as to make room for the traffic
to pass. Every moment I expected another salvo to come in
the same place, as they were shelling the road a little farther
down, and the Cloth Hall. In about a quarter of an hour
I got the road clear and the rest of the traffic was able to
get through. When things were quiet, late at night, I
had the harness stripped off the dead horses and sent back
in the mess-cart. At 1 in the morning Harvey arrived,
having brought up another wagon of ammunition and fresh
teams to take away the damaged wagons. Harvey is

really splendid ! He always does a nasty job himself. One of the teams, with a full wagon, bolted down the crowded street. It is wonderful it did not run into anything or fall into one of the numerous 17-in. shell-holes. One driver, who was hit on the forehead and knocked quite silly, found himself at the wagon-lines when he recovered, his horse having taken him seven miles straight home, although itself badly wounded in three places. I have not been able to find out what the total casualties are in the battery, as I don't know yet if some of the men have been taken to hospital. So far it is: Men, 2 wounded, and 3 missing. Horses, 5 killed, 2 wounded, and 1 missing.

YPRES, 12TH FEBRUARY, 1916

A wet and cold day. Nothing doing in the morning. At 3 p.m. a terrific fire broke out on our left. I have heard nothing like it since the bombardment of Loos. A few minutes later I got an urgent appeal for help from the infantry, also orders from the Group for Retaliation Z., which means a bombardment of the front-line trenches opposite Hooge. Now (at 4 p.m.) the bombardment is still raging, quite like machine-guns. Guns of all sizes are going hard at it. (7 p m.) The bombardment was terrific till dusk, quite as bad on a short front as Loos. All sorts of rumours are flying about. Some say that we have lost trenches ; others say that *we* attacked, and have done a big charge. It is impossible to know what the truth is. I hear that the Hun " barraged " the Vlamertinghe Road —they say that it smoked with shrapnel. I have my wagons to get through to-night safely. At 4.30 p.m. they turned a 4·2 battery on to my battery. They did not get any direct hits, but they put a lot of shells in among the guns. One pitched just in front of a gun and choked the bore up with mud. (Midnight.) We have had a very lively evening—they have shelled the battery and the Lille Gate the whole time, mostly with shrapnel, and a certain amount of 4·2. At 10 p.m. I was standing outside the mess when my excellent Q.M.S. Gill trotted up the street and said he had got four ammunition wagons just behind. I was horrified, as the whole of the town was alive with bursting shrapnel. They came up very smartly at a trot, and I got them close in under the houses on the safe side of the street. It was impossible to get any men over from the battery to unload the wagons, as they were plastering the bridge over the moat, and all the streets. Bishop and I and all the servants unloaded the ammunition—four times 76 rounds of high explosive. I never saw people work so hard ! We just dumped them in the houses alongside till it was possible to get them over to the guns. The Hun shrapnel was bursting all round the streets, and it was marvellous that neither horses nor men were hit. I should think we must have done the job in record time—certainly under a quarter of an hour. The moment the last round was out, we slammed the wagons shut, Gill jumped on his horse, and off the convoy went in fine style at a steady walk. I have tried to impress them with the fact that the Royal Artillery gallop into action and walk out. Considering that they are all young soldiers, with only about eighteen months' service, they are wonderfully steady. About 11 o'clock the Hun started on us with a bigger gun—probably a 5·9—which fired at us from Hill 60, right over the Lille Gate, and burst his shells just in front of my door. The concussion shook the whole building to the foundation. It is rather amusing being at the Gate, as we get a constant stream of visitors all day, who run in to take shelter from the shells. They will soon drink us out of whisky. However, we have another case on order—I hope it will arrive soon. (1 a.m.) Shelling still going strong.

YPRES, 18TH FEBRUARY, 1916

Fritz kept it up all night. It was impossible to get any of the ammunition over to the battery, and we are now trying to slip it over a round at a time, by daylight. (8 p.m.) I am sitting in the telephone dug-out, between two of the guns, as Bishop is completely done up, having been up all night. Perry is F.O.O. and I don't think he is enjoying it very much. Apparently he has gone into A Battery's O.P., close to ours, as they have put a shell through ours. As I am writing, the Hun is putting literally thousands of shells into Ypres. They are going over my head in a continuous stream; the shriek of one shell has not died away before the next begins, and the noise of the bursts sounds like one great thunder-storm. For the moment our guns are not very noisy, but every now and then they go off with deafening roars, in front, behind, and on each side. The Hun is heavily bombarding our trenches at Hooge, and has driven our infantry out. There is so much smoke that my F.O.O. cannot see to shoot. I have my guns loaded and ready laid on the Hun's front-line trenches, in case he assaults, which is very probable. This terrific bombardment must mean something of the sort. I hear we lost some trenches up to the north a couple of miles, but the Guards retook them yesterday. They certainly get their share of nasty jobs. (10.50 p.m.) I hear our trenches have been completely blown in, and the infantry cannot occupy them. We are " standing to," expecting the S.O.S. signal any moment. There has been a complete lull in the firing since dark. Coming after the tremendous bombardment this is very ominous. I shall lie down with all my clothes on. Thank goodness the Rifle Brigade are in !

YPRES, 14TH FEBRUARY, 1916

(11 p.m.) A horrid day. All the morning the Hun bombardment our Hooge trenches, with thousands and thousands of heavy shells. By lunch time there was nothing of them left at all. At 2 p.m. I got a message from Group H.Q. that things were looking very bad. The infantry reported that their trenches no longer existed at all, and that they were being badly shelled in their support and reserve trenches, into which they had withdrawn. They said they expected an assault any minute,

and that they would not be able to stop the enemy ; consequently it would all depend on us.   Soon after, the S.O.S. signal arrived, at the same moment as the S.O.S. rocket went up.   Instantly every battery started the most intense rate of fire possible.   This lasted in bursts, and periods of slower fire, from 4 o'clock till 7.10.   By 5 o'clock all the telephone-wires were cut, in spite of the fact that most of them were in triplicate.   It was a horrid sensation, being entirely cut off and unable to get any news of what was going on.   I got through 400 shells in the three hours.   The whole time we were bombarded by 4·2 howitzers and field-guns, the shells bursting all over us in a continual deluge.   It was almost impossible to get my orders passed from one gun to another.   The little foot-bridge connecting the ramparts with the battery was under a hell of a fire and I had to run across it.   I must admit I did not expect to reach the guns.   I have only had one man wounded—Miles, the Officers' Mess cook—who is very badly hit in the lung and head.   When I came back to the Mess at 9 p.m. for dinner I found a dreadful mess.   The little ante-room full of wounded and men who were taking shelter from the shells, the road outside my door littered with dead horses and men, and transport carts that had been knocked out.   Now, at 11 p.m., our guns (the big ones) are having a terrific duel with the German batteries.   The noise is simply wicked, and my head aches.   It is a real duel—they are firing as hard as they can—probably forty rounds a minute—and the German shells are bursting all round.   The house rocks like an earthquake, and the doors, etc., are rattling, and it never stops !   That is the dreadful part of it—there is no respite.   Hour after hour, those violent explosions, that shake the ground and every nerve in one's body.   I have just had a message from the Group Commander, Colonel Burne, to say that the infantry say we (the Right Group) have saved the day.   The Germans came out of their trenches, but could not face the fire of the guns. It must have been appalling !

I am now going to try and get a little sleep, but doubt

if it is possible, with this row going on. However, I am so tired I cannot see or think any more !

YPRES, 15TH FEBRUARY, 1916

A day of alarms. We have been expecting a great attack all day, but it has not eventuated. As it is impossible to cross the moat, I am spending the day in the telephone pit with the guns. It is very cold and raining, and the telephone pit is not a drawing-room ! We are " standing to," as an attack is expected, so I shall not leave the battery at all, as I might not be able to get back here. The telephone wires are all mended now, and I am receiving half-hourly reports from Perry in the O.P..

YPRES, 16TH FEBRUARY, 1916

At 2 o'clock this morning the S.O.S. signal came through. I rushed out of the telephone-pit and got the guns going in about twenty seconds or so. Immediately after, the order came through to stop. It turned out to be a false alarm. Our S.O.S. signal from the trenches is a green-coloured rocket. The Hun seems to use the same colour for some other signal. He sent one up and hence the mistake. However, no harm was done, as we were able to stop firing at once. This evening a Territorial subaltern turned up to be attached to me for a fortnight. His name is Clinton, and, oddly enough, he belongs to a brigade commanded by Hillier, who used to be my C.O. in the Essex Horse Artillery. The world really is small !

YPRES, 17TH FEBRUARY, 1916

A quiet night for once. This morning my colonel came round. He has relieved Colonel Burne with running the right Group. He said all sorts of nice things. It seems that the infantry have sent in a deuce of a good report on our work two days ago. They say we absolutely saved the Hooge trenches. There is no doubt that the Germans made a serious assault, and were only stopped by the terrific fire we opened. The general came in and said the same thing, and was most cordial. I have told the men, who are no end bucked up. I have examined the ground round the guns ; there are hundreds of fresh shell-holes all round. There is no doubt that we were subjected to a much heavier fire than I realised at the time. It is marvellous that nothing was hit. This afternoon I went down to the O.P. with Clinton, and tested the lines. I also took on a small house the Huns have built lately behind their lines—and hit it. Then we went on and called on the infantry, who are now holding the trenches in front of us. Fortunately we were not shot at, which is a wonder, as that road is very dangerous. The communicating trench has been badly knocked about, and there are many places where one is completely exposed to view from the Hun trenches at comparatively short ranges. Needless to say, I did not linger when passing them, and made Clinton follow a hundred yards behind me, so that one shell should not get both of us.

YPRES, 18TH FEBRUARY, 1916

A quiet day. I think they have only fired one shell at us, and that did not explode. I have been collecting materials for my new gun-pit. Gilmour is staying with us' to-night, so we had quite a cheerful dinner. Harvey was due to arrive here at 6 p.m., but did not turn up till after 10. I was getting very nervous, and began to think he must have been hit on the road up. It rained all day, so I did not fire.

YPRES, 19TH FEBRUARY, 1916

This morning I verified my corrector, and found it 184 for the 85 Fuze. The General (Philpotts) came round again, and said Capper had told him to say how pleased he was with the fight we put up the other day. Perry was in the O.P. to-day, and amused himself in registering various points. I sent Sergeant Pailthorpe down to have a look at the zone and do a little observing, in view of the fact that I have recommended him for a commission.

He is delighted. At 5 p.m. the Hun retaliated on us, and
put 50 4·2's into the battery. One went through the roof
of No. 4 gun, but providentially did not explode. At
11.30 p.m., just as I was going to bed, the infantry have
asked me to fire on my old friend, the machine-gun in
Eclusette House. I am going to give him beans !

YPRES, 20TH FEBRUARY, 1916

Quite a noisy day. We have not done much shooting,
but the Hun has. To-night I am going to pull down one
of the old gun-pits and rebuild it a little better. Personally, I think the gun position is impossible, but the general
wants it done, so there is an end of the matter.

YPRES, 21ST FEBRUARY, 1916

A horrid day. We were very heavily shelled about
4 p.m., both the battery and the Lille Gate. At one time
I really thought the whole place would come about my
ears. They were using 4·2 and 5·9. They got several
hits on the Gate and in the moat just outside. After
pulling down the old pit last night, I found it was impossible to make a new one, as the ground was simply an evil-
smelling quagmire.

YPRES, 22ND FEBRUARY, 1916

What a birthday !—my second on active service. If I
am still alive next year, I hope the war will be over. We
have had a terrific bombardment to-day. About 3 p.m.
it started. They knocked the mess about with 5·9's and
at the same time shelled the battery for all they were
worth. They hit the telephone pit with a 4·2. It struck
one corner and blew all the sandbags away. Harvey and
Perry were inside and had a very narrow escape. They
and the telephonists were blown into a corner, with sandbags and instruments on top of them. However, they all
got off with a bad shaking. Harvey was all right, but
Perry seems much upset. He could hardly speak when he

11

got over to the mess, and refused to eat anything. I spent three hours to-night repairing the damage and trying to get one of the pits improved. I have put in a lot of wooden ammunition-boxes into the walls, that I have fitted up in compartments, so that I can use them as pigeon-holes. It keeps the ammunition dry. I hear Brigade Headquarters were badly shelled, too. Corporal Carter, the brigade clerk, was killed, and three men wounded ; they are going to move to-morrow.

YPRES, 23RD FEBRUARY, 1916

(1 a.m.) A Zeppelin has just passed over Ypres, going in the direction of Poperinghe. I reported it at once. I wonder where it is going to drop bombs to-night. Thank goodness we have had a fairly quiet day. As I expected our battery to be shelled this afternoon, as usual, I spent the afternoon in the telephone pit, but except for a certain amount of shrapnel nothing happened. The Brigade Headquarters have had to move into Ypres, as they have been badly shelled. An R.E. Major came in to dinner ; he is going to put up an aerial railway for me, like I have at Wishaw. It will be a great blessing when I get it.

Gilmour dropped in after dinner for a drink and a smoke ; he is really an awfully good fellow. I am very glad he is near me, with so many casualties.

YPRES, 24TH FEBRUARY, 1916

A quiet day. There has been a good deal of snow and the place is all white. In the morning, I went down to Infantry Headquarters to see Colonel Conway, who commands the North Staffordshires. He could give me very little information. I called in at the O.P. on my way back, where Perry is F.O.O. to-day. It was very misty, and difficult to make out the Hun trenches. With my powerful telescope I was able to make out a white wooden cross in the Hun front-line trench. I suspect it of being put there to hide a periscope and shall have a shot at it soon.

YPRES, 25TH FEBRUARY, 1916

Nothing of interest to-day. I have sent Sergeant Pailthorpe to the O.P. for forty-eight hours, which pleases him
very much. Very few shells fired at us to-day.

YPRES, 26TH FEBRUARY, 1916

We fired a Group Retaliation to-night. A tremendous
burst of fire that must have been very uncomfortable to
the Hun. After three days of no letters, I have just heard
the sad news that Reynolds has been killed. He seems
to have been badly gassed and to have died at Le Touquet
on the 23rd. I am very sorry for poor Doris, who only
had her baby three weeks ago. I hear she and Flora went
over at once, but arrived too late. It is really too sad :
first her brother and now her husband. He was a very
nice fellow, and well earned his V.C. in the retreat from
Mons. As I have not heard of any gas attack on this
front lately, I imagine it must have been one of those
vile " K " shells that they have just started using.

YPRES, 27TH FEBRUARY, 1916

It has now begun to thaw and the place is more beastly
than ever. In this position, with the guns in a marked
place like they are in, I expect to be smashed up every
day. I am sure that when a big strafe comes we shall be
shelled out. We have no cover and nowhere that we
could withdraw to, even if it were possible to withdraw,
which it is not. We might have to fire the S.O.S. any
time, if the Hun assaulted again, and I could not think
of leaving the guns, whatever happened to us.

YPRES, 28TH FEBRUARY, 1916

It has been thawing again and the ground is in a horrid
state. The colonel came round and looked at my gun-
pits. Both he and the general are very taken with my
pigeon-holes made out of old ammunition-boxes. Our

heavy guns are still keeping up a tremendous bombardment of the Bluff.

YPRES, 29TH FEBRUARY, 1916

The odd day in Leap Year. Nothing of interest to-day except that Perry has seen a German artillery officer observing in their front-line trenches ; we shall knock him out to-morrow, if there are not too many aeroplanes over. Clinton goes back to England to-night. It must be very nice just to do a fortnight of war and then go home !

YPRES, 1ST MARCH, 1916

In a few minutes the battle for the recapture of the Bluff will begin, and I am now going over to take command of the battery. I have had one gun-pit hit this morning, and expect we shall have a bad time this afternoon.

(10 p.m.) There has been a terrific bombardment— almost worse than Loos, whilst it lasted. At 5 p.m. we all started off. As the attack is not on the front of our division, we only " demonstrated "—i.e. kept up a moderate fire on the Hun trenches. We must have had a tremendous collection of big guns on our right, as the roar was absolutely continuous. Things have quieted down. but we start again at 4 a.m. to-morrow.

YPRES, 2ND MARCH, 1916

I got up at 4 a.m. and went over to the battery. It was pitch dark and I nearly broke my neck crossing the little trestle-bridge over the moat. At half-past, to a second, the bombardment began with an appalling crash, hundreds and probably thousands of guns, from 18-pounders up to " Grandmamma," the great 15-in. howitzer, let fly together. For the next hour the noise was simply indescribable. It was almost impossible to distinguish the report of one gun from that of another ; the only thing it can be compared to is the roll of a drum. We have the ramparts of the town near us, and the noise was intensified by the continuous echo. It was quite impossible to make oneself heard, even by yelling in a person's ear. After an hour, it began to die down, and by the time I came over to breakfast at 8 o'clock it was fairly quiet. The Hun, to my surprise, took it lying down— at least, as far as our area was concerned, he did not fire at all. As soon as the bombardment began, we saw the German S.O.S. signals going up all along the zone that was threatened. There were red rockets bursting into red stars. Soon after, rockets of all colours went up—white, green, red, golden rain, and even red golden rain. I imagine these were meant to confuse us.

About 9 o'clock the wounded began to stream down the road. All those who could walk took themselves to the Field Hospitals. Only the bad cases can be taken in the motor ambulances ; these went by in streams also. Most of the men were very cheerful at the prospect of a slight wound that would take them home for a bit. They were principally men who had been hit through the arm or leg by rifle-bullets. They told us they had got back our lost trenches and also some of the old German trenches. They said they had been wonderfully supported by the artillery, whose fire had kept just in front of them as they charged. In spite of the bombardment, the German trenches were full of men, and they had to charge under a very heavy rifle and machine-gun fire. The Suffolks and Gordon Highlanders seem to have lost most. Some men of the former regiment said their battalion was wiped out; but men always say they are the sole survivors.

A little later, convoys of German prisoners came through under escorts with fixed bayonets—I should think between 200 and 300 in all, no officers. They were quite a good lot of men, in the prime of life. All wore the flat round cap— no helmets. They have been trying to get into Ypres for eighteen months, and now they have succeeded !

About 11 o'clock, the enemy began shelling the Lille Gate and road, and the fresh ammunition wagons had a bad time. The drivers of the 107th Brigade were very

good. They took their wagons forward over the bridge
at a swinging gallop, through the shells. Team by team,
they went out of the Gate, about 200 yards apart. The
Hun very nearly did for his own prisoners, who were coming
in at the same time. We have had a good many shells
over here this afternoon, but no one has been hit. One of
Sir Douglas Haig's A.D.C.s came in for shelter—a Major
Thompson, 17th Lancers. He had very little news, but
confirmed the report that the French have inflicted tremendous losses on the Germans at Verdun.

YPRES, 3RD MARCH, 1916

It has rained all day; consequently, we have had a
quiet day. We have not fired ourselves, as it is too misty
to see anything.

YPRES, 4TH MARCH, 1916

Colonel Burne, who commands the 109th, came up to
Ypres this morning and relieved Colonel Walthall. The
latter has gone back to rest. They seem to take a fortnight each in running the Right Group. It is a pity the
batteries cannot do the same.

YPRES, 5TH MARCH, 1916

A good deal of snow again, but it thaws as it falls and
makes the country even more muddy than usual, if that
is possible. We did a good deal of firing to-day, as I am
not satisfied with the old register and am taking a new zero
line. My fool of a look-out man did not notice that there
was a German observation balloon up. The result was that
at 5 p.m. three hostile batteries were turned on to me.
One was a 4·2 howitzer and the other two were field batteries. Fortunately they did not do any damage beyond
cutting my wire cable across the moat. However, they
put about a hundred shells all round the guns. We found
one of the fuses from the 4·2 battery, which gave its range
from the setting-ring. I was able to identify it on the map
with the aid of the aeroplane photos. So at 9.30 I turned

my guns on to the offenders and began to " search and sweep " for them. However, they would not stand it and opened fire on me again, getting a direct hit on No. 1 gun. The shell burst under the muzzle and made a beastly mess of the pit. No one was hit, and the gun does not seem to be much damaged. However, I thought I had better shut up, as they evidently had my exact range and were more likely to hurt me than I was to hurt them.

YPRES, 6TH MARCH, 1916

It started snowing this morning, but cleared up by 11 o'clock, and was extraordinarily bright. I went down to the trenches to call on the colonel of the Leinsters, whom I am now supporting. I did not think much of them, as they did not offer me any lunch although they were just beginning lunch when I arrived. I fired some twenty rounds from the O.P. on the new register but am not at all satisfied with it. I saw the smoke of a train behind Hooge, quite near the line.

YPRES, 7TH MARCH, 1916

It has snowed hard all day and there is nearly six inches of snow all over the country. It really looks very pretty and hides some of the millions of shell-holes. On the other hand, the town looks more forlorn than ever. I have taken advantage of the fact that the Hun cannot see me and have worked all day at the new gun-pits. I am having up thirty drivers to-night to help with the pits.

YPRES, 8TH MARCH, 1916

A gloriously bright day, with bright sun. Everything is white. The ramparts and moat are quite lovely. Every telephone wire is coated thick. We worked all night, and I did not go to bed till 7 o'clock this morning. It was the most awful job getting the gun out of the old pit. It was 4 feet underground and in soft mud, so that the more we pulled the deeper the wheels cut into the mud.

Eventually, after breaking two drag-ropes, forty men just managed to get it out. The new pit is excellent, and I have made pigeon-holes in the wall to hold 300 rounds. This afternoon I registered the gun, but was not able to finish getting all the guns on to their new lines as Perry was shelled out of the O.P. by 4·2's in salvos. Nobody seems to have been hurt. I hope to finish the other pit to-night, and am making it of steel arches.

YPRES, 9TH MARCH, 1916

Worked all night trying to get the new steel-arch pit made. It froze hard, and I was very sorry for the men holding the steel sections. We absolutely failed to get it together. Each section had to dovetail into the next, and unless you get them exactly right they won't fit. It was rather serious, as I had got a gun out of the old pit and it was out of action till I could get it into its new position. When daylight arrived I had to give it up and just hide the gun under brushwood and old sandbags.

POPERINGHE, 10TH MARCH, 1916

I have come down to the wagon-lines for one night as there has been a little trouble. I have a new Sergeant-Major, an excellent man, but a little too energetic. He has managed to fall foul of all the junior N.C.O.s. However, I managed to settle the matter without a row. I was glad of an opportunity to see how the horses and harness were getting on. I had tea with the Column.

YPRES, 11TH MARCH, 1916

Back to the battery after lunch. For once I had a perfectly peaceful ride up to the Asylum, where I sent back my horse and walked through the town. To my surprise and delight, I found that Harvey had managed to get the steel arches up after all. We have made quite a good pit and I shall use them at the next position I have to make.

YPRES, 12TH MARCH, 1916

The general came round and said he was very pleased with the new pits. A very peaceful day, till close on midnight, when I got a frantic message from the infantry, asking for retaliation. A few minutes later I got another request from a Lieutenant Somebody, which I naturally queried, as batteries do not fire at the request of infantry subalterns, the more so as Harvey, who is in the O.P., reported that everything was normal. However, I got more requests, and so gave them a few rounds. The battalion commander later sent a message that it was not really required. They seem to have a funny system in that battalion if subalterns can wire to the artillery over their own commanding officers' heads. I wish we had the Rifle Brigade back again—they were splendid.

YPRES, 13TH MARCH, 1916

I forgot to put in my diary that I have a new officer—Radmore—a very nice fellow of my own age. The colonel has gone to hospital with malaria—everybody seems to have it now.

YPRES, 14TH MARCH, 1916

Summer has arrived ! A lovely day, with a bright sun that one could actually feel. I was able to leave off my " woolly " for the first time, and sit in the sun. The aeroplanes have been very active. The " Archies " have had a field-day ; at times the blue sky has been absolutely dotted all over with their bursting shrapnel. About 3 p.m. the Hun began shelling our trenches pretty badly at Hooge, and we replied. I have fired over 200 shells this afternoon.

YPRES, 15TH MARCH, 1916

Another lovely warm day. I spent the morning cleaning up the battery position. After lunch we had the same thing as yesterday. The Hun shelled our trenches badly, and we replied with interest. I have discovered that whenever I fire at Belvaarde Island the Hun at once retaliates ; it is evidently a tender spot, so I shall frequently shell it now. `About tea-time, a lot of shells came over, but nothing fell very near the battery. I went round to Group Headquarters and had a talk with the Group Commander about various retaliations.

YPRES, 16TH MARCH, 1916

Sudden orders to leave this position. We are to be relieved by the Lahore Divisional Artillery. The battery commander who relieves me—Major Nornabell, 59th Battery—arrived this morning and went over the gun position with me. One section comes in to-morrow night. He stayed to lunch and then went back to his battery at Steenvoorde.

YPRES, 17TH MARCH, 1916

Nornabell arrived in the morning, and we made our arrangements for handing over. The Huns were very active, putting a lot of stuff into the town. Fortunately they were quite quiet whilst the relief was taking place. We found the new dial-sights exactly agreed with ours. Had a pleasant combined dinner.

YPRES, 18TH MARCH, 1916

Nornabell and I went down to the O.P. and the infantry H.Q. We had an adventurous journey down, as they saw us and pip-squeaked us all the way. They very nearly got us, as they burst several within a few yards. We tested the lines of fire and found them quite correct. In the afternoon, they shelled our battery, hitting three of the gun-pits, but did no damage beyond slightly wounding Bombardier Finch in the head. Ypres has done its best to live up to its traditions in the way of being shelled, for our last day, and none of us are sorry to leave it. The relieving section came up at 8 p.m., and we handed over the guns to them. As soon as all was finished, I handed over command to Nornabell and marched all my people to the Asylum, our kit and gun stores being brought down as far as that in D.A.C. wagons. At the Asylum we found a motor-lorry waiting for each battery, and we piled ourselves and our kit into it. It was some squash!—all the kit and over thirty men. Some clung on to the top, and two sergeants sat on the radiator. We reached Eecke at 11 p.m.

EECKE, 19TH MARCH, 1916

Had a splendid night, with no telephones. The relief is indescribable not to care what happens. It does not concern me whether the Huns assault Hooge or not.

Summer really seems to be arriving. The days are quite warm and the sun almost hot. We are delighted to be in France again. The change from Belgium is very great. The roads and farms are so much cleaner and better looked after, and the people nothing like so repulsive.

After lunch I went over to Eecke itself to call on the general. The colonel has been sick for the last week in hospital, so I have been in command of the brigade during the move. I told the general that the whole brigade had withdrawn without loss and that the arrangements all worked like clockwork. I had been told that the colonel was in hospital in the Trappist Monastery on Mont-des-Cats. I rode over there, five miles, but found that he was not there. However, it was a lovely afternoon and I had a delightful ride up the slopes of the hill. Hitchy-koo was full of himself, and we came back across country. Gilmour dined with us and the subalterns rode races round the table on bicycles.

EECKE, 20TH MARCH, 1916

Another glorious day. This morning I had an inspection of equipment and clothing. I was pleasantly surprised to find that there was not as much stuff lost as I expected. After lunch I inspected all gun stores. I am having all the wagons painted, and if the weather lasts we shall look quite smart soon.

Eecke, 21st March, 1916

The weather has changed, and is wet and cold again. A great disappointment after the last few days. Spent the day inspecting various things. The general called but did not look round. I have sent two of the Lahore Division guns up to them and am getting my own back in exchange.

Eecke, 22nd March, 1916

Wet and cold again. We have all to be inoculated again, against enteric. Gilmour came and did the officers and the Right Section. By tea-time we all felt pretty bad.

Eecke, 23rd March, 1916

I had an awful night; could not sleep at all, and a temperature of about 101 degrees. All the Right Section are sick, and the officers can hardly see. I got up about 11 o'clock and inspected the lines, but had to come in. To make matters worse, the weather has changed and we have 8 inches of snow and a bitter east wind.

Eecke, 24th March, 1916

I was much better this morning, but most of the others are still very sorry for themselves. It is bitterly cold, and we have all got a little fever still.

Eecke, 25th March, 1916

A lovely morning, with bright sun. I took Hitchy-koo across country, jumping the ditches. At 11 o'clock I was president of a Field General Court Martial at my own mess. I tried Wurtele's Q.M.S. and acquitted him, as the evidence against the man was so doubtful. I never met such a low class of N.C.O.s as there seems to be in that battery. I lunched with the colonel at H.Q.—beer, port, and Benedictine ! ! ! Gilpin dined with us and we had a merry evening till nearly 2 a.m. The subalterns had bicycle races round the dining-room table and cockfights on the floor.

EECKE, 26TH MARCH, 1916

Sunday. A beastly day, cold and wet.

EECKE, 27TH MARCH, 1916

Had a regular " beano." All the battery commanders of the 24th Division went up to the new front in motor-lorries. We started from Eecke at 9.30 a.m. and went via Caestre, Meteren, and Bailleul to Dranoutre, which is my new wagon-lines. It is just under Kemmel, the hill from which we do all our heavy observation. From there we motored right up to the gun position ! We had been told that we were coming to a land of milk and honey, where there were no shells. As we got out of the motor a 4·2 H.E. landed within 50 yards of us, and, immediately after, two more right into the battery I am taking over from. I am relieving the 11th Canadian Battery. I lunched with them and examined the position. I was very disappointed with everything. They have a very poor show, in spite of being lavishly equipped. Their gun-pits were mere shelters, and they have no zero line laid out. I can see that there is a great deal of work to be done there. After lunch we were heavily shelled by 4·2, 5·9, and 8-in. The house next to the officers' mess disappeared in a great cloud of red dust ! So much for no shells. We walked up to the top of Kemmel, from which there was a wonderful view. We came back at 5 p.m. the same way as we had gone, stopping in Bailleul for a bottle of wine at the hotel. On comparing notes we found that none of the Canadian batteries had had any drinks, so perhaps they are forbidden to have any alcohol.

EECKE, 28TH MARCH, 1916

Cold and wet. Birch dined with us and was very amusing. I have been promised my leave on the 3rd, I hope nothing turns up to interfere with it.

EECKE, 29TH MARCH, 1916

Perry went on leave to Ireland this morning. I can just imagine the wonderful tales he will tell about the horror of his experiences ! Bishop had a bad fall from his horse and has hurt his back ; I hope to goodness he does not to have to go sick, or it will leave me very short. One section moves on Friday and the other on Saturday.

EECKE, 30TH MARCH, 1916

Bishop is better and the doctor says he will not have to go sick, fortunately. Spent the day in packing the vehicles and getting everything ready for the march. As we have been lent two D.A.C. wagons, we shall have no difficulty in carrying our horse-rugs and spare kits.

KEMMEL, 31ST MARCH, 1916

At 10 a.m. this morning I marched out with my right section. After passing Eecke, I left the section to come on under Radmore and trotted on to Bailleul with Beart. We had a good lunch at the hotel, and went on to Dranoutre where my wagon-line is to be. Harvey met me there and showed me the lines. They are just what I expected— filthy. We are billeted in a convent, but all the nuns except ten were murdered by the Germans in 1914. To my annoyance I find that the 73rd Field Ambulance have stolen part of my billet and established themselves there. I will have them out or see the general about it. It is quite impossible to share a billet with another unit. The Section arrived about 4 p.m., and as soon as I had seen them settled in I rode on to the gun position with Harvey. At 8 o'clock the guns came up ; we got the two Canadian guns out with the greatest ease and ran my own guns in, in their places.

KEMMEL, 1ST APRIL, 1916

A lovely warm day. Harvey and I walked down to the trenches and registered our two guns on the German front line. They are excellent trenches, or rather breast-works here ; quite dry and very easy to get at. One can get right into the fire trench without being seen, and can go there any time of the day. What a change from Hooge ! On the other hand, one has to be very careful, as the trenches are only 85 yards apart at the centre of my zone, and Fritz has a playful way of throwing over bombs and grenades. After lunch I took over papers, maps, etc.

KEMMEL, 2ND APRIL, 1916

Sunday. In the morning Harvey registered the left section on their part of the trench. In the afternoon I had a great shoot. There is a little house only a hundred yards away from the guns, from which I can see the whole of the Hun country. I fired the whole afternoon, register-ing my new zero line. It was a lovely day, and I enjoyed myself immensely. The house I was firing at was obvi-ously used by the Germans as an observation post, as I could see men moving about in it. I put a quantity of high explosive inside the house, and destroyed a good deal of it. I hope it knocked out the observation party. After tea I rode down to the wagon-line, where I am spend-ing the night.

1, ST. JAMES'S TERRACE, 8RD APRIL, 1916

Home once more. I left Dranoutre at 8.80 a.m. and rode into Bailleul, getting to the station at 4.80, just an hour before the train was due to start. As I left the wagon-lines, all our heavy guns were firing for all they were worth. I cannot imagine what at, as so far as I am aware there is no attack coming off. The train started punctually but was dreadfully slow, taking till 10 o'clock to get to Boulogne. The boat was waiting, and we got away at once. A beautiful crossing—the sea was like glass. We landed at Folkestone at 1 p.m. and after a little delay got off, reaching Victoria at 4.80. It is impossible to describe one's feelings of delight in living in one's own comfortable house once more. I have seven clear days' leave in London, but have a lot to do—new clothes to get, dentist, and a hundred little things wanted for the battery. It is hard to realise that only this morning I was in action !

DRANOUTRE, 11TH APRIL, 1916

I arrived back here at midnight. Seven clear days in London is well worth having, although it goes very quickly. I had an immense amount of work to do, getting new clothes and various instruments for the battery.

I left Victoria at 9.30 a.m., being seen off by Mr. Peterson, who very nobly turned out at that awful hour to say good-bye. We had a quick run to Folkestone, where I found that the leave boat did not cross till 5 o'clock in the evening, so had to hang about for six hours. They might just as well have let us go down by a later train. A calm crossing, and just time to have a hasty dinner at the hotel before the train started. We reached Bailleul at midnight, and I found the mess-cart waiting for me. After an hour's drive, I arrived at my wagon-lines. A cold and wet night, but one feels depressed anyhow on returning from leave.

KEMMEL, 12TH APRIL, 1916

I inspected my wagon-lines in the morning and was very pleased to find that a lot of good work had been done since I was away. They have made a good road in the field and built an immense harness-room, with pegs for each set of saddlery. At 11 o'clock I had my horses and rode up to the guns. They seem to have had quite a quiet time and have registered various points. I handed over all the new instruments to Harvey. Colonel Walthall is at present commanding the 72nd Infantry Brigade, so I have taken over the 108th Brigade till he returns. Since I have been away Gilpin has become a major. Our Brigade H.Q. are in a dirty little farm.

KEMMEL, 13TH APRIL, 1916

A most energetic day. I started out at 10.30 with Bond, the Orderly Officer, and visited A, C, and D batteries.

Then I went on and called at the battalion in local reserve
(N. Staffordshire); there we had lunch. From there we
went on to H.Q. of the left battalion in our zone (W.
Kents). They gave me a guide to take up to the front-
line trenches. The trenches here are really very nice;
there is no necessity to get one's boots dirty, and as we
hold the top of the crest it is possible to walk up to the
front line across the open with perfect safety. As a matter
of fact, a sniper had a shot at us at long range from the
high ground on our left. However, the bullet did not go
anywhere near us. I had a very interesting afternoon
in the trenches, being passed along from one company
commander to another. I looked over the parapet every
few yards with a periscope, and got quite a good idea of
our front. On the right the trenches are a long way
apart, over a hundred yards; but on our left they are only
separated by some thirty yards. It does not do to talk
very loud there, or the Hun may throw over bombs. I
had tea with the colonel of the left battalion on my way
back. I did not get back to my farm till 6 p.m.—quite
a good day's walk.

KEMMEL, 14TH APRIL, 1916

A wet and cold day. A Battery were heavily shelled
this afternoon with 5·9's. One gun-pit damaged, but no
casualties. I am sure there are spies, as all the batteries
and Brigade H.Q. have been shelled lately. All leave has
been stopped—lucky I took mine.

KEMMEL, 15TH APRIL, 1916

At 11 o'clock I met the C.O. of the N. Staffs. at his
billet behind the trenches, and went all along his front
line with him, some 700 yards of trench. We examined
the German trench with periscopes and worked out a little
scheme of retaliation. It was all quiet on our right, but
on the left, where the trenches are only 80 yards apart,
there was a lot of bombing going on. I must say I dislike

12

bombs and rifle grenades. Their effect is very local, but very deadly. One has to be a little careful in approaching the trenches as there is a wonderful sniper on our left front who is an excellent shot and picks off a lot of people. He generally only fires at officers.

I lunched with the N. Staffs, and then went to my own battery, who were registering. I was very disappointed with the shooting—in fact, it was distinctly bad.

KEMMEL, 16TH APRIL, 1916

(Sunday.) I have had a very enjoyable day. This morning I sent for my horse and trumpeter and rode over to B Battery, who are acting as an enfilade battery some 3 miles on our right. I have presented Hitchy-koo with a blue saddle-blanket, a head chain, and brass bosses on his bridle. He really looks very fine now, as he has got most of his summer coat. I have not clipped him all the winter, and so now his coat will be beautiful. The dark blue saddle-blanket shows off his jet-black coat. I went to my wagon-lines first and inspected them. We have a new vet. who seems excellent—a man of forty who was with the Royals in South Africa and Egypt.

From Dranoutre I rode on to B Battery, who are in action some two miles beyond Neuve Eglise and on the edge of the famous " Plugstreet " wood. They have a good position in a hedge, and their observation post on the top of Hill 63, only a thousand yards away. The last 50 yards' approach to the O.P. is in full view of the enemy, so we crawled on our hands and knees. It quite reminded me of shooting in East Africa. It was a glorious day—bright sun and very clear : I could see the trenches for miles, with the bright strip of green grass which is " No Man's Land " in between. In places, the trenches are three and four hundred yards apart ; in others they seem to touch. Messines, which is only about a mile from there, looked as if it was only a few yards away. It was useful and interesting to see the zone of the batteries from a new direction. I was looking at the trenches from right angles to our line of fire. B Battery can fire right up the Hun front line. For once the Hun is in the salient and we can enfilade him properly.

I met Stanhope up there, who was having a look round with some general. I have not seen him since he and I were subalterns in the Grenadiers together. Now he is on the Staff and edits the *Daily Lie,* as the Intelligence Summary is called. It never contains anything except extracts from the *Daily Mail* of two days ago. I rode back about 5 o'clock and was much struck with the death-like silence of Neuve Eglise. The village is constantly shelled and nearly every house is in ruins. Not a soul is to be seen, and my horse's hoofs sounded quite weird as I trotted along the paved streets. The place is on top of a hill and can be seen from Messines, so the R.E. have put up high canvas screens at intervals along the road, to prevent the Hun from knowing when there are people passing; otherwise he sends over shrapnel. On my way back I passed an enormous gun near the road. I saw an officer belonging to it, and asked him to let me look at it. He said they were just going to fire and invited me to watch. They were firing at a German battery about 11,000 yards off. The gun—or, rather, howitzer—was pointed almost straight up to the sky, and when it went off made a terrific flash that seemed to go up to heaven. There was less noise than I expected. The shell was simply enormous—12 inches diameter and from 3 to 4 feet high. It weighs 750 lb. and is filled with high explosive. The gun travels in six parts and requires 25 lorries and five huge caterpillars to move it. I had no idea the thing was so massive. They say it is absolutely accurate and that they can give corrections down to 10 yards. Last week they were firing at a German field battery. One shot landed in the gun line, and two guns were seen to leap into the air and disappear in dust. Our trenches have been a good deal shelled to-day by 5·9's, so in response to appeals for help from the infantry, I turned three batteries on to Ontario Farm, which I believe is used as a battalion headquarters.

KEMMEL, 17TH APRIL, 1916

A vile and beastly day. Rain and a bitter wind blowing at 40 m.p.h. Our trenches were again badly shelled and I put all available batteries on to retaliating on a tender spot just behind their front line. D Battery was shelled with 5·9's at midday and a man wounded. The shells fell exactly in the gun-line, so I am afraid their position has been located. I had tea with C Battery.

KEMMEL, 18TH APRIL, 1916

The same weather continues. It makes life very disagreeable. I did not go out this morning and spent some hours bringing my nominal roll of the battery up to date. After lunch I went round A, C, and D Batteries. At the latter I found Birch, just back from leave, in the deepest state of depression. D Battery has been shelled with 5·9's twice a day for the last three days. The Hun has got them marked down to a yard, most of the shells falling right into the gun-line. Birch was very funny—quite unconsciously. I asked him when the next shelling was due. He replied : " At 4 o'clock," and took out his watch, adding : " That will be in two minutes from now." By a curious coincidence, the shells began to arrive at exactly 4 o'clock. Fortunately, they were a little too far over and did not hit us. However, I thought it would be as well not to take the short cut home, as they were shelling the road hard. I am more than ever convinced that there are spies about. We shall have no peace as long as the civilians are allowed round the gun positions.

KEMMEL, 19TH APRIL, 1916

The colonel came back this morning, so I have returned to C Battery, but if he goes on leave to-morrow I shall have to go to H.Q. again. However, I have had a very pleasant day with my own mess, and have been decently fed. We had a great dinner to celebrate my return and had a competition in smashing bottles with revolvers.

Not a very safe amusement, as the glass flew about the room and cut my hand. However, I hit my bottle with the first shot. We had the new tunes that I brought out on the gramophone. I miss it very much at H.Q.

KEMMEL, 20TH APRIL, 1916

The colonel went on leave this morning, so I have taken over command of the brigade again. I have got the most awful cold imaginable and can neither see, hear, nor speak. It is a great nuisance, as I have a lot of work to do. Stayed indoors all the afternoon with a thermometer in my mouth. I am sure I have got influenza.

KEMMEL, 21ST APRIL, 1916

Good Friday. My cold is a bit better, so I had my horses up at 10 o'clock and went over to the Ammunition Column to divide up among the batteries a draft of new horses. Quite a nice lot of animals, but all American and long in the back. After that I called on General Mitford, who commands the 72nd Infantry Brigade that we are supporting. He had very little news to give me. I rode over to B Battery's wagon-lines with Wilkins, and investigated a complaint by the farmer, who, like all the country-people in this part of Belgium, is openly hostile to the British troops. He said that he far preferred the Germans ! After lunch Nosworthy, the doctor, and I had a revolver competition. I won, but that was not difficult, as none of them could hit a haystack. Great excitement this afternoon, as one of the 109th Brigade's batteries burst two gas cylinders in the Hun front line trench, and the chlorine gas drifted about over the trenches. Now the wind has begun to change, so there is a " Gas Alert " on. There seems to be an idea that the Hun will attack soon near here. I have issued careful orders covering all eventualities as far as can be seen ; but it is rather an anxious moment. We have the 50th Division on our left, and they are Territorials. I wish we had a regular division next to us.

KEMMEL, 22ND APRIL, 1916

A pouring wet day. At 11 o'clock I rode up to our new battle headquarters with Nosworthy to meet General Philpotts and the brigade major. The work is getting on very slowly, and I have persuaded the general to lend me a party from the Div. Ammunition Column. It is most important that the work should be finished soon, as I should have to go there in case of a battle, in order to be near General Mitford, the infantry brigade commander. We are converting a ruined house into a strong room. Steel arches inside, then concrete and a great thickness of rubble and sandbags on top and at the side. The owner of the house will not recognise it when he comes back after the war. It has already had 5·9 burst inside it. In fact, this is the same house that I saw hit the first day I came up here to have a look at the position. After the general had gone I called on Harvey and had a look at all my instruments, which they seem to be using all right. The observations for temperature of the air, cordite, barometer, wind velocity, etc., are taken three times a day. It has simply poured all day, and I have not gone out this afternoon.

At 4 o'clock a terrific bombardment of our trenches began. It seems to be in front of Wytschaete, on the line held by the 50th Division (Territorials). I am afraid they must have had a bad time, as the bombardment lasted two hours and was very heavy. I hear they were using 5·9's and heavy trench mortars. They started firing into my trenches also, so I have retaliated with three batteries.

KEMMEL, 23RD APRIL, 1916

Easter Day. At 8 a.m. I rode over to C Battery. I breakfasted there and rode on to Dranoutre. I called on General Mitford, but he was out, so I saw his brigade major, who seemed very pleased with last night's retaliation. It seemed to have stopped " Minnie " for the rest of the evening. I inspected the Ammunition Column's Lines, also C and D's wagon-lines. With some difficulty

I found A Battery's new camp. All the lines are in a dreadful state after this heavy rain ; the unfortunate horses are standing in nine inches of liquid mud. After lunch I walked up to the top of Kemmel, where I found Condon and Hector in the Brigade C Post. It was a lovely day, and we could see Comines and Warneton, and Messines looked so close that one felt one was in it. I spent a couple of hours there studying the country with my powerful Davon telescope. We discovered a long red screen that looked just like the roof of a house, but on examining it more closely I was sure it was a canvas screen. Not far behind it there was a board, painted white and nailed to a tree. As we had had a hostile battery reported near there, I feel pretty certain that the screens are put there to hide their flashes. I at once 'phoned down to C Battery and ranged a gun on to it. The officer on Kemmel will keep an eye on the place after dark and see if any flashes come from there, in which case we will strafe it.

KEMMEL, 24TH APRIL, 1916

Another fine day like yesterday. Nosworthy went out this morning, so I had to stay in. However, there was lots to do. I have worked out a new retaliation scheme that will strafe a company headquarters and a battalion one at the same time. At 4 o'clock the usual appeal for help came from the infantry, so I had to put all four batteries on to my new scheme—10 rounds per gun, i.e. 160 shells, all practically on to the same headquarters in a few minutes. I hope it will keep them quiet for a bit. After tea I rode into Dranoutre to call on General Mitford. He seemed quite pleased with the support he was getting from us. We arranged details for a shoot to-morrow on their strong points.

KEMMEL, 25TH APRIL, 1916

A lovely day, with bright sun all the time and quite warm. I sent the Adjutant out all the morning to arrange about burying the armoured telephone cables. It is a tremendous business, as there are many miles of them. General Philpotts rang me up about 11 to tell me the details of the big combined shoot that is coming off this afternoon. I worked out my Brigade Operation Orders very carefully and got them out by hand by 1.30. It is not safe to send orders of that sort over the 'phone. It is extraordinary how the Germans get to know of our plans.

The idea was that at 4 p.m. our heavy howitzers would bombard three of the hostile strong points just behind their trenches. Our part was to open a heavy fire with shrapnel on all the paths and communicating trenches leading into these strong points, beginning ten minutes before the heavies. We hoped to drive the Germans into these fortified places by our fire, where they would be caught by the heavy shells. After it was all over I waited ten minutes and then gave them a few rounds of rapid fire with shrapnel in case any of them had ventured out of shelter. The aeroplanes of both sides have been very active to-day. The 60-pounder battery, 400 yards in front of my farm, has been heavily shelled all the afternoon. I don't think any great damage was done, as most of the shells were falling a little short of them.

KEMMEL, 26TH APRIL, 1916

" Gas Alert " still on, as there is a gentle breeze from the east. It is beautifully warm, with a bright sun. We have been sitting outside till 7 o'clock. Quite a change, considering only five days ago it was blowing a hurricane, with incessant rain. The trees are really coming out at last. There are very few leaves to be seen yet, but everything has a greenish look. This morning I rode up to C Battery, and from there went to the left and right battalions by bicycle. The *pavé* roads are vile, and I shall not ride a bicycle again there. It is not safe to ride beyond the line of the batteries, as, as soon as one gets over the crest of the ridge, one is in full view of all the high ground at Messines. I was very lucky, as they were shelling

Wulverghem church just before I got there, and they put two more shrapnel in as soon as I had got past. The colonel of the West Kents seemed very bored, as usual, and had no information to give me. From there I went on to the East Surreys and had a talk with Delafontaine, their colonel. He seemed very pleased with yesterday's strafe, and said that we and the heavies, between us, had made an awful mess of the Hun trenches and strong points. Our battle headquarters are getting on slowly; I don't think they will be ready for another week. We are building a steel-lined room inside one of the rooms of the house. There will be concrete and about 6 feet of brick all over it.

KEMMEL, 27TH APRIL, 1916

Last night was full of excitement. About 9 p.m. we got a message to say that two Poles had deserted from the enemy and come into our lines. They said that gas cylinders had been put into the enemy's trenches all along the V Corps front, and that if the wind had been favourable it would have been let off the night before. I at once sent out urgent orders to all batteries to be prepared for the " S.O.S." signal at any moment. I had extra food got up and the wagon-lines were warned to be ready to send up ammunition if wanted. The deserters reported that the gas attack was to have taken place between 3 and 4 a.m. Knowing that German time is an hour ahead of ours, I ordered the batteries to " stand to " at 1 a.m. After carefully looking to my own gas helmets, I went to bed. At 1 o'clock the telephone rang and C Battery reported that the electric syren was blowing (this is the signal for a gas attack). Immediately afterwards a tremendous fire broke out on our right, near Ploegsteert ; evidently the 9th Division on our right had given the S.O.S. I gave the alarm to all the people in the house, including the Belgian inhabitants, and dressed as quickly as possible. By this time the syrens all along the front were blowing. As the S.O.S. signal had not gone up we did not open fire. Shortly afterwards the infantry brigade rang us up and said that there was no gas coming into our trenches, and that it looked very much like a false alarm. The heavy firing continued for half an hour. I told the batteries that they could turn in beside the guns, one officer per battery and one man per gun remaining on guard. The rest of the night was quite peaceful.

After breakfast, General Philpotts rang me up and asked me to meet him at infantry brigade headquarters as soon as possible. General Mitford, General Philpotts, and I had a conference, and we arranged that some of the 108 batteries should register two roads leading to the German trenches, away up on our left, opposite the 50th Division. In case the Huns attacked near Spanbroekmolen we could bring fire to bear on these roads. On return I put A and C Batteries on to this.

KEMMEL, 28TH APRIL, 1916

Another night of alarms and excitements. The Staff seems to have quite made up their minds that a gas attack is imminent on our front. At 10 o'clock the brigade major of the 72nd Infantry Brigade rang me up and asked me to open fire on the German trenches on the left of our zone. He expected the Germans to attack about 2 a.m., and wanted me to start enfilading them at 1.30. As the trenches are so very close at this point, I was not very taken with the idea and rang up General Philpotts to ask him what he thought about it. He was not at all in favour of shooting so very close in the dark, so I decided to compromise and told Cammel, who commands B Battery, to fire occasional salvos at the German second-line trenches, which are some fifty yards in rear of their front line. I hear that the infantry are very pleased with the result. I got very little sleep, as the telephone rang every five minutes.

This morning the 60-pounder battery in front of us came in for a very bad time. From 8.30 to 11 they were fairly deluged with 5·9's. The German shooting was wonderfully accurate, but they had not quite got the range correct.

In spite of the fact that the majority of the shells were falling within a few yards of the guns, I don't think any damage was done. My farm is only about 400 yards from this battery, and quantities of pieces fell all around us. They come quite hard enough to do a lot of harm if they hit one.

KEMMEL, 29TH APRIL, 1916

Again, last night, we expected a gas attack, which did not eventuate. I must say I wish they would make it and get it over. The 3rd Division have come in on our left, and relieved the Territorial Division, which is a great blessing. If they had any chance of penetrating our lines before, I don't think they have now.

We have been issued with a new type of anti-gas helmet. It consists of a metal box, which is carried in a haversack and contains chemicals. There is a face-pad that goes over the mouth, with a clip that closes the nose. A thick white tube connects the chemical box and mouth-piece. The goggles are separate. I don't like the thing, and shall trust to the old-fashioned flannel bag that goes right over the head.

We found that the local inhabitants had only got four helmets between eight people, so we had to give them some old spare ones that we had. In spite of alarming messages that strong German reinforcements had been seen coming up behind Messines, nothing happened. However, I still believe they will attack within the next few days. They seem to have made a big attack on the First Army between Hulluch and Loos. This morning I went round the batteries with General Philpotts, who asked the unfortunate gunners fearful conundrums about the various fuses and explosives we use ; the poor men had no idea what the shells were made of !

I had quite a near squeak myself, riding up there. Two 5·9 shrapnel burst close to the road, not more than 80 yards on my right. I have just heard that I have got to lecture to young officers at the Divisional Technical School on the 1st May, on the subject of Artillery in Trench Warfare.

It ought not to be very difficult. Radmore goes on leave to-night, 11 p.m. Another deserter has just come into our lines and says that the Huns are going to assault with gas at 1 a.m. to-night. I am inclined to believe it is true this time, the more so as the wind is just right for them— less than ten miles an hour and blowing straight from their trenches to ours. I have sent round a special warning to the batteries to be ready.

KEMMEL, 30TH APRIL, 1916

The gas attack has come off at last, and was very serious whilst it lasted. By midnight last night, I had completed all arrangements and had drawn up code words for each battery, indicating what places they might have to attack according to how the German assault developed. At 1 a.m. I had just lain down in the hope of getting an hour's sleep, when the gas alarm syren on Kemmel Hill started. Immediately afterwards the infantry brigade rang up and said, " Gas attack on D 4," that is one section of trenches that we cover. I gave the alarm to the head-quarter men and the Belgian inhabitants of the farm. In the meantime, terrific rifle and machine-gun fire started from the trenches, followed a few seconds after by all the field-guns on the front. I laced up my boots as quick as possible and lit the lamp. I was only just in time. Suddenly the cattle and dogs set up a piteous noise and we smelt the chlorine gas. Helmets were put on immediately but not before I could feel the irritation in my throat.

The night was very dark, and it was very difficult to get about with the goggles over one's eyes. I had not expected to be shelled here, as the Germans have never sent any-thing near here whilst we have been here. However, within two minutes of the alarm being given, there was a terrific crash as a shell burst just outside the house. From that moment the shells came all round this farm at inter-vals of half a minute. They started with a field-gun, firing shrapnel, but a 5·9 howitzer very soon joined in. Considering that they had never registered they made wonderful shooting, shell after shell bursting within a few yards of the farm buildings. We had never expected to be shelled so far back as this, and consequently had not prepared any dug-outs. Our telephone switch-board was in a barn with thin mud walls and it was most alarming having all these shells bursting just outside.

There was a terrible scene with the local inhabitants, who had hysterics, and got in our way. They had not got enough masks to go round, and had refused to send away their children as I had frequently warned them for the last two days. It was not till the gas-cloud was just on us that they could be persuaded to fly to Dranoutre. The gas being very heavy travels along valleys, so I told them to keep along the ridge. Apparently they were not caught, as they had mostly turned up again this morning.

With our helmets on, we could not taste the chlorine, and in the darkness it could not be seen; but we knew it was on us by the way the howls of the dogs and the bellowing of the cattle ceased. The noise of our guns was like the roll of a drum, and the sky was lit up with the flashes. Every gun on the Corps Front must have joined in, from the 12-in. down to the field-guns. We were firing high explosive almost entirely, in order to break up the gas-cloud. I found the greatest difficulty in breathing with a gas helmet on, and speaking through the telephone was most tiring.

About 1.80 I got a message by a despatch rider that the trench D 4 and our salient at that point had been captured by the Germans, who had thus secured a footing in our trenches. The brigadier requested me to barrage the German trench opposite this place, in order to prevent reinforcements from reaching the assaulting party. The message also said that the 1/North Staffords were about to launch a counter-attack. Shortly afterwards we heard that the Huns had been bombed out and that our line was re-established all along.

The way in which the Germans got into our trenches is rather interesting, as it is the first time I have heard of this method being used, except by poachers. The gas-cloud was accompanied by dense volumes of black smoke. Under cover of this, the Germans came out of their trenches, crossed No Man's Land, which at this place is only 30 yards wide, and stood on the top of our parapet. They worked in pairs, one man holding a very powerful electric torch, the other having his rifle ready. As they stood on our parapet, the man with the lamp flashed it on to one of our men in the trench beneath him, so blinding him for the moment. The other man then shot him at 'point-blank range. This ruse was so successful that all our men in that part of the trench were almost immediately shot down and the Germans jumped down into the trench. They found a mine shaft there, which they tried to destroy by lowering a charge of dynamite with a fuse attached, but as there was a lot of water at the foot of the shaft, the fuse went out without setting off the dynamite.

To return to my own adventures :—About 2 o'clock, I heard from the brigadier that he was on his way to his Battle Head-quarters, which are strong bomb-proofs about three-quarters of a mile behind the trenches. I, therefore, started off with Dew, the Orderly Officer, to join him there. It was just beginning to get light, and we could see what an enormous number of shells the Germans had used to barrage the valley and so stop us from bringing up rein-forcements. There were quantities of holes all round our farm, and this, of course, did not include all the shrapnel which had burst in the air. After walking a mile across country we reached Battle H.Q., where I reported to General Mitford, commanding the 72nd Infantry Brigade, curiously enough the same general that I supported in the attack at Loos last September.

Things were pretty quiet by that time, and it was quite light. The Staff expected another attack about 5 a.m., so we all waited with patience to see what would happen. Reinforcements were on their way from all parts, and cyclists were being sent off to meet and guide the various battalions that were now coming to our help. I left Dew to represent me for a short time and went over to see how

D/108 were getting on. I found Birch in great spirits, having had only three casualties, all gassed. He was really the funniest sight I have ever seen. I am sure he has set up a record for battery commanders. He actually fought a battle in his pyjamas ! ! His get-up was positively the limit ; a cap, cloak, his pyjamas showing underneath his cloak, and bedroom slippers ! When the alarm went he had only just time to put on his gas-helmet and run out to his guns.

Some very gallant things were done to-day. A sentry in the front line, on first smelling the gas, gave the alarm to the other men by striking his gong before putting on his gas-helmet. The result was that he fell dead the moment the gas-cloud reached him. Also two of our telephonists, when the wire to their F.O.O. had been cut in many places, took a message through to him in the trenches and brought back the answer, having to pass through a hail of fire each time.

I also went over to C Battery to have a look at them, and tell them that all the batteries in the brigade had done very well. Our casualties were very light ; one officer slightly wounded and four men gassed, through not putting on their helmets quickly enough. I believe the battalion in front of us had about sixty casualties only. I stayed talking to General Mitford till 8 a.m., when he decided to go home, as it was too late for another attack to be probable.

I walked back to my farm and had breakfast and shaved. The Infantry Brigade had no further news, so I came back to my headquarters. After lunch I tried to get a little sleep, but had to give it up, owing to the telephone ringing all the time. I have had temporary wires laid into our own Battle H.Q., which is alongside the infantry ones, so that if there is another attack we shall be in communication with all the batteries from there. This morning I had to depend on orderlies. The day has been very quiet, hardly a shot fired. We have had about 500 casualties, I think, in our division. The gas cases were dreadful to see ; most of them will die.

KEMMEL, 1ST MAY, 1916

Another night of alarms and excitement. At 10 p.m.
I had just lain down in the hope of getting a little rest,
after being on my feet for forty-one hours on end. Suddenly a telephonist rushed into the room and said, " Gas
attack; the syren is going." Almost before he had finished
speaking the guns were all going for all they were worth.
At the same time, the infantry sent up the S.O.S. rockets,
which meant an attack by the German infantry. The guns
were firing " gun-fire " at about fifteen rounds per minute.
I put my boots on as quickly as possible and blew my
whistle to rouse everyone. In about five minutes the 72nd
Infantry Brigade wired through to say that the attack was
not on our front, but on a brigade a little way off on our
left. Accordingly, I at once ordered all the batteries to
cease firing till further orders. General Philpotts then told
me on the 'phone to " stand to " and await developments.
Presently I heard that the Huns were letting off smoke
in front of our trenches, but not gas. I therefore ordered
a slow rate of barrage fire to be kept up, to interrupt them
in case they were massing for an attack again. It all
fizzled out in a little more than an hour, and by midnight
all was quiet, except for a good deal of rifle-fire and a very
large number of Verey lights that were being sent up by
both sides. The colonel returned from leave some time
during the night and was much surprised to hear of the
battle we had had. After breakfast I returned to C
Battery. It really is an extraordinary coincidence that
each time the 108th Brigade is in a battle I seem to be in
command.

This afternoon I had to go to the Divisional Technical
School to give a lecture on " Artillery in Trench Warfare."
There are some thirty or forty young, or rather junior,
officers and as many sergeants at this school. They
practically all belong to the infantry. It went off very
well and the commandant seemed pleased and asked me
to lecture again.

It was most interesting seeing the effect of the gas-cloud

on the crops. It must have travelled in a straight line, as one could follow its path quite easily. We seem to have been just on the edge of it. There were large fields of clover that might have been divided in half with a ruler, one half bright green and the other a chocolate brown. I got off and picked a bunch of the burnt stuff as a curio. The gas they used this time was phosgene and is deadly poisonous. Cattle were killed several miles behind the line.

I got back to the battery just in time for dinner to find that everything had been quite quiet whilst I had been away. About midnight the infantry rang up to say that they were having a very bad time in my zone from the German machine-guns. Both sides were out in front of their trenches repairing their wires that had been cut in the assault. The German and English working parties must have been within a few yards of each other, as the trenches were only thirty yards apart at that place. They implored me to fire a few salvos to try and stop the Hun machine-guns. I fired about three rounds of gun-fire with high explosive, after which the infantry said that the machine-guns ceased troubling them and that terrible screams and groans could be heard, so there is no doubt we must have hit someone. They say that the men who assaulted our trenches were picked men of the Prussian Guard. Apparently, there was great difficulty in distinguishing Germans from English during the hand-to-hand fighting in the trenches, as both sides were wearing gas-helmets and it was a very dark night, added to which the Germans had mixed black smoke with the gas. Altogether, it must have been very unpleasant in the trenches at the time, as both sides were throwing bombs freely. The Germans not only managed to take away their own dead and wounded with them, but ours as well.

KEMMEL, 2ND MAY, 1916

Except for being called on twice to fire on the German machine-guns, we had a peaceful night. I did not get up till 9 o'clock. I had a look round the battery and was very

13

pleased with the way Harvey has run everything since I have been away. It is just a month that I have been away from the battery. First I was on leave for ten days, then I went in command of the brigade whilst Colonel Walthall commanded the 72nd Infantry Brigade, and since then I have had the brigade whilst he was on leave.

This afternoon I went up to the top of Kemmel Hill to try and register some new points, but it was so misty that it was impossible to see anything at all. I fired a salvo of H.E. into a house near Messines that produced an enormous volume of smoke. It hung about in a great black cloud and then drifted away. It is the second time this happened when I have hit that house. I cannot help thinking that it must be used as a bomb store, or perhaps the Hun has smoke cylinders in it. The infantry have 'phoned to say that after our salvos last night fearful screams and cries were heard, so we must have killed some at least.

KEMMEL, 3RD MAY, 1916

A perfectly peaceful night. We had a late breakfast, and in the course of the morning I was led down to the infantry headquarters near the trenches. I had a very unpleasant experience on my way there. As I was crossing the open, a bullet hit the ground at my feet, from the direction of Spanbroekmolen. Remembering what I had been told about the extraordinary good shooting done by this sniper, I ran for the nearest hedge as hard as I could. Before I got under cover another bullet just missed me. I followed the hedge for another two hundred yards and then had to cut across the open. Again, the brute had two more shots at me, all within a yard or so. The same sniper killed six men and wounded ten in a week at this spot.

In the afternoon I got a message to say that Colonel Walthall is going to command the 72nd Infantry Brigade again for ten days, vice General Mitford who has taken over the division whilst Capper is on leave in England. This means that I have, as usual, to take over the brigade. I am really becoming the permanent brigade commander,

at this rate. An additional complication is that Harvey
is ill. He has a high temperature and will have to go to
hospital at once. It is quite impossible to put Bishop in
charge of a battery in action, so I have sent Hector from A
Battery to take charge of C till Harvey is well.

DRANOUTRE, 4TH MAY, 1916

We have been trying to get good quarters in Dranoutre
to be close to the 72nd Infantry Brigade ; also my farm was
half a mile off the road, and across a ploughed field, which
made it very awkward to get at on a wet day. General
Philpotts telephoned after lunch to say that he would like
to visit the Brigade Observation Post on Kemmel this
afternoon and wanted a guide. I took him myself. We
were able to ride half the way up, which was a blessing, as
it is a hot day and the hill is very steep. The road was full
of deep mud-holes, into one of which the general's horse
put its foot and came down. The general was flung on
to the road, but did not seem hurt. We found Bishop in
the O.P., who pointed out all the sights—Wytschaete,
Messines, Menin, Comines, Tourcoing, Roubaix, and in
the far distance to the south the chimneys of the great
factories at Lille. It was a lovely afternoon, and the woods
were full of flowers, principally blue-bells. As we rode
down the hill we heard shells going over our heads and
bursting in the direction of Dranoutre. On arrival at the
latter place we were told that the Hun had been shelling
the village all the afternoon, but that he had not got any
shells into the houses ; they were fifty yards or so to the
north. I found that our impedimenta had arrived, but
that nothing had been done towards getting things straight.
I started the clerk and servants off with their work, and
walked across to the 72nd Infantry Brigade, who gave
Gilmour and me tea. The colonel was very cheerful and
seems to be enjoying himself as an infantry brigadier ; I
should not be surprised if he gets an infantry brigade of
his own soon. We have got quite a good room for our mess,
but it is at the corner of the square and very noisy ; one
can hardly make oneself heard when motor traffic is passing,

My bedroom is in the same house as our office, quite a nice room upstairs, with a bed.

DRANOUTRE, 5TH MAY, 1916

At 10 a.m. it was 70° F. in the sun. At 9 o'clock they started shelling the village again, this time bursting their shells right in among the houses. It is really very tiresome of them, as one has always imagined that this place was well out of range. They must be using their 5·1 naval gun, same as the one that fires into Poperinghe. It must be firing at something like six miles' range. After lunch I went to see A and C Batteries. Whilst I was having tea D Battery was badly shelled, and the infantry who were next door to them had to move out quickly as several 5·9's landed in their farm. In the middle of dinner we had a gas-alarm, syrens were reported to the south of us, and a heavy fire was going on. However, nothing happened as far as we were concerned, and the firing died down in an hour.

DRANOUTRE, 6TH MAY, 1916

This morning they shelled the village again. They have so far only managed to knock down the estaminet at the entrance to the village, and a couple of houses. Still, it is a bore if they go on like this, as the pieces go flying all over the wagon-lines. One battery had three horses hit. I dined at the 72nd Brigade H.Q., a cheerful party, including Nelthorpe, the brigade major, and Dugmore, who commands the N. Staffords. Whilst we were having our coffee after dinner a message came to say that a shell had landed on the rest billet of the N. Staffords and killed three and wounded fourteen men. An unlucky shell with a vengeance, as it could only have been fired blind in the dark. I at once turned on all our batteries in retaliation.

DRANOUTRE, 7TH MAY, 1916

Sunday. I spent most of the morning in the office going through various orders. We are going to do a combined shoot this afternoon at the Bois D'Enfer. The idea is that all our batteries will fire a *rafale* at 4 o'clock which will make the Germans run into their dug-outs and then the howitzers will break up the dug-outs. The observing officer who is on Kemmel Hill tells me that the shooting was excellent. All the batteries fired exactly together, with the result that the poor little wood simply disappeared in smoke from the bursting shrapnel. We fired a few salvos afterwards to keep them quiet.

DRANOUTRE, 8TH MAY, 1916

Rather a typical April day, showers and sunshine alternately. I have worked out another little scheme for this afternoon. All the batteries will fire a few rounds of gun-fire into the wood, same as yesterday, but, as the Germans will then expect the howitzers to go for their dug-outs in the wood, they will probably run out of the wood into some trenches and dead ground near. So, to-day, the batteries will then turn on to these places outside the wood. It ought to make the Hun very jumpy, as he will not know what to expect next time we fire at the wood. Montgomerie came to lunch with me, but went back to his battery in time for the shoot.

DRANOUTRE, 9TH MAY, 1916

Wet and bitterly cold. The enemy amused himself by dropping 5·9's into D 6 trench and did a good deal of damage to our parapet. I went round to the colonel of the Heavies and got him to turn some of the 60-pounders and 4·7 guns on to the offending battery. I also put two of our own batteries on to the German trench opposite to the place. After lunch Montgomerie and I went, with a party of officers of various regiments, by bus to Meteren. Here we were given a demonstration of the new machine that picks up telephone messages. It is a wonderful new invention of the French, though I believe the Germans have got it also. It has no wires, but only earth-pins. It overhears all conversation within 1,500 yards of it!

This means to say that everything we have been saying on the 'phone up to now must have been heard by the Germans. It is very serious indeed, as we are bound to use the telephone all the time; but it would be an awful business if we have to put all messages into cypher. We got out of the bus at Bailleul on the way back and had tea with Divisional Artillery Headquarters. From there I telephoned for our horses, and rode back in time for dinner. We had a great Wagner concert on the gramophone after dinner.

DRANOUTRE, 10TH MAY, 1916

The Hun has misbehaved himself very badly to-day and I have had to deal severely with him. All the morning I got appeals for help from the infantry. After lunch I went to the Brigade Observation Post and had quite a little battle. The Hun was " crumping " our trenches, so I strafed his. As I was using four batteries and he only one, I think that, on the whole, we had the best of it. It was really quite an amusing game as I turned on the fire of one battery after another on to various sore places in his lines. From the height I was on I could see all his roads and back trenches. I called on A Battery and had tea with C. From there I went on and had a drink with Birch at D Battery. Having foolishly sent away my horses, I had to walk back three miles on the *pavé* road, in nailed boots. Gilpin and Trydell (the new Vet.) dined with me, and we had an amusing evening till 1.30 a.m.

DRANOUTRE, 11TH MAY, 1916

The weather is much warmer again and I have been able to leave off my waistcoat. We have had a great deal of trouble lately with our telephone-wires being cut by spies. I telephoned over to the Provost-Marshal—Captain Oliphant of the 12th Lancers, whom I knew in India —he rode over and went into the matter. It is very difficult to catch these spies, as they do their work after dark and never cut a wire twice at the same place.

DRANOUTRE, 12TH MAY, 1916

I went round some of the horse-lines this evening—D, H.Q., and C Batteries. My black horses are beginning to look beautiful again. I refused to clip them all the winter and have had them standing out in the open all the time, wet and cold included. I have not had a single cold among them, and, now that their woolly-bear coats are coming out fast, they are going to look magnificent, and, more important, are all in hard condition.

DRANOUTRE, 13TH MAY, 1916

It has rained all day and generally been beastly, though, thank Heaven, it is still warm. The new organisation of the Divisional Artillery came into force at noon to-day. D Battery is transferred to a new brigade, and we get an howitzer battery instead, commanded by a Captain Hart. He came to see me to-day and arranged for his zones for the various retaliation schemes we have in this brigade. My command is growing ! I have now got under me four batteries of 18-pounders, one battery of 4·5 howitzers, and an ammunition column. In all some thirty officers, nine hundred men, and about a thousand horses, with twenty guns. Quite a decent-sized command for a major. The Hun has been on his best behaviour to-day and has not annoyed us much; perhaps he is beginning to realise that he gets more than he gives. We have got Saxons against us now, and they are much less aggressive than the Prussians.

DRANOUTRE, 14TH MAY, 1916

Bishop goes on leave to-day, so I am getting him to take my diary home up to the present date. There may be a battle any time, and one never knows what may happen. As a matter of fact, I generally carry it in my pocket on the move, but I should hate to lose it. That is the advantage of having loose leaves. I can always take out as much as is finished. Another miserable wet day.

DRANOUTRE, 15TH MAY, 1916

Have spent a lazy day, marking up German gun positions on my large-scale map. We have just got a new list of them, at least a hundred. The difficulty is to know which are occupied at the moment. The Germans have an excellent system by which each battery has several alternative positions and sometimes fires from one, sometimes from another. We prepare one alternative position but never seem to use it.

DRANOUTRE, 16TH MAY, 1916

Bright sun. General Capper is coming back to-day, so General Mitford will relieve Colonel Walthall with the Infantry Brigade and I shall be able to get back to my battery, which I have only been with for two days since we came into action here.

KEMMEL, 17TH MAY, 1916

Very muggy and tiring day. I was thoroughly dissatisfied with the night-lines of the guns and have spent the day altering them. It is very nervous work firing at the German parapet when it is only 30 yards from our own. The minutest error on the part of anyone concerned would cause the shell to go into our own trenches. Radmore was F.O.O. and must have had an exciting time ranging the guns. He and Beart are feeling very ill, and Harvey is still in hospital. I believe it is all the dead rats in the trenches ; they were killed by the gas-clouds and now are being more disagreeable even than they were when they were alive.

KEMMEL, 18TH MAY, 1916

We had a disturbed night. At half-past twelve all the gas syrens started blowing ; we turned out as quick as possible and put on our gas-helmets. After " standing to " ready to fire for two hours, I let the men go to sleep again. Nothing happened, and I believe it was a false alarm.

To-day has been gloriously hot and one can really say that summer has arrived. I have spent a really lazy day going round the battery. Harvey has come back from hospital ; he says they made him very comfortable there in a large château.

KEMMEL, 19TH MAY, 1916

I had meant to go down to the trenches this morning, but the colonel telephoned to say he was coming up to see me. I find that we are all to make several new battery positions in case these are required for reinforcing batteries. I am expected to make two complete battery positions ! I don't know how long it will take. However, I started off this afternoon and put up a huge green canvas marquee, so that we can work by day without being seen by the Hun aeroplanes.

KEMMEL, 20TH MAY, 1916

We came on duty to-day, so I have an officer on the top of Kemmel, instead of an F.O.O. in the trenches. Perry has gone up for three days. It is really hot, 75° in the shade at breakfast.

KEMMEL, 21ST MAY, 1916

This morning Radmore saw a working party of Germans in Hell Farm. We worked out all the corrections for air, charge, barometer, shell, angle from zero, angle of sight, etc. We have never fired at this target before. However, I put great faith in the calculations and decided to give them the most rapid rate of fire possible, without giving them warning by ranging in the usual way. We fired sixteen shells as hard as we could. Of the sixteen, fifteen burst in the house and one just outside. There is not much the matter with the gunnery of the New Army evidently. We have worked steadily on at the new gun-pit, and it is beginning to take shape. The walls are nearly done.

KEMMEL, 22ND MAY, 1916

Soon after midnight the infantry reported that they were being annoyed by a minenwerfer, so I fired a few rounds into their front-line trench. This morning General Capper inspected the battery at 7.30 ! What an hour for a general's inspection ! He was very cheerful and seemed quite pleased with everything. Being a sapper, the only thing that really interested him was the construction of the pits. He made several very useful suggestions, but talked far over my head, about stresses of beams. He thoroughly enjoyed going into matters that were his own trade. He is going to make out a specification for a model gun-pit. General Philpotts was more interested in my coloured cards for denoting different kinds of ammunition.

KEMMEL, 23RD MAY, 1916

Very hot but muggy. I feel very slack—liver, I think. We worked all day at the new pit; it is taking much longer than I expected. I dined with Montgomerie at A Battery. An excellent dinner, but I suffered from the gramophone; they had nothing but rag-time, etc. Got back to my battery at midnight and checked the laying of guns on their night-lines. I was glad to find that they were all right. Just as I was starting to go to A Battery, Birch rang up on the telephone and said, " Gas alarm ! " We all put on our gas-helmets and awaited further news. Eventually we found that one of our own batteries had burst two gas-cylinders in the German trench. It shows they still have the gas there.

KEMMEL, 24TH MAY, 1916

The new pit is practically finished and has turned into a very fine affair, with roller blinds to close the mouth and the entrance at the back. I have painted a large canvas screen to represent a hedge ; this closes the gap in the real hedge. It cannot be seen from 200 yards off, let alone 2,000, from which an aeroplane would be looking. There was a meeting of battery commanders in Dranoutre, to which I went. We had tea with the colonel, and I went over my wagon-lines afterwards. In the afternoon the men cut a great quantity of turfs to cover the roof of the new pit. I had a wagon up to cart them to the position, but it rained hard and we could not see to work.

KEMMEL, 25TH MAY, 1916

A wet and misty morning. I had a G.S. wagon up to finish the turfs, but I am afraid it must have been seen by a Hun balloon or aeroplanes, as we have been heavily shelled all day with shrapnel. I had a near escape as the first shell of all burst just over my head. I at once ordered all the men into the pits and ran behind a tree myself. I had hardly got there when two more shells came and burst twenty yards in front of my tree. The tree got the full benefit of it, and the bullets and pieces whistled past me on both sides. Fortunately it was just thick enough to protect the whole of my body. After two or three more, I thought it was too hot, and retired into a dug-out, running across the open to get there. The fuse of one shell buried itself almost at my feet, and on being dug up showed a range of 5,050 metres, or 6,275 yards. I was also able to get the angle from Magnetic North, by the marks on the trees. We were, therefore, able to tell almost exactly where the German battery was. I at once 'phoned to Headquarters and asked for the heavy batteries to be turned on. The horses of the G.S. wagon had a near escape also, but fortunately were able to get away safely. This afternoon they have had a regular strafe all over the country. Our heavy guns have been firing hard all the time, so that it has been noisy. One of my best signallers—Gunner Quayle—has been wounded by shrapnel in the face.

KEMMEL, 26TH MAY, 1916

We worked on the second new pit as usual all the morning, and after lunch I climbed up to the top of Kemmel

Hill. Perry, who has been up there all the week, reported that he saw large bodies of German troops on the road from Hollebeke to Wytschaete. I worked out the angles, etc., and tried to hit them, but found, as I expected, that my shells were several thousand yards short, although I had extreme elevation on the guns, added to which I had allowed an extra 400 yards for the mark of shell, so that we must have been firing at 6,600 yards. Whilst I was up there, A Battery was badly shelled by 7·7 cm. shrapnel, and had a man seriously wounded.

KEMMEL, 27TH MAY, 1916

A fine day, but much colder. The wind is changing round to N.E. and I am afraid if it goes round any more we shall be just right for a gas attack. As we burst gas cylinders in their front trenches a few days ago, we know that they have brought their cylinders back again, and I am very much afraid that they mean to repeat their attack of the 30th of last month. They have also been registering all our roads and batteries the last few days.

KEMMEL, 28TH MAY, 1916

No gas attack last night, although the wind seemed just right for it. This morning General Capper looked in on his way back from the trenches. I asked him to give me his opinion on the completed gun-pit. He was very technical about the strength of beams, etc. However, he gave me quite a lot of useful information. I am trying to carry out his suggestions in my next pit, but am quite certain I shall never get enough timber out of the R.E. It makes one realise why the Israelites got fed up with their brick-making job.

KEMMEL, 29TH MAY, 1916

Sergeant Meecham and I went down to the trenches to register a new part of the Hun line. I used H.E. with terrific results as far as the Hun was concerned. It was very difficult to see, as the German trench slopes away at an angle at that place. After a few rounds that went too far over, one fell right into the middle of the trench and detonated with a roar. I have never known an 18-pounder shell do anything like it. The place it hit was some seventy yards from where I was standing, but the air all round us simply whistled with pieces. I could see timber, sandbags, and earth going up in fountains. I put several more shells into the same place, with the result that ten yards of the German parapet was levelled to the ground, not only exposing the head of a communicating trench, but the bottom of the trench. They did not reply whilst I was down there, but when I got back I found a message to say that it had annoyed the Huns so much that they were plastering our trenches with 5·9's, 4·2's, 77 mms., minenwerfers and grenades ! It seems as if I only got away just in time.

KEMMEL, 30TH MAY, 1916

Harvey went on leave to England last night. I rode into Dranoutre to see the colonel after lunch, and inspected my wagon-lines. I went to see a section of model trenches that have been dug in exact replica of a section of German trenches. A Captain Kempthorne and his sergeant-major arrived this evening to be attached for fourteen days' instruction. They belong to the 335th Brigade—67th Division (Second Line Territorials). I told Radmore (F.O.O.) and Bishop and Perry to finish registering the trench I started on yesterday, whilst I went to Dranoutre. But they made such a horrible mess of the job that it will all have to be done again to-morrow.

KEMMEL, 31ST MAY, 1916

I sent Perry down to finish the registration that he was engaged on yesterday, whilst I wrote down the angles, etc., on the guns myself. It seems that it is a very " tender spot," as the Hun at once retaliated again very heavily. Quite a warm day, with a westerly wind, so that there is no gas alert on for the moment. The second pit is getting on slowly. General Capper's idea is doubtless very good, but it takes much longer to build and requires an enormous amount of material. I am using something like 80 pit props, good strong ones, too, same as they use in the pits at Wishaw. The steel helmet that Grizel sent me is very comfortable. I don't feel the weight at all now. General Philpotts came round at tea-time with the colonel to see the new pits. He was delighted with it. Capper sent a message to say that he was very pleased with the turn-out at his inspection last week.

KEMMEL, 1ST JUNE, 1916

Another fine sunny day, with a westerly wind. The 9·2 howitzers took on Muskrat Mound, which is a concrete fort at the nearest point to our trenches. For weeks we have been worried by machine-guns and snipers at this place. However, fifty-five 9·2 shells on to the same spot have settled it for some time. It was a glorious sight. Fountains of red earth and timber going up a hundred feet into the air. I watched it from the ridge above my battery. However, as might be expected, the Hun was not pleased, and retaliated, a 4·2 battery firing on me. The first shell pitched between my two new pits. The next went into the farm where my signallers live ; there were a dozen men and a horse in it, but fortunately none were touched. I made the men stay inside their dug-outs and kept in the entrance to my telephone-pit myself, dodging in like a rabbit whenever I heard one coming. Perry, who was F.O.O., brought in the 9·2 subaltern to dinner. It was very interesting hearing all about how the big guns work. There is no doubt that they have much more fun than we do in this war.

KEMMEL, 2ND JUNE, 1916

A lovely day, just warm without being hot. The new pit is getting on very slowly, as we have got to a stage when we can only work on the roof when it is dark. I am making shelves in the recesses for ammunition. Each pit will hold two hundred and fifty rounds. The heavy batteries have had a tremendous strafe on all day, making a deafening noise, that has given us all headaches. I have been trying to get time to write some letters home, but have not had any to spare for days. The bombardment has continued all the evening and is still going on now at midnight.

KEMMEL, 3RD JUNE, 1916

All last night the big guns roared ; the few remaining panes of glass in my room were broken. It was quite impossible to sleep till after 3 a.m. There is a rumour that the Canadians lost the Hooge trenches yesterday afternoon, but that they were retaken and also the German first line, and support trenches back to Bellewaarde Lake. I hope it is true. There was certainly a tremendous strafe about midnight. Every gun on the Corps front to the north was firing hard, and all our heavies, too. The adjutant has been in this morning and says that not only have the trenches been lost but Maple Copse and Observatory Ridge. If this is so, it means that the four guns we left up there have been taken too.

KEMMEL, 4TH JUNE, 1916

The news from Hooge is worse. Our counter-attack with two Canadian Brigades failed, and far from taking any German trenches, they still hold right up to Maple Copse, including all Sanctuary Wood and most of Observatory Ridge. The fighting is so intricate that the artillery on neither side can fire. The trenches are said to be completely blocked with German dead—and presumably ours also. We have just got the depressing news about the naval battle. Last night we had our battle. For days we have been preparing for this attack. The West Kents were to have entered the enemy's trench under cover of a very intense artillery fire. It was timed to begin at thirty minutes after midnight, and punctually, to a second, the whole of the batteries opened on the German front line. At the end of three minutes we ceased firing high explosive

and changed to shrapnel at the same range. Under cover
of this our infantry were to creep forward as close as they
dared to where our shells were bursting. At the end of
two more minutes all the guns suddenly " lifted " on to
the German support trench and formed a barrage there.
This was to be the signal for the infantry to rush forward,
blow up the German wire and jump into the trench. They
were to collect prisoners, gas cylinders, etc., and come back
in ten minutes, when we dropped back on to the front line
again. As far as we were concerned it all worked perfectly
and we kept to our time-table exactly. Unfortunately,
the infantry failed to blow up the Gernan wire and never
got into the trench. I expected to have a heavy fire turned
on to me, but was pleasantly surprised to find that only
one field artillery battery devoted itself to us, doing us no
damage. It was very noisy indeed. After lunch I rode
into Dranoutre with Kempthorne and had a look at my
wagon-lines. We had tea with Headquarters and heard
all the latest news.

KEMMEL, 5TH JUNE, 1916

A tremendous hurricane is blowing with the wind at
85 feet per sec., which will make shooting very difficult
if I have to fire on the front line to-night. The infantry
have taken to asking for retaliation every time a machine-
gun fires, which means that we get very little sleep. Work
on the new pits is going on steadily. I have now got five
rows of earth sandbags and two rows of brick bags on the
roof. This ought to keep out a direct hit from a 4·2 at
any rate.

KEMMEL, 6TH JUNE, 1916

A hurricane still blowing—85 feet per sec., which makes
it very difficult to calculate one's range. After lunch I
took Kempthorne down to call on the Infantry Headquarters. For a wonder we did not get sniped. I took
the precaution to keep close under the hedges, as I have
now a wholesome respect for the Spanbroekmolen sniper,
who has lately acquired an automatic rifle. We heard a

good many shells, large and small, going over towards the battery, and, when we got back, found that they were shelling our officers' mess. They put one within five yards of the door and made an awful mess of the clerk's office, besides filling the rooms with lumps of mud. Fortunately, they hit nothing.

KEMMEL, 7TH JUNE, 1916

Fine, but still blowing pretty hard. As it is from the west, there cannot be a gas attack till it changes. The news from Ypres is very bad ; the Canadians have lost all the Hooge trenches now and only hold a line 150 yards behind the Culvert. As they have lost Sanctuary Wood and Observatory Ridge also, it will be very difficult to keep the Germans back if they make another serious attack. The 60-pounders are roaring just behind me ; it is the worst noise I have ever met, and gives me a headache after a dozen rounds. We are just in front of them and get the full blast of it. It even breaks the glass. As we seem to be fixtures here, we are planting nasturtium seeds round the pits !

KEMMEL, 8TH JUNE, 1916

Harvey came back from leave this morning. In his week he managed to get invested with the Military Cross by the King, and also to be married. The wind has gone down to a normal five foot-seconds, which means that the cyclone is nearly over. As soon as the wind changes to the east I expect we shall have another gas attack. The news from Ypres is worse again. They have lost more of our trenches, and a prisoner says that they would have attacked with gas if the wind had been in the right direction. Why do we never use gas ? I suppose that the precious Nonconformist Conscience does not approve of gas, in the same way it does not allow of retaliation for Zeppelin raids. We have just had orders to fire a retaliation with the Hun plane up. I reported that the German machine was over us, but was told to carry on. I expect he saw our flashes.

14

KEMMEL, 9TH JUNE, 1916

After lunch Sergeant Meecham and I went to my little
O.P. near the battery to register a gun that has been away
for repairs. We had hardly got there when a 4·2 burst
just in front of the house. We waited to see what would
happen, and another burst forty yards behind, giving the
German battery a hundred-yard " bracket." I said to
Meecham, " This is no place for the likes of us." We
picked up the telephone and fled back to the battery. We
hardly got clear of the house before the next shell burst
full on top of it, sending up clouds of red brick dust. They
hit it again twice more, but we were safely back in our
dug-outs in the battery. I wonder if our flashes were seen
last night, or if we were seen to go into the house.

KEMMEL, 10TH JUNE, 1916

In the early morning the infantry saw a working party
just behind the German trenches ; we fired on them by the
map, and dispersed them with the first salvo. I don't
know if any were hit or not. Radmore tried his hand at
cutting wire in front of the Hun trench. I think he found
it a more difficult job than it sounds.

KEMMEL, 11TH JUNE, 1916

Sunday. Inspected my wagon-lines in the morning.
Bishop is in charge there now. I rode up to Kemmel
Hill and had lunch with Perry and Kempthorne, who are
in the O.P up there. It was very misty, but with great
difficulty I was able to verify my registration on Zero Farm.
I left the O.P about 4 o'clock to walk down to the battery.
When I arrived I heard that the O.P. had been shelled
by 4·2's just after I left.

KEMMEL, 12TH JUNE, 1916

I have been ordered to cut wire in front of our trenches
with my shrapnel. It is a very difficult thing to do, as it

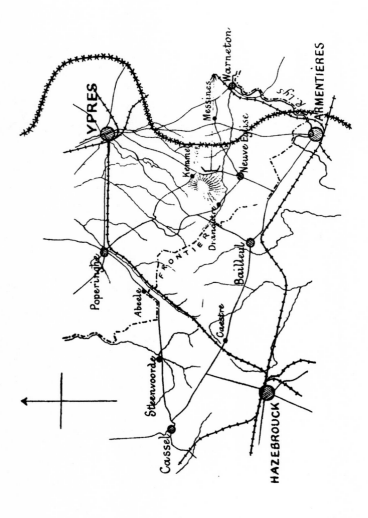

KEMMEL, JUNE 1916

is necessary to burst the shell right among the wire. It is also an unpleasant job, as one stands a very good chance of being killed by one's own shells, which are only bursting some 20 yards or so in front of one. To say nothing of the fact that of all things that annoys the Hun most, smashing up his wire and parapet is the greatest. He usually immediately retaliates by throwing over trench mortars, grenades, and bombs of all sorts. I fired 39 rounds, making a horrible mess of his wire and trench for a space of about eight yards. Fortunately he was sleepy after his lunch, or bored with the war, as he did not trouble to do anything. Kempthorne and his sergeant-major returned to England to-night, on the conclusion of their fourteen days' attachment.

KEMMEL, 13TH JUNE, 1916

At 1 o'clock this morning there started a terrific bombardment up towards Ypres; it was kept up most of the night. We have no means of telling whether it was our guns or the Hun's shells. The Germans replied with 5·9's near us, and altogether made such a hideous noise that t was impossible to sleep. The 60-pounders immediately behind us made the most painful ear-splitting noise I have ever heard. It is really wicked to allow them to take up a position so close behind another battery. When they fire it not only gives everyone a headache, but it actually hurts like being rapped over the head with a stick. They have shelled us all day, more or less, nothing very close. Their favourite spot is a place on the road about two hundred yards off. They must have burst several thousand shells there in the last two months.

KEMMEL, 14TH JUNE, 1916

A wet day. My newest pit, which has not got the roof on yet, was flooded out and became a sticky mud-hole. It has turned very cold and we have to have a fire for dinner.

KEMMEL, 15TH JUNE, 1916

Cold and misty. Radmore went down to the trenches and amused himself cutting wire. He fired about a hundred shots and seems to have made an awful mess of the Hun parapet, as well as the wire. I walked into Dranoutre, and had a look at my wagon-lines.

KEMMEL, 16TH JUNE, 1916

This morning General Philpotts, with the C.R.E., Colonel Craven, came to my gun-pits and gave a lecture to battery commanders on building pits. We were very gratified to find that our newest one is said to be about perfect. It has taken more material than three ordinary pits.

KEMMEL, 17TH JUNE, 1916

In the early hours of this morning we had another gas attack by the Germans. We had just gone to bed at half-past twelve when very heavy machine-gun fire broke out, immediately followed by the gas-syrens on our front. I jumped out of bed, seized my steel helmet and gas-helmet, and ran to the battery. They were already firing hard by the time I reached them. I went to the telephone and tried to find out what the situation was, but could only hear that gas was coming over our trenches very thick. As it is our turn to man the Brigade O.P. on the top of Kemmel Hill, I had no one in the trenches at the time. We kept up a steady rate of " barrage fire " on the German first and second lines for two hours, when the infantry reported that all was then quiet. We fired four hundred and fifty rounds in the time, which was not bad ; some of the wounded told me later that the Germans had tried to come out of their trenches but had not been able to face the machine-gun and artillery fire. Our casualties seem to have been heavy; one battalion is said to have lost two hundred and another a hundred and sixty. But I have heard nothing definite yet. We ourselves were extraordinarily fortunate; no casualties, although we had a tremendous number of shells round us. There was so much noise going on with our own guns that it was difficult to distinguish one shell from another. They gave us a great number of shrapnel and 5·9's and to-day I have found two enormous craters just behind my telephone-pit that could only have been made by 8-in. shells. It is the first time they have used these on this part of the line. I am glad they did not land on my head !

KEMMEL, 18TH JUNE, 1916

Sunday. I rode into Dranoutre in the morning, and went round the wagon-lines. This spell of cold weather has put back the horses' coats a good deal. They had nearly finished getting their black summer coats, and now they are looking a bit rusty again. We worked last night till 3 a.m., and got the roof of the third new pit finished, all except a few layers of sandbags. Also I rebuilt the front and roof of one of the present pits that had been badly knocked about by a shell during the gas attack. I am afraid our casualties seem to be far larger than we heard at first; so many men seem to be affected the day after the attack who were all right at the time. The figure given is now nine hundred, but no one knows for certain. One thing seems quite clear, and that is that the gas experts do not know what gas the Germans are using.

KEMMEL, 19TH JUNE, 1916

A splendid day—that is to say, the wind is from us to the Germans ; the clouds are too low for the aeroplanes to go up, and it is misty ! We have, therefore, had a quiet day, except that I stirred up the mud at tea-time by knocking the Hun parapet about. Perry went on leave last night; I should think he will be about the last to go before leave is finally stopped for the summer.

KEMMEL, 20TH JUNE, 1916

We had two gas alarms last night : one at half-past twelve and the other at 3 o'clock. Both turned out to be false alarms. The syrens were heard just the same as on the real gas attack night. My guns opened up immediately and had wasted a good number of rounds before I heard that it was a false alarm and stopped the firing. At any rate, it showed both the Hun and our own infantry that we were all ready. We very likely caught some of the enemy who must have been working on their parapet which has been badly damaged by our fire. These alarms are very trying; one wakes up to hear the mournful scream of the syrens and fairly falls into one's clothes. I simply stick my feet into my field-boots without lacing them up, seize two gas helmets which are always beside my bed and run to the telephone pit in the battery, putting on a gas-helmet as I go. With an ordinary gas wind one only gets about seven minutes' notice before the cloud arrives. In the trenches, of course, it is only a matter of five seconds or so, and they have to keep their helmets always rolled up on their heads. They say the gas was mixed with smoke, and it was like a November fog in London.

KEMMEL, 21ST JUNE, 1916

A lovely day, with a west wind, so for once gas alert is off. General Philpotts came round this morning and had another look at my pits. They seem to fascinate him. He tells me that Cowan, who commands an howitzer battery in the division, built a very strong pit with a roof that was to keep out 5·9's. Unfortunately, it collapsed with its own weight. At present I am making the telephone-pit, having finished three out of four pits for the new position. It is very tedious work, as so much has to be done by night, because of aeroplanes. We seldom stop work before midnight, and often later. A glass of port and a slice of cake, with a few tunes, takes us till 1 a.m., " and so to bed."

KEMMEL, 22ND JUNE, 1916

Bright sun and little wind, which means that we have been plagued by hostile aeroplanes. There was a very pretty battle this morning. A German machine was observing for one of his batteries that was ranging on us. Suddenly two of our newest and fastest machines appeared like specks far above him, and side by side they dived right on top of him. The Hun was not standing still, but our planes seem to be going three times as fast. They seemed to absolutely be touching, and as they shot past his tail they let fly with their machine-guns. The Hun simply crumpled up and fell to ground some 8,000 feet like a pheasant that had been shot. Still working on the telephone-pit; it is going to be " some " pit when it is done.

KEMMEL, 23RD JULY, 1916

A quiet day till 8 p.m., when the Hun started a tremendous bombardment of our trenches. At the same time he shelled A and C Batteries with 5·9's and field-guns. Fortunately for us, his range was a hundred yards too long, and most of the shells fell on the roads and fields behind and did us no harm. I fired H.E. into one of his trenches that I completely enfilade. The bombardment lasted till 3 a.m., so we got little sleep. I managed to do a little work to the new telephone-pit, but of course any work in the evening was impossible. To-day I got a letter from the War Office saying they had antedated my commission as major back to 5th August, 1914, so that makes me very senior.

KEMMEL, 24TH JUNE, 1916

Last night's bombardment cost the East Surreys twenty men, who were buried under the trenches. The Hun seems to have sent some streams of the largest minenwerfer bombs, which make a bigger explosion even than an 8-in. shell. Several of the men were buried so that they could not move, but with their heads out. They say that two German officers came across and tried to get them out to take as prisoners, but could not get them clear in time. It sounds a rather tall story, but cannot be verified, as both men have died since. Some men were buried under

7 feet of earth, and have only just been found. I went down to the trenches to observe for my guns, as we had to cut the enemy's wire. I fired four hundred rounds. It is always a difficult job cutting wire, especially if the trenches are only 50 yards apart, as they are at this place. Unless the shell falls actually into the wire it does not cut it. I managed to make a good job of it over about a hundred yards of front. In fact, I could not see a vestige of wire after I had finished.

KEMMEL, 25TH JUNE, 1916

Sunday. Rode into Dranoutre and looked at my wagon-lines. My hand has been getting rather painful where I got a small wound from shrapnel on the night of the gas attack. As it is showing no signs of healing up, I looked in at the Field Ambulance and asked the medical officer to tie it up properly. He insisted on injecting anti-tetanic serum into my chest, as he says that anyone who is even scratched must be inoculated against tetanus. It was very painful, as he used a large and blunt needle. It made me feel rather sick for a time. My quartermaster-sergeant (Gill) has gone home to get his commission, and they have sent me a sergeant-major instead. He is a dear old gentleman with several medals, but I don't think he has been in action since the Boer War. I have brought him to the gun-line, and left my quartermaster-sergeant's clerk to carry on with the work of that department. After dark we had several alarms caused by hearing gun-fire to the south. Wurtele, who was my adjutant at Loos, came in and took me to see an anti-aircraft gun.

KEMMEL, 26TH JUNE, 1916

Feeling very ill, and my eyes are so swollen I can hardly see out of them. I suppose it is the inoculation ; also my hand does not seem to be getting any better. At 6 o'clock this morning the Hun started bombarding A Battery with 5·9's and kept it up hard till 10. He has done a lot of damage. I can see one gun knocked out completely.

I have not heard yet what casualties they have had. (Later.) A Battery came off better than I had expected, only losing one man. Considering that about a hundred and fifty 5·9 shells landed practically in their gun-line, it is wonderful they were not knocked out altogether. Only one gun was damaged.

KEMMEL, 27TH JUNE, 1916

We had a tremendous bombardment last night. The brigade on our left did a raid on the German trenches. My battery had to put up a flank barrage to protect them. I fired five hundred rounds in half an hour—not bad going. It meant keeping up " section fire, 5 seconds " for the whole time. The Hun did not retaliate much on us, but one shell burst on a gun-pit and set it on fire in spite of a tropical downpour of rain. The detachment managed to put out the fire before it reached the ammunition. As usual, we did not get to bed till after three. To-night we shall have to work on the new position till daylight. I hear the raid failed, but have not heard the reason yet.

KEMMEL, 28TH JUNE, 1916

We worked all night long, and by 4 a.m. had got seven layers of bags on to the roof of the telephone-pit. I think everyone is getting very tired of everlastingly building pits. We have had another quiet day. I suppose both sides are getting up ammunition for the next strafe.

KEMMEL, 29TH JUNE, 1916

Another tremendous night of noise. The Queen's carried out the raid that we have all been preparing for for so long. As they entered the German trenches in my zone, we were the all-important battery, as all depended on whether we had cut the wire properly or not. Also everything depended on our " lifting " at the moment of the assault. I am glad to say the whole thing was a huge success. We fired 638 shells in about an hour ! When the infantry got to the German wire, they could not find it—not a single piece. Consequently, they were able to walk straight into the trench. They found thirty Germans in dug-outs under the parapets, all of whom were bombed except five who surrendered, and were brought in as prisoners. We used our gas this time, but I have not heard if it was successful. The wind was just right, but as it had been very unsteady till just before the time, we were not sure if it would be possible to use it. This morning I received a telegram of thanks from the infantry brigadier and another of congratulations from the Army Corps commander. The Hun did not shell my guns much, only a certain amount of shrapnel.

KEMMEL, 30TH JUNE, 1916

At 9 o'clock last night the enemy started a terrific bombardment of our trenches, sending over streams of shells of all sizes. Our trenches were badly knocked about. We fired hard for a time, but it was no good shooting 18-pounder shells at them to stop a bombardment of that sort. We therefore ceased fire, and stood by ready to put up a barrage if the Germans attempted to come out of their trenches. Everyone expected that they were going to attack. However, by midnight it all died down without any assault developing. Bishop and his telephonists had a pretty bad time, but were not touched, although dug-outs all round them were knocked in. To-day we cut wire again, this time entirely clearing away all traces of wire over a width of forty yards or so. Bishop did the observation in the morning and Radmore in the evening. At 9 o'clock at night a furious bombardment was started on our right and also on our left. Radmore could see dense clouds of our gas sweeping across the enemy's lines from left to right. As usual we are working all night.

KEMMEL, 1ST JULY, 1916

We worked till dawn, and did not have breakfast till 11 o'clock. We are all absolutely tired out with this incessant working all night and shooting all day. The Germans had a great strafe at a section of 4·7 guns not far behind my battery. They must have put at least two hundred 5·9's on to them in the course of the day. They only managed to damage one gun and that not badly. It was very unpleasant for us, as we got all the pieces round our heads.

KEMMEL, 2ND JULY, 1916

(Sunday.) Rode into Dranoutre and took the colonel to see my horses. I hear a 5·9 shell landed in my wagon-lines last night, but fortunately did not go off. It went down 13 feet into the earth, and almost vertically, which shows that it must have been fired from a great distance off. As we are working so hard and every night, I have instituted a system of holidays on Sundays.

KEMMEL, 3RD JULY, 1916

As Bishop and I were standing outside our house after breakfast this morning a 77 mm. shell landed 10 yards from us on the road. It made a very small burst, and did no harm at all. A very peaceful day, and we have been able to do a lot of work.

KEMMEL, 4TH JULY, 1916

A great day. I have moved three of the four guns into the new pits and registered them on zero and their night lines.

KEMMEL, 5TH JULY, 1916

As usual, worked till 4 a.m., getting to bed about 5. At 5 o'clock in the evening I got sudden orders to start cutting wire. Radmore went to the trenches and observed, getting well shelled by minenwerfers. At 7 o'clock orders came for a battle to-night—another raid. I just had time to get the place registered before dark.

Kemmel, 6th July, 1916

Last night's shoot was a splendid baptism for the new pits. The Germans put a great amount of shrapnel over our heads ; everyone enjoyed the feeling of perfect security. I have put in speaking-tubes to the guns from the telephone pit, so can give all my orders without going out into the open. The telephone room is so far under ground that we would hear very little of the shells and other guns ; only our own. It is a great blessing to be able to hear easily on the telephone in spite of outside noises.

Kemmel, 7th July, 1916

Worked as usual till daylight. General Philpotts came round this morning and said that we must hurry up and make more and more pits. He admired my position, but seemed to think that the work was too good—he has not got to sit in it, when 5·9's are falling about. Having made the actual gun-pits, with 6 feet of cover on the roof, I am now linking them all up so as to form a continuous rampart with chambers for extra ammunition in between the guns. I want to make space for a thousand rounds per gun. Prideaux-Brune—the second-in-command of the Rifle Brigade—dined with us. We have many mutual friends in London, and had a very pleasant evening.

Kemmel, 10th July, 1915

For the last two days we have had no excitement, and have been working steadily on the position. In the afternoon General Capper and Kenny came round and crawled into all the ammunition shelters, etc. He seemed delighted with the whole place.

Kemmel, 11th July, 1916

Last night we had another battle ; the Rifle Brigade raided the Hun trenches at the Bull Ring. It was very successful. They killed eleven Huns and brought back a great quantity of equipment, including the mail which had evidently just arrived. They were just carrying out a relief and their trenches must have been full of men, so it is thought that the artillery fire must have accounted for a good many more.

KEMMEL, 12TH JULY, 1916

Generals Humphreys and Philpotts visited me and informed me that I have now got to build another position a mile from here, with infantry labour. A horrible prospect, as it will mean an officer standing over them all the time, as they have no idea what a gun-pit looks like. I went to see the place, and found that it is in full view of the German lines. On my way back I met the general again, and Philpotts asked me what I thought of it. I replied that I was glad *I* had not got to fire from it. There was a dreadful pause, and Walthall said in a stage whisper : " General Humphreys chose it." No battery commander would have chosen such a place. I hear that Dranoutre was shelled by a long naval gun this afternoon, but no damage was done. Bishop was hit by shrapnel this morning whilst doing F.O.O., but it is very slight, and he will not have to go sick.

KEMMEL, 13TH JULY, 1916

Started off at 7.30 this morning to teach the infantry how to make gun-pits. It is bad enough to work night and day on my own, but it is far worse to have to do foreman of works to infantry who have never seen a gun-pit in their lives. They were very bored with the proceedings, and quite the laziest lot of men I have ever met.

KEMMEL, 14TH JULY, 1916

I got a telegram to say that General Franks, G.O.C., R.A., 2nd Army, was coming round to-day, so I sent Harvey on the fatigue in the morning, and went there myself in the afternoon. It is heart-breaking work, trying to make these lazy infantrymen build decent gun-pits. I should think the work will be finished about Christmas with any luck. Just as I had finished at 6 o'clock, General Philpotts arrived and asked me to reconnoitre another area with him. We wandered all over the country and looked at large numbers of possible (and impossible) sites for new battery positions. Got back in time for dinner and another night's work.

KEMMEL, 15TH JULY, 1916

To-day we have had a great shoot at the enemy's wire, cutting away some 120 yards. He is getting very angry over so much of this sort of thing; all the batteries on this front have been doing the same thing to-day. He started shelling my guns at the time, so, as I have a fair idea of who the offender is, I retaliated. The range is 7,800 yards, which is the longest we have ever fired. I hope to-night's work will about finish my own position, then we shall have to start on the next one. The men are wonderful; they must be as dead tired as I am, but they are very cheerful in spite of everything. Thank goodness we have good weather.

KEMMEL, 17TH JULY, 1916

For the last two days we have been cutting wire. We finished all the wire on our front yesterday, but as we were ordered to fire another two hundred rounds to-day, we amused ourselves by knocking out two machine-guns. The guns shot beautifully and we burst round after round of H.E. on top of the emplacements, eventually smashing them to pieces and leaving nothing but heaps of earth to show where they had been. The poor Hun worked all night long repairing the breaks we had made in his parapet and put in some real good work, pit-props and more sand-bags. To-day we have knocked it all down again, and left it worse than before. Also the infantry keep machine-guns on the breaches all night. After lunch I took Perry to see the new position that I am making at La Polka with labour supplied by the Leicesters. After which we started to reconnoitre the ground towards Wytschaete.

We got to within about a thousand yards of the front line when I asked an R.E. subaltern if the road we were on was moderately safe by day. He assured us that it was. I did not feel very happy as we were in full view of the German lines, less than half a mile off, and it was very clear. When we were right out in the open a shrapnel burst 50 yards in front of us, and all the bullets flew round our heads. By some miracle we were neither of us touched. We at once dived into a little cottage near us. Of course the Hun F.O.O. had seen us, and no doubt had recognised us as officers. He put two more right into the cottage, so I thought it was time to go. But the moment we tried to bolt out at the back, he spotted us again and drove us in with another shell. It was really a most silly position, as we could not get away except across two hundred yards of perfectly open ground. We waited twenty minutes, till I thought the Hun observer would be bored with watching our cottage, and then bolted for the nearest hedge, one by one. I got very hot, and quite lost my temper.

KEMMEL, 18TH JULY, 1916

We have done a lot of firing to-day, principally at working parties who were trying to mend the breaches we made in their parapet the day before yesterday. I have the place registered to a yard, and can always burst my first salvos right on to the spot. There was another raid on Spanbroekmolen last night, and although we did not fire ourselves, we came in for some retaliation on the part of the Hun. However, we do not mind in the least now that we are in our beautiful new pits. It makes all the difference, knowing that you have got 6 feet of timber, earth, and brick over your head.

KEMMEL, 19TH JULY, 1916

Great excitement ; we are going out of action. There is no news as to where we go, but everyone assumes that we shall go south and join in the great battle. I do hope this is so, as it would be very ignominious to miss the greatest battle of all, after having been in all the others so far. I went down to Dranoutre and found my unfortunate wagon-lines being shelled by a heavy naval gun. The shells were falling among the horses, but by the greatest luck only one horse was wounded. The horses were sent away until it was over. I have gone through all the stuff in the Quartermaster's Stores and had everything issued out, as we shall have to travel very light. After dinner, Wilkins, who now commands B Battery, came to see me and stayed till 3.30 a.m.

KEMMEL, 20TH JULY, 1916

A glorious hot day. Everything is very quiet. Very little shelling going on. I think the Hun has sent most of his heavy guns down to the Somme. We are to be relieved. An officer of the Ulster Division has just arrived in advance of his battery. What is left of them has come from the Somme, where they were in the great assault on the 1st July. Their guns are due to-morrow.

KEMMEL, 21ST JULY, 1916

The relieving battery has arrived and is now at my wagon-lines. C/172, commanded by Major Murray, p.s.c. —a very nice fellow. We are arranging all details of the relief between ourselves. If only the people above will leave us alone it will go off all right. It is a ticklish job to hand over a place in the dark to strangers, the more so as there is a gas-attack wind. We shall take out two guns at a time, and keep my other guns on their lines and loaded till the new ones are ready to fire. Murray is delighted with the pits, etc., as well he may be. General Philpotts came in to tea with the relieving general. Philpotts said all the right things. He told General Brock that he considered mine the show position of the division.

EECKE, 22ND JULY, 1916

The relief came off all right. We got down to our wagon-lines in Dranoutre about 1 o'clock this morning.

Very tired, but very glad to hand over the responsibility of holding the line for a few days. We slept at Dranoutre and marched off from here at 9.45 a.m. this morning. We had an uneventful journey, and reached our old billet here at 2 o'clock. It is four months less a week since we left here. It is extraordinarily quiet and peaceful, not a shot to be heard, not a gun. It sounds very strange. We have no news of our next move, but I expect we shall entrain for the south at once.

EECKE, 23RD JULY, 1916

A glorious peaceful day. No telephone, and no excitements. I have really enjoyed myself pottering round the horses. Rode into Eecke village at tea time to see the colonel. Perry is ill; I suppose he has eaten too much. I know where we are going, but cannot write it down; anyhow, I am very pleased about it. The horses are really looking well.

EECKE, 24TH JULY, 1916

We have overhauled all the guns to-day, and find that they are not improved by all the firing they have done. Bishop has rejoined, he was left behind at the last position to show the new people how the place worked. We march off to-morrow morning at 7.30 a.m. and entrain at Godewaersvelde for " somewhere." This is the place where Prince Max of Hesse is buried. He was killed on Mont-des-Cats in September 1914. I have left my complete 5·9 shell and fuse with the farmer here, and hope to pick it up after the war is over, if ever I come back to see the place again. The farmers' name is Monsieur Elie Stoffoes, Kiecken, Commune d'Eecke, Department du Nord, France.

CROUY, 26TH JULY, 1916

Here we are at last on the Somme. We entrained at 10 a.m. at Godewaersvelde lafter a three-mile march and meandered southwards all day. We came via Hazebrouck, St. Omer, St. Pol, Doullens, and Amiens. We

15

detrained at Saleux, a small station three miles south of the latter. We arrived there at 9 o'clock at night and got the horses out before it was dark. It was a very difficult job with the wagons, as there is no platform, and we had to build ramps with sleepers. However, we were ready to march off a little before 12. It was a pitch dark night and I had a section of the Divisional Ammunition Column with me, so we were a pretty long column. We passed through Amiens, being challenged by excited French sentries with long, wicked-looking bayonets. The sentry rushed at me and shouted " Qui vive ? " to which I replied, " L'artillerie royale." It was rather difficult finding my way in the dark, as there were no sign-posts and not a soul about. However, we struck the tramway which enters Amiens by the Abbeville road, and I knew we must be right, as I have often motored along it in happier times. After an eighteen-mile march we reached this place at 5.30 in the morning, very tired and sleepy. It is a delightful old village, full of gardens, with lovely roses and hollyhocks —very different to the beastly Flanders that I hope we have left for good. As an example of staff work, our journey was typical. We actually passed within 50 yards of this camp in the train twelve hours before we reached it ! Heaven knows why they could not let us detrain at a station only a mile up the line.

CROUY, 27TH JULY, 1916

We are having a very pleasant rest in this place before being flung into the " dog fight," as everyone calls the terrific battle that is raging on the Somme just east of Amiens. We don't know what day we go into action, but probably it will be in two or three days' time. This morning I took the battery staff and officers out on the hills near here, and did some open warfare. We had a really good gallop, the first for many months. In the after-noon I had battery gun drill. I am appalled at the ignorance of all the officers of everything appertaining to open fighting. They are very good at trench warfare, but I tremble to think what will happen when we eventually get the enemy on the move. There has been tremendous firing all day. I hear we are still attacking hard and have gained more ground and prisoners.

CROUY, 28TH JULY, 1916

Glorious hot day, with bright sun. After lunch I took the battery up on to the downs and did open warfare, after which we had some driving drill. Finally, I dismounted all the gunners off the vehicles and had a few minutes' horse artillery galloping drill, just to wake everyone up a bit. Hart dined with us.

CROUY, 30TH JULY, 1916

To-day (Sunday) Bishop and I had a holiday. We rode into Amiens during the cool of the morning and sent our horses back. We spent a long time examining the cathedral; it was very interesting as Bishop, being an architect, was able to explain it all to me. They have sandbagged up most of the best carvings for fear of an attack by Hun aeroplanes. The organ is magnificent. We had lunch at the Hôtel du Rhin, where I have often stopped when motoring. I have seldom enjoyed a meal so much. After living on tough beef and boiled potatoes for months on end, it *was* a change. Eggs in aspic jelly, fried sole, etc., and a bottle of Pommard. Whilst we were having tea we heard the news that the division was moving up immediately into Corps Reserve. We therefore got a train back to Hanghest, which is a mile from here and came back at once. Apparently we move to-morrow morning. Both the English and French have done very well to-day; we have taken several more villages.

VECQUEMONT, 31ST JULY, 1916

We left Crouy at 1.30 p.m. and marched here, via Amiens. The heat was tropical, with the sun on our backs. The roads were three inches deep in fine white dust. As it is twenty miles, the whole march was very trying. The horses suffered a good deal with the heat and weight of the guns and ammunition wagons. We came through three or four miles of the lowest class of suburb, worse than the outskirts of Glasgow. I felt quite done up myself by the time we arrived, and was off my feed. The whole of the artillery of the division are packed together on some low ground on the banks of the river Ancre, just where it runs into the Somme. We are bivouacking here, sleeping in the open among the horses.

VECQUEMONT, 1ST AUGUST, 1916

I had quite a good night; it was very warm and I did not even want a blanket. There are fifteen batteries altogether, with some 3,000 horses on a piece of ground 400 yards long by 200 wide. Some crowd. My chargers are picketed alongside my bed, and they wake me by blowing into my face. Hitchy-koo, my first charger, is very amusing; he gets furious if I don't give him sugar or bread all day. Four German aeroplanes came over this morning and dropped bombs. Fortunately not on our heads, or there might have been a stampede. We are not moving to-day, which will give the horses a rest. I expect we shall go into the battle to-morrow.

IN BIVOUAC AT VECQUEMONT, 3RD AUGUST, 1916

We have had two days' complete peace here. Of course, it is not comfortable, as we are living in the horse-lines and sleeping in the open. Fortunately the weather is quite dry, and it is no real hardship. I have taken up my abode under a poplar-tree, but it gives very little shade, and the sun has been tropical all the time. To-night, at 8 a.m., we move up twelve miles nearer the " dog fight." We do not know yet when we go into action.

BIVOUAC. BOIS-DES-TAILLES, 4TH AUGUST, 1916

The whole Divisional Artillery marched in the early hours of the morning, when it was nice and cool. We arrived here at 9 a.m. and have gone into bivouac in a small wood. The guns and horses are just outside. We are about 5 miles from the fighting here, and the noise of the guns is very clear. We came through Corbie and by the road on the north bank of the Somme. We are on the dividing line of the British and French zones. The road was thick with French transport, and I noticed that a large number of German prisoners were being employed in road-making and in unloading a train. There did not appear to be any guard over them, and they were working very contentedly under their own N.C.O.s. They certainly were not over-exerting themselves. This is quite a nice little wood of the usual kind. We have established ourselves in a small clearing. As long as the fine weather lasts it is quite the pleasantest method. All my guns have now gone to be repaired, so that now I am quite unarmed !

Bois-des-Tailles, 5th August, 1916

I have had a most exciting day. This morning all brigade and battery commanders met the general at the Citadel, which is a collection of huts and tents in the middle of the plain. After a conference we all went up to see the ground we are to take over. We were able to ride nearly up to the old British front line. Here we found that the heavy guns had established themselves. There were rows and rows of them. We went along the broad white track and soon came to the old British front line. We passed through the remains of our wire and were in " No Man's Land," which is about eighty yards wide here. Then we crossed the German front line, and found ourselves in a maze of trenches and shell-holes. One could see what a terrific bombardment there had been, as the whole place was one mass of shell-holes, large and small. In fact, it was most exhausting work walking about, as one was climbing in and out of the holes every step. In many places the trenches had ceased to exist, and at no place could one see a single square yard of the original ground surface. The shelling by the Hun was very heavy, by far the heaviest

I have ever seen since Loos, nearly all 5·9 H.E. They were falling all round us, and it seemed impossible that one should not be hit; but I did not see a single casualty that day! I think some of the shells must have been 8-in., as the detonations were very loud and the clouds of smoke enormous. No doubt this was partly accounted for by the fact that the ground was so dry that an immense amount of earth was thrown up. We went as far forward as the southern corner of the famous Trônes Wood, but did not go inside, as they were shelling it very heavily with salvos of four 5·9's. We selected various gun positions, which we shall occupy when we go into action. It was very hot, and walking was most exhausting. By 3 p.m. we had seen all we wanted and started back. It was with a considerable sense of relief that I got back to the quiet part behind the line. We picked up an empty motor which brought us part of the way back to our horses. After a hot and dusty ride over the chalk downs, we got back to bivouac in time for tea.

Bois-des-Tailles, 6th August, 1916

Sunday. I did not get up till 10 o'clock. It is probably the last good night's rest we shall have for some time. Parade service in the wood this morning. I intend to have a really lazy day, and do nothing but write letters and sleep. I believe the Germans threw a lot of shells in this direction last night, but I slept much too well to know anything about it.

Bois-de-Tailles, 7th August, 1916

After lunch I took Radmore to see the German trenches. We rode to Fricourt and left our horses at the foot of the hill. The old German front line comes down the slope of the ridge on the south of the village, and then passes through Fricourt itself. The ground is so torn up by the terrific bombardment of the five days before the assault that it is very hard to make out what was front line and what was supports. We wandered about the trenches for three hours, eventually getting to the top of the hill, from where

we had a splendid view of the greater part of the battle-
field. To the north we could see Bazentin le Grand.
Mametz lay at our feet, a sad wreck—in fact, it was quite
difficult to make out the remains of the village; there is
not a wall 6 feet high in the whole place. In the distance
we could just see High Wood, where the 7th Dragoon
Guards and Deccan Horse did their charge. Montauban,
Bernafay, and Trônes Wood could be seen, whilst to the
south was Carnoy and Maricourt. Some of the dug-outs
were marvels of science and industry. One, which had
obviously been an officer's dug-out, was over thirty feet
deep; two flights of steps led down to it, the whole sides
and roof being timbered with 6 × 4 wood, and logged
together. On arrival at the bottom, we found ourselves
in a good-sized room, with a passage leading off to the left.
We had no electric torch with us, but made our way along
by striking matches. After about ten yards we found
another flight of steps leading upwards. Ten 9-in. steps
brought us to another little room, with a passage leading
out of it. This eventually landed us at the bottom of a
long flight of stairs ending in the trench we had descended
from, but some twenty yards from where we went down.
The air at the bottom was quite sweet, and it was delight-
fully cool and quite clean. There were several mine-shafts
which went down to incredible depths and led away
towards the old British trenches. The enemy had no
time to fire them, and they are still charged.

Bois-des-Tailles, 8th August, 1916

To-day has been a very hard day. We are now going
into a different position. The colonel and the battery
commanders went up to choose positions this afternoon.
We started at 1 o'clock, and rode 4 miles to Carnoy.
There we left our horses and walked. We had to go
4 miles, climbing in and out of German trenches and
scrambling over the millions of shell-holes. Eventually
we crossed the Caterpillar Valley, where there is a German
railway train completely smashed up. We found a little

valley near Longueval, which we selected. It is not a very nice place, as it is close to Delville Wood, which is shelled all the time. However, the whole area is badly shelled night and day, and one place is much the same as another. The cleaning-up parties had not finished their work so far up to the new front, and there were many signs of the battle lying about. Great quantities of abandoned equipment and a certain number of dead. B Battery had to begin by burying the men who were lying where they wanted to dig their gun-pits. As these wretched men had been lying in the sun for probably a month, it was a most unpleasant job. There were two abandoned guns lying there also with the dead gunners beside them. One poor devil was lying across the trail of a gun in two halves —head and shoulders in one piece and the rest of him the other side. Wilkins was as sick as if he had been on a Channel steamer. We had to wait there all the afternoon till our working parties arrived at 8 p.m. Bishop and Perry brought mine, having lost their way and wandered about all over the battle-field. We marked out everything and explained what was wanted and then we—the battery commanders—started to walk home. Soon after 8 we saw the S.O.S. signal go up from the trenches, and both our artillery and the Germans put up a terrific barrage. The whole front line for about a thousand yards was one continuous sheet of flame from the bursting shells. The wind was blowing towards us and the smoke and dust came back like an impenetrable fog. The noise was dreadful, and it really seemed as if the lid had come off the top of hell. We struggled back the 4 miles to our horses and reached them more dead than alive. The heat has been tropical, with a blazing sun, and no air in the bottom of the white chalk trenches. The dust lies a foot deep over everything, white or khaki according to the soil. I have seldom been so utterly exhausted, as we had had nothing to eat or drink all day. We called in at Divisional H.Q. on our way back, and asked the general for a drink. After he had filled us up with whisky and soda, he broke the news to us that the whole scheme has

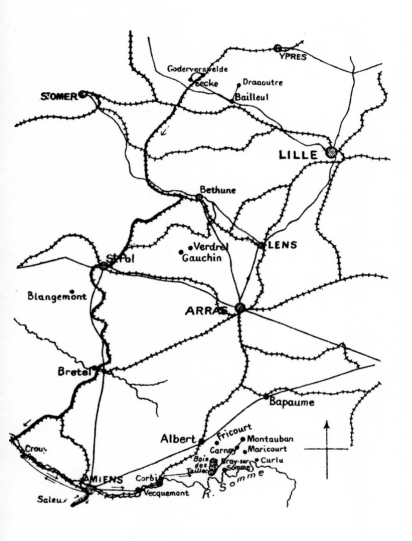

AMIENS – LILLE, AUG. 1916.

been changed and that we are not going into this position
after all. However, someone will no doubt benefit by our
labours later on. We got back to camp about 11 o'clock,
and went straight to bed, after arranging to send out
wagons at dawn to fetch in the working parties.

Bois-des-Tailles, 9th August, 1916

Harvey brought in the working parties about 10 o'clock.
They seem to have had a hard time. They were shelled
with 5·9's and shrapnel all night. I have lost the best
gun-layer in the battery—Gunner Clarke—who was hit
in four places by shrapnel. They got him away all right
to a dressing station. At 6 p.m. I got orders to reconnoitre a new place, and started off at once on another
of these pilgrimages. It was not such a long walk this
time, and it is a more or less made position, as there is a
battery in there now. We shall probably relieve them
to-morrow. It is not a place one would choose for a rest
cure, but it might be worse. The difficulty will be to get
the horses and guns up to the place, as there are so many
old trenches and shell-holes that it will be impossible to
get there by|night, and the German's balloons will see us
by day. However, just after dawn there is generally a
ground-mist. The smells here also are very trying.

Bois-des-Tailles, 10th August, 1916

We did not move up this morning, so I have had a good
sleep, not getting up till 9 o'clock. There was great excitement, as the King was seen motoring past on the road to
the front. I hope he won't go too far up, as they shell
the roads a long way back. I have just received orders
to go into action to-morrow morning at 8 a.m. (Later.)
This evening I took Radmore up to reconnoitre the route
and find the exact position. It might be worse.

German Trenches near Maricourt, 11th August, 1916

In action again. I started at 6 a.m. this morning from
my bivouac and brought two guns and four ammunition-
wagons into action, relieving a section of C/157 Brigade

(Major Parsons). The latter is a brother-in-law of Hugh O'Neil, and therefore a cousin by marriage. He has been able to do little to improve his battery position, which in any case is a bad one. We had quite a peaceful ride across the downs, but, as there was a thick white fog on, it was not easy to find my way. We entered the line at Carnoy and from there had to make our way over the trenches to our position. Fortunately they were not shelling that part of the battle-field at the moment. I found no preparations had been made for our arrival, and no officers about. We got the guns in at last, and the horses away. I started work at once on improving the place. The first thing that had to be done was to make " slits " for the men. These are very deep and extremely narrow trenches in which the men can take shelter during a bad shelling. I laid these out and also started improving the gun-pits. There was no place for the officers at all, as B Battery have taken over the former battery's mess. I have started digging out a deep hole which will be covered over so as to be at any rate shrapnel-proof. After lunch Parsons took Wilkins and me up to the front line to register the guns on their zero-line. It was by far the most ghastly thing I have done yet. We went up for about two miles across the open, having to pass through two 5·9 barrages on the way. At one time the shell-fire was so heavy that we had to lie flat in the open for twenty minutes. The big shells were bursting all around us, and our only chance was to keep flat on the ground out of flying splinters. The ground was dotted all over with dead, mostly in khaki. The cleaning-up people had not reached this part yet. The whole country is strewn thick with equipment of all sorts—rifles, belts, tin hats, bombs, etc. We eventually came to the front-line support trench, where the real horrors of the day began. This trench was packed with men, and was so narrow that it was impossible to pass one another. The infantry were mostly asleep on the floor of the trench, and we had to step over them. It took about twenty minutes to work our way along a hundred yards. They shelled us and the whole area all the time. The heat was terrific and the smells simply too awful for words. The only thing that I can at all compare it to was the rhino that G. and I shot just before leaving East Africa, and that was mild in comparison to this. The trench had been blown to pieces in many places and one had to climb out and run across the mounds of thrown-up earth. In many places the men who had been killed a week or ten days ago were lying in the bottom of the trench, and one had to walk and crawl over them. Many had been half buried by the shells, and only their faces or hands or feet could be seen. They had been trampled into the soft earth by the many reliefs who had passed along the trench since they were killed. Many of the bodies were not complete ; in one place a pair of legs were lying on a path and no signs of the rest. To add to the horror of it all, there were millions and millions of flies everywhere. As we climbed along over the heaps of corpses they rose in dense black clouds round us, with a hum like an aeroplane. I was nearly sick with the stench and sights. We reached a place at last from whence we could see Guillemont and Guinchy. Sergeant Meecham and Gunner Quayle, who had come up with us, had laid out a telephone-wire with extraordinary rapidity and coolness. To my surprise it proved not to have been cut, and we got communication with the battery at once. It did not take many shots to get the guns on their zero-line, but Wilkins and I had to wait for each other, and I have seldom if ever spent a worse half-hour. We were all crouching at the bottom of his horrible little trench, full of dead, and only 18 inches wide, whilst the shells from both sides were screaming over our heads in a continuous procession. Thousands of shells must have gone over us ; both sides were shelling the hostile front lines, and noise and dust made up as good an imitation of hell as anyone is likely to meet with this side of the grave. As soon as we had finished our registration we came away, and, after struggling back through the crowded trench, got back into the open and made for the battery. It seems nothing short of a miracle that the whole of our party got back safely.

TRENCHES NEAR MARICOURT, 12TH AUGUST, 1916

What a "12th"! Last night was very disturbed. I slept in the open trench, in a little burrow 3 feet deep under the parapet. Several times I had to climb out to take shelter in a deep slit, whilst the 5·9's burst all round. As far as shrapnel was concerned, I was fairly all right, as the bullets buried themselves in the back of the trench. Still, the noise of the shrapnel bursting a few feet over my head was enough to make it difficult to sleep. To-day I have spent in digging trenches and improving the position. The remainder of Parsons's battery took themselves off this morning, and my other two sub-sections came in. As I have one gun away at the workshops at present, it makes me one short. We have lost two battery commanders to-day, Montgomerie and Wilkins. The former was badly hit, and was taken away on a stretcher, and Wilkins, though not dangerously wounded, had fifty-five pieces of shell that drew blood. Harvey has taken over command of B Battery, and Hector succeeds to A. It is a great blow to me losing Harvey, as he was very valuable to me and ran my wagon-line. We have dug all day, and are beginning to get some protection. I am sinking a mine 20 feet under ground and with two entrances, so that I can have the telephone well protected and, if necessary, take most of the men down there in case of a heavy bombardment, just leaving the minimum necessary to work the guns. Before dinner I went over to another battery to call on their major. He is going to take me up to a good observation station to-morrow. I always hate walking about a strange battle-field without someone who knows the way.

TRENCHES NEAR MARICOURT, 13TH AUGUST, 1916

Perry and I started at 6 a.m. with the other battery's people and went to Waterlot Farm. We went past Bernafay Wood and then across the horrible Caterpillar Valley nearly to the place we originally started to dig a gun position. It was quite a good trench, and had not been badly shelled. It was a long way round, and we arrived very hot. Apparently the Hun has breakfast between 6 a.m. and 8 a.m., as he fires very few shells at that time. The farm is, of course, only a heap of ruins, and we did not know when we had reached it. The trench runs along the railway line, or what is left of it, and at the station were the remains of several engines ; they were practically unrecognisable and were merely masses of twisted and rusted iron. We found a battalion that we knew very well holding the line. The whole place is as usual one mass of crump-holes, and the trenches have been so knocked about that one is more or less exposed walking about there. However, the German snipers all seemed to be asleep and I was able to stand on the fire-step of the trench and look over the top with my glasses. After months of observation always through a periscope, it was a very great joy to be able to use one's field glasses. I had a glorious view of the area, as for once we are on a slight crest and look down on the Boche country. I had no telephone run out, and so was unable to register. Before starting I had arranged with Bishop that he should fire a few salvos at a certain time, in the hope that I should see them and note down any corrections required. As it happened this was practically impossible, as so many other batteries were firing at the same time that I could not definitely pick out my own shells. I was determined to go as far as the nearest point to Germany, and visited a bombing post in an old Hun trench. We walked up to a certain point, and then there is a barricade of sandbags blocking the trench. I looked through the sentry's periscope, and fifty yards off could see another barricade behind which were the Hun bombers. Quite near there was an overturned railway truck, under which I was told lived a German machine-gun. After we had seen all we wanted we started back by another way to that by which we had come. It is rather an interesting situation from a military point of view, as just to the south of the farm our line bends back at a right angle, and then bends again the other way. This brings Waterlot Farm actually behind the German trenches on the right. One has a fine view of Guillemont and Guinchy, as the one is on the immediate right and the other just across a narrow and shallow valley to the front. On our way back we passed through the notorious Trônes Wood, and there I had the intense pleasure of seeing a German 8-in. howitzer which had been captured. It had evidently had a direct hit from a 9·2 or 8-in. of ours, as it was lying half buried, upside down, and with its carriage on top of it—a very cheering sight, as I have not forgotten how the 8-in. howitzers smashed my battery to small pieces at Voormezeele last November. We also went through Bernafay and called on the Headquarters of the R.B., whose colonel gave us a cup of tea. I wanted it very badly, as by then we had tramped over six miles in the hot sun, and had nothing to eat or drink. The two tunnels are getting on well and are already some yards in from both ends. I hope they will join up in a couple of days.

Trenches near Maricourt, 14th August, 1916

We have had a very peaceful day, with only a few 5·9's and shrapnel near us. We have been digging hard and making ammunition dug-outs, etc. I have now got accommodation for about eight hundred rounds per gun. That ought to last quite a little time, even in a big battle, it is everything to have sufficient ammunition on the premises, not to have wagons and horses up while the battle is actually taking place.

Trenches near Maricourt, 15th August, 1916

No special excitement yesterday; we worked as hard as ever on the position, and as usual were shot at on and off all day and night. To-day I suddenly got orders to be prepared to fire on the quarry in front of Guillemont. Radmore, Harvey and I at once started for the trenches. The only moderately safe time to go up to the front is at 6 o'clock in the morning; however, as it was vitally important that we should have the place accurately registered, we had to go. After passing the Briqueterie we entered the 8-in. barrage, and for the next mile it was simply damnable. The great 8-in. shells were falling regularly every minute, and as they were searching and sweeping the whole valley side it was impossible to dodge them. There was a 5·9 and a field-gun firing on the same area. When we got half-way up we passed a deep support trench, in which we rested for a couple of minutes. We agreed that as the thing had to be done it was no good waiting, so decided to go on across the open, leaving Trônes Wood a little on our left. By the time we reached the sunken road, which runs past the south corner of the wood, we were through the barrage, and fortunately the front line was not being shelled much at the time. We found a place just behind our front line from which we had a splendid view of the Hun country. For once we are in a position to look down on to the enemy. The ruins of Guillemont lay just in front of us and across the shallow valley at a distance of 400 yards. The place we were at was so " unhealthy " and I had so short a time to finish my registration and get back to the guns, that I dispensed with the periscope and observed through my glasses over the parapet. As a matter of fact, I don't think the Bosch snipers spotted me, as very few rifle-bullets came over. The chief thing I had to do was to register the quarry, but I had great difficulty in locating it. There is nothing to be seen except a line of chalk, as the quarry itself is hidden by a slight fold in the ground. Whilst I was hunting for it, one of our 9·2 shells came over my head and burst with a terrific noise in the quarry; it was quite obvious that it was the place I was looking for, as one could see the smoke and dust rising out of the whole crater. It did not take me long to get my guns on to the right spot, and I had the satisfaction of seeing them go in one after another, throwing up dense clouds of dust and splinters of chalk. As soon as Harvey had finished his registration also, we packed up the telephones and made for home. I told the telephonists to abandon the wire if they were shelled. It is easier and cheaper to replace wire than one's experts! We ran the gauntlet of the 8-in. barrage successfully, and got back just in time to work out the time-tables for the shoot which began soon after we got back. To-day we did two short shoots, very intense while they lasted, but intending to mystify the Hun ; the infantry did not attack at all in front of us. The French on our right made a fine assault, and are said to have reached the village of Maurepas. Their organisation seems to be excellent ; they always seem to succeed in their attacks.

Trenches near Maricourt, 17th August, 1916

We have had another short bombardment of Guillemont and the country behind early this morning and again at midday. The Hun must wonder what it all means ; he will know in time, and I hope he will like it. He has taken to shelling us at uncertain times with field-guns, which is a nuisance if there are men about in the open, but quite harmless to those in the bottom of the deep slits. In the afternoon he also turned a 5·9 battery on to us, and put about a hundred shells in. Fortunately they were 40 to 50 yards to a flank, and so did no damage at all.

Trenches near Maricourt, 18th August, 1916

We have had a really big battle to-day. At midday, I got orders to be ready for anything that might happen and soon after got my written orders. The Corps are to attack Guillemont to-day and to-morrow and it is hoped to carry the whole place by 10 a.m. to-morrow. The programme of our bombardment is very complicated ; there are at least twenty phases in it. We are doing what is known as a " creeping barrage "—that is to say, we " lift " as the infantry advance. First there is a period of intense bombardment, hundreds and hundreds of field-guns firing at the rate of six shells a minute, with all the heavier guns firing in proportion. During this time our infantry leave their trenches and charge across " No

Man's Land " right up close to our barrage. They know they will lose some men from our fire, but they are prepared for that in order that we may keep down the German machine-guns till the last moment; after that we lift our shells 50 yards every minute till we reach the next barrage. After a time the whole process is repeated until the final objective is reached, when we cover them with a curtain of shrapnel for twelve hours or so, whilst they are digging trenches. The ball opened at about a quarter to five this afternoon. Up to that moment everything had been normal—that is to say, there was just the usual daily shelling by both sides. Exactly to the second hell broke loose, and thousands of guns went off at the same moment. Never have I heard anything like it, or could have imagined such noises possible. It is quite impossible to describe to people who have not experienced it. It actually hurt, and for a time I felt as if my head would burst. All talking was impossible, and the telephones were useless. After a time I retired to my telephone-pit, which we have dug 20 feet down into the solid chalk, and 30 feet in from the entrance. There matters were almost worse, the noises were not so violent, but the vibration was so great that at first I thought my heart was going to stop, from being so jolted. If one could imagine the vibration of the screw of a ship intensified a thousand-fold, it might give some idea of my sensations. Hour after hour it went on without a second's pause. Sometimes there seemed to be a comparative lull, and then immediately it was off again worse than ever. Now at midnight we are firing much slower, a shell every minute, but there are so many hundreds of batteries engaged that even that rate is one continuous roar. The men are very tired, and the layers nearly exhausted, although we have changed them as often as possible. My guns have already fired nearly a thousand rounds each and are red-hot. We have to keep swilling them out with our precious little stock of water. Every now and then I have to stop one gun to allow it to cool, meanwhile increasing the fire of the others. We are taking it in turns to be awake, dividing the night into

16

watches. I have now got more or less accustomed to the noise, and my head no longer hurts.

TRENCHES NEAR MARICOURT, 19TH AUGUST, 1916

At 3 in the morning I got a telephone message to say that the remainder of the programme was cancelled, and that I was to drop back to my normal four hundred rounds a day. Since the attack began we have not been much troubled by the Hun ; he has been busy in front. We have no news of what has happened, but fear that the attack has been held up.

(Later.) I hear that we have captured four hundred prisoners, Machine-gun House, Guillemont Station, and best of all the Quarry. Our losses are said to be very heavy, one battalion only having three officers left, but that was expected. Radmore has gone up to the front line as F.O.O. for the brigade. They have managed to get the telephone cable working again, and I have been able to check my registration. I was greatly relieved to find that I was only 25 yards off my target after all the switches and alterations yesterday. Now I have got an exact registration from a zero point in Guinchy, and can quite confidently fire on any new point off the map. The great difficulty is to keep the guns supplied with ammunition, and at the same time not to get the horses and drivers killed in coming up. During yesterday's bombardment I saw a great 5·9 shell burst right in the middle of a team of six horses, who were bringing up a wagon to a neighbouring battery ; it was a horrid sight. A German aeroplane was shot down by one of ours this morning and fell in flames in our lines. The officer who was F.O.O. yesterday had a wonderful view of the whole attack. He saw our men go across the open, falling fast from machine-gun fire and then reach the German trench. He says he could distinctly see them all fighting with the bayonet in the Hun trench. At the time they did not shoot much at our trenches, but I fancy they must have had a bad time later on.

Trenches near Maricourt, 20th August, 1916

This morning the colonel rang me up and asked me to go forward to the infantry brigade headquarters and find out exactly what the situation is at present. It is by no means clear how far we have penetrated into Guillemont ; at the same time we telephoned to Radmore to go right forward to the Quarry and see what he could see from there. I found General Mitford at the bottom of the 30-foot German dug-out. It must have been the headquarters of a German regiment, as it was a regular rabbit burrow, with any number of little rooms underground, all leading into a central passage. The atmosphere was very dreadful, as there does not seem to be any arrangement for letting air in. Radmore came back this afternoon ; he had a bad time last night. He says the trenches are full of dead and that they are lying all over the place. We have finished the tunnel and now they are making a room for the telephone and one leading off it, and nearly twenty feet underground. Last night they put a number of shrapnel over my trench. They seem to have a gun which is exactly on the officers' mess ; they put out my lamp four times in as many minutes with the blast of the shells ; after that I gave up writing as hopeless, and went to bed in my tunnel.

Trenches near Maricourt, 21st August, 1916

To-day the sun has come out again and things look more cheerful, but it is still distinctly chilly. On the whole of this great undulating plateau there is not a single green tree or blade of grass, nothing but yellow earth and white chalk. Trenches, both English and German, have been dug everywhere ; there is not a single acre for miles that has not got trenches in it. Another feature of the landscape is the miles and miles of tangled barbed wire everywhere. It is an open question whether it is quicker to walk in the trenches or across the so-called " open." This afternoon we are again attacking Guillemont, I hope with better luck than our previous attempt. This time, at any rate, we start in possession of the Quarries, which have always been so costly to us. The attack was launched at 4.30 p.m. and as usual every one of the thousands of guns concentrated here opened fire together. I am writing this now at 5 o'clock at the bottom of my tunnel beside the telephone. The noise is simply dreadful; it gives me the curious sensation of my heart being jolted about inside my body. The vibration down here is not unlike a fast train going over a badly laid line, only much worse. It is very difficult to use the telephone, as there is quite as much noise at the F.O.O.'s end as here. I have just had a message from him, so the line is not broken yet. My chief difficulty is to keep my nasty little tallow candle burning; it has been put out three times since I started this page. They have just begun putting shrapnel over us. So long as they don't send anything heavier we need not mind. The roofs of the gun-pits will keep out that much, and all the spare men are at the bottom of my 8-foot trenches. I shall have to give it up, as it is impossible to keep the candle burning, and matches are valuable.

TRENCHES NEAR MARICOURT, 22ND AUGUST, 1916

A disastrous day. Perry went to the Brigade O.P. this morning and had a job to get there. As usual he had to go through the 8-in. barrage to get there. Apparently he sent off two of his signallers to mend the telephone-wire; they left him at 12 o'clock; since then nothing has been heard of them. Moore and Quayle—the two men in question—were about my two best telephonists. All that has been found up there is Moore's water-bottle. I shall have to report them as " missing." They may have been wounded and made their way to the field dressing-station. As against that all inquiries at the field dressing-stations have been fruitless. The other possibility is that they may have been blown to pieces by an 8-in. shell. Another horrible possibility is that they may have taken shelter in a dug-out which has been blown in and buried them. If they are wounded they will write to us from England, meanwhile, nothing more can be done.

Trenches near Maricourt, 23rd August, 1916

Perry got back safely this afternoon. I never really expected to see him again, as the trenches near the Brigade O.P. have been strafed the whole time with every sort of heavy shell. He seems to have had a bad time. I am much distressed to hear that Hill, one of the company commanders of the N. Staffords, has been killed. We saw a great deal of him and his company at Dranoutre, and liked him very much.

Trenches near Maricourt, 24th August, 1916

On the whole a quiet day that we have spent in more digging. The position is getting like a rabbit-warren. There are slits 9 feet deep and roofed all over, connecting up not only the gun-pits but the ammunition stores, etc. I lost my way this morning and emerged into daylight in quite a different place to what I had expected. My own bedroom and the telephone room which are off the tunnel have been neatly lined with art green canvas and look really very comfortable. Sergeant Meecham and Bath, my servant, have made me a comfortable bed, 9 inches off the ground, out of a sheet of steel netting. I have sent in Bombardier Hibberd's name for "immediate reward" and hope he will get the Military Medal.

Trenches near Maricourt, 25th August, 1916

Yesterday evening there was another attack right and left of Guillemont. We have not heard the result, but I fear that we have not gained much ground. I fired an enormous number of rounds again, and hope they did some good. The colonel came round this morning and was much astonished at the amount of tunnelling and digging that had been done. I have got my No. 14 Periscope at last, after indenting for it for over a year. It is a beautiful instrument, and Bishop has taken it up to the trenches to-day for its baptism—of fire. I only hope that neither Bishop nor the periscope get broken. Yesterday B

Battery's F.O.O. was hit, and when they sent another officer to relieve him, he was hit too. Bad luck for B Battery to have three officers wounded in a week. D Battery also had an officer very badly wounded.

(10 p.m.) Three-quarters of an hour ago, my rocket guard rushed in and said that rockets were going up over our side of Trônes Wood. I at once opened with an intense rate of fire, and reported that the S.O.S. had gone. The Hun at the same time started on us with shrapnel. We had an alarm this afternoon that counter-attack was imminent, so I suppose this is it. We have been firing steadily ever since. I am at the bottom of my tunnel, sitting with the telephone to my ear. I can catch all the messages going through on the various lines. Our wire to the F.O.O. is cut as usual, but there are men out mending it ; I hope Bishop is all right, but I saw a large number of shells bursting in his direction.

TRENCHES NEAR MARICOURT, 26TH AUGUST, 1916

Fritz has taken a violent dislike to this place. He has sent over shrapnel at one-minute intervals for the last twenty-four hours. His bursts are quite good, and have swept this trench time after time. It is really miraculous that he has hit nothing. The men have been working on the pits and in the trenches round, and I have expected that someone would get caught all the time. They put a few shells near Brigade Headquarters this afternoon, and damaged two orderlies. This evening it has begun to rain and the white chalk dust has turned into a horrible sort of slippery vaseline ; it is almost impossible to keep one's feet. I have begun to put down " duck boards " to walk on. These boards are laid at the bottom of all trenches, and are like 6-foot ladders with square rungs, a couple of inches apart. The water runs away underneath them.

TRENCHES NEAR MARICOURT, 27TH AUGUST, 1916

To-day has been beastly, cold and wet, and the trenches are in a horrible condition. Last night I heard from the medical authorities that one of my missing signallers had been found. Moore is wounded in the face, leg, and arm, and is probably in England by now. Quayle, on the other hand, has never been heard of at all, and I am now afraid that he was blown to bits. Fritz started on us with 4·2's just as we had finished tea and burst several uncomfortably near. The mess dug-out was full of mud and smoke. I had to take all the men into the deep slits and tunnel for half an hour.

TRENCHES NEAR MARICOURT, 29TH AUGUST, 1916

Yesterday was an unfortunate day. I finished checking my zero-line and S.O.S. at 4 o'clock in the afternoon, when they started shelling us with 4·2's and shrapnel. It did not worry us in the least, as we think we have got good enough cover now to keep those out. But they shortly turned on a 5·9 battery. We all took cover in the slits and tunnels, and felt fairly safe. Suddenly there was a terrific roar and the whole place rocked, earth and timber came flying all over us. At the same time shrieks and yells for help started from down the slit, 8 or 4 yards on the left of where I was standing. I found that a heavy shell had burst in the trench and blown in the side of the slit, burying about six men. It was very difficult to work at digging them out, as the slit is only little more than a foot wide, and only one man can work at a time. I left Perry and Selwyn to try and get at the buried men on that side, and went through the tunnel and started a party to dig in from the other end of the slit. I was standing on the top of the stairs leading into the tunnel when there was another and much worse explosion down the trench some 10 yards off. I afterwards found that a 5·9 had landed in one of my ammunition pits and blown up 400-odd rounds of high-explosive shells. Something hit me an awful whack on the side of my steel helmet, and the blast of the explosion blew me down the stairs and right into the tunnel. The remaining events of the day are more or less a confused blur to me, as I was knocked quite silly by the concussion. As soon as the 5·9's had wrecked the place they put in some gas-shells, which got into the slit and made the men working there unconscious. I have a confused recollection of pulling a man out of the slit by his heels who had dropped down unconscious from the fumes, and I gather that soon afterwards I collapsed myself. I eventually found myself on my bed in the tunnel, with various people, including the doctor, giving me brandy. I had a violent pain in my head and felt ghastly ill. They got all the men out in just over three hours, and, strange to say, all were alive. Gunner Alexander, my clerk, is badly wounded in the head, shoulder, and arm, and about eight or nine more are suffering from the gas or shell shock. I have recommended Sergeant Meecham for immediate reward, as he appears to have behaved in a most gallant manner ; had it not been for him, the men would have died.

Trenches near Maricourt, 30th August, 1916

I feel fairly all right to-day, but a bit shaky ; the others who were gassed have gone to the wagon-lines, and I have not heard how they are. The colonel came round this morning and said that he watched the whole thing through his glasses. Our ammunition store seems to have gone up with a tremendous burst. To-day it is raining hard and the ground is in a dreadful state ; the trenches are beginning to fall in. The narrow passage leading into our mess dug-out is coming away in large lumps that fall flop into the pools of muddy water at the entrance. It is also very cold, and I have had to sit in our damp dug-out wrapped in my cloak. Probably owing to the wet the Hun has been very quiet during the day. After dinner we had two S.O.S. alarms, and all batteries round opened an intense fire. We can see the rockets quite well from here, and so get the news quicker than it can be sent round by 'phone.

Trenches near Maricourt, 31st August, 1916

It is exactly a year since the division sailed from Southampton. What a lot we have seen and done since

then ! Neuve Chapelle—Loos—Voormezeele—Ypres—
Kemmel, and now the Somme. I have been going through
my roll to see what the casualties in my battery have been ;
I find that it amounts to fifty-six in all. This number
cannot be considered excessive under the circumstances.
The infantry must have lost at least 100 per cent., some
battalions far more. Two of my guns are in hospital now ;
I am not surprised, considering the very heavy firing
they have done. At Dranoutre I fired 10,000 shells in three
months ; and if we stay here a little longer I shall equal that.
Perry was Brigade F.O.O. to-day and started for the O.P.
at midday ; at 3 o'clock he and Bombardier Carter were
brought back here in a state of collapse, they having been
caught in a gas-shell barrage in the middle of Bernafay
Wood. I sent Bishop up instead, and telephoned for the
doctor. I got them away in the mess-cart, after dark. I
hope they will be all right after a day or two's rest in the
wagon-lines. Radmore is coming up to-night ; in the
meanwhile I am the only officer left in the battery. The
Hun has been very active to-day, both in the air and with
his artillery. He has bombarded my poor little trench the
whole of the last twenty-four hours. He as near as possible
killed Bishop this morning with a shrapnel that missed his
head by a yard and burst in the trench. Yesterday we
had three S.O.S. alarms and have already had two to-day.
Personally I don't think either side could attack in the
present state of the ground. All the trenches are full of
water, and the rest of the ground, which consists of millions
of shell-holes, large and small, has now become a complete
series of little lakes.

TRENCHES NEAR MARICOURT, 1ST SEPTEMBER, 1916

A year ago this morning the battery landed at Havre.
Then, with about half a dozen exceptions, none of the
battery had seen a shot fired. Now they can all claim to
be veterans. I am the only officer left who came out with
the battery. An analysis of the battery casualties shows :
5 killed, 30 wounded (including gassed), 1 missing, and 20

sent down to the Base, sick. Radmore arrived here from
the wagon-lines at 10 o'clock last night, having had a
very exhausting walk from Carnoy, as he says that the
whole valley is under water, and that one sinks into the
slime up to the knees ; in addition, it was a pitch dark
night. He had hardly got here when Bath rushed into my
dug-out to say that there was gas in the trench. It was
quite true, and we at once roused up all the men and made
them put on their gas-helmets. The smell rapidly got
stronger, and my eyes and nose began to stream; it also
hurt my throat and chest. I ordered blankets to be
stretched across both entrances to the tunnel, and retired
to the telephone. Fortunately it was only the Lachryma-
tory Gas-shell, and not particularly dangerous. It was
very weird, as we could hear nothing but the whistle of the
shells. With these shells there is no explosion ; they just
break open on striking the ground and liberate the fluid,
which at once turns into gas. They must have fired thousands of shells, as one could hear them whistling about all
along the line, and they kept it up for two hours. What
good they expected to do I don't know, as there was no
infantry attack. The principal object of these shells is
to hinder our gunners from seeing through their sights
during an attack. The gas contains chloroform and makes
one very sleepy.

TRENCHES NEAR MARICOURT, 2ND SEPTEMBER, 1916

To-day we have carried out the preliminary bombardment for a general attack to-morrow. We have fired
intense bursts of about a dozen rounds at odd times all
day. Every one of the thousands of guns in the district
together. It is very impressive, comparative stillness and
then this sudden roar from everywhere, which stops as
suddenly as it begins. The idea is to make the Hun think
each time that the attack is coming. Some time or other
we shall " lift " without stopping, and then our infantry
will assault seriously. We have tried to get Guillemont
now half a dozen times, and each time been driven back

with very heavy losses. This time it will be done on a very large scale, as part of a big scheme to attack all along the line. I am increasing my ammunition with the guns to 800 rounds per gun to-night. We have had very few shells to-day, but, as usual, a lot of gas-shells at night.

TRENCHES NEAR MARICOURT, 3RD SEPTEMBER, 1916

Since yesterday evening we have isolated Guillemont with a curtain of fire, and at times have increased our rate to " intense." All the time our 15-in., 9·2's, and all the other heavy guns have been pouring their enormous shells on to the place. Both Guinchy and Guillemont have been invisible for smoke and dust for the last twenty-four hours. (Later.) Late this afternoon the great attack took place. The artillery opened a terrific fire and kept it up for four hours, " lifting " a few yards at frequent intervals. The latest news is excellent—Guillemont is ours, and our infantry have reached Leuze Wood, nearly a mile farther. Contrary to all expectations, the Hun made little resistance. He appears to have been over-whelmed by the heavy shells we have been pouring on to him. As we lifted our fire the infantry followed up close behind, within a hundred yards of our shells, and most of the garrison were trapped in the deep dug-outs. Large numbers were captured, and I have already seen several hundred pass here. Everyone is very pleased, as every-thing seems to have gone off like clockwork. We have just heard that the French have been equally successful, and gone forward a long way. No news from Guinchy yet, where the 7th Division are attacking. We are still keeping up our barrage.

TRENCHES NEAR MARICOURT, 4TH SEPTEMBER, 1916

Unfortunately it appears that we could not hold Guinchy and were bombed out of it early last night. However, we are still in the western edge of the village. The failure on our left placed our particular front in a dangerous posi-tion, so we withdrew from Leuze Wood, and dug in on the

Wedge Wood-Guinchy road, where they still are. This afternoon I believe another attempt was made to get Guinchy, but failed. There is a report that the remains of one of our battalions is surrounded, but still holding out in the village. Our expenditure of ammunition is terrific, but the German fire is slacking. It looks as if their guns were retiring. Our infantry have gone forward to the western edge of Leuze Wood again, and are consolidating there. I gather that, as Guinchy is not taken yet, the left of our infantry line is " in the air," and being prolonged by our barrage. A truly extraordinary situation.

TRENCHES NEAR MARICOURT, 5TH SEPTEMBER, 1916

At 5 a.m. this morning I got information that we are to be relieved at once, one section this morning and the other to-morrow. At 11 o'clock the new battery commander arrived, and looked round the place. It is C/76 Brigade of the Guards Division, the same people who followed us at Loos (Major Marryat). As a matter of fact they did not arrive till 1 o'clock, having been hung up by a French division on the road. He has left two subalterns with me in charge of his two guns. Soon after tea we got the S.O.S. and, in common with everybody round, opened an intense rate of fire. Soon after we got the order to lift 300 yards, and again and again, later. We are now firing almost at our extreme range of 6,200 yards. (Later.) Great news : The German is in full retreat and we and the French are in hot pursuit. Combles has fallen to the French, and we are out beyond Leuze Wood and looking down on to the promised land beyond. We are out of action now, as our infantry have passed beyond our extreme range. Three days ago I was firing at the Bosche at 8,200 ; now I cannot reach him with 6,200. It is the biggest advance by far since the 1st July. I am delighted we were in at the death, after so many attempts had been made to take Guillemont. Fresh guns are going forward now, to take up the fire. We have ceased firing for the first time for three days and nights, and have got rid of some five thousand shells in the time. I hear the French have captured a 4·2 battery and are still pursuing.

TRENCHES NEAR MARICOURT, 6TH SEPTEMBER, 1916

In the middle of the night I suddenly started the most violent toothache I have had for years. I suppose I have got a chill in my face. Five grains of aspirin produced a wonderful effect. I was rung up at 7 a.m. to be told that orders for the relief were cancelled and that the relieving brigade were not coming here, but going straight forward. We have to stay here till this afternoon to cover their advance. Fritz has woke up now, and is shelling all round here, just at the moment that I am expecting the teams. I shall be very thankful if we get the guns away without an accident. It is ridiculous to relieve batteries in broad daylight, with German aeroplanes over our heads.

BOIS-DES-TAILLES, 7TH SEPTEMBER, 1916

We got out of action all right, although they were shelling the valley we had to pass through. After a mile of wading through mud up to the axles we found the rest of the horses waiting for us near Carnoy. It was a great relief to climb up on to Hitchy-koo once more. It is just a month since I saw him. I came here via Bray, so as to keep on the hard road all the way. We are not in quite the same place as last time, but on a wooded slope in a small pine wood, quite a nice bivouac. The five-mile ride here was most amusing. We were on the main road that divides the French and British armies. They do not appear to have any road discipline at all. The motor-lorries race each other and dash past transport on the wrong side, etc. We had a great excitement when a convoy of immense motor-lorries came past at about thirty miles an hour. The French divide their wagons up into different convoys, each with a large picture of an animal. Whilst the monkey column was passing, the elephant column came up behind. The result was a race in which the lorries cut in and out of the traffic with a recklessness that took one's breath away. I expected to be knocked down any moment. They were ammunition wagons, both English and French. Blue French forage wagons with three horses abreast, Turcos and Senegambians, French cavalrymen and English gunners, all in a desperate hurry and all very cheerful, yelling to each other and generally driving at a gallop. It was just like a Derby Day.

BOIS-DES-TAILLES, 8TH SEPTEMBER, 1916

I have been suffering with violent toothache for some time, so to-day I took the opportunity of being out of action to go to the dentist. Gilmour—our brigade medical officer—came with me, to protect me from his brother doctors, whom I was afraid would try and send me sick. We rode to the Main Dressing Station, some three miles back, and there got into a motor ambulance taking wounded to Corbie. There we found a dentist attached to a Casualty Clearing Station. He found I had got a septic abscess in the tooth, so it was not surprising that it had hurt. We lunched with the doctors and, after buying some papers in Corbie, came back to camp the same way we had gone. (Later.) We have just heard the sad news that General Philpotts and Crippen, the Brigade Major, have both been killed this afternoon at Guillemont. He will be a great loss to the division, as he was a fine soldier and charming person to deal with.

BOIS-DES-TAILLES, 9TH SEPTEMBER, 1916

This morning practically all the officers of the Divisional Artillery rode over to the Citadel for the general's funeral. The two coffins were carried by sergeants of the various brigades, and covered with Union Jacks. They were buried side by side in an already enormous military cemetery there. It has been a lovely day, with hot sun. I have done absolutely nothing, and have given the men the day to clean themselves and their kit.

Bois-des-Tailles, 10th September, 1916

(Sunday.) I have let the men spend the day doing nothing. They will soon be working hard again. The news has just come that the Guards have taken Guinchy and the whole ridge beyond. But there is still a battalion of Huns between Guinchy and Leuze Wood. It looks as if they would be surrounded and cut off. We may go forward again any moment now. The flies are an awful nuisance, and my new fly-sprayer seems to have no effect on them.

Carnoy, 11th September, 1916

Brigade commanders and B.C.s rode forward this morning at 7 a.m. to reconnoitre the new position. We were told that we had to get to the Cemetery between Guillemont and Leuze Wood. We rode as far as the old position and then walked on. The Hun was very active and was putting up a very large barrage of 8-in. and 5·9 on the Maltz Horn Ridge. He had spotted one unfortunate battery and was giving it hell. We passed within a couple of hundred yards of it, and every thirty seconds an 8-in. shell landed right on the guns. Just as we were passing one big shell hit an ammunition store of high explosive, which blew up with a terrific explosion. After passing Arrow-head Copse we came under very little shell fire, but the sights and smells were worse than anything I have yet seen. I thought last time I was at this place that it was pretty terrible, but when we crossed No Man's Land beyond the thing was beyond description in writing. Of the hundreds of corpses lying everywhere, none were complete, but had all been blown to pieces. It was nothing but a collection of heads, legs, arms, etc. There is a German " strong point " here with wire round it, and there our men were lying in a row, just outside the wire. At one place there were thirty or forty of them in a perfect line, as though they had been dressed on parade, all with their heads towards the enemy. Evidently they had been mown down by machine-guns. As soon as we crossed the ridge at Arrow-head Copse we were exposed to view from

Guinchy Telegraph, and before long the German shrapnel began to burst quite uncomfortably close to our party. We spent some time examining the ground, and the colonel and I came to the conclusion that it would be quite impossible to get guns and ammunition through the chaos of shell-holes, and, moreover, as long as Square T.20 was held by the enemy it would be suicide to attempt it. We got back to our horses and arrived at Carnoy just as the brigade was marching in. The next difficulty was water. The Staff had brought up thousands of mounted troops to this place, but had not arranged for water, with the result that the existing water-troughs ran dry at once. My horses then had to go back to the Citadel—two miles in rear—where they again found no water left. Eventually they had to go to Fricourt, after marching about the country for four hours in search of water. All day we have been expecting to go up into action ; we have reported to the division that it is out of the question to get guns to the Cemetery at present, and have suggested that we go into action at the southern end of the Trônes Wood. It is raining hard now, and the ground is like vaseline.

CARNOY, 12TH SEPTEMBER, 1916

All to-day we have been waiting for orders to go forward, but can get nothing definite. I have had a wagon out all day collecting material for the new position. Our own division having gone away to rest, we are nobody's child, and neither the Guards nor 6th Division will help us ; however, we have managed to loot a certain amount of stuff from various dumps. This evening a new officer arrived for me, by name of Stewart ; he is a man of over thirty, and should be very useful ; he belongs to Beardmore, the great ship-building firm on the Clyde. We have only one small bell-tent for six officers to eat and sleep in, so we are none too comfortable. However, it will not be for very long.

CARNOY, 13TH SEPTEMBER, 1916

Late last night I got orders to again reconnoitre the Guillemont Cemetery, as we have positive orders that we must get there to-night at all costs. I took Stewart with me, and started at dawn. We rode up as far as Arrowhead Copse this time, and sent the horses away at once. We found that a rough track had been made over the ridge leading down into the valley at Wedge Wood ; we followed this for about a mile till we got to the valley behind Combles, and not far from the western side of Leuze Wood. Working up this valley we eventually reached the crossroads at the cemetery. There is nothing left of the roads at all, and as a matter of fact we passed the place without knowing we had reached the road. I did not feel at all happy about it, as I knew the situation had not been cleared up here. We have certainly got Guinchy and some part of Leuze Wood, but I had been told that the Germans were still holding out in shell-holes on our side of the Telegraph. We picked our way through the craters and eventually came on to a platoon of our infantry in a shallow trench. They gave me the pleasing news that we were within 400 yards of the Germans, and that they had not been cleared out of slope yet. This was soon confirmed by bullets which flew past my head, and which were evidently fired from quite near. However, as I had definite orders to select a battery position, I stuck some rifles in the ground by their bayonets to mark the places where the guns were to be. As I had quite made up my mind that it would be impossible to get horses from where the track ended at Angle Wood owing to the way the ground was torn up by our heavy shells, I decided to come back by Guillemont, and see if it would be possible to get through that way. We came on an old German trench where there were some men of the Suffolks with their colonel, who assured me that they had cleared the whole slope that morning. In view of my own knowledge and the fact that I had just been fired on at very close range, I was certain that he was wrong. We climbed in and out of the usual shell-holes and eventually reached the sunken road near the western side of Guillemont. The Staff may say what they like, but until tracks have been made it is not possible to get horses and guns through that country,

17

quite apart from the fact that it is close in front of the German machine-guns. It is all very well for the Staff to sit miles behind, with their map, and say " Go there." I wish they would come and show us how to do it. Eventually I chose a position near the village itself, which is close to a road that can be made passable for guns without an enormous amount of labour. During our morning's walk I had the good luck to find a German helmet with its brass spike and all complete. I have been looking for one of these since the beginning of the war. We found a motor lorry at Trônes Wood that was just ready to start, so we got a lift back as far as the Briqueterie, where we had sent our horses. On arrival in camp I reported to the colonel what I had seen, and strongly advised the brigade going into action in the Guillemont position. He went off to Headquarters and the general agreed to this. After lunch I sent Perry with a party of men to get places ready for the guns and to make a road up to the position. We are going up with the guns late to-night.

Guillemont, 14th September, 1916

Last night was a nightmare. We were due to start at midnight, but it suddenly began to pour with rain ; however, we got off punctually. The ground was like vaseline, and it was only with the greatest difficulty that we got the guns on to the main road. They had to go along the side of a little hill ; the guns started slipping sideways and skidded down, dragging the teams after them. Fortunately there was enough moon to see where we were going. I was told to go by the Maricourt road,- but, after being blocked for two hours without moving a yard, I realised that I had no chance of getting into action by daylight. We, therefore, turned off the main road and made our way to Montauban and thence via Trônes Wood to Guillemont. We arrived at 8 a.m., and found that Perry had mended the road sufficiently to get the guns into position, and had made four holes in the mud for emplacements. There was fearful confusion, as all three batteries arrived together with our forty wagons of ammunition. The track was too narrow to turn, and on each side were enormous shell-holes. The last vehicle was unloaded and got away just before the mist lifted enough for us to be visible to the enemy on the ridge two thousand yards in front. We worked all day and put up wire cages over the guns, made out of rabbit-netting, with pieces of sandbag and old German overcoats tied on here and there, to make them invisible from the air. I sent Radmore and Stewart to Guinchy to register the guns on zero, which I made Les Bœufs Church. They had a bad time in Guinchy, as the place was heavily shelled. They say the sights there are, if possible, worse than here. We have established our Officers' Mess in a hole in the mud, some 6 feet square and 5 feet deep, with a leaky tarpaulin stretched over it. The state of Guillemont is indescribable; no trace of a house is to be found, not even a brick that we could make into a platform to put under the wheels. As for the roads, one cannot trace them at all; nothing but an unbroken sea of shell craters, one touching another. I am beginning to realise how heavy the German losses must have been; there are hundreds and hundreds of dead all round, and, for every one that is lying on the surface, there must be a dozen or more buried under the debris. It is really most unpleasant, as, every time one puts a spade into the ground to dig a trench or gun platform, it turns up a leg, or hand, or head or something. One's sensibilities become quite blunted and one can no longer look on them as dead human beings, but simply as horrible, obscene things to be hastily covered over with a spadeful of earth and chloride of lime. It is a fortnight at least since they were killed, and except for the grey or khaki uniforms it is impossible to tell if they are English or Germans. Our own dead are still lying just as they fell; no attempt has been made yet to clear the battle-field. Thousands of rifles, bombs, bayonets, steel helmets, etc., etc., everywhere.

GUILLEMONT, 15TH SEPTEMBER, 1916

To-day there has been another great battle, which seems to have been nothing less than a victory for us. I cannot talk about the " tanks," as our new armoured caterpillars are called. These astounding machines arrived last night, and halted under cover of Trônes Wood. By dawn they had got into position in the front line. They are huge armoured forts, weighing over thirty tons. They have no wheels, but move like the caterpillar, on endless chains. They can go over any ground, however broken up. When they come to a bank they just rear up on end, get the front part on, and fall on their noses on the other side. They are the most alarming things imaginable and are so heavily armoured that they are impervious to rifle or machine-gun fire ; nothing but a direct hit from a gun can stop them. They are armed with light naval guns and also machine-guns. As soon as it was light enough to see at all our bombardment began along the whole front with tremendous violence. As it became lighter we could see four of the new monsters on t h Guinchy ridge just in front of us. When they advanced we could see them crawling towards the German trenches on the crest. They were rolling and pitching on the rough ground like ships at sea, but kept steadily on at about a mile an hour, till they reached the German parapet, hoisted themselves over and were lost to sight on the other side. Accounts vary very much so far, as to how they did, but I think on the whole they have been a great success. We could see our infantry attacking, line after line, especially the Guards on our left. They went forward in perfect order at a walk, breaking into a run when they got near the German .positions. The wounded began to come back very soon, hundreds of the slight cases, all very cheerful and bringing the news that we had taken the first line of trenches and gone on towards Morval. Soon after the prisoners began to come, all streaming past my battery. Several hundred passed in the first hour. They are no trouble, and one wounded man will act as escort to thirty unwounded Germans, who follow him like sheep. The usual order is the Englishman limping along in front, carrying his rifle and smoking a cigarette, and talking to a Hun, followed by the rest of the party, two

and two. An amusing story is told of one party
who lost their escort. After wandering about for some
time, the German sergeant halted his men, and, going
up to an English officer, saluted and said: "Which
way are the prisoners to go, sir?" I talked to a
lot of wounded Bavarians who had been in front of us;
they said that our fire had been terrible and that they
had been taken by surprise. Our barrage of shrapnel
crept across the country, lifting 50 yards every minute,
and the infantry followed 50 yards behind it. The result
was that the Germans who had had to take shelter
in their dug-outs and under their parapets looked up to
find our men standing over them. The Germans have put
up a wonderful fight. Prisoners tell that they have been
cut off from their friends for twelve days and had only
seven days' food with them. We have fired a tremendous
amount of ammunition: my own guns have fired off
three thousand shells to-day. (Later.) The attack on
our right and left was a great success, but our men were
held up by a machine-gun fort straight in front of us.
At midday I got a message to go at once to Headquarters
with a telephone. On arrival the colonel pointed out a
trench in front of which our men were lying in shell-holes.
They had failed to take it, and I was told to shell it at once.
I put a number of shells into it, and other batteries from
all round also switched on to it, including the 15-in. It
seemed impossible for anything to live there. We could
see our stretcher-bearers going out and picking up the
wounded, and all the time the Hun machine-guns were
firing on them. It was a very fine sight, and it is not often
in this war that one gets such a view of the fighting from
a battery position. The one thing that leaves me dumb
with astonishment is why the Hun did not shell my battery
for the last two days, as he held the sky-line and was
looking down on us all the time at 2,000 yards. One
of the officers of B Battery, who were 40 yards on the
right of my battery, was killed by a chance bullet that
hit him in the eye.

GUILLEMONT, 16TH SEPTEMBER, 1916

It rained all night and we were wet through, as we have
no gun-pits or mess. The tarpaulin we have put over our
hole in the ground leaks like a sieve, and the water dripped
through on our heads; the hole is also rapidly filling
with water. We have put in a layer of empty cartridge-
boxes, which has so far kept us above the level of the
water; to add to our misery, the sides of the hole are
caving in and large pieces of the wall fall into the water
with a flop. Every moment I expect some horrible part
of a corpse to be exposed and stink us out. The four of
us spent the night huddled up in the mud and water.
It was bitterly cold, with a chilling wind, and I expect we
shall all have pneumonia after it. This morning we have
taken the Quadrilateral, as the system of trenches just
in front is called; we put up a tremendous fire, and the
infantry got in without much loss. The Hun garrison
must have been badly shaken by yesterday's bombardment.
We took three officers and over a hundred prisoners there.
I talked to them when they came in, and they say they are
starving, having neither food nor water for five days.
Hindenburg sent them a special order that they must hold
on at all costs. They certainly did their best. The unwounded Huns were used to carry in both their own and
our wounded. I went to see the dressing-station, which
is just behind my guns. It was most interesting. The
wounded either walk or are carried on stretchers as far as
this advanced dressing-station. If the ground is good
enough the horsed ambulances go as near as they can
to the firing-line. On arrival at the advanced dressing-
station they are put in rows alongside the road, and the
doctors dress the wounds. There is a chaplain with them,
and if the case is hopeless the doctor gives the padre a
sign, and he gives the man the Last Sacraments. When
I passed I saw a priest, with the violet ribband round his
neck, over his khaki, ministering to a dying Irish Guards-
man. As soon as it was seen that yesterday's advance had
been a success a number of batteries came up, and, passing

us, dropped into action on the ridge in front. This afternoon they were heavily shelled by 5·9's and at times were hidden by smoke. They got a hit on an ammunition dump, which blew up with a' great bang and huge clouds of black smoke. There is so much German equipment lying about that I have been able to collect several nice souvenirs. A couple of helmets, one with a brass spike, and another with a dozen shrapnel holes in it. This I was interested in as it was lying just where my No. 8 gun was firing all the time we were bombarding Guillemont. I also got a couple of German steel helmets, which are much better than ours, as they protect the neck and back of the head ; a good rifle and several bayonets of different sorts, including one of the barbarous things with a saw on the back edge. I also picked up a complete anti-gas outfit, nearly new. I hope to get them safely home.

GUILLEMONT, 17TH SEPTEMBER, 1916

A fairly quiet day. Both sides are probably exhausted after the last few days' heavy fighting, and are doubtless replenishing ammunition of all sorts. A labour battalion has arrived here, to try and find the road and repair it. They have identified it as passing a couple of yards from our mess-hole. The only result of their digging, so far, has been to make life unbearable for us. The corpses are all right now, so long as you leave them alone, but this wretched road-making has dug up dozens of them, and the place is simply unbearable. We could hardly eat our lunch, as they found half a one just at our door. One of their captains is a Close, who lived at Kirklington in Oxfordshire ; he used to be in the Rifle Brigade. He came to lunch and gave me yesterday's paper, which is full of our exploits. We were warned to register by aeroplane, but as usual, after waiting several hours, we heard the plane had gone home. The sergeant-major (Skeat) has got his commission, and dined with us.

GUILLEMONT, 18TH SEPTEMBER, 1916

To-day we had another battle, and stormed the remaining part of the Quadrilateral ; the whole of the high ground is now in our hands. It has been raining hard, and the place is simply a water-logged bog, so slippery that it is impossible to keep one's feet. I don't know how we are going to keep up the ammunition supply. The roads are completely blocked with transport and no one seems to be attempting to regulate it. So far they have not seriously shelled us, but if they get on to our road with shrapnel, it will be very unpleasant. Two brigades of artillery passed us last night, and, as the road ends in nothing, of course they got into a hopeless mess, and dawn found them still struggling. To add to the confusion, four caterpillar tractors, with heavy guns, blundered into the place ; they at once fell into the ditch and there they are— I imagine till the weather is fine. Radmore did a very good reconnaissance this afternoon, and got up close to the Germans. They have no regular trench now, but are just lying out in crump-holes, with their machine-guns. I have lost one of my best linesmen—Samways—whom I have twice recommended for gallantry. He was hit in the head with a rifle-bullet. The bullet is still in his head, but he insisted on walking all the way back.

GUILLEMONT, 19TH SEPTEMBER, 1916

Still raining, and more beastly than ever. We have not fired to-day and they have sent over very little, but one 4·2 burst within 5 yards of Harvey without touching him. This evening it cleared up and there was a tremendous air battle. There were five German machines and about eight of ours. They circled round and round each other, up and down, firing their machine-guns all the time. Another of my guns is now out, so I have only two left. I am to hand them over to Harvey, and take the rest of my people back to the wagon-lines for a few days' rest. It will be a great thing to get clean.

CARNOY, 20TH SEPTEMBER, 1916

After a beastly night in my sopping wet cloak and blanket, I woke at 6 o'clock with a start. A shell had landed within 20 yards of me and the mud and pieces were falling all round. I lay there for some time to see what would happen, and in a minute or two another one came. It was most unpleasant, as we have absolutely no protection, and one place is as safe or dangerous as another. There was nothing to be done, so, after seeing that the men were down in their slits, I returned to my mud-hole and read the remains of a wet and muddy *Observer*, with my steel hat on. After all, the country is large and the chances are against a shell landing exactly on one's head. I now know what the infantry have to put up with in the hasty shelter trenches they occupy. At 11 o'clock I got a message from the colonel to hand over my two remaining guns to Harvey and, take the rest of my battery back to the wagon-lines for a few days' rest. We got back without much difficulty, although the road was being shelled intermittently by 4·2's. As our mess was on the move and no lunch available, we broke up and asked the various sections of the D.A.C. for a meal. Gilpin gave me an excellent lunch, for which I was duly grateful. We are a horrible sight, not having washed or shaved for four days, and being plastered from head to foot with mud. It is still bitterly cold with a sharp north-east wind, and, as we have only got one bell-tent for the five of us to eat, sleep, and bath in, it is not exactly luxury, even in the wagon-lines. But at any rate it is a great relief to have a few hours' rest from the continual anxiety of holding the line, and firing S.O.S. at all hours. Even here we get a certain amount of shelling. The Germans have got a long-range naval gun, probably on a railway, which shoots at our railway and wagon-lines here. It is not the least dangerous, and only amuses people, especially as most of the shells fail to explode in the soft ground. We have a 12-in. naval gun close here that makes a terrific noise every time it goes off; it literally shakes the earth and wakes one up with a start.

CARNOY, 21ST SEPTEMBER, 1916

A fine and almost warm day at last. I had a glorious hot bath in a shelter we have rigged up with a large sail

cloth that we have " acquired " in the night; what a
relief it is to be clean again! At 7 o'clock this evening I
got orders to report immediately to the Divisional Headquarters. Apparently there is a big battle to-morrow
morning, and the general wants me to do liaison with the
infantry general. I found General Sheppard (our new
C.R.A.) and Major Crozier, the new brigade major, just
starting dinner. I had an excellent dinner with them and
after a pleasant evening rode on to the Briqueterie, which
is the Headquarters of the 18th Infantry Brigade, which
we are supporting for the attack. I found the general
and his staff, and arranged to join him first thing to-
morrow morning. I had a beastly ride, as it was as dark
as pitch, and the road was absolutely packed with transport, mostly motor-lorries. I had to force my horse
through the crowd with an electric torch in my hand.
Fortunately they were not shelling the road at the time ;
they had just stopped when I got there and there was a good
deal of broken-down transport about. I got home to
camp before midnight and found my excellent officers
waiting for me with hot whisky-and-water.

CARNOY, 22ND SEPTEMBER, 1916

I was at the Briqueterie in good time but heard on
arrival that the battle has been postponed; so I have left
an officer to represent me there till active operations
begin. The roads are in a terrible state with all this rain
and shelling, and it takes fourteen hours to get our ammunition up to the guns and back. I am afraid if something
is not done soon all the horses will die of over-work. The
poor brutes are in a terrific state. I had sent away my
horses before I heard that the battle had been postponed,
so I had to walk back. I took Sergeant Meecham with me
and he insisted on taking me via Maricourt to see a monster
gun there. I told him I did not want to see the wretched
thing ; however, he insisted, and off we tramped 8 miles.
It very nearly was the end of us, as the enemy started
shelling the place with their long-range naval gun, and
dropped half a dozen within a hundred yards of us. Even-

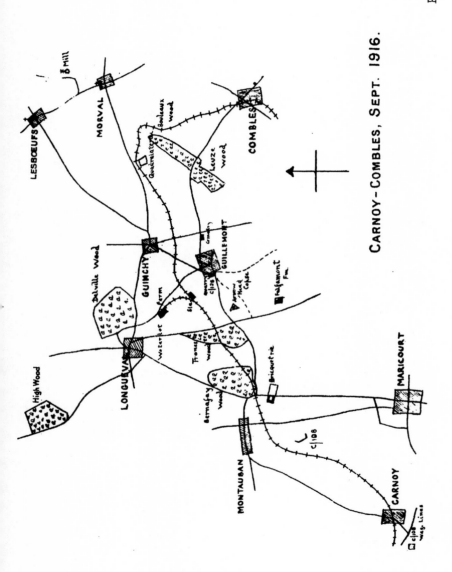

CARNOY-COMBLES, SEPT. 1916.

tually we got on to the main road and caught a bus, or, in other words, climbed on to the back of a motor-lorry. This got blocked on the road just where they were shelling, and several burst alongside us. It was very hot walking, and we decided to risk the shells rather than tramp along the rough road any more. Our lorry deposited us near our own camp, and we got back in time for tea.

CARNOY, 23RD SEPTEMBER, 1916

To-day has been beautifully warm without a breath of wind, and I have spent a gloriously idle day, doing absolutely nothing. In the evening Stewart and I walked over to the D.A.C., and called on Colonel Talbot to borrow some teams from him, to save our own horses, who are on their last legs. Our friend, the naval gun, had a few shots at us this evening; but, as usual, failed to get his shells to explode even. It is a great joy to have the gramophone again. I was delighted to hear, this evening, that my bombardier, Hibberd, has got the Military Medal. He earned it during the attack on Guillemont, where he was linesman and continuously mended the telephone-wires for hours at a time, under a terrific fire of heavy shells. Our wire ran across the German barrage, and was cut to pieces all day.

THE BRIQUETERIE, BERNAFAY WOOD, 24TH SEPTEMBER, 1916

A warm autumn day. I spent the day in camp, resting, as I shall get little sleep during the coming battle. After tea Perry and I rode up to the Briqueterie and arrived there without any adventures. The Hun is very quiet to-day, and we met no shells. I dined with General Bridgeford and his brigade major, who is a brother of the Master of Kinloss. During dinner we heard that four prisoners had been taken near Morval and I offered to examine them. I was given an old German dug-out to sleep in; it was quite 30 feet deep, and quite clean, with a rabbit-netting bed. The prisoners arrived about midnight, and were brought to me. I had a good deal of trouble getting any-

thing out of them, but was able to establish for certain
that there were two lines of trenches between us and
Morval and Les Bœufs. They belonged to the 240th
Regiment, and have been at Ypres for the last seventeen
months. They all agreed that this place is far worse than
Ypres, and seemed extremely glad to have been taken
prisoners. One fellow—a stretcher-bearer—who was a
well-educated man, was somewhat truculent and refused
to give any information. I was very anxious to find out
if they were digging a new line of trenches in rear, so asked
these prisoners. My truculent friend refused to tell me,
so I jeered at him and said that, now that we had got
through all their three lines, there was nothing more to
stop us till we got to the Meuse. He got very excited and
angry, and said we should be able to advance for another
15 kilometres and no more. When we got there we
should come on their newest line, which is very strong and
well wired. I thanked him for the information and wrote
it down. When he realised that he had given himself
away, he was perfectly furious. I handed them over to
the escort of military police at about 3 a.m., and lay down
in my boots and spurs, with just a blanket.

GUILLEMONT QUARRY, 25TH SEPTEMBER, 1916

I breakfasted with the general out-of-doors, the table
being a cable-reel. At 11 o'clock we walked forward to
Guillemont and found that they had made some quite
good dug-outs in the side of the Quarry, also most of the
corpses had been cleared away. Unfortunately, they had
not been able to get rid of the smell. The battle began at
12.30, and by then I had all my wires connected up, and
was in direct communication with my group and also
Divisional Artillery Headquarters. My job was to act as
" liaison officer " for the three brigades of field artillery
who were supporting the 18th Infantry Brigade. It was
most interesting being able to follow all the stages of the
fight. The day has been more successful than the most
sanguine had dared to hope. We gained our first objective
with hardly a casualty. For the first time the German

did not fight well. The moment our artillery barrage
lifted, and our infantry went forward, the enemy left their
trenches and came to meet our men with their hands
above their heads. Morval and Les Bœufs were taken
an hour later with little more trouble. It is really quite
extraordinary, as the places were very strong. The Hun
has carefully prepared them with deep trenches and
enormous dug-outs capable of holding a hundred men each.
We have taken hundreds of prisoners. Almost immediately after our attack was launched we saw them coming
back over the ridge, in whole companies. I am sure I
must have seen at least six hundred at one time. It looks
as if the Hun had had enough, and was refusing to fight
any more. Of course it is only an isolated instance, but
it is very encouraging ; it is the first time that the Germans
have surrendered to us in this wholesale manner. All
the afternoon we got messages to say that the attack
was successful all along the line. It is reported that the
French are advancing on our right, and that we have
joined hands with them behind Combles, which means
that the latter place is cut off, and will have to surrender.
I was kept very busy all the time, as the messages were
pouring in and had to be passed on at once. After we had
got our first objective patrols were sent out to the front ;
these advanced a further half-mile and reported that they
could find no Germans ; the aeroplanes also reported that
the enemy is retiring all along the line. We are in close
touch with the Guards on our left, and they are advancing
too. After dinner we had some of the prisoners in and I
examined them for the general. Most of them belong to
the 240th Regiment, and had been sixteen months at
Ypres. They say that this is far worse than anything
they had there, and that their losses have been terrible.
It is quite certain that no trenches can stand the sort of
bombardment we are doing now. We have hundreds of
guns concentrated on this small area, including the heaviest
of all. Nothing can stand up against it. The prisoners
all agreed that Germany has no hope of reaching Paris
and London now, but that we shall never get into Germany

either. They do not seem to realise that our great offensive is only just beginning, or that we are prepared to keep up the fighting for another two years or more, if necessary.

CARNOY, 26TH SEPTEMBER, 1916

They did their best for me, but it was not a very comfortable night. The general and I had stretchers, the others lay on the floor ; however, the Hun was very quiet and we were not disturbed. I got a message from the colonel after breakfast that there was no necessity for me to do liaison any more, and that I could go back to the wagon-lines. I went over to see him at his new Headquarters and found him in an underground palace—quite the best dug-out I have yet seen. It had a low concrete entrance with a flight of steps leading down some 20 feet ; at the bottom was an iron plate door, and inside a series of three or four rooms, very comfortably fitted up and the walls lined with canvas. There was another entrance leading out of a telephone-room. I got a lift on a motor-lorry that landed me at Carnoy, close to my wagon-lines. I was much struck, in passing through Montauban, by a life-sized statue of the B.V. Mary which had been rescued intact from the ruins of the church there. There is not a house or even a wall left standing in the place. This statue seems to have been the only thing unbroken in the whole village. The men who had been collecting bricks for mending the roads had made a pedestal of timber 6 feet high or so, and put the statue on it, facing the road. The effect was very strange, as the pale blue and pink of her robes were the only touch of colour in the whole wilderness. It is an extraordinary but undoubted fact that all over the country one sees crucifixes absolutely untouched standing in places where every other thing has been smashed out of all recognition. I hear that when dawn broke large numbers of Huns were seen in front of our lines, running about in the open and only waiting to be allowed to surrender. Our infantry could not resist treating them as running deer and shot at them, but orders have been sent to cease firing and let them come in. The

Hun seems to be completely demoralised and has made no attempt to counter-attack in front of us. I suggested to General Bridgeford that our guns might do a creeping barrage backwards for a change. I want them to put up a slow curtain of fire starting a thousand yards in front of our line and creeping slowly back to within a couple of hundreds of yards from our trench. If at the same time we put up standing flank barrages on each side, all the Huns who are in the net will be driven back on to our trench, and if the infantry refrain from firing we should get a good haul of prisoners. The general is rather taken with the idea, and I went to talk it over with the colonel before coming away. On arrival at Carnoy I heard the welcome news that Combles and Thiepval had both fallen, and a further large number of prisoners taken. It is said that we have taken ten thousand unwounded Germans in the last week. The latest is that the enemy is retiring and that the Guards are in full pursuit. If there is going to be a pursuit, I shall be sorry to miss it.

CARNOY, 27TH SEPTEMBER, 1916

A quiet, fine day in the wagon-lines. We are coming out of action at once and going to join our own division in a new area. The relieving batteries came in this morning and have camped alongside my wagon-lines. One of my sections has arrived this afternoon and the rest will follow to-morrow morning.

BOIS-DES-TAILLES, 28TH SEPTEMBER, 1916

We had a very nasty experience last night. Just before midnight a German aeroplane came over the wagon-lines, flying very low. As soon as the first bomb fell there was a general chorus of " Lights Out," and I have never seen an order obeyed quicker. We could hear the thing coming, and from the sound of the engine it was obvious that he was flying very low, probably only a few hundred feet up. He started dropping bombs half a mile away, and I realised at once that he was coming straight for us. The sound of the plane got louder and louder, then there was a tremendous explosion, 60 yards from where our tent was and right on my horse-lines. The next second another bomb fell less than a hundred yards behind me. I went over to the horses and was relieved to find that none of them had been hit. The bomb fell only a few yards from them and right in the middle of the relieving battery, who had nine horses killed. Two were dead when I got there and the others I shot, as they were hopelessly wounded. It was a horrible business shooting them in the dark, as there were hundreds of men and horses all round, and the wounded horses would not keep still. One can only make certain of killing them dead if one can get them to put their heads down, so that the bullet will be certain to go into the brain. In the end we had to tie their legs together and throw them. As soon as they were down it was easy enough for me to put my revolver to their heads and make a certainty of it, without danger of the bullet glancing off the skull. This morning I heard that the bomb that fell behind me killed fifty-one of the horses of another battery. These bombs are much worse than shells, as they do not go into the ground and all the pieces fly sideways. The Guards Artillery lost over a hundred horses at the same time. I got orders in the middle of the night to take the brigade, less the sections that are still in action, to this place. We marched off at 8.30, and, as there was the whole day before us and the roads were congested with motor traffic, I decided to go across country. Of course, I got into difficulties with the old trenches that are dug all over the place, and at last found myself stopped by a deep and wide trench that cut me off from the road that I wanted to get on to. It was a fine morning, and I had great fun in building a bridge out of material that was lying about. We got across safely and everyone enjoyed doing something a little different from the usual work. The whole brigade is camped on the edge of the large wood, and as we have no tents or huts this time, we have put up a shelter made of a large sail-cloth stretched between two trees. We have had a very cheerful evening, dining practically out-of-doors, and a gramophone concert. We have not been able to use the gramophone all this time, and it is a great pleasure to hear it, instead of the whine of shells.

TALMAS, 29TH SEPTEMBER, 1916

A very long and hard march. We must have done at least twenty-four miles. It rained the whole day, and the colonel tried to take a short cut, with the result that the provost-marshal of the corps turned us back. It would have been lovely country, as it was hilly and well wooded, but no one was in a mood to enjoy the scenery. Talmas is quite a small village, and, as the whole divisional artillery is here, we have not much room.

BRETEL, 30TH SEPTEMBER, 1916

A short march of eight miles, starting after lunch. There is no village here, only a few cottages. We have one small room for all of us, but it is only for one night.

BLANGERMONT, 1ST OCTOBER, 1916

(Sunday.) Another long march of about eighteen miles. The country is very hilly, and it is very hard on the horses, who are completely done up after their terrible time on the Somme. It was fine, and a pleasant march ; we are beyond the fighting area, and can no longer hear a gun. Except for the complete absence of able-bodied men, there is no sign of war. We are billeted in a clean house in a small village, and I have a real bed with sheets.

CAMBLAIN, CHATELAIN, 2ND OCTOBER, 1916

The colonel rode on to meet General Sheppard, so I brought the brigade along. It was pouring wet, and a horrid march. We passed through St. Pol, which is a quite uninteresting place. I halted for lunch on the open road, and we ate our sandwiches under the lee of a wet haystack. We have now reached the mining district, and the country is disfigured with coal byngs and tall chimneys. Our billet is in a small estaminet.

18

VERDREL, 3RD OCTOBER, 1916

To-day our A Battery was broken up, one section going to me and the other to Harvey. We have, therefore, now each got a six-gun battery. General Capper reviewed us on the road and was very complimentary. Birch's battery in the 109th Brigade having also been broken up, he has joined me as captain. I have now got seven officers.

CARENCY, 4TH OCTOBER, 1916

Into action again. I rode on ahead with Stewart and the men of the battery followed in G.S. wagons. We have exchanged guns, and I have had to take over six rubbishy old things that have been in these pits since the year One. The position itself is very good, being at the entrance to a little valley. I fire over the bottom of one of the spurs of the hill. The pits are very strong and well made, and the officers' mess is dug into the side of the hill. I think we shall be very comfortable. We relieved the 9th Divisional Artillery, who are going back to the dog fight for the second time. We are facing the famous Vimy Ridge here.

CARENCY, 5TH OCTOBER, 1916

My Observation Post is on a ridge about half a mile to a flank of the guns. It is a most uninteresting zone, as the Boche is on the top of the whole ridge and looks down on us. It is impossible to see anything behind his front line, and very little even of that, as there are so many mine craters that the trenches cannot be distinguished one from another. I managed with great difficulty to get the guns registered on a small mound that the Survey people have tabulated.

CARENCY, 6TH OCTOBER, 1916

General Sheppard came round and saw the place. Bishop has gone to an infantry course for ten days. I don't think it will be much use to him. After lunch I went up to the O.P. to try and register Fosse 6, which is a pit-head

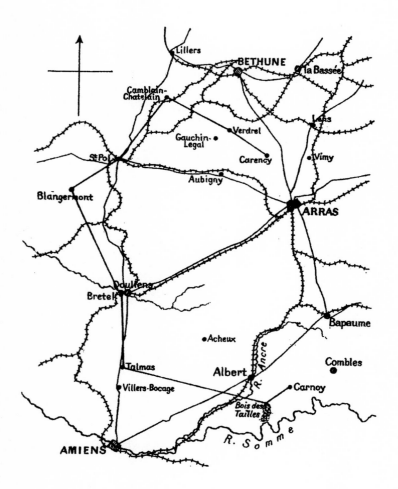

AMIENS – ARRAS, OCT. 1916.

away on my right. In the far distance one can see all the houses of Lievin and Lens. Loos is only just the other side of tne ridge of Notre Dame de Lorette, and not more than 5 miles off. It is just a year since we left there.

CARENCY, 7TH OCTOBER, 1916

(Sunday.) We have got a new battery of howitzers that has just arrived from England to join us. They are Territorials ; it seems a funny idea to put them into a Regular Brigade, but much sounder than having complete Territorial Brigades. None of them have been out in France before, and are very green. I hope they won't shoot our own trenches ; it would be quite easy to do so here.

CARENCY, 10TH OCTOBER, 1916

We are fast turning into vegetables. There is nothing to do, and neither side ever seems to shoot. The colonel has had to put off his leave, and has offered me the 12th. I jumped at it, and sent a wire to Grizel at once to expect me.

CAMBLAIN L'ABBÉ, 11TH OCTOBER, 1916

This afternoon I rode to my wagon-lines at a place eight miles from the guns. I found Birch had not got my letter, and consequently had not gone to the gun-lines. General Capper had heard that I am going on leave to-morrow and kindly invited me to dine with him at Divisional H.Q., sleep there, and motor to Boulogne with him to-morrow. We had a very pleasant dinner—the general and I had a heated argument on Wagner, which he considers vicious and depraved, whilst I think there is nothing like it. Most of the General Staff were there, including Bayford, 18th Hussars, and Pope, 17th Lancers, so we were quite a cavalry party.

1, ST. JAMES'S TERRACE, 12TH OCTOBER, 1916

Home once more, after just six months away. We started at 7.30 a.m., and did a fast non-stop run to

Boulogne, arriving there at 10.30. The boat sailed at 11, and I was in London by 4 o'clock.

BOULOGNE, 21ST OCTOBER, 1916

On completion of my leave, I have returned to France. The train left Charing Cross at 4.20, and as I arrived there by 4 o'clock I had expected to get a good seat. However, I was too late, and had to be content with a second-class carriage. The boat sailed from Folkestone in connection with the train, and we landed here at 9 p.m. As the only train up-country starts at 7 p.m. I shall have to wait till to-morrow evening. I have gone to the usual hotel near the station, and had quite a good dinner.

VILLERS-AU-BOIS, 23RD OCTOBER, 1916

I spent yesterday in Boulogne. It was very cold and I was very bored with nothing to do and no one to talk to. I went to the cinema and saw the War Office film of the Somme battles. It was really very good, as many of the films must have been taken in the front line. One saw our shells bursting in the German wire a hundred yards or so in front. It was really a good representation of the real thing, minus the noise. It was a curious feeling to be sitting on a comfortable chair in perfect safety and seeing 8-in. shells bursting a few yards off. After an early dinner I caught the train and travelled up-country with Cowan of the 107th Brigade, and young Smith who used to be in my battery. We had an old second-class carriage and were very cold. The journey seemed endless, and we only reached Béthune at 3 in the morning. I found my horses and trumpeter waiting for me ; also the mess-cart. After a cup of coffee at the hotel, I started in the pitch dark and arrived at my wagon-lines at 7.30, very cold. Perry gave me breakfast, and afterwards I inspected everything there. All the horses and men are now under cover. When I had finished I got fresh horses and rode up to Brigade Headquarters, which were in a wood some mile and a half behind the batteries. I found the colonel

there, who told me he was just off to Divisional Headquarters to take over the duties of C.R.A., as General
Sheppard went on leave this morning. Our Brigade
Headquarters are moving to-day and going to Villers-
au-Bois so as to be near the infantry brigadier, and also
as tents in a wood are more comfortable in summer than
in winter. I went on to lunch with my own battery, and
found them all very cheerful. Nothing exciting seems to
have happened whilst I have been away, except that
Carency has been once shelled. This is quite an event
for this quiet place. They put over three 4·2's as I
was riding up, but they were nowhere near me. I sent
my horses back to the wagon-lines and spent the afternoon with the battery. After tea I walked over to Villers-
au-Bois, about a mile in rear.

VILLERS-AU-BOIS, 24TH OCTOBER, 1916

Our new Headquarters are in a ruined cottage in this
village. The Pioneers have done their best to make the
place habitable and have really been quite successful.
At any rate, the roof seems to keep out the rain and we
have a good fireplace. There is no glass, so they have made
windows out of calico soaked in oil. Altogether, one
might be worse off. Colonel Spiller has taken over the
Group, consisting of the 107th and 108th Brigades, which
are commanded by Cowan and myself respectively.

VILLERS-AU-BOIS, 25TH OCTOBER, 1916

It is bitterly cold and wet. I have got a violent cold
in my head and chest, and feel very sorry for myself.
Fortunately there is nothing for me to go out for.

VILLERS-AU-BOIS, 27TH OCTOBER, 1916

My cold still very bad, but it is no good nursing it, so
I shall go out. Our division has been relieved and gone
to Loos, whilst they have been replaced here by Canadians.
The Canadian Artillery is still on the Somme and we shall
have to stay here till they relieve us—probably a fortnight.

Apparently we are going back to Grenay, to almost exactly the same positions we were in during the battle a year ago. We shall have covered a good deal of ground by then— St. Eloi, Ypres, Kemmel, and the Somme.

VILLERS-AU-BOIS, 28TH OCTOBER, 1916

I rode over to the batteries for lunch and saw the new pits they have been building. My battery is getting on very slowly and I have told them they must hurry up. After lunch Birch and I went up to the trenches to call on the battalion commander who holds our section of the line. It was most exhausting, as we had to go in communication trenches the whole way—some two miles. The Hun is on top of the ridge and can look down on us, so that one has to keep underground all the way. I found a very young Canadian major in command, who gave us a drink that we were glad of after our tiring walk. The duckboards were wet, and so slippery that it was difficult to keep one's feet, especially going up or down hill.

VILLERS-AU-BOIS, 29TH OCTOBER, 1916

My cold is very bad still, so I have not gone out. Hart came to tea. His battery is detached from the brigade and is close to Loos. He says it is a delightful place and quite quiet now. Since I have been away my battery has been changed from C to A. I am very angry about it, as we have made our name as " C " and got into the way of thinking of ourselves by that name. A was broken up to make the other two 18-pounder batteries up to 6 guns. Now we have got a new howitzer battery. They insist on calling it " C," and I have had to take the vacant letter, so that A and B may be 18-pounders and C and D howitzers.

VILLERS-AU-BOIS, 31ST OCTOBER, 1916

My cold is still very bad, and is on my chest, which makes me feel very wretched. It has been raining more or less ever since I came back from leave, but, as it cleared up after lunch, Spiller and I walked down to Carency to see how the new positions are getting on. Each battery has to make one position in case it was ever necessary to have reinforcing batteries here. I was not particularly pleased with any of them. We had evolved a very good sort of pit at Dranoutre and I cannot see why the batteries cannot copy them. I shall have to have some of them rebuilt. I found a very regrettable incident has happened in my battery. A telephonist on duty was caught asleep. I shall have to try him by court martial, and it is more than likely he will be shot. A warning came round only yesterday about this sort of offence. There is no distinction between a sentry asleep in his front line and a telephonist asleep at his instrument in a battery. It might cause a disaster if the guns did not get an S.O.S. immediately.

Villers-au-Bois, 1st November, 1916

Yet another wet day. I have stayed in all day except for a short walk down a muddy road in the afternoon. I understand Colonel Walthall is coming back here to-morrow.

Carency, 2nd November, 1916

I was very late for breakfast this morning, and just as I came into the room General Sheppard and the colonel arrived. The general wanted me to go on to the batteries with him, so I got no breakfast ! I hadn't the face to admit that I had only just got up. The general has brought his brother out with him for a week's visit. He is an admiral, lately commanding H.M.S. *Neptune.* The colonel has relieved me at Brigade Headquarters and I have returned to the battery.

Carency, 3rd November, 1916

My cold is a little better, and I do not feel quite such a worm. I have spent the day trying to straighten things out. It was very clear after lunch, so I decided to test my zero-line, which is laid out on a mound of earth on the sky-line, just over four thousand yards off. I have discovered a place not more than a hundred yards from the guns from which I can see as well as from the O.P. I had just finished the first four guns when they rang up to say the colonel had arrived, so I put off doing the other guns till to-morrow. I am much more comfortable here than at Headquarters, and we have the gramophone.

CARENCY, 4TH NOVEMBER, 1916

I finished testing the other guns this morning, and was glad to find there is not much the matter with their line. We have to fire on the German roads and communication trenches all night. It is a great nuisance to me, as my dug-out is 50 yards in front of the muzzles of the guns and the noise is horrid. We fired six times last night at intervals of about an hour, and I woke up each time. So many artillery officers have been lost on the Somme that they have taken away all our supernumerary officers: Selwyn has gone to the Lahore Division, Swain to take charge of a dump, and Stewart is going to trench mortars. It is very annoying when one has trained them.

CARENCY, 5TH NOVEMBER, 1916

(Sunday.) I rode over to Camblain l'Abbé to see the staff captain. I have to lecture to-morrow evening at Gauchin-Légal, and I am trying to borrow a motor to take me there. Soon after I got back here a cypher message arrived from Perry to ask for fire to be brought to bear on a certain point. Apparently the heavy trench mortars want us to cover them whilst they fire. It is blowing a hurricane to-day, and very cold.

CARENCY, 6TH NOVEMBER, 1916

Pouring wet and a high wind. I had to lecture to-day at the Artillery School on " Co-operation between Infantry and Artillery in Trench Warfare." I rode over to Divi-

sional H.Q., and had tea with the general and his brother
the admiral. They went to Guillemont yesterday for a
joy-ride, but said there was nothing much doing. I
borrowed the general's car to take me to Gauchin-Légal
and back here. The driver was a gentleman who owns
several cars of his own and who, not being medically fit
for the Flying Corps, has come out as a serjeant on the
Motor Transport. He has now been chauffeur to three
C.R.A.s of the 24th Division—Sir Godfrey Thomas, poor
General Philpotts, and General Sheppard.

VILLERS-AU-BOIS, 8TH NOVEMBER, 1916

The colonel went on leave this morning, so I have taken
over the brigade again. To-day I went to Loos to have a
look at the positions we are going to take over there.
I rode to Divisional H.Q. with Harvey and found an old
London omnibus waiting to take a party of us. It took
a little over an hour to get there. First I went to the
Headquarters of the brigade we are relieving and got a
guide. The adjutant of that brigade took me round and
showed me the various batteries in the Group. We went
through Les Brebis to Grenay and passed the old position
that my battery occupied during the great battle fourteen
months ago. I went into the little garden near my old
headquarters and found Colonel Butcher's grave. To
my relief, it has been very well looked after; someone
has put four cut stones at the corners of the grave and a
stone curb all round. The inscription on the cross also
was easily legible. When we get there I will have it
repainted. We passed Grenay Church where Colonel
Butcher was killed, and I very nearly was, and visited the
various batteries. Afterwards I went on to the O.P.s
and had a look at the German trenches some four hundred
yards in front. The O.P. I went to is next door to my old
one, but looks out to the left of the " Double Crassier."
I arrived back at the Brigade H.Q. very hot after my long
tramp in a waterproof. Parsons, from whom I took over
on the Somme, has just got command of this brigade. It
is rather funny taking over from |him again. The bus

picked us up soon after 8, and deposited us at our door in time for tea.

VILLERS-AU-BOIS, 9TH NOVEMBER, 1916

Colonel Spiller has again taken over the Group and come to live with us. I am feeling very ill with my old complaint, but hope to be able to stick it out. I have never got over those days and nights at Guillemont when I sat in the water in my horrible shell hole.

VILLERS-AU-BOIS, 10TH NOVEMBER, 1916

The general called here this morning and said that he was bringing General Mercer to see the 108th gun-pits this afternoon. I telephoned to all the batteries to have the place specially well cleaned up in honour of his visit, and to see that all his little foibles are carefully attended to. Every general has his own little likes and dislikes, and the careful officer who wants to get on makes a study of them.

VILLERS-AU-BOIS, 11TH NOVEMBER, 1916

I felt so bad to-day and have been in such pain that I have decided it is no good hanging on any longer. Last night the doctor had to give me morphia, which I hate. I went to see the general and found him very sympathetic. He quite agreed that I had better get operated on at once and get back as soon as I can. I shall, therefore, go to hospital to-morrow.

SECOND CANADIAN FIELD AMBULANCE, LES QUATRE VENTS, 12TH NOVEMBER, 1916

I went sick, after all, to-day. I am getting worse every day and the doctor says I must get operated on at once. After lunch I rode to the nearest field ambulance at Grand Servins, taking Bath and my kit in the mess-cart. They would not take me in there, but sent me on two miles by motor ambulance. This hospital consists of a collection of wooden huts, one of which is an officers' ward. There

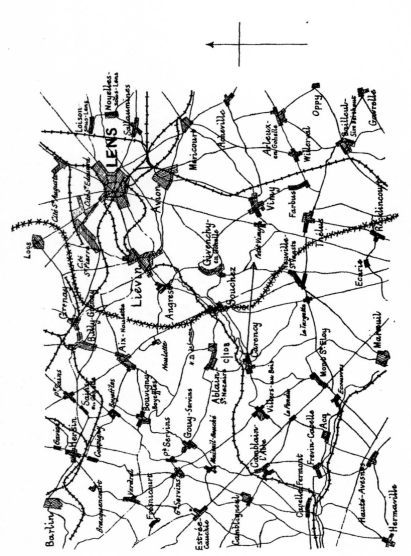

WEST & SOUTH OF LENS, NOV. 1916.

are four Canadian officers in here—mostly with rheumatism or influenza. I have got to stay here to-night and then get passed on down the line to the Casualty Clearing Station. The food here is very primitive, but all that one really requires. I am going to be very bored.

ETAPLES, NO. 20 GENERAL HOSPITAL, 14TH NOVEMBER, 1916

I left the Canadian Field Ambulance after lunch yesterday, and motored in an ambulance to the clearing station at Bruay. This is near Nœux-les-Mines, where my wagon-lines were during the battle of Loos. I was examined on arrival, and told that I should have to go on to the Base. They have only one train a week when there is no fighting going on in our part of the line. It happened to be the day for the train, but the medical officers said it was too late for me to go by it as my name had not gone in. However, I made a great fuss, and got off all right. We started at 6 p.m., and had a comfortable but slow journey to the coast. It was a new hospital train, well fitted up for 600 wounded. We had a number of Germans on board, to whom I talked. There were two German field artillery telephonists, who gave me a lot of interesting technical information. We arrived at Etaples at 3 a.m., and were driven to No. 20 General Hospital. I had hoped that it would be in a comfortable hotel, but instead it is a collection of draughty tents among the sand-hills. I have seldom been so cold, as all the tent doors were open and a bitter wind swept through. I had a hot bath immediately on arrival, but had to go out into the open to get to the bath hut.

ETAPLES, 14TH NOVEMBER, 1916—9 P.M.

I have been examined again and, to my disgust, I find that they refuse to operate here, and insist on sending me to England. It is a great nuisance, as I shall be evacuated from the 24th Division and may be sent anywhere when I am well again. They don't know when the next boat goes, but say we must be prepared to start at any minute.

7, MANDEVILLE PLACE, LONDON, W., 15TH NOVEMBER, 1916

I was woken up at 3 a.m. and told to dress quickly, as we were to start at once. It was horribly cold, and we had to wait in a tent for an hour. The train started about 6 o'clock, but did not reach Calais till after 11. We went straight on board the hospital ship and got to Dover at 8 o'clock. I made friends with the Medical Landing Officer, and got him to send me to London instead of to Manchester, like the rest of the officers who came over with me. We waited at Dover till 6 o'clock before starting, eventually getting to Charing Cross at 9 p.m. I was driven straight to this nursing-home.

1, ST. JAMES'S TERRACE, 15TH DECEMBER, 1916

I was discharged from hospital to-day, and have been given six weeks' sick leave. I was operated on by Mr. Fedden, of St. George's Hospital, on the 22nd of last month, and have been flat on my back for three weeks. I am all right now, but so weak that I can hardly stand. I shall be quite glad of a rest in my own house. The next thing will be to try and get back to the 24th Division as soon as I am fit again. Anyway, I get Christmas at home.

S.S. " FRANCE," 30th APRIL, 1917

Off again at last. After weeks of delays waiting for medical boards, etc., I at last got my orders to return to France. I left London at noon to-day and embarked on this boat in the evening. We sailed at 9 p.m. with a half-moon and a dead calm sea, so we have quite a good chance of being submarined. I have got my life-belt beside me and carry it about everywhere I go. This is a very fast little turbine boat of under a thousand tons, which is supposed to go too fast for the submarine to have much chance of hitting her. We are all reinforcements and drafts, mostly gunners. There is no accommodation for officers, so we have to sleep on the floor of the hold. It is not worth unrolling my bedding as I have no servant with me. There is a doctor on board who was on the hospital ship that was sunk a few days ago. It sounds very unpleasant, although he was not actually in the water, having been taken off by a destroyer that arrived in time. Southampton must have made a fortune out of the war, judging by the prices they charge—*3s.* for a cab from station to the boat, about four hundred yards, etc., etc. Having a vivid remembrance of the last time I crossed from Southampton, I took care to buy a supply of chocolate. However, we can get food of a sort on board, so are not hungry. If we are lucky, we ought to reach Havre by daybreak, and shall then have to get orders from the R.F.A. depot.

HOTEL CONTINENTAL, HAVRE, 1ST MAY, 1917

We arrived just before sunrise this morning, and berthed in the outer harbour. I landed at 8 o'clock and was told to find my way to the R.H. and R.F.A. depot at Harfleur. Things are well organised here now, and there was a party to unload the officers' kits and a motor-lorry to take them out to the camp. We walked into the town and got a train which landed us at the camp in about an hour. The R.F.A. depot is an enormous place, with over eight thousand men waiting to be sent up-country as required. I have had a real stroke of luck, as the Depot Adjutant turns out to be the late Quartermaster-Serjeant of F Battery, and who was a member of my Masonic Lodge at Sialkot. I asked if it was possible for me to send a telegram to General Sheppard to tell him I had arrived, but was informed that no one was allowed to send private telegrams. However, my friend arranged matters somehow and the wire has gone. There is no accommodation in the camp for field officers, and they are allowed to live in the town. After we had been issued with gas-helmets, steel hats, identity discs, etc., another major and I started back for Havre. We lunched at a little local hotel near camp, and had an excellent and very cheap feed with a bottle of red wine— just the sort of place one stops at when motoring. Our luggage was sent back to Havre in the evening. We have

to telephone twice a day to the depot to ask if any orders
have come. It is extraordinary that an important place
like Havre should have no hotels of the first class. There
are nothing but the most wretched places, and they charge
one rather more than the Ritz. Freddy Lister is in this
hotel; apparently he has been waiting over a week. Havre
is a very uninteresting place; good shops, but nothing of
interest to see. I would rather have stayed at Rouen,
where one can spend days seeing the old cathedral. I
dined alone at the hotel, and then had a " bock " outside
the principal café. It seems funny to be sitting out-of-
doors at night without an overcoat, after the bitter cold
of ten days ago at Leeds. I must find out how one sends
letters home; one cannot use the French post office.

HAVRE, 2ND MAY, 1917

I rang up the camp both morning and afternoon, but
there were no orders for me yet. The submarines have
been very active. An English destroyer and a large
Norwegian cargo boat were sunk this morning, just outside the harbour. I am afraid there was much loss of life,
as they say only five men were picked up from the destroyer.
I did not see it, but understand she was torpedoed quite
close to the entrance of the harbour this afternoon. Caddick and I went for a walk round the docks. It was very
interesting, as we saw ships of all sorts being unloaded.
German prisoners were doing most of the work. We also
saw a French submarine being built. We dined at the
Tortoni Restaurant, which is not as good as our own hotel.
We were discussing problems of gunnery before going to
bed, when suddenly all the electric lights went out. We
went downstairs to see what had happened and found
that there was an alarm on. All the lights in the town
were out, and men running along the streets putting out
the gas as well. Presently the French bugles began
sounding the " Alerte," shortly followed by the " Garde
à vous." We waited some time watching the search-
lights playing all over the sky. About 11.80 there were
four heavy explosions, which sounded as if they were about

three miles off. Ten minutes later a gun in the fort near our hotel started firing, so we thought it as well to go inside the house. Even though there were no bombs about, it is always as well to be under cover, in case of splinters from the shells of our own guns. By midnight all was quiet, and the electric light came on again. I suppose we shall hear to-morrow what the excitement was about. A large red motor has just dashed along the street, with a bugler sounding a new call—probably meaning that it is all over—whatever it was.

HAVRE, 3RD MAY, 1917

Another glorious hot day. I have not been able to find out yet what last night's excitement was about. There is a rumour that there was a Zeppelin raid on Rouen. I went to the English Officers' Club this morning, to see what it is like. The first person I saw was Dr. Mitchell, who looks after G. in London. He had landed this morning and was much depressed at the way he had been treated on the voyage. Although a Harley Street specialist, he has only been commissioned as a subaltern in the R.A.M.C. Apparently he also had to sleep on the floor last night, and is quite indignant. I have still not got any orders yet as to my destination. Caddick and I spent the morning under the trees in the public gardens, reading the English papers. Mitchell lunched with me at Tortoni's, and we are dining with him this evening.

HAVRE, 4TH MAY, 1917

No more excitements. Someone said that there was a Zeppelin raid on Rouen the night before last. It is very hot, and I have done absolutely nothing all day. This is the most expensive place I ever met. Everything is at famine prices. I got some food and a spirit-lamp for the journey up-country. I gather that it may take several days, and I don't suppose we shall stop at a station. These troop-trains usually halt half-way between two places.

HAVRE, 5TH MAY, 1917

Caddick came into my room whilst I was dressing and said that the camp had telephoned that we are to start to-night; and that I am posted-back to the 108th Brigade. Someone must have been working the strings. I wonder if I shall get my old battery again. We start at 10 p.m. to-night in a troop-train, and have arranged for a taxi to take us to the station (4 miles).

ROUEN, 6TH MAY, 1917

We got off last night in a troop-train with some thousand men, who were reinforcements for all the divisions. We were five in the carriages, which are meant for four, so it was not very comfortable. I managed to get about an hour's sleep sitting up. We arrived at Rouen at 7.30 a.m., and had a dreadful time with the luggage. Of course I had to look after it myself. There are no porters, but I managed to get a couple of men to help and we piled it up under a shed. The small things we put into a store near the gate. Even so, Caddick has lost his haversack. After having been so crowded last night, we were determined to do all we could to get a compartment to ourselves this time. We got to the station long before the train started and " arranged " matters with the corporal who was chalking the names on the doors. As soon as we arrived at Rouen in the morning we had gone to the Hôtel d'Angleterre and washed and had breakfast. After that we had to go back to the station and report to the R.T.O. and find out when our train started again. We were told we must be at the station by 3 p.m., so, it being Sunday, we thought we would go to the service at the Cathedral. It is a magnificent old building, and we spent a long time examining it. We got quite a good lunch at the hotel, and did ourselves well, as it may be a long time before we get another meal. As we had no servants, we had to do everything for ourselves, including cooking. We bought two Etnas at Havre and managed to boil a plum-pudding and make tea on the floor of the carriage.

I managed to cut my thumb down to the bone in opening
a tin of bully beef. Fortunately Caddick is a doctor, and
he was able to tie me up at once.

Fouquière, 7th May, 1917

As we were only two in the carriage last night, we
managed to lie down and get a fairly good night. At
7 o'clock in the morning we found ourselves in a siding at
Etaples, where we stayed for an hour. We took the opportunity of the train being still to shave and cook our breakfast. In the course of the day we meandered on, passing
through Marles, where I was when the 24th Division first
landed, St. Pol, etc., and reached Béthune at 4 p.m. There
I got out, extracted my kit with great difficulty, and found
out where the 108th Brigade were. The R.T.O. said they
were in action at Grenay, where I had left them, so I rang
up the I Corps and asked if they could arrange to send a
car for me. I was told that the brigade was resting at
Fouquière, only two miles south-west of Béthune. I
waited about the station for some time, till I saw a likely-
looking motor, whose driver I bribed to take me and my
kit out. We found the place all right and I introduced
myself to Colonel Drake, who has succeeded Colonel Walthall in the command of the brigade. They have got a
splendid billet in a large house, where they spend the time
playing tennis with three young ladies who own the place.
Gilmour took me round to my old battery, where I found
Perry and Bishop still there. The battery is now commanded by a major called Denniss. He has only just
come out to France for the first time, so cannot know very
much about the job. I dined with them and went on
to a Sergeants' Concert. I had a most touching reception
on coming into the room. All my old sergeants insisted
on shaking hands and singing. I did not get away till
1 a.m., when Perry, in a state of great excitement, insisted
on driving me back to Brigade Headquarters in a
victoria.

19

Fouquière, 8th May, 1917

The brigade major from I Corps came over this morning and said that I was to remain here attached to Brigade Headquarters till there was a vacancy for me. I do not know whether they mean to give me another battery or a brigade. I shall try and get in touch with General Sheppard again. This morning I went down to the hospital to get my thumb dressed, and Gilmour insisted on giving me an injection of anti-tetanic serum. As he had a very blunt needle, it was distinctly painful. Fortunately this inoculation, unlike the para-typhoid one, does not make one feel at all ill. Bath came to Headquarters this afternoon, and we sorted out my kit, and made up a set of saddlery. The advance parties went up to Loos to-day and part of the batteries go into action to-morrow.

Fouquière, 9th May, 1917

A glorious day, sunny and quite hot. Last night there was a heavy bombardment about midnight, which seemed to be in the direction of Vimy. At 10 o'clock orders came from the corps, cancelling our move and ordering us to be ready at a moment's notice to go to some new place. It sounds as if we were going into the moving battle farther south. I think I should prefer it, as I have a horror of Loos, and the moving battle is much more interesting. Gilmour fitted me with a box respirator; it is a horrid thing that one has to carry on one's chest; but they are said to be much better than the old flannel bags that went over the head. We still have to carry one of the latter in addition. I am having great difficulty in getting Hitchy-Koo out of Radmore; he has no right to him at Corps Headquarters, as he always was a 108th Brigade Horse.

Fouquière, 10th May, 1917

Very hot and sultry. The Germans have bombarded Nœuz-les-Mines again to-day. Colonel Drake was over there at the time. I also heard a good many shells dropping in Béthune this evening. The Hun has brought up some long-range heavy guns that reach far back behind our lines. They do not do much damage, but are very irritating to people billeted in the back areas. No letters from home yet, which I cannot understand, as I wrote from Havre and told them where I was going. Colonel Walthall has been made a general and posted as C.R.A. 34th Division; he passed here yesterday on his way south, but unfortunately I missed him, as I was at the hospital at the time, having my hand dressed. He told Colonel Drake that he had recommended me for the command of a brigade, so I hope to get one eventually. Meanwhile, I am very bored with nothing to do, and expect to get a battery in this brigade. I went to see the new C Battery yesterday, which is the one I am most likely to get, as their major is at Boulogne in hospital. I was not very much taken with them, but doubtless they could be worked up with a little time and trouble.

FOUQUIÈRE, 11TH MAY, 1917

We are still sitting here waiting to move to an unknown destination at a moment's notice. It is an indescribable comfort to have got Bath back; he knows my ways and can always find anything I want at a moment's notice.

(Later.) We have just heard that we are to stay on here for the present, which is a relief, as it is so pleasant here that one does not want to leave. The brigade has been continually in action since January 1916, when we went to Ypres, so a rest is doing them all the good in the world. This afternoon I rode over to Gonnehem, a village some 5 miles from here to the Army Remount Depot, to try and get a charger. They had nothing at all, but promised to let me know if anything came up from the Base soon. It was very hot and dusty, and as it is the first time I have been on a horse for six months, I was distinctly tired by the end of it. Gilmour and I dined with Harvey at B Battery and had an excellent dinner; we sat out in his garden, smoking and talking till after midnight.

Fouquière, 12th May, 1917

I woke at 7 o'clock this morning to find the Huns having shots at us, with a long-range naval gun. It was a very high velocity gun, as the shells arrived at a tremendous pace. He only fired about a dozen rounds, none of which fell within 500 yards of us, and all except one were " duds." I suppose it amused him and did not hurt us. After breakfast a Hun plane came over and gave the anti-aircraft guns a little fun ; needless to say, they did not hit him. I am trying to borrow a car from the Corps to chase General Sheppard half across France. The 24th Division has left this area, and I am very anxious to see him to try and get him to apply to General Headquarters for me to get a brigade. Walthall says he recommended me before I went home, but I am afraid that is not much use, as it is so long ago. I expect we shall have a thunderstorm to-night ; the air is as heavy as lead.

At 5.30 p.m. this afternoon the brigade staff and all battery staffs went out to do a little scheme. It was a distinctly humorous situation if one thinks of it. There were we having a field day, like in England, and all the time we are well within range of the German guns. Hart, who commands D, our howitzer battery, came to tea. He is a major now, as he has got six guns. He is still in action near Loos, and seems to have had a pretty disagreeable time there.

Fouquière, 13th May, 1917

(Sunday.) We had a brigade inspection this morning at 7.30. All the three 18-pounder batteries. It took over two hours to go round them all, and inspect their harness ; I was not much impressed by any of them. Harvey's battery was much the best. I cannot help thinking that my poor old battery has gone down very much. They were nothing like so well turned out as they used to be. My arm that was inoculated has swollen up like a leg, and is very painful. Gilmour thinks that I must have been bitten by something on top of the anti-tetanic injection. This evening all the battery commanders came to tea, and discussed the best way to carry various extra things on the march. My arm is more swollen than ever, and I am convinced that it is poisoned.

FOUQUIÈRE, 14TH MAY, 1917

In the middle of the night we woke up to hear a tremendous crash. At first I thought it was a bomb, but soon realised that it was only a thunder-clap. It is again very sultry to-day.

BRANDHOEK, 16TH MAY, 1917

Just before midnight last night, a telegram came from General Headquarters ordering me to report to 24th Division at once. I sent Michelmore into Béthune before breakfast to find out from the R.T.O. when there was a train. I went round the batteries to say good-bye and got off at 12 o'clock. As my train did not start till 1.30, I had lunch at the Station Hotel with a Naval Division Staff Officer who was going on forty-eight hours' leave to Dunkirk. We got to Hazebrouck about 3 and found there was no train going north till 4.30. I left Bath at the station in charge of my baggage and went for a walk in the town. I have not been there since I was at Staple with the 2nd Life Guards in 1915. No one seemed to know where the 24th Division were as they are on the move. The railhead for them is Abeele, which is the Belgian frontier. I had a great deal of trouble with my kit, as I have got a lot of stuff and there were no porters. Bath and I therefore had to carry it ourselves. We were deposited at Abeele about 5.30, and I rang up the 24th Divisional Artillery on the R.T.O.'s telephone. They told me to go to Corps Headquarters, which are in the same town I was at, and ask for instructions. After a lot of trouble I found that the Headquarters were at Brandhoek, which is a camp quite close to Vlamertinghe and only three or four miles from Ypres. Eventually I got the loan of a motor to take me out, but as I had to give a lift to Colonel Doyle, our A.Q.M.G. and one of our G officers, there was not room in the car for all my kit. I therefore deposited my heavy box of instruments and saddlery in the corps guard room. We passed through Poperinghe, which did not look very different to what it did a year ago, in spite of the heavy shelling it had had since I was there last. Brandhoek is quite a small place, which has been turned into a Divisional Headquarters by putting up a collection of leaky huts. As the Headquarters had only arrived this afternoon, they were all upside-down. General Capper has left the division to take command of all the tanks of the British Army. General Sheppard is officiating as Divisional Commander for the time being. I found him at dinner with the G mess. He said he was very pleased to have me back, and told me that he had asked for me. I dined with the R.A. mess in a very primitive fashion, as they had not got settled in yet. I am posted to command A/106th Brigade R.F.A. They are in rest near Cassel at present, and I am to join them to-morrow.

CASSEL, 16TH MAY, 1917

After breakfast this morning I was lent the R.A. motor and with Bath and my kit was driven some fifteen miles to this place. The colonel is on leave at present, and I ought to have taken command of the brigade, but as I want to get to know my new battery, I asked the Divisional Artillery to leave Ryder, another major, in charge for the moment. This is Bridgeman's old battery, which he left on taking up brigade major of the 47th Divisional Artillery. The battery has been commanded by an acting major called Maskell ; he is a ranker who has got on very fast, having done very well. It is very bad luck for him to have been supplanted, but no doubt he will get his promotion again very shortly, as I gather there is every chance of my getting a brigade soon. I always understood that it was a very good battery under Bridgeman, and as far as I can see it is pretty good now. My officers are a regular subaltern called Dallas, whose father is a colonel, and three others besides Maskell, who becomes my captain. Besides these, I have a Yeomanry major attached, who is supposed to look after the horses whilst the guns are in action. Also the brigade veterinary officer lives with us, so we are eight in the mess. The battery is billeted in a small typical Flemish farm, less one complete section which is in action at the Lille Gate, in my old position.

Cassel, 17th May, 1917

It rained hard all the morning, so I had to cancel a drill order parade that I had meant to have. However, this afternoon I was able to have laying, signallers, range-takers, etc. They all seem pretty good, but naturally there are many small things that I shall want to alter. Every battery commander has his own methods, and I shall have everything done precisely as in my old battery. The mess is very bad, quite unnecessarily uncomfortable, and the cooking vile. I have put Bath in charge of the mess, and he will have to look after everything. I went over to Headquarters to see Ryder this afternoon.

Cassel, 18th May, 1917

As it was fine this morning, I was able to have my drill order inspection. I was fairly satisfied with the turn-out, but there is room for improvement. Afterwards, I sent the horses out for exercise and took the battery staff out for a little practice in director work, etc. I called on Hobday who now commands our B Battery; he used to be adjutant of this brigade when we came out from England. After lunch I had the signallers, etc., out and lectured to the N.C.O.s on the director, proving to them by demonstration how the rules worked out. Three of my sergeants have distinguished themselves by getting run in by the A.P.M. for buying rum in a cantonment. Very annoying for me just as I take over command. Chalk has gone up to the guns to-day to relieve Rentell.

CASSEL, 19TH MAY, 1917

A fine day, but cloudy. I took the battery staff and a section out for exercise this morning and did a " fleeting opportunity " on the road, just to see what they would do. They are not bad at all, but nothing to boast about. Maskell is probably getting another battery soon, which is a good thing, as there is not room for two majors in one battery. I think Dallas will make a good captain, although he is only twenty-one. My third subaltern turned up this morning, having been with my detached section at Ypres. He is a ranker called Rentell, and was one of Birch's serjeants in D/108. Various padres have been round to-day arranging for church parades for to-morrow. As usual, when one is out of action, half the day is taken up answering official letters.

Very hot to-day and a bright sun. I had no idea the weather could be so nice in this beastly Flanders. I rode into Cassel to-day ; it is a pretty little town on the top of a very high hill. It stands up like a rock in the plain and dominates the country for miles in every direction. It has a rather interesting old church, built of brown brick, and very much better decorated than any other in Flanders that I have seen. I imagine that it must have been built about 1700 or so. Dallas has gone on special leave to London and should be there to-night. They are still giving a certain amount of leave, but only in special cases. It leaves me with only three officers at the moment, which is too few.

CASSEL, 21ST MAY, 1917

A fine day. I meant to have a drill order parade, but had to send 80 men to Steenvoorde for baths. Last night Hobday, who commands our B Battery, came to dinner, and we sat up very late talking shop. After dinner I gave the officers a little practice in flash spotting with my patent director. I sent Bath about a mile off with my electric lamp, with instructions to flash it towards us for a second at a time, from various points. It worked very well, and we all read the flashes off to within thirty minutes of each other. I am having great trouble with the farmer's wife ; she has put in a claim for fr. 8,000 damages to the grass of one field. The whole field is only about ten acres, and we do not use more than a couple of acres. These Flemish peasants are all the same—out to make all they can from us.

CASSEL, 22ND MAY, 1917

Raining hard, so I was able only to have exercise. Maskell has got orders to join C/147 and has gone off. I have just heard that Chalk, the subaltern I sent up with the section to Ypres, has been badly wounded. The position was shelled by 5·9's and he withdrew the men to the Ramparts ; apparently he was caught by a splinter of a shell in the hip. I have had to send up Cooper to replace him. As Dallas is away it leaves me alone with Rentell, who has only just got his commission from the ranks. As I do not know the N.C.O.s or men, it will be very difficult to go into action so short.

(3 p.m.) Orders have just come to be prepared to move up to-morrow to close to Ouderdom, which is not far from Brandhoek. I have got a charger from the trench-mortar people, in exchange for a draft-horse. He is a big grey horse about 16·2 and very powerful ; not at all bad-looking, and up to my weight. If he turns out well he ought to be an acquisition.

(10 p.m.) Orders have come that we don't march till 8 p.m. to-morrow ; this gives us all day to get ready.

CASSEL, 28RD MAY, 1917

A fine day. We have been packing up and getting ready to move at 8 p.m. to-night. The farm people have been living up to the best traditions of the Flemish population. We had agreed to pay them fr. 2 a day for the use of a room to mess in ; however, they claimed three when we went, and followed the officers about shouting abuse. It is extraordinary the way the British Army is made to swallow any insults from the civilian population. If we

had been Germans these people would grovel on the floor,
As it is they have never been so well off before.

OUDERDOM, 24TH MAY, 1917

We started at 8 p.m. last night and marching via Winni-
zeele, Watou, and Poperinghe reached this place at
2.30 a.m. It was about 16 miles, and good going till we
reached the frontier, when of course the roads became the
worst form of *pavé*. There was no moon, but there was a
little light from the stars, and we had no difficulty in
getting along. Ryder, Shuttleworth, and I rode at the
head of the column, and had a cyclist party on ahead to
find the way. We had some trouble in getting into our
wagon-lines here, as the field is very small, and there is
very little room for four six-gun batteries. I have only
one gun at present ; two were handed over to another
brigade, two are in action on the Ramparts, and one was
blown up yesterday by two direct hits with 5·9's ; fortunately no one was hurt.

OUDERDOM, 25TH MAY, 1917

The colonel and battery commanders rode up to the
area we are going to occupy in a few days. We had to
get off our horses at Café Belge and walk from there, as
it is not safe to ride any farther up. I am to go into a
spot in the open, not far from Zillebeke Lake. We started
at 3 a.m. and got up there by 5.30. I had a good look
round and saw how much ammunition there already was
up and then walked back with the other B.C.s. We
passed my old position which I was shot out of in November 1915. There is a 60-pounder battery in it now.
Perhaps they will have better luck. As I passed by No. 4
gun-pit, I saw various twisted pieces of No. 4 gun that the
newcomers had evidently dug up when they rebuilt the
pits. I had got back in time to wash and shave before
9 o'clock breakfast. On return I heard the sad news
that Stewart, one of my subalterns in C/108, was killed
at the Lille Gate last night. He had been transferred
as captain to B/107. His body had been brought down

to the wagon-lines in a G.S. wagon and was alongside
my camp. I went across to see him—he had been hit in
the back of the head by a piece of 5·9. I am very sorry
about it ; I liked him very much, and had been talking
to him only a few days ago. The funeral was at Reninghelst at 4 o'clock and General Sheppard and I went over
for it.

OUDERDOM, 26TH MAY, 1917

I have been very busy all day in the wagon-lines trying
to sort people out, and struggling with masses of official
papers. I must have had half a hundredweight in the last
two days at least.

OUDERDOM, 27TH MAY, 1917

The colonel, Ryder, and I rode part of the way up this
morning. We only got as far as " Den Groenen jager "
mounted, as they were shelling the road in front very
heavily with 5·9's. From there we walked to the corner
of Zillebeke Bund, where we got a guide who took us up
to the front lines, near Sanctuary Wood. We passed
within 30 yards of Zillebeke Church, but as we were in a
great hurry, I did not go to see Peter Petersen's grave.
It was a good thing I did not stop, as a shell burst just
over the place, less than a minute after I passed. The
trenches in this part are in a dreadful state, worse than anything I have yet seen. At many places we were quite
exposed to view, and I was surprised that the Hun did not
snipe us. After walking quite three miles in communication trenches, we reached the Sap from which we were
to observe. Only one of my guns came up last night ;
however, I wanted to register it on zero. We are not
supposed to have any telephone-wires of our own, as the
corps has laid out a most elaborate system of buried cables
and exchanges manned by R.E. operators. On arrival
at the O.P. we found a Major Powell of another brigade,
who was cutting wire. He showed us the zone and pointed
out various targets and places on the map. The trenches
are about a hundred yards apart at that place, and we can

get quite a good view of them. We tried to get through to my gun, but failed altogether, as the R.E. man at the exchange said he had never heard of my battery. After waiting an hour and a half, I gave it up, and walked back to Brigade Headquarters, where we were given tea. I was very hot and tired, as the heat in the trenches was simply tropical.

After tea we started to walk back to where we had told our horses and trumpeters to meet us. It was quite three miles more. By the time we reached our camp I was more dead than alive, having ridden some eight miles and walked about fifteen. It was a long day for me just after getting out from England after being on the sick list for five months.

ZILLEBEKE, 28TH MAY, 1917

We had a very exhausting night, as the Hun shelled our camp with 8-in. shells from 11 o'clock till daylight. Fortunately, only one shell fell in our lines, but he completely wrecked the next camp alongside us. I had to turn out the men and take the horses off the lines, in case it became necessary to file out. In the middle of it the guns to our south started firing an S.O.S. and the gas syrens blew. I think we must have been just about on the edge of the gas-cloud, as, although I could smell it, it was very faint. Of course we had to put on our gas helmets as it was phosgene, which is very dangerous even when weak. I did not go to bed until after four, and even then the Hun was dropping shells near our camp. After breakfast the adjutant brought a new officer to join me, by name of Ellis. He is an Australian, and seems competent. After lunch Ryder, Ellis, and I rode up as far as the White Château, and, leaving our horses, walked up to the gun positions. I found very little had been done to improve things, and we shall have to put the guns in the open, under rabbit-wire, just as at Guillemont. Last night's strafe by the Hun on our roads cost me one driver wounded, one missing, and seven horses. I hope it will not happen every night.

ZILLEBEKE, 29TH MAY, 1917

We had a dreadful night, as we were heavily shelled, and we have no head cover beyond a tarpaulin. I got no sleep till dawn, and then only an hour. A new officer arrived in the middle of the night, by name Franklyn. He has always belonged to this battery, but has been in hospital for some time. Just before the ammunition wagons came up—at 2 a.m.—we had been heavily shelled and I expected a disaster every moment. However, the Hun was kind enough not to begin again till they had got away. It was a very dark night, and as the whole place is a honeycomb of deep shell-holes, it was very difficult to get the wagons the 800 yards from the road to the gun-pits. During the night I had a telephone-wire run out to the front line on my zone. This morning very early I went up to the trenches and registered two of my guns on their zone. I also did some wire cutting. There is not much wire in front of my bit, and I spent most of my time sweeping away bundles of it. It is rather amusing work, as one's shells fall only 50 yards in front of one's nose, and give one the feeling that they are going to go down one's neck. To my immense surprise the Hun did not seem to mind. I expected he would retaliate at once, but he seems quite tame as far as wire cutting is concerned. All his energies seem to be devoted to trying to knock out the batteries behind. We had dinner in my new mess-house, which consists of four walls of sandbags and a tarpaulin over the top. All the afternoon they had been registering on Bedford House, a ruined château not far from me. I noticed that they were firing guns of all calibres, first one and then another. This made me suspicious, and I was not surprised when, at 9 o'clock, a perfect hurricane of shells arrived, large and small mixed. They kept it up for half an hour or more, but they were nearly all two or three hundred yards over me. Suddenly they stopped and began a creeping barrage right across the flank of my battery and on my mess. Franklyn, the doctor, Bath, and I rushed out and threw ourselves down flat in a little trench outside. It was only 18 in. deep and the same width. The hurricane of shells lasted about five minutes, mostly shrapnel bursting in air and 4·2's bursting on impact. There must have been dozens bursting at the same moment, all round and over us. I have never seen anything like it before, except our own barrages on the Somme. We were covered with earth and sods that were being flung up, and the shrapnel bullets fell on the ground all round just like a hailstorm. Suddenly there was a tremendous roar and the whole country was lit up like day. We put up our heads to see what it was and found that one of my ammunition dumps had blown up. The concussion set off another dump near it, but, instead of blowing up, it started burning, the H.E. shells going over in dozens just like a Chinese cracker, only each crack was an 18-lb. shell. The pieces of shell were flying in every direction, adding to the awful noise of the barrage, which was still going on. We were 200 yards from the battery, and it was absolutely necessary to get back to the men. Franklyn and I agreed to risk it and ran as hard as we could past the burning ammunition to the battery. How we got across alive I don't know; neither of us had the smallest hope of surviving. It was dark, and the place was full of shell-holes. Three times I was knocked over by shells bursting almost under my feet, and my own ammunition was popping off all the time. At the same time the air was full of shrapnel. Something hit me on the right wrist, but needless to say I did not stop to examine it. When I was quite out of breath I flung myself down in the bottom of a big hole and waited till I could continue my rush. Eventually I got to my guns; the barrage was on a very short front, and had only caught one of my pits; fortunately its gun had not come up yet. The men had gone down to the other end of the battery, where they were quite safe. So far as I could tell no one was missing; however, as the barrage had crept on by that time, Franklyn and I were able to go along from pit to pit and see if anyone had been killed. We got off with the loss of six hundred rounds of ammunition, which is serious, as we have to get a large quantity up by a certain date. The drivers and horses are having a hard time ; they have to come up every night, some six miles each way, and the Hun shells the road all night. I am losing two or three men and four to six horses every night. Last night it was particularly bad. I am told that early this morning the roads were strewn with wagons, motor-lorries, dead horses, and men. The figure I heard was four hundred in this particular area. My farrier sergeant, a sergeant, and two drivers, were killed, and two more wounded. It is really getting a very serious problem, the getting up of ammunition.

ZILLEBEKE, 30TH MAY, 1917

I went up to the trenches again and cut some more wire. I took Ellis with me to show him the way. I have never seen such bad trenches as they are near Hill 60. In places they simply don't exist, and one has to expose oneself to the view of the Hun front line. We seem to have adopted the German system of only keeping posts in the front line by day. So it is very uncanny, as there is a dead silence all along, and the place seems to be deserted. I never go up there now without my pistol ; it would be too ignominious to be caught by a Boche patrol and be unarmed. This evening they gave their attention to strafing the place where our Headquarters are. We watched from a distance, till the adjutant rang me up and said the colonel had been wounded. I at once collected my cloak and a few odds and ends for the night and went off with the faithful Bath to Headquarters. On arrival I found a dreadful mess ; the whole place was wrecked and there were huge craters made by 8-in. armour-piercing shells everywhere. The colonel had already been carried off to the Field Ambulance ; but I gather he is not seriously wounded. It seems that when his dug-out was blown in a heavy beam of wood fell on him and crushed his leg. I do not suppose he will be evacuated, but on the other hand he will probably be away for some considerable time. I am very glad he is not badly hurt, but I confess that I hope he will leave me in charge for at least fifteen days, as in that case I shall automatically get the rank of lieutenant-colonel. It would be nice to have it, if only for a few days. It gives one a better chance of getting it permanently. The colonel left a message for me to say that he advised me to change the Brigade Headquarters at once. As I saw Colonel Walthall's Headquarters shot out of the same place eighteen months ago, I was not surprised at what happened. I at once set to work to find another place, and eventually got a home for the night not far off. I have only got a tiny cabin some 9 feet by 9 in a tunnel under a railway embankment. We got all the papers and the office table (made out of ammunition-boxes) across and were established in our quarters in a couple of hours. These six dug-outs are allotted to Colonels de Satche and Spiller. We had an uncomfortable night, as there is little room to work, eat, and sleep. The floor is made of " duckboards," under which is a sheet of water, so it can be imagined that the place is a little damp. My wrist is rather painful where I was wounded the other night, but I think it will heal up all right in a few days ; the wound is not deep, only a small gash about 2 in. long across the inside. Lissant—the adjutant—and I worked till 4 o'clock in the morning getting our papers sorted, and getting orders for the batteries.

ZILLEBEKE, 31ST MAY, 1917

The 70th Infantry Brigade are at this place ; General Gordon, who commands, has been most kind, giving me breakfast and lunch, as our mess was blown up. The brigade major called this morning and was horrified to find what a pig-sty I was established in ; he has offered to have some proper dug-outs built for me outside in the open. At tea-time I had a conference of all battery commanders and explained various matters to them. As my Headquarters are so small and quite dark except for a candle night and day, I met them at D Battery's mess, which Ryder allows me to use for such purposes. Except for this I have not been above ground all day, as I have been too busy putting the office on a more business-like footing. We are always getting into trouble with the division for not answering letters, etc., punctually. I have started files, etc., and have now got things on a little better.

ZILLEBEKE, 1ST JUNE, 1917

Spent most of the day in my cellar. Last night about midnight I got orders from Divisional Artillery for a practice barrage to take place that afternoon. I worked out the programme for all the batteries, and this afternoon it came off. I sent Welch (the major of our C Battery) up to the trenches to report on it. He says it looked very good, but, owing to smoke, etc., it was difficult for him to see much. I am known as the " Wire King," as I am in charge (for wire cutting) of all the batteries on this front, no less than six brigades. That is some twenty-four batteries of six guns or howitzers each. Not a bad command for one major ! All day various battery commanders have been calling to get their instructions from me as to where they are to cut wire. I allot them tasks, from the reports I get from the infantry, as to where there is still wire that wants cutting. From seven to ten to-night we have been subjected to violent and intense shell-fire. The dug-out rocked under it. I thought that this place was strong enough to keep out an 8-in. shell, but the compartment next to my office was blown in and the dirt flew all over us. An unfortunate signaller, who was standing at the place to keep under cover, was buried under debris. By the time we got him out he was dead ; his spine was broken by the fall of timber. My little dug-out rocked like a ship at sea under the terrific blows of the 8-in. and 5·9 shells that were bursting at the rate of half a dozen a minute all over us. I was writing a letter to G. during the beginning of the strafe, and told her that my dug-out was crump-proof. I had hardly closed the letter when a large shell burst just outside and blew in the tunnel about three yards from my compartment. The dressing-station

20

outside was blown up and all the medical people with the
wounded poured into the tunnel. The whole place was
in a pandemonium, dead and wounded everywhere, and
blood in pools all along the passage. It quite prevented
me from doing my work. It lasted about three hours,
during which time they fairly pumped heavy shells into
us. All the dug-outs on the surface were crumped in,
including the bedroom of the infantry general, who was
wounded in three places.

ZILLEBEKE, 2ND JUNE, 1917

Towards dawn things quieted down and we were able
to get a couple of hours' sleep; but, as there were five of
us in a space of 9 feet, including two large pillars and a
big office table, it was not very comfortable. The brigade
major called in this morning and cheered us up. He was
horrified to find what a pig-sty we were living in, and is
going to send up material and an A.C. party to-night to
make me a dug-out somewhere out in the open. It is a
case of the devil or the deep sea. I am sure we are too
uncomfortable, but fairly safe from anything except direct
hits with really heavy shells, and in the open we shall
have no protection from anything except shrapnel, but
we shall be much more comfortable. We have heard from
Colonel Balston ; he seems to be badly shaken and bruised,
but the X-rays show no bones broken, so perhaps he will
be back in a week or so. My wound is rather troublesome,
the glands under the arm are swelling and the wound
itself is inflamed, but it does not worry me so much as
the inoculation I had against tetanus. I am so stiff all
over my chest that I can hardly move.

ZILLEBEKE, 3RD JUNE, 1917

To-day we had another practice barrage, very intense
whilst it lasted. I cannot imagine what the object of it
is, as it tells the Hun exactly what to expect on the real
day, and I do not suppose we hit anyone, as they are sure
to be at the bottom of their dug-outs all the afternoon.

We are having a terrible time getting up ammunition
every night. I lose horses and men every time. Last
night the farrier sergeant and another sergeant were killed,
besides two drivers and several more wounded. The
Hun shells our roads all night, and, as there are tens of
thousands of horses and wagons moving all night, he is
bound to hit something. The D.A.C. party have arrived
and started work on my new Headquarters; there are
three iron-roofed dug-outs in a field near B Battery.
I sit at my office table with a candle for about eighteen
hours a day, and occasionally find time to dash out and see
the batteries. The faithful Bath always goes with me as
escort, as it is too dangerous for anyone to walk about this
horrible Salient alone. I have never seen such terrific
shelling in my whole experience; the Hun seems to have
countless batteries of 5·9's and unlimited shells.

ZILLEBEKE, 4TH JUNE, 1917

What a 4th of June ! I wonder if they are having the
procession of boats at Eton to-day; certainly we can
compete with them for fireworks; there has been nothing
like it before. Our guns and the Germans' roar night and
day and never stop for a moment. To-day General Sheppard had a conference of group commanders at his Headquarters in the vicinity of Poperinghe. He sent a car
to meet us near the Asylum on the road to Vlamertinghe.
Colonel de Satche and I walked over to meet it and had a
rough time, as the Hun was shelling the whole area heavily.
We had to make detours to avoid burning dumps of ammunition, which were exploding gaily in all directions. We
were nearly caught going through Kruistraat, a big shell
hitting a house not far off and blowing out the whole of
the side of the house facing us. It was tropically hot and
we had to keep off the roads because of the shelling. The
fields are thick with long tufts of grass and full of shell-
holes, so by the time we had done 3 miles I was about
exhausted. It was a relief indeed to reach the car. For
the first mile or so the car had to pick its way among the

holes in the road, but after that we bowled along the road merrily, and reached Divisional Headquarters, which are a collection of well-made huts. The general and everyone asked after my wound, and we adjourned to their mess for our conference. General Sheppard read out a letter from the army commander saying that he realised what a bad time the gunners were having and much appreciated the good work that was being done. We discussed every detail of our plans and the general made several excellent suggestions. I saw our brigade major and staff captain and made all sorts of arrangements, and asked for all the maps I wanted. They are a delightful staff to work with —always anxious to help in every possible way. This is not the case with all staff officers by a long way. After the conference we drove to our wagon-lines, where I had tea and saw the horses. They are looking much better than I had expected after the tremendous work they have had. C Battery horses were caught last night in a gas-shell barrage and had a bad time. Their horses were still gasping for breath and looking very sick, but none have died and they will probably be all right in a day or two. After tea I had my trumpeter and an orderly with a horse-holder and started back for the line. I took the new sand track and was able to canter for the first two miles without drawing rein. I could have ridden farther, but when I got into the area that is shelled at night there were so many dead horses lying on the road that my mare began to object. I don't blame her, as she could not hold a handkerchief to her nose like I did. I accordingly got off and sent the horses back. The orderly and I walked the last two miles to Bedford House. I passed a 6-in. howitzer battery in my old position near Voormezeele and inquired whose it was ; to my surprise I found Birch in command—now a major. He was my captain in A/108 when I went home in November last. He gave me a drink and we exchanged news. He is very lucky, as, being " silent battery," he has not been spotted by the Hun yet, and has had a peaceful time since he arrived here. On arrival at my own brigade I found that A and D

had been heavily shelled whilst I was away. D had
bad luck, a 5·9 shell crashing into one of their gun-pits and
killing two and wounding seven men. I do not think it
was meant for them at all, but was a bad shot for A
Battery. The Hun has " bracketed " them with a 25-
yrd.¹ bracket, so I have warned Dallas to look out for
trouble. The general has given me two more officers, both
of whom I have posted to A Battery, as they are very
short. To-night the Hun has put a large number of gas-
shells round our dug-outs. I did not put on my gas-
mask quickly enough, with the result that I got a nasty
whiff of it that made me cough and splutter. It catches
one by the throat and the eyes are affected, so that tears
pour down one's face. Our new gas-helmets are a great
improvement on the old flannel bags. I was so tired that
I half went to sleep with it on. The Hun has shelled my
Headquarters intermittently all day, but has not caught
many people fortunately.

ZILLEBEKE, 5TH JUNE, 1917

A black day. A and B Batteries have been shelled
all day, and it is still going on now at 11 p.m. Ellis, my
best subaltern, has been mortally wounded in the head
by a piece of a 5·9. As for the battery position, it has
practically ceased to exist. They have put several hundreds of 5·9's right into the gun-line and blown up hundreds
of rounds of ammunition. At 7 o'clock this evening I
went over to the guns to see what the damage was, but
the guns are so covered up with earth and bits of wreckage
that it is impossible to see if they are damaged. Poor
Dallas has had to take his men out into a field to flank.
I hear that since I left them they have again had another
bad strafe. The German heavies seem to have registered
them to a yard ; the whole ground all round the position
is just one large series of holes. One of the high-explosive
dumps of D/106 has been hit and the crater made by the
explosion is some 15 feet deep and quite 40 feet across. I
am afraid that a lot of ammunition has gone " west."
We did another practice barrage to-day, but it does not

seem to have had any effect on the Hun, he is going on shooting up our batteries. Another of my men has been killed by a hit on the head ; at this rate we shall soon be very short of both horses and men. I went over to see my new Headquarters, which are quite a nice collection of dug-outs ; they would not keep out a direct hit even of a pip-squeak, but they ought to be good enough for shrapnel. I had a drink with Welch and Hobday, who are all quite cheerful. I have no doubt now that this is a good brigade ; they have all risen to the occasion well, and are working all out, in spite of the bad shelling we are having. At present our principal work is wire cutting, and I think we have made a good job of it. There does not seem to be any wire left now in front of the German trenches. In fact, most of his tracks seem to have been flattened out too. At one time I was " Wire King," as they call me, with the call on the guns and howitzers of six brigades at my disposal. It was very interesting, but it entailed more work than was possible for three people to manage in a small cellar. The amount of writing and circulating of instructions is simply appalling, at least three times as much as in normal times. We ourselves have had a fairly quiet day, except that the Hun has set fire to a farm some 200 yards from us. As there are fifteen hundred rounds of H.E. shells in it, we expect a terrific burst up at any moment. It is just a question if the tunnel will be wrecked or not. The three group commanders who live here have had a conference, and we have decided that, as the thing may not blow up for hours, we cannot abandon our Head-quarters indefinitely at this crisis ; so we are going to risk it, and hope that the main force of the explosion will be upwards and downwards. Still, I expect we shall get well shaken.

ZILLEBEKE, 6TH JUNE, 1917

Dallas came over to see me early this morning to report the extent of his damage. By some miracle none of his four guns have been hurt, although they have been blown round so that they point in all directions; the loss of

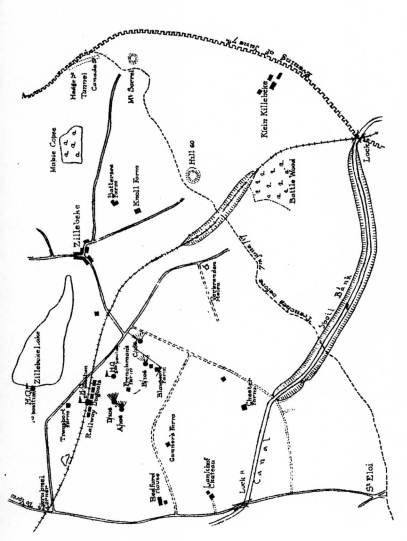

ST ELOI – ZILLEBEKE, JUNE 1917.
Showing northern battery positions.

ammunition is more serious, as there is little time to get any more up. At 8 o'clock I went over to his position and found that last night's shelling had made the place into even more of a mess than ever. Two more guns have arrived in the wagon-lines and I have told Dallas that they must be brought up to-day, even by daylight. I am afraid that they will be caught on the road, but we must make the attempt. Yesterday, Wilmot, a subaltern of D Battery, did a fine piece of work for which I have recommended him. His battery commander was up in the trenches whilst the battery was firing the practice barrage. Just before zero time D and A were heavily shelled by 4·2's and 5·9.'s, some of D Battery's dumps being blown up. Wilmot rallied his men and took them back to the guns and carried out his fifteen minutes' programme, in spite of the hostile bombardment of the position. I have made all the final arrangements and am having a last conference with the battery commanders to-night. There is nothing more to do but to drink " Confusion to the Hun." At 11 p.m. I closed my office in the tunnel and at the same moment opened communication from my new Headquarters, which are a collection of dug-outs in the open, close behind B and C Batteries. I myself synchronised watches with the staff officer from Divisional Headquarters, and on my arrival at the new headquarters sent for an officer from each battery and gave him the correct time, to within one second. After that I lay down and tried to get a couple of hours' sleep before the battle. I was doomed to disappointment as the battle began farther to the south soon after twelve and the noise was tremendous, to say nothing of the fact that the Hun put a gas barrage on us, and I had to wear my gas-helmet. The officers of the batteries did not all arrive together, so I got only half an hour's sleep before zero.

ZILLEBEKE, 7TH JUNE, 1917

At exactly 3.10 a.m. Armageddon began. The timing of all batteries in the area was wonderful, and to a second every gun roared in one awful salvo. At the same moment the two greatest mines in history were blown up—Hill 60 and one immediately to the south of it. I cleared everyone out of the dug-outs and was watching for it. Never could I have imagined such a sight. First, there was a double shock that shook the earth here 15,000 yards away like a gigantic earthquake. I was nearly flung off my feet. Then an immense wall of fire that seemed to go half-way up to heaven. The whole country was lit with a red light like in a photographic dark-room. At the same moment all the guns spoke and the battle began on this part of the line. The noise surpasses even the Somme ; it is terrific, magnificent, overwhelming. It makes one almost drunk with exhilaration, and one simply does not care about the fact that we are under the concentrated fire of all the Hun batteries. Their shells are bursting round now as I write, at 3.40 a.m., but it makes one laugh to think of their feeble little efforts compared to the " ausgezeichnete Ausstellung " that we are providing. We are getting our revenge for 1914 with a vengeance. It is now beginning to get light, but the whole world is wrapped in a grey haze of acrid fumes and dust.

(6 a.m.) It is as noisy as ever. The wounded have been streaming past for the last two hours. They say that we are getting on well, and have taken the German third line. We are also reported to be half-way across Battle Wood. Up till half an hour ago the enemy had not attempted to reply to us seriously ; now they are beginning to get to work on our batteries. I have just had a telegram from the Casualty Clearing-station at Poperinghe to say that Ellis died of his wounds yesterday afternoon. I am very sorry ; he was an excellent officer and A Battery will miss him much. My battery did a fine thing yesterday afternoon, bringing two guns into action in the open in broad daylight under 5·9 fire. I wish I had seen it. I hear that it was seen and admired by dozens of batteries round. They galloped up the last few hundred yards in the approved Horse Artillery style, unlimbered, and gave " Half-action Right," and the teams trotted away. There were no casualties, and it is a fine thing for the moral of the

men. I have been out of communication with Divisional
Artillery Headquarters for two hours, and am much
worried ; I have sent out six linesmen to lay out a new
cable to the nearest test-box, half a mile away, but now
hear that the main buried cable is cut still farther back.
I have also sent in telegrams by runners to Infantry Brigade Headquarters to try and get through from there. It
is very serious, as I can get no orders in case of emergency.
If the infantry are held up anywhere it may be necessary
to do a rebombardment of some place. Our wounded say
that the wire on my zone is thoroughly well cut, both on
the front and support German lines—that is a relief to
know. We have been firing something like 4,000 shells a
day into it for the last week.

(10.30 a.m.) Telephone communication with Divisional
Artillery has been re-established. I have spoken to our
brigade major, and, fortunately, nothing happened during
the break that we were wanted for. He also told me that
the attack is doing well down south ; from which I gather
either Wytschaete or Messines has been taken. Our
wounded are still coming past me and say that we have
got our final objective, a certain black line on the map.
The red and blue lines were captured earlier this morning.
All accounts agree that the Hun is not putting up much
of a fight, and as usual is receiving our men with hands up.
I have this moment had orders to put up a new flank
barrage, so I suppose the enemy are preparing to counter-
attack. We must expect to be heavily attacked this
afternoon and to-night, as it is inconceivable that they will
give up Hill 60 and all the ridge without a great effort.
At the present moment the Ypres Salient does not exist, for
the first time since October 1914.

(11.20 a.m.) Enemy are bombing along front line from
extreme left of attack ; I have put B Battery on to this
place. It is rather close shooting, as both our people
and the Germans are fighting in the same trench. Rate
of fire has been increased to two rounds per gun per minute.
A Battery have no luck at all ; the new subalterns
Wallace and Harrison, whom I got for them yesterday,

have both been wounded this morning. This again leaves Dallas and Rentell alone. In the last two weeks my battery has now had one officer killed, four wounded, and two gone sick, as well as myself gone away to command the brigade.

(1.10 p.m.) Rentell has come over to report, and says that their casualties to-day are two officers severely wounded, three sergeants and four men, also one gun. I don't know how Dallas will carry on. R—— has distinguished himself by firing several hundred rounds of smoke-shell that he was given for the practice day. I told him he might just as well have fired blank. It is simply priceless. The only thing is, the Hun probably thought it was some new form of lethal gas, as he could not possibly imagine anyone would calmly fire harmless smoke at him in a great battle like this.

(9 p.m.) The battle is over, and the victory is with us. We have gained the whole of our objective along the entire front of the attack; Hill 60, St. Eloi, Wytschaete, and Messines are all in our hands. The 24th Division is also said to have captured the Oostaverne Line, which is a long way behind Messines. On our own front (Hill 60) everyone is delighted; they took the first two lines of trenches with hardly any loss at all. The wire is said to have been entirely cut and gave no trouble anywhere. This afternoon the general rang me up and said he wished all ranks to know how pleased he was with the work of the guns.

ZILLEBEKE, 8TH JUNE, 1917

We all expected a great counter-attack last night, but, to my intense surprise, nothing happened. It was the quietest night we have had since we have been in action. I was very thankful, as I was just as tired as I could be. No sleep at all the night before, and the awful noise of our guns all day. This morning I sent for battery commanders and arranged to have a Brigade Observation Post manned in turn by the four batteries. The difficulty is to keep the telephone-wire going, but I have established a chain of block-houses along it, and, as they have to test the line every five minutes, it will be known at once if it is cut.

Also the parties on each side of the break will know where the break is. There are sufficient linesmen at each post so that they can send men out working towards the break, and, at the worst, they will find it by the time they meet half-way between their posts. I have just heard that we are through on the new line right to our front-line trench. Unfortunately, one of the men laying the wire was killed and another wounded. The casualties of the brigade to date since we came into action here are about fifty. At 7.30 this evening we got the S.O.S., and everyone for miles round started firing as hard as they could. The noise was as bad as yesterday. I stood in my command post from which I can see all my batteries and also the sky-line. I watched the S.O.S. rockets going up all along the front. After about an hour I got a message from the Divisional Liaison officer, who is with the infantry, to say that the Hun had reached our trenches, some 500 yards on the south of my zone. As nothing happened on my own front, I then slowed down the rate of fire to one round per minute per gun or howitzer. A little later the brigade major told me the general wanted my howitzers to fire on the road at Klein Zillebeke. This is where Petersen and Arthur O'Neill were killed on the 5th November, 1914. If we advance another quarter of a mile we shall reach the place, and I shall cause inquiries to be made by the infantry and my own F.O.O.s as to whether there are any graves of officers of the 2nd Life Guards who may have been buried by the Germans. The Germans are generally very good about marking our people's graves. I heard that we found lots when we advanced lately, near Bapaume. (11 p.m.) We are still firing very slowly, otherwise all is quiet. The counter-attack must have broken down under our heavy barrage.

ZILLEBEKE, 9TH JUNE, 1917

We had a horrid night. I finished all my work soon after midnight and went to bed—that is to say, I wrapped a blanket round me and lay down in my boots, etc. About 1 o'clock the Hun started to shell us and kept it up without stopping till 4. I do not know what it was meant for, but

the shells were falling exactly on the line of my Headquarters. They were 4·2 howitzer shells. Dozens fell within
10 yards of us and dozens more burst in the air over us.
Fortunately, none of the percussion ones hit us quite,
as we have nothing but two layers of sandbags over our
heads. It is just enough to stop shrapnel and small splinter,
but no more use than paper against a direct hit, even with
a pip-squeak. It quite prevented me from going to sleep,
and I lay there counting when it was time for the next.
For the first hour they came regularly, one every four
minutes ; then they quickened up, and arrived every thirty
seconds. They searched up and down the hedge I live
in, some bursting 100 yards to the right and some a hundred
to the left ; others close on to us. In the morning I found
lots of holes within 20 yards of my shelter. I am afraid
it is his ordinary barrage across the valley, and he happens
just to have selected the line we are on. In this case we
shall get it every night the same. The medical officer
had gone to the wagon-lines to get whisky for the mess,
so I was all alone in my dug-out. My liaison officer, who
was in the trenches with the infantry last night, says the
latter were delighted with the S.O.S. barrage we put up.
The Germans seem to have attacked up the Klein Zillebeke
road, but never reached our trenches at all ; they seem
to have melted away under our shrapnel. I am told
that an enormous number were killed. We have so
much artillery up here that it is almost hopeless for Fritz
to attempt to face our curtain fire. The same glorious hot
sun continues every day, and makes life just bearable.
My new line to the trenches is working beautifully, and we
have been able to check the registration of all the batteries
to-day. There were a large number of aeroplanes up this
evening, and I watched some quite pretty fights in the air.
My F.O.O. says the German trenches are crumped to pieces
and can hardly be found. As for round Hill 60, when the
great mine went up, not only was every dug-out wrecked,
but the trenches simply filled themselves in, and must
have buried hundreds of Germans alive. They say we
have got over six thousand prisoners and straightened out

the south side of the Salient. It has not affected the German guns to the north, who are still firing at us just the same. The enemy seems to have an unlimited amount of ammunition, as he is firing all day. He no longer has the old deliberate shoots of thirty rounds or so at a time. Now he starts suddenly with two or three batteries at a time on the same target and pumps it in as hard as he can for a couple of hours on end. It is very unpleasant, as one has no warning, and it is impossible to move if one happens to be caught in the barrage.

(10.80 p.m.) The night hate has begun again ; I suppose there will be no sleep for us again. They are falling some 800 yards off at present, but he is searching the whole valley that we are in.

ZILLEBEKE, 10TH JUNE, 1917

Another disturbed night. All night long the Hun searched the valley with his 4·2's. None of them were very near us—that is, within 20 or 80 yards, but he must have put fifty within 100 yards and three or four hundred within a radius of a quarter of a mile. When you have only two sandbags between your head and the shell it is too near to be pleasant. Every time I managed to go to sleep I was awakened up again by a horrid crash, which one always imagines in the dark is much closer than it really is. Things quieted down before dawn and I got a couple of hours sleep then. Last night I got a letter from G. to say that she had had a telegram from the War Office to say that I was wounded, but giving no details beyond the fact that I was still at duty. The extraordinary thing is that I wrote to her the same day as I was hit, in the hope that she would get the letter first. Naturally she is rather worried. As a matter of fact, my wrist is practically all right now, and I have no longer got it in a sling. It is about a fortnight since it happened, and I expect in another week it will be quite healed up again. To my horror, this morning I found that a section of anti-aircraft guns had come into action, not more than 40 yards away from me. This was really too much of a good thing, so I

wired in to the division and got them to ask the corps
to have them shifted. They belong to the Army, so it is
quite a job to do it, but in the end they were made to move.
One gets shot at quite enough as it is, without having it
made a certainty by these people blazing away all day
alongside one.

Richardson, the brigade major, came again this afternoon and said that our own division will come into the
line here to-night and that therefore there was no chance
of our moving. This is rather sad news, as we had all
been hoping to get away from this horrible place as soon
as possible. We had quite a tea-party to-day—Shuttleworth rode up from the wagon-lines to see how we were
getting on and Hobday and various people came in to
talk things over. I have arranged to go up to the new
front line at dawn to-morrow with Botham of D
Battery who has been there already. I have got to find
two more Observation Posts for two of the batteries ; the
existing Brigade Observation Post will do for the third.
I have sent in Dallas's name for immediate reward for his
excellent conduct during the recent operations. I hope
he will get something.

ZILLEBEKE, 11TH JUNE, 1917

Last night as usual we were shelled the whole time.
Several 5·9's fell within a few yards of us. It is beginning
to get on everyone's nerves, as it is quite impossible to
sleep. One lies in the dark and listens to the whine of
the shell, which seems to take hours before it arrives.
Then there is a horrid crash which makes the dug-out
rock. To vary the monotony a little, Fritz gave us two
goes with phosgene-gas shells, which made us put on our
gas-helmets. He kept it up till daylight at 4 a.m., when I
went to sleep, only to be called by Bath at 6 o'clock. I
had arranged to go up to the new front line with an officer
of D Battery, who was supposed to know the way.
We started very early, as things are usually quiet then.
We passed through the cross-roads of Zillebeke itself, and,
as everything seemed quiet, I thought I would go to the

churchyard and see if Peter's grave was all right. I had
got to within 50 yards of it, when I heard the whine of a big
shell. We had just time to crouch down in a hole when it
arrived. After that I decided to get out of the village
at once. We had a long walk up to our old front line,
which is so smashed up that it is hardly possible to get
along it, except by walking along the top of the parapet,
which is too dangerous. My zone is the extreme flank
of the late attack, so there is a place in the old Boche front
line where we touch. We have built up a barrier in the
trench here, and we hold one side whilst the Hun is a few
yards off on the other. We have made a communication
trench across No Man's Land, near the flank of the attack
so that it is possible to get across into the former German
trenches without exposing oneself to fire from the part
of the German front line when we did not advance. Unfortunately, my guide made a mistake and took me out
by a small sap, some way to the north of the communication trench. When we got half-way across, the sap
suddenly came to an end, and we found ourselves high
and dry in the middle. I realised what had happened,
but thought it would be better to go straight on and drop
into the German line as quick as possible. I was not
certain where the barrier was, and it was pure luck if we
struck the trench on our side or the German. I unloosened
my automatic pistol in its holster and made for the wire,
which had not been properly cut so far to the flank. We
got through it somehow and jumped into the trench, not
knowing if we should find Germans or our own people.
As a matter of fact, there was no one there, but we heard
a shout and saw an English officer running up the trench
towards us. He thought we were quite mad, as he had seen
us walking across No Man's Land. He told me we had
only just missed crossing beyond the barrier. I can only
suppose that the Huns must have been asleep not to have
seen us. They could have shot us like rabbits if they had
seen us. I don't know what would have happened if we
had jumped into a German bombing post—probably
there would only have been half a dozen men, and, as we

both had our revolvers, we might have shot them down before they recovered from their surprise. I found the German trenches in an awful state, very much like Guillemont. The whole place was a mass of huge craters. There are lots of wonderful concrete dug-outs, that had doubtless been built into the parapet of the trenches, but now that all the trenches are flattened out those dug-outs stand up like large white houses. They are 4 feet thick, of solid concrete and iron, but many of them are broken to pieces like eggs. Everywhere was the well-known stench, and many half-buried Germans lying about, with legs and arms sticking out of the earth. Thank goodness the place is quite dry ; it would be truly terrible in wet weather. We made our way down the remains of the trenches towards our new front line. It was a laborious process, as whole platoons of infantry were sleeping on the floor of the trench, which was only some 18 in. wide. One has to step over them, and as they generally lie head to tail, it takes ages to get along a few hundred yards of trench. I called on various company commanders, but was not able to get much information from them as this battalion had only come in last night. We are not holding a regular front line, like in ordinary peace warfare. The support line is very strongly held, but in front we have only posts at intervals. It is quite easy to walk out between the various posts without seeing them, in which case one would find oneself in the Hun lines without any warning. My principal object in going up there this morning was to find some more Observation Posts, in case we take over a zone more to the south. I found one very good one, with a good concrete dug-out that would do for the F.O.O. and his party to retire to, in case of a strafe. Botham and I climbed up to the top of the dug-out and lay flat on our stomachs on the top. I am not sure how far we were from the Hun, but I think quite 400 yards. The infantry warned us to be very careful, as the snipers were very active. We moved as little as possible, and just lay there, studying the country through our glasses. We continued our pilgrimage, and as we were going along

I saw a German sniper's vizor lying on the ground. I rescued it at once and carried it about all day. It is the front part of the German steel helmet, and fits over the ordinary one. It is very heavy, and made of the hardest Krupp steel. The German snipers fasten them in front of their helmets, and so get a double thickness of steel protecting the forehead and top of the head. I should imagine that if the helmet gets a direct hit from a bullet it would give the man a bad headache. I also found a German paper of the 5th May. It gives most wonderful accounts of the battle of Arras, from which one would gather that the Germans were driving us back. Not a word about their appalling losses there. On my way back I called on Colonel Dugmore of the North Staffords, whom I used to know very well at Dranoutre a year ago. He is living in a series of catacombs in a hill, for all the world like a coal-mine—a horrible place, with an atmosphere you could cut like cheese. We had a tiring walk back to the guns across country, climbing in and out of deep holes and old trenches. We could not use the main road we had come along, because it was being heavily shelled by 8-in. shells. Just before I got back I saw a 6-in. howitzer battery and found that it is commanded by Cammell, late of B/108. He had two lorries blown up last night. From there I went to call on Welch to ask what his losses were last night. He had a gun hit and broken, also three killed and two wounded. They had not cleared up the gun-pit yet, and the detachment were just lying dead beside their gun. It was a horrid sight, and the pieces had to be collected in a blanket. A shell struck the lower part of the shield, and, after penetrating it, burst in the pit. It was horrible, blood everywhere, and these men lying across their gun, just as they were caught. The gun is badly damaged and will have to go away. I went back to my dug-outs and had breakfast. General Sheppard with his brigade major and staff captain came round soon after, and the general simply overwhelmed me with compliments as to the work of the brigade. He visited A and D Batteries and spoke

21

to the men and officers. I have never known such congratulations after a battle before, even after Morval and Les Bœufs. I have been told to send in the names of men for recommendations and have been very busy all day compiling the lists. I am afraid it will only mean that two or three of the men will get Military Medals, and, possibly, one subaltern a Military Cross. As for the battery commanders, they are neither fish, flesh, nor good red herring. Being field officers, they are not eligible for Military Crosses, and not being on the staff or in a departmental office they are not likely to get D.S.O.s. We had just finished lunch when the Hun commenced a furious fire with two and, I suspect, three 5·9 batteries on a battery of the 107th Brigade, only 100 yards away from me. Many of them were falling quite close to my dug-outs, and covering us with smoke and dust. It was more than I could stand, so I gave the order for everyone to withdraw till it was over. I myself at once went to the 298th Brigade Headquarters with some orderlies and opened up temporary communication with Divisional Headquarters from there. About an hour later the medical officer, Bath, and I went back to see if it was all over, but they started again as soon as we got to our place. They stopped about 5 o'clock, and we went back for tea. Having had no sleep the previous night and my long walk in the sun before breakfast, as I was about done by 10 o'clock I went to sleep, not waking till 8 o'clock this morning. I don't know if they shelled us or not; I don't think salvos of 17-in. would have disturbed me. I have had to finish writing this up to-day.

ZILLEBEKE, 12TH JUNE, 1917

I had hardly finished shaving this morning when Richardson came in to say that General Reed—the X Corps Artillery Commander, was here. I went round the batteries with him, and had a repetition of yesterday. He told everyone what fine fellows they were and how well the brigade had done. I suppose the army commander had said the same to him. Blame is always carefully passed on down the "chain of responsibility" and sometimes praise is also. All the morning Fritz has been throwing huge shells into the middle of Zillebeke Lake, raising huge fountains of water 100 feet high. It is quite harmless, and if it affords him any amusement to see the splash, by all means let him go on as long as he likes. After lunch I got orders for a new battle and had to go and see the brigade commanders of 104th and 107th Brigades. Before doing so I sent for my battery commanders and had a conference with them about what has to be done. Whilst we were all sitting in my little dug-out the Hun landed a salvo of 4·2 shells all round and over us. One burst two or three yards from the door and covered us with dirt. What a bag he would have made if he had only been those few yards nearer—the group commander, adjutant, orderly officer, and four battery commanders. I had tea with the colonel of 104th and met the C.R.A. of the 47th Division there. Just as I was getting near my own headquarters, on my way back, I saw 4·2's bursting all over it, and had to wait till it was finished. When I eventually got there I found that nothing had actually been hit, although there were fresh holes all round. It certainly is quite the most unhealthy place I have ever lived in.

ZILLEBEKE, 18TH JUNE, 1917

This morning all the group commanders who have been covering the 23rd Division in this battle were sent for by General Babbington. We walked to Ypres Station and were met by motor there, which took us to the Divisional Headquarters. General Babbington said all the usual things, that we had covered his infantry splendidly, etc., etc. He told us to let everyone know how pleased he was. General Sheppard was there and introduced us. After that I motored on to my wagon-lines and had a bath, which I wanted more than anything else in the world. I had a look at all the horses and was surprised to see how well they looked, after all their hard work. The wagon-lines are moving to-day up near to Dickebusch Lake. I walked back to my Headquarters from Bellegoed Farm and

got back without incident, beyond being nearly killed by
an 18-pounder that was firing across the road I was on.
I did not see it till I was almost in front of the muzzle
and about ten yards in front; at that moment it fired.
I was knocked backwards by the blast of the gun and nearly
had the drums of my ears broken. People ought to look
out before firing and see that the place is clear, especially
when they are firing across a main road that is used all
day. Whilst I was talking to Ryder in his mess the Boche
put over some of his high-air bursts, which always means
that he is registering on something. I had hardly got
away when the hurricane began, right on top of poor A
Battery again. Salvo after salvo of 5·9 and 4·2 shells;
they disappeared in smoke and dust, so it was impossible
to tell exactly where the shells were falling. I have never
seen a more vicious or more prolonged hate. It was kept
up for two hours and a half almost without a break. I
telephoned to D Battery to ask for news, but all they
could say was that they believed Dallas had got all his men
away in time. Later I heard that he had lost one bombardier killed and three gunners wounded. After dark
Dallas was able to go back and take stock of the damage.
By another miracle none of the guns were hit again, although there are fresh shell-holes all round them. As on
the previous occasion, the main point of impact was some
80 yards over the gun-line, and at least 90 per cent. of the
shells pitched beyond them. When he had finished with
A, the Hun shortened his range and strafed another
battery near my Headquarters. We were having dinner
and some of the shells fell alarmingly close to us; the
nearest was some 50 yards away. I picked up my gas-
helmet, and collected my Zeiss glasses and cloak, so as
to have them ready if it became necessary to clear out.
Fortunately we were able to finish our dinner, by which
time it was dark and the Hun stopped shooting. Dallas
came over to see me and was no more perturbed than if
he had been playing tennis. I have seen the general
about him and have every hope that I shall succeed in
getting him a bar to his Military Cross. I am also trying

to get something for Hobday and Welch. They have all done so well that they richly deserve some reward. As the attack has been such a success, there is a chance that the Authorities will be a little more free with decorations.

ZILLEBEKE, 14TH JUNE, 1917

For once we had a quiet night, at least I slept well ; perhaps I am getting accustomed to this shelling in the open ; at any rate, I feel much better now that I have had more sleep. The brute refrained from giving us gas-shells for once. Colonel Russell, who commands 189th Brigade, called at breakfast time and stayed talking for a couple of hours. On the whole, it has not been a bad day, though we have had the usual amount of shelling all round us. This afternoon the Hun started putting his " woolly bears " over us, which always means that he is registering a fresh target on that line. Just before dark he started in on us with 4·2's and field-guns, mixed up with a few 5·9's. So far as the shrapnel was concerned, it did not worry us at all, as our sandbag roof will keep out that. The howitzer battery which planted themselves in the open behind me, some 50 yards off, had a bad time, and had an officer killed outside my dug-outs. B Battery had two men wounded in Blaupoort Farm and sent for the doctor. Mortimer picked up his shell dressings, called his orderly, and went across at once. The place was still being shelled by 5·9's and 4·2's, but he was not caught. He got the wounded men out, dressed their wounds, and took them off on stretchers to the Field Ambulance. I have strongly recommended him for the Military Cross.

ZILLEBEKE, 15TH JUNE, 1917

At 10 o'clock this morning I had orders to meet the C.R.A. at Lock 8, so took Lissant and went off there. We passed Bedford House on the way in perfect quiet. We had hardly got beyond the place when the Hun began one of the most vicious strafes I have seen yet—salvo after salvo of 5·9's on the road we had just passed. The whole landscape swiftly disappeared in a thick brown fog of smoke and dust. Every now and then we could see trees leaping into the air. As we were 100 yards off before it began, we were all right and sat down beside the road near Lankhof to wait for the general. When he arrived he gave us the welcome news that we were to move as soon as possible to a new area, a mile or two away. He allotted me an area and Lissant and I went out to reconnoitre it. I climbed the slope we have looked at for nearly three years and sat down in the former German trenches by the famous Mound at St. Eloi. From there I looked back ¡at¡;our͙ old;¦positions and wondered how it had been possible for us to live there at all. The Germans could see every detail of our country spread out like a map in front of them, right away to Ypres. My old position at Voormezeele that I had in November 1915 was clearly visible even to the naked eye in summer, so no wonder they saw us in the winter, when there were no leaves on the trees. I selected various places and went back to my Headquarters for lunch. After lunch I 'phoned for the battery commanders and gave them their approximate positions and sent them off to choose the exact spots for themselves. A complete new scheme came in by despatch rider and I spent the afternoon in working out all the new zones. After tea the colonel arrived ; he is looking very ill and still very lame. I don't think he ought to have come back so soon. I stayed to dinner—I had to, as Fritz was plastering the whole valley with shrapnel—and then returned to A Battery. I have told Dallas to carry on for the next day or two, as I don't know anything about his angles, etc., and it is not worth going into it all, as the battery will be moving to-morrow. Also the colonel wants me to be handy to tell him all that is going on. The new A Battery mess is large but frail, and I had an excellent night on a canvas bed. The Hun behaved well for once.

ZILLEBEKE, 16TH JUNE, 1917

This morning I got a message from the colonel to say that he had been driven out of Headquarters and had

taken refuge in D Battery. He wanted me to go
round to the brigade—the 64th—that we are now linked
with and then take him to our new Headquarters. We had
a very hot walk, as my thermometers are showing 85° F.
in the shade. The colonel is still very lame, and weak
after being in bed for a fortnight ; I am afraid he felt the
heat a good deal. I have adopted the usual kit for the
forward area now—khaki shorts, puttees, and a shirt open
at the neck and no tie. It is a strange kit to fight in, but
very comfortable in this sort of weather. I left the colonel
with the infantry general of the 122nd I.B. and came back
to my battery to lunch. All the afternoon the Hun has
been heavily shelling the ground round the old Headquarters. Huge masses of smoke and dust are rolling
down on us as I write. He is putting a concentrated
5·9 barrage right across the valley, some 400 yards in front
of me, and only about 50 yards in front of the old Brigade
Headquarters. It is quite time we left this spot. We
have had a hundred men killed and wounded in this
brigade in the last two weeks.

St. Eloi, 17th June, 1917

A very strenuous night. As soon as it was dark we
brought four of our " Tarpons " (code name for guns)
over to the new position. Fritz must have got wind of it,
as he strafed the roads badly. Fortunately my teams got
through without any casualties, but I hear other batteries
were not so fortunate, and lost a large number of men and
horses. We have dug the guns in and covered them with
" camouflage "—wire netting with bits of canvas tied all
over it. We got up eight loads of ammunition before dawn
and then lay down in the open to get a few hours' sleep.
I managed to sleep from five to nine and then shaved
and had breakfast in an old trench. I have put my guns
practically in our old front-line trench.

At 11 o'clock Welch, Coates, and I went forward along
the bank of the Canal to register the guns of our respective
batteries. We found an old concrete gun-pit of the Boche,
and looked over the top. We had a wonderful view of the

back country that the Hun has retired to, all green fields and red roofs. There is no sign of war, and one can see miles of growing crops. I selected a bridge under a railway embankment and fired at that; three guns hit it with the first shot, which was really wonderful as the line had only been laid out by map and compass. The Hun evidently saw us, or else guessed where we were observing from, as he soon began to burst shrapnel and H.E. over our heads. The business did not take long, and we cleared out. The banks of the Canal are very high and steep and the Germans had honey-combed them with tunnels. Horrible smells were coming out of the mouths of the tunnels, so I did not look in. There were a certain number of dead Germans lying about, but most of the mess had been cleared up already. The Canal is full of water, with steep sides, and on our way home Coates and I ·had a glorious swim. I swam up and down for half an hour, and have not felt so fresh and clean for a long time. The sun was simply scorching, and I was dry almost before getting out of the water.

Shells were falling a few hundred yards off, but nothing just where we were. I got a message from the colonel soon after my return to the battery to say that he had gone sick again, and that I must take over the brigade once more. I walked across and found him just off to hospital in a car. He has not recovered from being blown up the other day, and will have to have a long rest in England before he is fit again. Meanwhile, I do not know if I shall get the permanent command of the brigade or not. Colonel Spiller of the 107th Brigade has got a D.S.O. for the late battle. We have got a sandbag house as a Headquarters, that is quite moderately comfortable, though not very safe.

St. Eloi, 18th June, 1917

I am commanding two brigades now : the 106th and 64th Brigades, which are grouped together and fire on the same zone. The colonel of the 64th is resting in his wagon-lines, so I have eight batteries now under me, quite a nice little lot. This morning I called on the 64th

Brigade, and made the acquaintance of their battery commanders. I also worked out some retaliations on the batteries that I suspect as being the ones who are annoying us most. This afternoon I turned seven batteries on to one place and fired hard at it. As the Hun only increased his fire on us, I suppose I had not got the right battery, so will try another. D Battery, who did not move across with the rest of us from the old positions, have been badly knocked about. Botham, the subaltern who reconnoitred the German trenches with me a few days ago, was very badly wounded—I am afraid, mortally—and several men. Ryder came over to see me and was much shaken by the bombardment; I have told him to have a few days' rest in his wagon-lines, and let his captain carry on.

St. Eloi, 19th June, 1917

D Battery were caught last night by 8-in. shell fire as they were moving to their new position and were badly shelled. Botham was dead before he reached hospital; I am very sorry, as he was a first-class officer, and was a great help to Ryder in running the battery. I have recommended him for the V.C. He behaved in a most gallant manner; the battery was heavily and violently strafed and one of the ammunition dumps caught fire. There were several hundred shells filled with high explosives lying near the burning cordite. Botham and Ryder managed to extinguish the fire with water and so saved the whole position from being blown up. We have had a quiet day here on the whole. This morning I went to see the general of the 122nd Brigade of infantry. He complained bitterly of my putting a howitzer battery alongside his dug-out, and said the noise would disturb him. However, I went to see him again this afternoon, and found that he was asleep with the howitzers firing hard. I saw him again later and he had to admit that he had not even known that they had fired! A large number of German aeroplanes flew very low over us this evening, but the Archies' fire does not worry them at all. The infantry brigadier of the 73rd I.B., who was out in front reconnoitring this morning, suddenly met a young German artillery subaltern. He promptly covered him with an unloaded revolver|and brought him in as a prisoner. The German officer admitted that our artillery fire has been awful.

ST. ELOI, 20TH JUNE, 1917

All the group and battery commanders were sent for this morning to see our new Divisional Commander, Major-General L. J. Bols, C.B., D.S.O. He and the C.R.A. made speeches and paid us the usual compliments on our late efforts. He said that the whole of the infantry agreed that · the [barrages had been perfect. General Sheppard called me up and told me that he had applied for a Brigade for me, and that I should shortly get it, though not necessarily this one. Of course I would rather have this one, if possible, as they are very good and I have already commanded it for three weeks in this battle. Dallas and I walked back to my Headquarters and came in for a road strafe ; one or two shrapnel were uncomfortably close to us. This afternoon I called on General Gordon, of the 123rd I.B., whose extreme left I am covering. He was very civil, and has promised to find me some better billets in the tunnels near him. At 6 o'clock the S.O.S. was sent up on our left and a very heavy bombardment of our trenches commenced. I at once opened a slow rate of barrage fire on my own front with all my eight batteries, and went over to my own Infantry Brigade Headquarters. However, it soon quieted down and I came back. Colonel Cardew called to see me; he is commanding the group of the 41st Division on my right. I asked him to restrain his people from driving G.S. wagons about near my batteries, in full view of the German balloons. It has been raining a little at intervals for the last two days, so the ground is like ice, very difficult walking.

I sent out an officer's patrol to reconnoitre for new Observation Posts to see the Zandvoorde line; they had an exciting time, being chased into a trench by a German aeroplane, who flew over them at not more than a hundred feet up. They say it was most unpleasant as they could

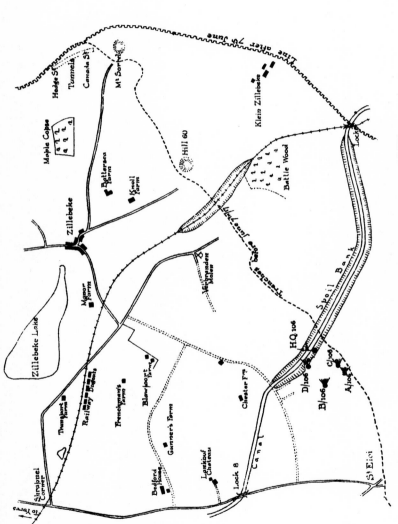

St. ELOI – ZILLEBEKE, JUNE 1917.
Showing southern battery positions.

do nothing but lie still, whilst he emptied his machine at them.

St. Eloi, 21st June, 1917

It has been a good deal cooler with some rain. We have been somewhat bothered by German aeroplanes, which have been flying very low. There is a squadron of specially fast German planes here, which drive down our machines. We cannot imagine why all our own fighting machines have left this district. One of the brutes flew over us this morning at about five hundred feet up. He fired his machine-gun at us as he passed. The infantry near us replied with theirs and the Lewis guns, but without effect. As for our Archies, they might just as well fire blank, for all the good they do. I have been round the batteries to-day, and seen how much work they have done. A Battery has done most, but that is not saying much ; the difficulty has been the want of material. However, we are beginning to get timber and corrugated iron, so it won't be long before we are at any rate shrapnel and splinter proof. Cammell came to lunch to-day ; he is bringing his 6-in. howitzers in alongside of us. We have already got 8-in. and 60-pounders, so this will be a noisy corner soon. We have had a few small shells near our Headquarters to-day for the first time, so I suppose the Hun has spotted us.

St. Eloi, 22nd June, 1917

To-day we have had one of the worst bombardments that I have yet met. At 3.30 a.m. I woke up with a start, to hear a horrible crash outside my little sandbag house. Another and another followed ; it soon became obvious that the Hun was ranging on us and nothing else. I got up and put on my boots, gas-helmet, and coat. Things became so noisy and near that I sent a telephone down into a wet and stinking tunnel near by, and, as soon as it was connected up, I sent all the men down and went down myself. I was nearly sick with the horrible stench down there, but at any rate we were quite safe in there from shell fire. We had to stay there for two hours whilst the Hun burst 5·9's just outside. About 6 o'clock we were able to emerge and went back to our little mess. Bath got us some hot cocoa and biscuits, and we went to bed (in our boots). Nothing more happened and at 9 we got up and had breakfast. I then shaved, and had nearly finished that boring operation when the shelling started again. Each time I heard the scream of a shell coming I hastily put down my razor on the table. They put several 5·9's within 30 yards of us, so I again gave orders to get into the tunnel. The doctor was dressing at the time the shelling began. His dug-out was hit, and blown in on him, but he was not touched. D Battery, who are quite close to us, had two men killed, and one of the headquarters servants was wounded. We got off very lightly. This settled my doubts about moving Headquarters into the deep tunnel next to the Infantry Brigadier. By lunch time we had taken everything across, and we connected up to all the batteries, brigades, etc. In the afternoon I went out to see the batteries and find out how much digging they had done last night. When I had finished I tried to get back, but found that the Hun was strafing the place to such an extent that it was impossible to get near it; 5·9's were arriving at the rate of twenty a minute and seldom less than a dozen a minute. I took shelter with C Battery for two hours and managed to slip in at last in a lull in the storm. Soon after 5 o'clock the new colonel arrived— Colonel Street, lately brigadier on the General Staff in Egypt. He wants to become a C.R.A., but has to learn the work by being a brigade commander first. I spent all the evening explaining the position to him, and telling him about the brigade.

RENINGHELST, 23RD JUNE, 1917

The colonel wanted to go round the batteries before breakfast, but I explained that in this part of the world the batteries work all night and do all their pit building, etc., in the dark. They go to bed in the early morning, and it would be rather unkind to inspect them at 7 o'clock.

We therefore went round after breakfast. He did not seem particularly pleased with anything, and seems to have very definite views on everything. I am afraid we battery commanders will have a bad time till we get into his ways. As all the other battery commanders have had a day or two's rest in the wagon-lines, I have come down too. I shall only stay forty-eight hours, to get clear and sort out my kit, etc. I had my horses and the mess-cart up at 5 o'clock, and rode down to Dickebusch, only to find that the wagon-lines had been shelled and had gone another two miles back. They had left a guide for me and I went on. Dallas was just settling down into the new camp, getting the divisions, etc., put up. We dined out-of-doors, but it is much colder.

RENINGHELST, 24TH JUNE, 1917

I had an excellent night's sleep, in spite of the fact that even right back here we get shelled. I woke at 2 o'clock to hear a big shell coming along. It fell some thousand yards off, but made a great noise as it passed right over my camp. They only sent us half a dozen or so, and none were at all near. I had a ride this morning, otherwise have done absolutely nothing.

RENINGHELST, 25TH JUNE, 1917

The new colonel came down from the Line this morning with Mortimer. He walked round the wagon-lines and seemed quite pleased with the horses. They certainly are looking very well, after all the fine weather we are having. Mortimer and I rode to Poperinghe for lunch. It was rather a long and dusty ride—seven miles. We lunched at the Officers' Club, which is a large house with a nice garden. It was crowded with officers of all units and branches of the Service—the A.S.C. naturally predominating. We got quite a good lunch of the typical British variety, but a good bottle of wine. We bought a lot of food at the Field Force Canteen for the messes. I found my late Q.M.S. of A/108 (Aisthorpe), who gave me all the news of that brigade. They were in action near

Kemmel, and seem to have had few casualties. Sergeant Holton, who was the King's footman before the war, has been badly wounded. He was an excellent N.C.O., and would have shortly become quartermaster-sergeant. Whilst we were in the town the Hun shelled the Belgian hospital just outside, but I did not hear anything fall in the town itself. Since I was here a year ago there has been a lot more damage, and now most of the houses have been more or less hit. I bought a huge basket of excellent strawberries for 4 francs, which is the only cheap thing I have ever seen in Belgium. Everything has gone up to famine prices, owing to the enormous number of troops in Flanders now. The Belgians must be making fortunes; they sell half-bottles of soda-water at a franc each, eggs at 80c. each, and penny English newspapers at 60c. Six-penny magazines are 2 francs. On our way back we went to Busseboom to try and find the field cashier to get some money, but drew a blank. The arrangements for drawing money are very bad. The nearest field cashier is at Abeele, quite 15 miles behind the Line, and occasionally he goes to a Divisional Headquarters, but one can never find out when he is coming up. It rained hard this evening, but if it does not last too long it won't do any harm as the dust is very bad.

St. Eloi, 26th June, 1917

I stayed in the wagon-lines till after lunch, when Rentell and I rode up to the guns. We got as far as Kruisstraat-hoek, when we began to meet shells which were too near to be comfortable. We sent our horses back to camp and walked the rest of the way. The transport evidently got caught last night, as there were a lot of dead horses lying about. We arrived in time for tea and found Dallas, Cooper, and Harper there. I took over everything and had a look at the gun-pits. We have not been able to make proper pits, but only sandbag emplacements with wire netting " camouflage " over the ground. They have managed to find enough brick from ruined farms to make good platforms, as otherwise the wheels sink into the soft

ground and the shooting becomes unsteady. Dallas meant
to have started back for the wagon-lines before dinner,
but they were shelling a battery on the way, so I advised
him to wait. By 10 o'clock things had got very bad.
The Hun was strafing savagely all round this area and shells
have been bursting within a few yards of my mess. So
far, most of it seems to be a little to my left, but I have
already had one man badly wounded in the head. Dallas
got away at 11 o'clock, during a lull in the storm, but he
must have got into the middle of it before he had gone
far. I shall be glad to hear to-morrow that he got through
all right. (Midnight.) It is really getting intolerable,
more and more German batteries are concentrating on
this bit of country, and shells are arriving at from ten to
twenty a minute. The dug-out is rocking with the concussion, and the place is full of fumes and earth that has
been blown through the door and window. The corner
of my mess had been hit and the trench outside in several
places. The servants' shelter has been blown in and they
were buried. We have no protection except a row of sandbags that might just keep out shrapnel. It is only a matter
of time before we are hit.

St. Eloi, 27th June, 1917

A damnable night, about the worst I have ever known.
Not for a single moment has the shelling stopped and now,
at 10 a.m., it is still going on worse than ever. My mess-
cook has been hit and fell outside the door ; everyone is
badly shaken and every line down. We are completely
isolated—I cannot even get the nearest battery on the
'phone. I have twice had the wire to C Battery
mended, but it is cut at once ; and it is simply murder,
sending men outside in this storm of steel. The barrage
seems to have moved a little to my left and to have length-
ened. We are only getting the shorts now (11 a.m.) and
a certain number of air-bursts. I think they are on to a
heavy battery now. The valley behind us is full of black
smoke, out of which one sees the red flashes of the explosions. This is far and away the worst strafe I have seen

yet. It is even worse than anything at Blaupoort, as it has already lasted twelve hours and more without a break. Talk of the Hun being short of ammunition !

(10 p.m.) After midday the German batteries took a rest and so did we. We are all getting savage with our own heavy batteries ; they might as well not exist for all the good they are to us when we are being shelled.

St. Eloi, 28th June, 1917

We only got intermittent shelling last night, but had an S.O.S. call soon after midnight, so I got very little sleep as usual. They have started a horrible system of making batteries send in an Intelligence Report at 6 in the morning; it is perfectly maddening as it means that I have to be called at that hour, having probably only gone to sleep about 4 o'clock. After lunch I felt energetic, so took a couple of telephonists and went out to look for a new O.P. I started by climbing to the top of the famous " Bluff," and had a look at the great mine-crater there, that we blew up about Christmas 1915. It certainly is a stupendous hole ; it must be 50 or 60 feet deep and a hundred yards across. From the top forward lip of the crater one gets a fairly good view, but I could not see the part I wanted, so went forward into old German trenches that we took on the 7th inst. The difficulty was that one was in view of the high ground east of Klein Zillebeke. It was rather like big game shooting; I had to go from shell-hole to shell-hole, keeping under cover, and bending double or crawling when crossing open places. I got very hot and exhausted after about an hour of it. In the end I found myself at our own O.P., where the colonel happened to be also. There was a subaltern of a heavy battery who imagined he could see a German battery. I watched the place for a long time, but could see nothing. Later, I went still farther forward and tried to register a house on a hill near Zandvoorde; but the battery had to stop firing so often because there were German aeroplanes over it that it was too tedious, the more so as I was being shelled all the time. The place I went to had been a

German field-gun pit, made of solid concrete. I had been there before and liked the place, as I could get inside if they started shelling; but, unfortunately, the Hun has managed to smash it in now—I suppose he suspected we should use it for observation purposes. On my way back I stopped at the Brigade O.P. and told the subaltern there that he ought to be very careful as the place was often shelled. He was very optimistic about it, and said that it was never shelled now. I had not got more than 300 yards away when a perfect tornado of shells fell all round the O.P. The bits were all whizzing past my head. So much for boasting.

St. Eloi, 29th June, 1917

Another horrible night. Intermittent 5·9 fire all the time after midnight. It is all very well when one has properly constructed gun-pits and dug-outs for the officers and men, but here we have nothing but wire netting over the guns, and no cover for the men beyond a sheet of corrugated iron. We had just finished breakfast when the shelling began again. It was evidently meant for a heavy battery quite close to me ; I imagine that, in three hours, some four or five hundred 5·9 howitzer shells fell on the place. I put up with it for about an hour, and then the Germans seemed to alter their line and the shells came nearer. C Battery are just alongside me, with their telephone pit about 30 yards from my mess, where I was at the time with my officers. A shell fell on C telephone pit, completely wrecking it, and burying all the men inside. After that I felt I really must withdraw the men, as we were not shooting. I accordingly sent out a telephone to a place in the flank of the battery, away from the shelling, and to which I had previously had a wire laid, I then gave the order for the men to withdraw under their Nos. 1 to the flank place. I also went myself, and had not left the mess two minutes when a shell pitched clean through the roof and burst inside. If there had been anyone there they must have been killed on the spot.

22

Welch had to take his men away too, and we spent the next two hours in watching our batteries being strafed. I don't think the German was after us at all—it was the heavy battery who was getting most of it. Still, the shooting was very bad and a great many shots fell in our batteries. After a couple of hours or so they stopped, but I was not born yesterday, and refused to go back at once. He did his usual low trick, of waiting twenty minutes till he thinks we have all gone back to see the damage, and then puts over another burst. As soon as the final burst was over we went back and were disgusted to find that our mess was completely wrecked and everything inside blown into small atoms. Fortunately most of my kit was in a corner and escaped. Now we are homeless.

I boarded out my subalterns on C Battery and went over to Headquarters for lunch. It was a great relief to spend an hour in complete safety, and be able to take off one's steel hat. The new Brigade Headquarters, I found just before the arrival of Colonel Street, are miles underground, lit by electric light and would keep out a 17-in. Personally, I have reached a stage of exhaustion that is not far removed from collapse. I have been exactly a month now living under incessant shell-fire, without any protection whatever. It is the entire absence of sleep more than the shelling, or rather a combination of the two. It is quite impossible to sleep if one is lying under a tarpaulin with 5·9's and 8-in. falling within a hundred yards. To begin with, there is the suspense of waiting between shells, which may vary from five seconds to ten minutes. Then there is the four or five seconds beginning with the first faint whine of the shell in the far distance, which rapidly rises to the well-known rushing scream ; then there is the crash as it lands, which makes the whole place shake for a couple of hundred yards, and finally the angry "zip" of the flying splinters, which may be any size from a match to the size of a large meat-chopper, weighing up to 20 lb. and with jagged edges like fish-hooks all over them. As soon as the pieces have finished flying, one looks out and

inquires, " Where did that one go ? " Or, " Are you all
right over there ? " One sees heads popping out of the
ground everywhere, just like rabbits in a burrow. Welch
and I walked back to our batteries after lunch, and were
very nearly caught by some salvos of 4·2's ; we were
walking in a trench at the time and the things landed just
on the edge. I spent a wretched afternoon, having no
mess to go to, and there were too many Boche planes up
to do much work before dark. We selected the site for a
new mess in an old trench close to No. 1 gun ; by building
two sandbag walls we shall be able to make a place about
10 feet long by 6 wide. I am going to put pit-props on
that, corrugated iron to keep out the rain, and one row of
sandbags, that will stop shrapnel. Last night's heavy
rain has fairly put the lid on everything ; the country
has suddenly returned to its normal condition of thick
yellow pea-soup. The trenches and shell-holes are full
of water, and, as what small part of Flanders is not shell-
holes is trench, the state of affairs can be left to the
imagination. Even that is, I fear, hopeless ; no one who
has not had the misfortune to experience the mud of this
vile country can hope ever to realise what it means. In the
good old days of trench warfare at least we had duckboarded
trenches ; now there is nothing but millions of shell-holes,
or rather ponds. In order to get anywhere near the front,
it is necessary to flounder from hole to hole. Although
we have most of the high ground, we can still be seen from
various vantage points in the Hun lines, so that one's
progress consists in crawling through the mud from crater
to crater. I have had to take to my gum-boots again,
which I hate as they are so tiring to walk in, and also, if
one attempts to walk fast, the boot remains embedded
in the mud. I am wet to the waist, and slimy from head
to foot—and still the rain comes steadily down. Last
night I had up an extra 2,400 rounds of ammunition, all
in boxes. But the track had been shelled all day, and
what with the holes and the rain, Dallas and Coates were
unable to get it up to the guns. It had all to be dumped
down some 300 yards away, and to-night we shall have to

carry it over by hand. In the fine weather, dry shell-holes make ideal dumps for ammunition and I had 3,000 rounds nicely hidden away in holes, and lightly covered over with earth to hide them from planes. Now all these places have turned into pools, and we have spent the day in digging them out and putting the ammunition into dry little shelters. So many thousands of rounds have been blown up lately by the shelling that I have given orders for not more than a hundred shells to be put in one dump. Our new mess is not ready yet, so I am living in a tent, which does not give one the feeling of great security. As I write the Hun is shelling the usual spot, some three hundred yards on my left rear. So long as he stays there I feel quite safe, but unfortunately every now and then he puts one quite close here. I suppose it is careless laying by one of his gunners.

St. Eloi, 1st July, 1917

A quiet night for this place. The four of us slept in the new sandbag house; by putting down our beds in a row we were just able to all get in. I believe they put some shells close to us, but except for two lots at 2 and 5 o'clock, it did not wake me. I suppose one can get accustomed to anything in time; but I never would have believed that I could sleep under a sheet of corrugated iron only, in a place that was shelled night and day. Yesterday evening and to-day we have had more air-bursts than crumps; they make more noise and are very deadly if you happen to be under them; but they are much less alarming than the things that land in the ground and then blow up a huge fountain of mud and debris. We are being relieved on the nights of the 3/4th and 4/5th (thank goodness), and then go back to the neighbourhood that I was in with the 2nd Life Guards. The country ought to be very pretty at this time of the year, and at any rate it will be peaceful. We have had very little rain last night, and the ground is beginning to dry up—that is to say, it is more like butter and less like cream. I have got my 6,000 rounds of ammunition up now, which completes my establishment. It is entirely due to the energetic Dallas, who has brought up convoys of wagons every night. One reason I am looking forward to our rest is that we shall have an opportunity of making up the mess-kit; at present, all our cups and plates are broken and the enamel chipped off.

St. Eloi, 2nd July, 1917

A quiet night till 8 o'clock this morning, when the usual 5·9 battery in the Kortwilde group opened up on C Battery. I put up with it for some time, but as the shooting was very wild and shells were getting on the edge of my battery, I gave the order to withdraw. We all went to the old front line, a hundred yards on the flank of my guns. We had to stay there for two hours whilst the Hun pounded C Battery and the wood beyond. Two guns were put out of action and a dump of ammunition blown up. By 10 o'clock we were able to go back and have a belated breakfast; at the same time, battery commanders were sent to headquarters. On arrival, we were told that the zone had to fire right up on the north; this means a 25° switch for me. The worst of it is that it will be impossible to see the place to register, except by going right up to Hedge Street, which is somewhere near Hooge. This will mean some 5,000 yards of wire, running parallel to the old trenches and just behind them. As the whole of the back of the trenches is strafed continually, I do not see much chance of keeping the wire open. It will also be a horrible walk in the sun, in and out of crump-holes. The new scheme does not come into operation till the morning of the day we go out, so it is a pity they did not wait till then, as the new people will have to do it all over again. Their dial sights will probably not be quite the same as mine, so necessitating registration.

We were just having our coffee after lunch when the "hate" began again. The same battery was firing, only this time on B Battery, which is just behind me. His shooting was quite excellent, every shell bursting with a terrific crash right in the gun-line. Over a hundred shells must have been fired and I saw several pits hit, also ammunition blown up, but I have not heard yet what the damage is. I am afraid several guns have been knocked out. There is no doubt that the Hun is getting savage : but what are our own counter-batteries doing ? It is the same here as in our late position ; day after day we are shelled by the same battery, and no one ever seems to take them on.

(3.30 p.m.) He has now started smothering us with shrapnel.

St. Eloi, 3rd July, 1917

We were shelled out at 8 o'clock this morning, but fortunately he did not hit the battery, and we were able to get back in time for breakfast. We have suddenly had our zone altered and now have to fire 26 degrees further north. It is a great nuisance, as I had to go all the way up Maple Copse to reregister. I left the battery soon after 10 with my telephonists and had a dreadful walk. It was very hot, and, as there is no lateral communication, I had to go across country. There is not a square yard of the country behind the trenches that is not a crump-hole, so I was climbing in and out of craters the whole way. I eventually got into the old English front line some thousand yards to the south of the O.P. I was making for. For a long time I could not find anyone in the trenches to ask my way of. Eventually, after climbing about the remains of what used to be trenches, I found a man sunning himself at the top of a dug-out. He suggested that I should descend into the pit and find his officers. I went down a steep flight of steps for about 20 feet, and found myself in a narrow mine gallery not more than 5 feet deep. It was pitch dark, and although I could see nothing I felt that the place was full of people. After shouting for some time a man came along with a candle-end and took me to his company commander. It was almost impossible to get along the gallery, as it was packed with sleeping men lying on the floor. One had to climb over them and push past their equipment, which was hanging on the walls. It seemed hours before we reached a light, which came from a candle in a recess at the side of the passage. Here the company officers live, in a hole 5 feet high, about 10 wide, and 5 deep. They told me that I was a long way from where I wanted to get to. They said it was impossible to get there overland as the trenches were completely broken up, and one was in full view of the Huns to the north. They said I should have to go all the way underground. I borrowed a guide who took me as far as their Battalion Headquarters. Here I got another guide who took me another 500 yards, to where one had to emerge into the open air. Although I only walked about half a mile, it took me an hour and a half, and I was quite exhausted, as one had to push past hundreds of men, in the dark and an awful atmosphere of concentrated dirt and sweating humanity. Eventually I emerged into daylight at the top of another steep staircase. As my head came level with the ground a shell burst on the parapet above, smothering me with earth. Needless to say, I went down my hole like a rabbit at the sound of a gun. As nothing more happened for five minutes I ventured out again, and walked along the trench for a few yards before again going to ground. Here the same process was repeated as in the other tunnel, and after another half-hour I finally reached the O.P. I was not surprised to hear that all the wires were down and that it might be hours before we got through. We have only one line of our own to this place, as we only took on this zone to-day. We were using the wires of another brigade, where we had to get connected on to our brigade and thence plugged through to my own battery. A very long way round and room for many things to go wrong. I went back to Battalion Headquarters and asked for lunch. I had an excellent lunch and a glass of port, after which I scrambled back to the O.P., and was overjoyed to find that one line had been repaired, and I was able to get through to my guns. From that moment the wires behaved beautifully, and I quickly registered all the guns on Graveyard Cottage, which is close to Klein Zillebeke. The real O.P. had been knocked in yesterday, and I had to stand at the top of the stairs in the open and use field-glasses. It is not so dangerous as it sounds, as, although the place is only a hundred yards from the nearest Huns, they cannot see it, owing to a high bank of earth on the left. To the front, where one is fully exposed, there is no German trench within 500 yards. The only thing to remember is that one must move as little as possible. I scarcely moved a muscle except to raise and lower my glasses very slowly. In spite of the big switch the guns were almost dead on their line, and as soon as I had got a direct hit on the target with each gun, I sent down the order to register. Just as I had packed up and was starting back, I got a message from the adjutant asking me to register our 4·5 howitzer battery. I had never registered howitzers and was rather amused. It is much easier than with 18-pounders, as the burst is so big. A great fountain of earth and smoke goes up each time. Meanwhile Hobday had arrived, so I left him to finish the last three howitzers and started back again. I had the same horrible scramble in the tunnel and emerged to find that the Hun was crumping the trenches round with 5·9's. Whilst I was having tea with the infantry two of the tunnel entrances were crumped in, but we managed to get out safely and lost no time in getting away from the trenches and into the open, where one only has to risk meeting an odd shell. I reached my battery in time to change before dinner. I was completely done up with the heat by that time. The relieving battery commander has arrived and is staying with me for the night.

At 10 o'clock one section of the new battery arrived; we got my two guns out as quickly as possible, limbered up on to the other batteries' gun limbers, and got them away in about ten minutes. Rentell and I got the new guns on to the S.O.S. lines and we all went back to my mess. Some very curious letters have been captured from the enemy, some found in dug-outs and on dead men, and others on prisoners who had not had time to post them before being captured. The following is the translation of a typical letter, and shows the state of the moral in the German Army at present. Allowance must be made for the fact that it was written under our bombardment on " Y " day, i.e. the day before our great attack. This sort of reading consoles one for the horrible time we have had ourselves.

TRANSLATION OF A GERMAN CAPTURED LETTER

" A Shell-hole in Hell,
"6/6/17.

" Thanks for your kind letter. I am still well, but quite discouraged. I have just received fifty cigarettes from Corporal Karl Neiss from Louvain in Belgium, a sausage and twenty cigarettes from my sister; the day before yesterday, fifty cigarettes, writing materials, and sweets from my Täubchen. In dejection I shared them out with my companions in misery. You have no idea what it is like—fourteen days passed in hellish fire night and day. In this marvellously beautiful weather we crouch together and await our doom. The dead here are piled up by their artillery alone, which is far superior to our own. The night through we lie prepared for action, with gas-masks on our faces, as the enemy fire gas-shells and 3 or 4 per cent. aerial torpedoes all night. No trench work, as it is not to be thought of with shrapnel all night; the wounded and poisoned are continually being grouped and sent off —many dead too from gas poisoning. Up to now our division, only three regiments, has lost 3,400 men in barely three months. The fourth regiment is in Macedonia. We are quite helpless against the English. Thirty men have been buried in mine galleries and are burning into the bargain. Every day the English fetch over some of those in the front line, or rather hole. What are the poor fellows to do ? Everyone refuses to go to the front line. We wait all night in increased readiness for action; we can no longer sit or lie down, our heads ache from gas. Cigarettes taste of gas. The 28 cm. steel shell would drive a lion mad, and their effect is indescribable. Our artillery cannot fire in the daytime; Tommy notices it at once and it all dies away. A terrible, devastated region! Three days more, and we shall go right up to the front line again for five days. We all look forward to being taken prisoner. We do not touch the hand grenades; it would be useless. Nowhere can a man be worse off, not even among the Hottentots. Such a pitiful life! No food, no drinking-water all day, and the sun burns. At midnight, dinner, and at 3 in the morning coffee; but not always, as in all acts is danger to life. If we are not soon relieved we shall go mad, we are already muddled. There are artillery-men, infantry, and flying men from Arras here.

They say Arras was the golden age, compared with this time in Hell. At least they had galleries there; we have absolutely nothing here. The English want to shoot us down, not make peace. They do not need infantry, their artillery is enough. We dare not let a glimpse of us be seen in the daylight. Fifteen to twenty-five flying men are 15 to 30 metres over our position; as soon as they catch sight of us, they signal with their machine-guns, and for half an hour the heaviest shells are whistling over us. Here and there, half a dug-out is to be found. Dear Otto, if ever I get back out of this position for rest, I will write you more and then answer your letter. My head hurts dreadfully from so much gas; the stuff does not pass off so quickly. Excuse my bad writing; the place is too narrow and there is no light."

RENINGHELST, 5TH JULY, 1917

We have got out of action at last. At 10 o'clock my remaining two sections were relieved and we got away without mishap. I was very nervous about having so many horses up there, as they always shell that part every night. As soon as the two first guns were out of their pits we ran in the new battery's guns and sent off mine under Cooper. I waited till all the new guns had been

checked on the lamps, and then followed the rest of my
battery on foot. We had hardly got away when the Hun
started his usual shelling; I was afraid he might add a
bit to his range and just hit us. Rentell and I walked
all the way back to Dickebusch, and found all our horses
waiting for us. It was a great relief to be on a horse again,
as I was completely done up with the long walk. We
reached camp about 1 in the morning and heard that all
the teams and wagons had got safely through. Dallas
had very thoughtfully got drinks ready for us, after which
I went to bed, and was instantly asleep.

RENINGHELST, 9 A.M.

We are just starting, and expect a long day, as it is
fifteen miles across country.

BORRE, 10 P.M.

We had a very trying march, as it was hot and hilly.
We got here at 4 p.m., and the men had their dinner before
stables. I am so sleepy I cannot see to write any more.
We were supposed to march as a brigade, but we soon got
blocked on the road ; I managed to water and feed on the
way. At various intervals I got messages from the colonel
about halting for ten minutes, etc., but I soon managed to
get completely out of touch with the rest of the brigade
and came on steadily and very slowly. All my gunners
had to walk, as the vehicles are fully loaded up with forage,
etc., and I do not want to take too much out of the horses.
Just as I was leaving camp I suddenly saw Jock Hann,
the riding master of the 3rd Hussars. We were mutually
astonished at meeting in such strange circumstances. He
is looking after the horses of the Heavy Artillery of the
Xth Corps. I had heard that he is out here from General
Reed, who is C.R.A. of the Xth Corps. Hann was much
struck by the turn-out of my battery, and said that it
was the smartest he had seen. I have found out where
he lives and must get hold of him when we come back
next week. We arrived at Borre at 4 p.m. and found

everything ready. Quite a good billet in a farm in the village. It feels quite funny to have a roof over one's head again. It is the first time the whole battery has been together since I took it over. We sat down to dinner eight—my own six officers and Shuttleworth and Towell, the vet., who both live with me.

RACQUINGHEM, 7TH JULY, 1917

I had a comfortable night in a bed with white sheets, but, as there was only one thin blanket, I was very cold. Another hot, sunny day. The camp is quite settled down and I have arranged for watering at a river half a mile away. There is a small common here on the top of a hill, and the whole Divisional Artillery is crowded into it— the 106th and 107th Brigades, the D.A.C. and the A.S.C. It would have been much nicer to have had a quiet farm as one generally has, instead of all being cramped together; but still, anything would be a relief after that awful Salient. We are all thankful for a rest before going back to the place. I have spent the day going into rolls of N.C.O.s inspecting horses, guns, etc. One of my guns has got to go to the I.O.M. to-morrow to be repaired.

RACQUINGHEM, 8TH JULY, 1917

It rained hard last night, and the unfortunate men had a very uncomfortable time, as the authorities have only provided five tents for about two hundred men. Last night I dined with General Sheppard, whose Headquarters are close here. There was only the A.D.C. and signalling officer, so we had a long talk about all sorts of things. I gathered that we are likely to stay here about a week, before returning to the Line. To-day being Sunday, I have done very little with the battery, beyond stables. I meant to have had a kit inspection, but it was too wet to lay out the things on the grass.

RACQUINGHEM, 9TH JULY, 1917

Rather cold and wet. This morning an inspection of guns in the gun park. Dallas has got a bar to his Military

Cross, which I am delighted at, as he has richly deserved it. It is not many young officers of twenty-two who could successfully command a six-gun battery in a great battle like Messines. Hobday and Harper have also got the M.C., so some of my recommendations have gone through after all. I am still hoping that the doctor will get his too, and various N.C.O.s and men.

RACQUINGHEM, 10TH JULY, 1917

Another fine day. I have spent the day in general reorganisation and cleaning up, inspection of gas-helmets, etc. Ryder has gone home. He has been a territorial and volunteer for over twenty years. He has very kindly taken two refills of my precious diary with him. He has promised to take them actually to the house, so I hope G. has got them by now. I shall be very nervous till I hear that they have arrived safely. I would rather lose anything than my diary, especially the interesting part I have just sent home, from the time I came back from sick leave to now.

RACQUINGHEM, 11TH JULY, 1917

To-day we have had the good news that the Russians have made a big attack and captured 25,000 prisoners. I did not think they had a kick left in them. We had a great dinner party this evening, the colonel, Welch, Grieve, Lissant, etc., making up twelve. We got it cooked by a Frenchwoman across the road, and it turned out a huge success. Bath superintended the waiters, and it was almost a civilised meal.

RACQUINGHEM, 12TH JULY, 1917

A new officer joined me this morning, called Ryves. This gives me a major, a captain, and five subalterns—none too many to start a big battle with. We have got orders to move to-morrow, which is a great disappointment, as we shall only have had six days' rest in this peaceful spot.

Borre, 13th July, 1917

Our holiday is over and we have started on the return march to the battle. Yesterday evening we had brigade sports for the men and races for the officers. I did not encourage any of my officers to ride, as I cannot afford to have them breaking limbs or their horses' legs, just at present. We started at 8 o'clock this morning and had an easy march here via Eblingham and Hazebrouck. We have not got the same good billet this time, as the D.A.C. wanted our old one; but it is not bad as Flemish farms go. Of course there was the usual row with the pro-German farmer, who objected to our coming into his farmyard. He began to get so noisy that my sergeant-major had to remove him out of the gun park. We cannot hear any firing here, which is curious, as we are so close.

Reninghelst, 14th July, 1917

As we had to march at 5 a.m. I ordered reveille for 3 a.m., but the Hun called us at 2 o'clock by dropping bombs on our heads. We were only just outside Hazebrouck and he was after the station there. There must have been several planes as a great number of bombs were dropped and a lot of damage done. When he had done with Hazebrouck he let go a final three really heavy ones close to our wagon-lines. We marched here via Bailleul and Locre, arriving about 11 o'clock. It was a disagreeable march, as there was an enormous amount of motor transport on the road and it rained most of the way, making the *pavé* roads very slippery. Just before we got to Bailleul, a cyclist handed me a leave warrant for Sergeant Porter. There was a train that I knew left in a few minutes, so I told him to hand over his horse, jump on to a passing motor-lorry, and get straight off.

We are camped quite close to where I had my wagon-lines before we went into rest. By a curious coincidence, Hann has his tent within 30 yards of my gun park. I took him round my horses and he dined with me to-night. We had a very cheerful party, as it is the last night's rest we

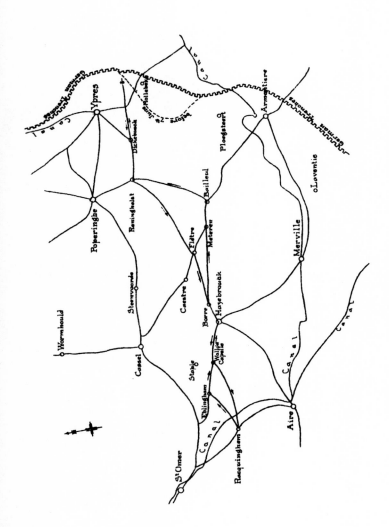

St. Omer – Armentieres – Ypres, July 1917.

shall get for some time. They have not given us a single tent, but we have a large number of waterproof canvas sheets, 18 × 15 feet, which make into excellent bivouacs for four men. My wheeler-corporal made us an excellent mess out of a couple of them and some planks he found.

RENINGHELST, 15TH JULY, 1917

The colonel and the four battery commanders went up to reconnoitre the positions this morning. Our worst fears are realised. We have to go into the old Blaupoort positions, or, at least, within a few yards of them. My own position is exactly where Welch was at the time of the late battle, before we all moved over to St. Eloi—a horrible prospect indeed. We rode up nearly as far as Spoil Bank, and then, as they were shelling a dump on our right, we left our horses and walked the rest of the way. We found the Blaupoort Valley simply alive with shells, quite in its best form. Dallas and I at once went to our map location and decided to utilise Welch's old pits, most of which were still standing. We made a thorough examination and then walked back to our horses. The rest of the day I spent quietly in the wagon-lines.

RENINGHELST, 16TH JULY, 1917

This morning the colonel has changed all the battery positions, owing to having misread the map, and putting B Battery into the 107th Brigade area. All our battery commanders, therefore, had to go up again and choose fresh positions. Dallas and I went up again and are putting our guns practically into the same place, but with our left flank thrown back. We had a horrid time whilst we were marking out the gun-pits. Hundreds of 5·9's fell just beyond us, most of them within two hundred yards, but, thank goodness, nothing actually on the position. The pieces fell all round, but it is wonderful what near escapes one can have without being touched. We got back by 3 p.m., having had lunch with a 9·2 battery, who are near my old 1915 position. I have sent Rentell and a large party up this afternoon to begin to dig the gun-pits and collect the ammunition which is lying about all over the place.

After tea, Hann and I rode over to a place a mile beyond Reninghelst, where the Xth Corps Cavalry are camped. This is a composite regiment of yeomanry of N. and S. Irish Horse, commanded by Colonel Goring, late 3rd Hussars. We had a long talk with Whitla, who is second in command of the regiment. He looks very old and worried. I had not seen him since Sialkot, when he commanded our A squadron.

BLAUPOORT, 17TH JULY, 1917

As soon as it was dusk I sent up all six guns in two parties under an officer each, and followed them after dinner myself. I rode as far as Bedford House and then sent back the horses. I walked past my old position and got to the old Brigade Headquarters near Blaupoort Farm without incident. We then came under fire from 5·9 howitzers and gas-shell. As it was pitch dark, it was very unpleasant. I was very nervous that if I was hit the man with me would go for help but would never find me in the dark. I kept telling him where we were, but he was an absolute fool and could not recollect any landmarks, although he had just spent a month at this very place. Eventually we reached the position all right, and I was immensely relieved to find the guns had all arrived without accident. Four pits were ready, and by dawn we had got some sort of emplacement dug round the others. There is no question of making shell-proof pits here : all we can do is to build a sandbag wall 4 feet high all round the gun, which will save the men from splinters of shells that burst near. Over the top we have got fishing-nets with bits of green canvas tied on in places. It makes excellent cover from aeroplanes and is practically what I did at Guillemont.

FRONT-LINE TRENCHES, 18TH JULY, 1917

After breakfast I went up to the trenches to register the guns. We had been told that the Brigade Headquarters had arranged communications, but when we got there found that it was impossible to get through on the telephone. We had a very disagreeable time going up, as we had to pass through a 5·9 barrage to do so. The O.P. is in the same old place, which one approaches through an enormous tunnel half a mile long and 15 feet deep. The gallery is only 5 feet high and 3 feet wide. It is packed with hundreds and hundreds of men. In spite of its being lit by electric light it is very difficult to get along, and most exhausting. Communication was eventually established at 7 p.m., and I let the howitzer battery then register as he had to shoot next morning. By the time he had finished it was too dark to see any more. I did not want the horrible walk back to the battery to-night, and have to come up again at dawn. I therefore decided to remain where I was for the night. Of course I had nothing with me except what I walked up in, and no food. The tunnel is very warm, not to say hot, and I asked the colonel of the infantry battalion to give me some dinner. I had a very pleasant evening with him till about 2 o'clock, when a tremendous barrage of 5·9's came down on us. We were quite safe in our tunnel, but no one could get in or out, and the place rocked and shook as in a continuous earthquake. It was very alarming, as every telephone wire was at once cut and we were completely isolated without means of knowing what was happening. We were very much afraid that it was a Hun attack, and all the men were made to stand to, with their equipment on, and bayonets fixed. It died down soon after midnight, and I found a corner to lie down in and snatched a little sleep.

BLAUPOORT, 19TH JULY, 1917

At 7 a.m. I went along the tunnel and found my telephonists ready for me. The wire was cut as usual, but I sent two men out along it, and in half an hour we were through to the brigade, who then connected us on to the battery. The lines were well laid out and the guns shot properly and in a very short time I had got them all on to their zero-line, which was Graveyard Cottage. When I

23

had finished No. 6 I gave " one round battery fire, 5 secs.,"
just to make sure, and was delighted to see all six guns
hit the target. Baker, who commands D Battery,
had joined me, and after he had registered his last two
howitzers we started back. On our way we visited a new
O.P. that has been made by the R.E. A tunnel has been
driven into a mound and two giant periscopes put in a
shaft. It is exactly like a submarine. You sit at the
bottom of a shaft in the dark, and look into the eyepiece
of this periscope which is some 10 feet long. We called
on Brigade Headquarters on our way back and saw the
colonel. We have to begin serious firing now, 300 rounds
per battery each day and 300 more at night—all road
strafing. Fritz will have some difficulty in getting up
his rations. We have had a fairly lively time in the
battery. The Hun has changed his tactics. We no
longer get any real set strafes like we used to. Now he
throws a couple of rounds in one place and then somewhere
else. I am not sure it is not more unpleasant. It never
stops night or day ; 5·9's, 4·2's and ·77 high explosive and
gas-shells—about one every five minutes, and all over the
place. It is no use trying to dodge them, as they may go
anywhere. Whilst I have been writing this a bomb has
just been dropped 10 yards from where I am sitting.
Coates, Ryves, and I jumped up to see what it was, and
found one of our H.E. shell dumps burning merrily. We
all rushed over and began pulling away the burning boxes
and throwing earth on the smouldering stuff. I turned
round to get another sandbag, and saw a man lying beside
me. He appeared to be quite dead, so I went on with the
work. However, Ryves, who is a medical student, discovered that he was still alive, so we put him on a stretcher
and carried him under cover. It was quite hopeless, and
he died in under five minutes. My own impression is
that he was dead all the time and only the muscles moving.
He was hit in the heart, head, stomach, both legs and both
arms, and his neck broken as well. The nearest place
to bury men is at Bedford House and that means sending
a party twice through the barrage across the valley. The

G.S. wagon arrived at that moment with pit-props and the rations, so we hastily emptied it and put the dead man in, and sent him down to the wagon-lines to be buried there. Four other men were wounded, but only two had to go to hospital.

RENINGHELST, 20TH JULY, 1917

Poor old R. is to be tried by General Court Martial for losing some secret papers during the battle of Vimy, and has asked me to defend him at the trial, as I know more about military law than most of the officers in this brigade. Accordingly, I came down to the wagon-lines this afternoon to help him to prepare his defence. Late last night I got a telephone message from the colonel telling me to reconnoitre the German wire early this morning. I nearly had a fit, as it is usually considered to be the business of the infantry rather than of a battery commander. As soon as it was dawn Coates and I went off. I had studied my coloured contoured map over-night and decided that there was only one place that was worth going to for the purpose of seeing the German wire (always supposing there is any left). First of all we made for Hill 60 and picked up a guide from the infantry. I met a young infantry subaltern who volunteered to show me the way to the most advanced post. He said that one could only get there at night, as it is in full view of the Germans. We got up to within a few hundred yards without much difficulty and then found a bit of old trench that helped. Eventually we reached a spot only a hundred yards from where I wanted to go, but the ground in between was on a forward slope and in full view. I therefore left Coates and the infanteer in a shell-hole with all my equipment except glasses, which I carried in my hand. I told them to stay there till I got back. I have done a good deal of big-game shooting and am pretty good at stalking. I am sure I never took so much trouble to stalk any impalla with the finest head as I did this morning. Either the Boche did not see me or he did not want to fire and so give away his own position, but I got into our advanced Lewis

Gun post after half an hour of crawling flat. I was nearly arrested as a spy by the officer in charge, who naturally wanted to know who I was and how I had got there. I showed him various letters and note-books that satisfied him, although any German could have produced letters from off a prisoner or dead English officer. I was repaid by a wonderful view of the Hun country, spread out like a map in front of us. From Klein Zillebeke to Gheluvelt the whole panorama was laid out. If it is possible to establish an O.P. up there, it would be the easiest thing in the world to shoot up the whole place. When I got back to Coates I found that he was starting out to look for me, thinking I must either be captured or lost. We got back to Bde. H.Q. by 9 and I made my report, and then made tracks for the breakfast that I hoped was waiting for me. Dallas was to have relieved me about 11, but there was such a heavy barrage across the valley that he could not get through it till 12. Bath and I waited till there was a lull in the storm and slipped through by way of Lankhof Château. My horses had gone to the wrong place, so I had to walk an extra mile and did not reach the wagon-lines till nearly 2 o'clock. After lunch the first thing I did was to have a bath, and then went on to see R. I have questioned all his witnesses and am fairly confident of getting him off. He appears to have lost a few papers that were not very important during a move forward in the middle of the Vimy Battle. Our own general wants to get the whole thing quashed, but some red-tabbed and red-hatted staff officer on the Army Staff, thirty miles behind the lines, is out for blood.

RENINGHELST, 21ST JULY, 1917

Hann and R. dined with me last night, and I got to bed early. I had a glorious sleep in pyjamas and breakfasted in bed, with the result that I feel a different person. I rode into Div. H.Q. this morning and saw Fox, the staff captain. He told me that the trial would be at 2 p.m. on Monday, but that he had not got all the papers in the case yet. I spent the whole afternoon in reading up my *Military Law*. I am fairly confident of the result, but at the very worst R. will only be reprimanded, which means nothing in a case like this.

RENINGHELST, 22ND JULY, 1917

Our guns have been firing all day and night, and the Hun is replying, but I imagine we are putting over a great deal more heavy stuff than he is. I was awakened this morning by a large number of heavy shells falling round my camp, but as they were not within two or three hundred yards I did not worry about them.

After breakfast I rode into Reninghelst. Whilst I was at Div. H.Q. I could see that heavy shells were falling very close to my camp, so was not surprised on my return there to find a huge chasm in the road not 20 feet from Hann's tent. A number more had fallen in the lines, wounding horses. I at once gave the order to file out, and took the horses some half-mile down a side-road out of the line of fire. It stopped in about an hour and we went back. I think they are using 8-in. armour-piercing shells, fired from a long-range naval gun, probably mounted on a railway truck.

RENINGHELST, 23RD JULY, 1917

The great excitement of the day has been the trial. We put up the best defence possible, but it was no good and poor old R. was convicted. There was no getting over the fact that the papers had been lost, and that some of them were secret. At the worst, R. will get a simple reprimand, which does not matter in the least in a case of this sort ; and in any case he is going home.

At 10 o'clock to-night we got the alarm of gas, and I found out from some R.E. signallers near here that a gas cloud was coming over from the direction of Ploegstreet and had already passed Kemmel. I got all the men out of their tents with respirators in the alert position and warned the hospital and other units near. However, it did not reach us and we got to sleep about midnight. Ellis Bishop came over to tea ; the 108th Brigade are not far off. He is the only one of my officers left now. Perry has gone home with shell-shock and so has Harvey. Sergeant Meecham has been badly gassed and is in a very dangerous condition in hospital. Apparently most of the signallers have been killed or wounded. Hart had five out of his six howitzers knocked out. Altogether they seem to have had rather a rough time of it. There has been a pretty heavy bombardment all day, but not what I should call really intense.

BLAUPOORT, 24TH JULY, 1917

I held a Board this morning to test some men for appointment as saddlers, and got Hann to assist. After lunch I rode up to the guns with the Padre, Neaves, Rentell and our horseholders. It was such a large party that I made them split up when we got into the danger area. Bedford House was being badly knocked about with 8-in., so I turned off and came by a different route. The country stinks of the new German gas, and before I reached the battery I had all the symptoms of violent hay fever, in spite of the fact that there had been no gas-shells about since the preceding night. We reached the battery all right; and I took over from Dallas as quickly as possible. He had just brought the barrage tables back from Brigade Headquarters — four sheets of small figures ; they look like logarithm tables. I sent Ryves down with Dallas for a few days' rest. They seem to have had a horrible time since I was away—gas-shells all night and strafed all day. We have been losing men every day. This afternoon my assistant clerk was wounded on his way to Brigade Headquarters. He was taken away to the Field Ambulance on a stretcher and of the men carrying him one was killed and the other wounded. We had hardly finished dinner when the shelling began on our position. A succession of 4·2's and ·77 gas-shells.

They were all round us but did not get a direct hit, which was fortunate as this place would not keep anything out. The gas shelling was the worst I have experienced. We sat with our gas-helmets on hour after hour. Each time I raised the face-piece to try the air I got a horrible mouthful of it. Our eyes and noses were streaming, and the back of the throat burning till it was nearly intolerable. At the end of a couple of hours the pain from the nose-clip and elastic bands round the head nearly made me scream, and I felt almost ready to tear the beastly thing off. About 2 o'clock the gas-shells ceased and we lay down on the floor as we were.

BLAUPOORT, 25TH JULY, 1917

I woke up with a start at 5 o'clock this morning with a feeling that something was very wrong. There was a fearful pain in my throat as if I had swallowed a spoonful of mustard powder. I realised at once that the place was full of gas. I shouted to Coates, who was lying beside me, and got my gas-mask on as quickly as possible. The shelling had just begun again and the sentries were rousing everyone. It did not last very long and I went to sleep again. This new mustard-oil gas is the very devil. It is not very poisonous itself, but it produces violent hay fever in a few seconds, and then they send phosgene, which is deadly. The real danger is that the mustard gas paralyses the nerves of the nose and one cannot detect the phosgene till too late. Coates and I worked in our nasty little dark dug-out from 10 a.m. to 8 p.m. making out the barrage tables. It is the most complicated thing I have seen yet. I am very nervous that these young N.C.O.s won't understand what to do. Welch had terrible bad luck last night. A shell burst in his sergeant's mess, and out of the six sergeants it killed three and wounded the other three. C Battery have now lost no less than fourteen sergeants out of their establishment of seven, all in the last six weeks. Bath has made me a wonderful gas-curtain that lets down across the door of my dug-out,

that may keep most of the gas out to-night. (10 p.m.)
It is time for the enemy shelling and gas to begin.

BLAUPOORT, 26TH JULY, 1917

A fairly quiet day. We have been shelled at intervals
with 4·2's and ·77's much as usual, but less of it. Grizel
has sent me a set of little flags, 9 inches square. Each gun
has four for its aiming posts—two on zero and two on 180°.
The idea is that every gun should have a different colour
so that the layer can always pick up his own aiming posts
quickly. We had a practice barrage this afternoon, which
is said to have gone off very well. A party of seven of
our infantry went over to reconnoitre a German " strong
point " at Klein Zillebeke and brought in twelve unwounded
prisoners.

BLAUPOORT, 27TH JULY, 1917

Another quiet night, strange to relate. I cannot make
out why the Bosche is so unnaturally quiet. We are
keeping up a very heavy bombardment, night and day, and
to-day we had a special counter battery shoot. Every gun
on the Corps front had been firing hard at German batteries.
I have developed violent toothache in the last four days
and scarcely know how to bear myself. It is a great nuisance, as I do not want to leave the gun-line at present.
This afternoon I sent Coates to the wagon-line for a rest
and have got Dallas up to replace him. At 11 p.m. we
got orders for an elaborate barrage at dawn to-morrow.

BLAUPOORT, 28TH JULY, 1917

Dallas and I spent most of the night sitting up working
out the new barrage tables. They were amended no less
than twice. Really one would have thought that they
could settle what they want done within twelve hours of
the battle. It is always the same thing—one works out
everything in good time, and then at the last moment the
programme is altered. I am suffering excruciating agony

with my tooth. I could not even lie down last night, and have had absolutely no sleep whatever. We commenced the barrage at 5.15 this morning, and have been making a dreadful noise. It was really just like the Somme. From 9 o'clock till lunch we had to fire over four hundred rounds more at a German battery near Hooge. We evidently annoyed them, as by 2 o'clock we were taken on by a 5·9 battery. Most of the shells fell on C Battery, who had to clear out. My toothache was so bad that I had to arrange to go to a dentist. The colonel was going down to the wagon-lines, so he arranged that we should go in the same car. He had just rung me up at 4 o'clock to say that he had started and would meet me at D battery, when a 5·9 arrived just near our mess. I told Dallas to take the men out if any more came. I had got about 40 yards away when another great 5·9 fell half-way between the mess and me. It knocked me flat on my back, but nothing touched me. As I got up I could see that Dallas was all right, so I waved my hand to him to let him know I was untouched, and ran as hard as I could so as to get away before the next shell. However, the brute had altered the line of his gun, and the next shot fell just behind me, not more than 10 yards off. Again I was flung down in the dust. After that he had two more shots pretty near, though not like the first two, and I did not wait for them but lay down as soon as I heard them coming. I met the colonel hurrying down a sunken road, pursued by gas-shells. It was really extremely funny ; as we walked (very fast) down the road, a gas-shell fell 50 yards behind us, and this happened four times in about two hundred yards. These gas-shells make very little noise arriving, and burst on the ground with a little " pop " like pulling the cork out of a bottle. It was the first time I had seen one burst, although I have heard thousands in the dark. There was no smoke, either black or white ; just the dust thrown up by the shell striking the dry ground, and then a small cloud of yellow green vapour—much the colour of jade. We walked to Voormezeele and arrived very hot in spite of the fact that

I was wearing cotton shorts. It is much more comfortable in this weather, and nearly everybody does it this summer. We found a car waiting for us and motored to the wagon-lines, where I was fortunate in finding Mortimer, our doctor, having tea with Coates, whom I sent down as he had been gassed. Mortimer got a motor ambulance and took me off to Poperinghe to see the dentist at No. 10 C.C.S. (Casualty Clearing Station). He was a very rough-handed individual, who hurt me abominably by prodding an exposed nerve with a long pin. He then put in an arsenic dressing to kill the nerve, and said I should have no pain after a few hours. Mortimer and I dined at the Officers' Club at Poperinghe and got a very bad dinner. However, there is a nice garden and it was a change from Blaupoort.

RENINGHELST, 29TH JULY, 1917

A nightmare of a night. Instead of getting better, my toothache was much worse by the time I went to bed, and M.O. gave me some morphia. Then, just as I was going to sleep, a Hun 'plane came along and dropped bombs all round the camp. The morphia had got hold of me by then, and the bombs did not stop me from going to sleep. The next thing I remember is someone shaking me violently and shouting " Gas attack ! " and pushing my gas-helmet into my hands. I woke up just enough to realise that the tent was full of phosgene, and by instinct at once put on the gas-mask, after which I promptly went to sleep again with the thing on. Some hours later I woke up again and took off my gas-helmet and found the air pure. As the toothache was worse than ever, I again borrowed a car and went to the C.C.S. The dentist was out and could not be found, so I tried the next hospital, where I was lucky enough to see an excellent man, very young, and quite the most skilful fellow at his horrid trade that I have met. He quickly announced that the trouble was from another tooth altogether than the one attended to yesterday. He advised me to have it out at once and have done with it. He got hold of a doctor and they gave me gas. In ten minutes it was all over and I had the consolation of knowing that it was the right tooth all right this time, as there was a large abscess under it. After tea with the doctors I motored back to camp. Selwyn, who was in my battery on the Somme, joined me to-day. He wrote to me long ago and said he wanted very much to come to my new battery and I asked General Sheppard if it could be arranged. The general wrote to the C.R.A. of the I Corps and got his agreement, and then applied to General Headquarters for him. I am very glad to have him, as I can depend on him in an emergency, and he is a smart young officer of the Old Army type. It has been raining hard and the place has become a muddy field again.

BLAUPOORT, 30TH JULY, 1917

The colonel, Mortimer, Selwyn, and I all motored up this morning, walking from Voormezeele. It rained hard last night and the ground was very slippery; one could hardly keep one's feet even on the duckboards between the tramway lines. When we got to the ridge overlooking the Blaupoort Valley we saw that the usual area shoot was in full swing. All our batteries were being shelled by 5·9's and we had to make a deviation to get to them. I was nearly knocked down twice before I reached the mess. I was met by Bath, wearing my field-glasses and pistol, and looking very shaken. The first thing he told me was that Dallas had just been badly wounded in the gun-line. He was talking to Rentell and some tank officers when a ·77 high explosive burst close to him and hit him in both knees. I am afraid it is serious, but I hope not dangerous. He was taken away on a stretcher and put in an ambulance at Spoil Bank, since when we have heard nothing of him. He is a great loss to me, as he was an excellent captain and had been in the battery since it came out in 1915. We have had one of the most poisonous days I have ever known—shelled all day with every calibre from 8-in. downwards. I have been very busy, putting the last touches to everything, ready for to-night. I have not dared to mention the great battle that is coming even in my beloved diary, but now that the day has arrived there is no more need for secrecy. To-night begins the greatest battle of the war. We commence at some time before dawn and attack all the way from here to the sea. If all goes well, there will be no Ypres Salient by this time to-morrow. Hann was coming up to stay the night with me and see the great bombardment start, but has not been able to manage it, for which I am thankful, as we are having such a horrible time. Another man has gone mad. This makes two since we have been in this position. There is no doubt it takes an iron constitution and a strong will to stand this sort of thing. We all thought the last position was the worst we had ever been in, but this beats everything. The whole place is ploughed up with fresh shell-holes and it is a perfect marvel that we have not had every man and gun hit. So far I have only had two guns actually knocked out here. It is now after midnight, and I have just got zero time and filled in all the barrage tables. There are no less than 45 " lifts," each involving a different range and angle for each·gun. It would be simple enough if one had a room with a table and good light to work with, but here in a mud-hole and a guttering candle it is very difficult indeed.

BLAUPOORT, 31ST JULY, 1917

" Z " day at last. We opened up at 3.50 a.m. this morning and have fired without stopping all day. The first reports were very good. The infantry got their first objective all along the line and reported the barrage as very good. But about 10 o'clock, when we ought to have started lifting for the attack on the second line, we began to get rumours that we had been held up in the centre of our division and we were not to lift any more. The situation is still very obscure, but there is no doubt

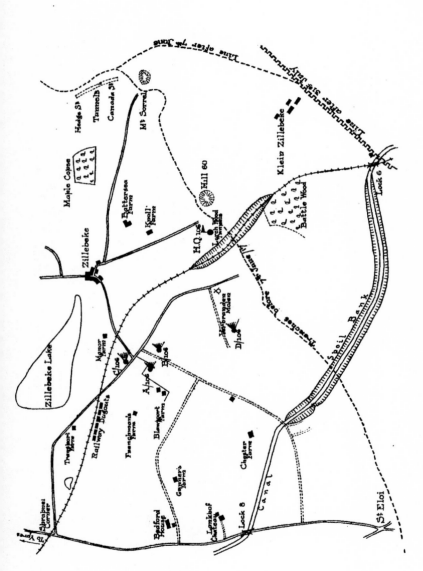

St Eloi – Zillebeke, July 1917.

that we have not got as far as was intended just here. I have only seen about a couple of hundred German prisoners, but I believe a great many have been taken. They have no doubt gone back by a different route. On the other hand, I believe we have done very well up to the North, which is the really important thing. We have used a great number of tanks, but I am not sure if they have been a great success this time. There are a lot of stranded ones all round the country. The weather is against them, as I believe they find it difficult to get along in the mud. They have been passing through the middle of my battery at intervals all day. I got one of them to give me a ride for a hundred yards. It was a very interesting experience. The driver, who was anxious to show off the paces of his prehistoric peep, headed straight for the largest shell-hole he could find, which was an 8-in. crater about 10 feet deep and 15 wide. The beast paused on the edge to take breath and then fell in nose first. I held my breath and clung on to something handy, expecting an awful crash, but to my surprise nothing happened. It was just like a ship at sea. We came down quite gently, and the beast's nose began to rise at once, and in another moment we had crawled out on the far side. The thing that struck me most was the tremendous heat inside. Late in the afternoon I heard that the attack of the brigade we are covering has been definitely held up and that the remainder of the programme has been cancelled. We are now keeping up a slow rate of barrage fire in front of the infantry to protect them whilst they consolidate the ground they have already won. I am afraid our casualties have been very heavy. The Leinsters are said to have the colonel, adjutant, and doctor only left. Other battalions nearly as bad. They seem to have been caught by machine-gun fire from a strong point that was not captured. Very few shells have come over us to-day as we expected. During the actual attack the hostile artillery devote themselves to the infantry. Our hard time will come to-morrow.

BLAUPOORT, 1ST AUGUST, 1917

We had a quiet night, but kept up a very slow fire all the time. At 10 o'clock this morning the Hun really began to attend to us. From that time till 6 this evening we have been simply deluged with shells. It has been one of the worst day's shelling I have yet known. C Battery was shelled out this afternoon, and Welch and his people took refuge with me. As my little dug-out is exactly 6 foot square, and there were eight of us squatting in it, there was rather a crowd. The difficulty here is that if one is heavily shelled there is nowhere to withdraw to, as the shelling is promiscuously scattered over the whole district. We are still barraging slowly, but there is no news of what is going to happen here. From all accounts we have done very well up to the north, and places like Pilkem and St. Julien are again in our hands after nearly three years. The Salient has not quite gone yet, but it is a very flat curve now. Meanwhile, the unfortunate batteries in this valley of death are slowly being smashed up.

BLAUPOORT, 2ND AUGUST, 1917

Another black day. We have been pounded by guns of all calibres from 10 o'clock this morning till now (5 p.m.). My faithful Bath has been hit at last, very badly. It got so bad at 11 o'clock, when they were actually dropping 8-in. among my guns, that I had to take the men away. At that time there was no shelling on the immediate right of the battery, and I took all the men there, about three hundred yards away from the guns. I left them there and went to B Battery to tell the brigade by 'phone that I had had to leave the guns. On my return I found that poor Bath had been hit by a fragment of a high-explosive pip-squeak. It had gone in behind the right ear and at the top of his neck, cut his tongue badly and lodged in his left cheek. We got him over to the dressing-station, where fortunately we found Mortimer and another doctor doing nothing. So they set to work on him at once. He was nearly choking with the blood running down his throat, but Mortimer said that that would quickly stop. They can't tell how bad he is yet ; it all depends if the wound becomes septic or not. He has a good chance of living but I am afraid he is very bad. He is a dreadful loss to me, as he has looked after me since just after Loos, and has been a devoted slave, anticipating everything I could possibly want. Now at 5.30 p.m. the shelling has become intense, and my office has just been hit. Several more men killed and wounded. I wonder how long we shall be able to stand this sort of thing.

BLAUPOORT, 3RD AUGUST, 1917

The shelling of this place was kept up last night till 6.30 ; then we had a rest till 10 o'clock and managed to fire a good many rounds ourselves. But at 10 o'clock it began again and was still going strong when I went to bed at midnight. We had comparative peace this morning, but now at 3 in the afternoon 5·9's and 4·2's are falling fast all over this part of the valley. Another man has gone off his head, but I have refused to allow him to leave the guns. It is simply a matter of everyone having to control their nerves. I am very sorry for the man, but if the idea once gets about that a man can get out of this hell by letting go of his nerves, Heaven help us. My clerk had a near escape with all his papers last night. A shell came through the wall of his dug-out and buried itself in the floor without exploding. We are getting very few duds, and if this had gone off I should have lost all my papers and my clerk into the bargain. I have had a new captain posted to me *vice* Dallas—Lissant, who was my adjutant all through the battle of Messines.

.   .   .   .   .

I have had a double blow—first losing Dallas, who was quite excellent as a captain, and now the general wants to

take Coates, my senior subaltern, as his A.D.C. I wanted
him as captain—a post he is quite fitted for.

BLAUPOORT, 4TH AUGUST, 1917

The country is now a morass—it is almost impossible
to move. We were shelled again last night, and Welch
has lost another gun. A third man in my battery has gone
off his head. I have been feeling horribly ill myself all day
—very sick and a bad headache. It is all owing to the
beastly gas. Baker, who commands D, and his captain
have both been badly gassed and gone away. I had
a letter from Dallas this evening, written in hospital.
I am afraid he is very bad and in great pain. They
have already operated on him. I wish I could get news
of Bath. I am very worried about him.

BLAUPOORT, 5TH AUGUST, 1917

We got gas-shells again in the night, but only for an
hour or so at midnight and a short time at dawn. My
zero-line is Graveyard Cottage, but as we have now advanced beyond it, I must find something else. Lissant
and I went to the O.P. this afternoon and had to pass
through a heavy barrage going. We lost our way in the
hopeless wilderness of shell-holes and had to move about in
full view of the enemy. The mud is simply too awful for
anything. I really think it is worse even than in the
winter. The ground has been churned up to a depth of
10 feet, and, before the rain, was like powder ; now it has
turned into a material of the consistency of porridge. It
is only possible to get along by walking along the edges of
the craters, which, as on the Somme, are so close that they
touch each other for miles. It is really very dangerous,
as the middle of the craters is so soft that one might easily
sink over the head. As it was, I got stuck to-day and it
was all the combined effort of my party could do to pull
me out. I was quite alarmed as I felt myself sinking
deeper and deeper and could not move either foot. By

the time B Battery had finished registering, the line was cut and, after waiting a couple of hours, I gave it up and went home, calling at Brigade Headquarters on the way to complain of no attempt being made to mend the lines. I arrived back at the battery at 8 o'clock, very tired and wet through from head to foot with mud and sweat. The whole forward area is getting very unpleasant now it is wet, as there are numerous dead floating about in the shell-holes and there must be hundreds, if not thousands, of German dead buried everywhere in ruined dug-outs. Their own shells are now reploughing the district and turning them up.

BLAUPOORT, 6TH AUGUST, 1917

We had just finished dinner and were having our cigars and coffee in our mud-holes when the S.O.S. broke out all along the front. The first thing we knew was that the Hun barrage came down like a clap of thunder on our trenches. I at once gave the order to " Stand to," and waited with the telephone to my ear. As a matter of fact we saw the S.O.S. signal before I got word from brigade, and we were firing hard before the order came. Even on the opening day of the battle I don't think there was such a noise as there was then for an hour. Nothing could possibly get through such a fire, and the counter-attack melted away at once. If the Boche came on in much strength his losses must have been tremendous. I got off several hundred shrapnel myself with a certain amount of delay-action high explosive thrown in for luck. We have had a fairly quiet morning, but a battery a quarter of a mile away took it badly in the neck. I saw an 8-in. land square in a gun-pit, and all the rest of the men of the battery digging frantically to get their buried men out, but they must have all been dead. Whilst we were shooting last night in the S.O.S. I saw a horrid sight. A gunner of some other battery ran right through the intervals of my guns. How he managed to avoid my shells I don't know. I could hear him making queer noises as he passed, and by the light of the gun-flash I saw that he was holding

24

one wrist from which the hand was missing. I yelled to him to stop and would have tied him up, but he ran on into the dark. I suppose it will be another case of " Missing," as I don't suppose his body will be found for weeks in the wilderness of shell-holes behind the battery. I have still no news of Bath, and consequently am still hoping that he is alive. If he lives a week or ten days, Mortimer says he has a good chance. He says the two great dangers are, first, shock, and secondly septic pneumonia from the quantity of dirty blood that got into his lungs and was making him choke. Lissant and I again went forward this afternoon to reregister on the new zero. We had a worse time even than yesterday, as we had to go through a 4·2 barrage on the way up and right through the middle of a 5·9 one coming back. I studied the barrage very carefully and took a line that would only necessitate passing under the fire of one gun. He was dropping shells at exactly one-minute interval, all on the same line, but at varying ranges. I took the jump at right-angles, so as to be under his line as short a time as possible. We got to within about a hundred yards of his line, and then crouched down in shell-holes for the next shell. As soon as the mud and pieces had fallen, we got up and clambered over the shell-holes as quick as we could so as to get on as far as possible before the next one. We managed to be in the immediate danger zone of that gun for only about three shells. On arrival at the O.P., which is a huge mine crater, I connected up and proceeded to register my guns on to a certain German strong-point about a mile from me. An extremely incompetent battery commander was also shooting on a place near, and bursting his shells at least two degrees in the air. At first I thought they were my own, and was very angry with the laying ; but as the corrections I gave had no result, I soon saw that it must be some other battery. As a matter of fact, my shells were falling in some thick scrub where I could not see them. When in difficulties, I always range with high explosives and did so to-day, at once seeing great black bursts. We had a very nasty walk back to Brigade

Headquarters, having to pass through the barrage again. Then we had to wait underground at Headquarters whilst they dropped 4·2's on the entrance ; and when we finally did get away they followed us up all the way to S.P. 9, so that we had to take shelter in an old concrete dug-out near Verbrandenmolen. Being thoroughly tired and wet through, I have come down to my wagon-lines for forty-eight hours' rest.

RENINGHELST, 7TH AUGUST, 1917

Except for a few 9-in. shells from the same old naval gun, nothing has disturbed us here, and I am thoroughly enjoying my holiday. I got a letter from Dallas late last night to say that he was too bad to be moved and was still at No. 41 C.C.S. at Godewaersvelde, so Selwyn and I rode over to see him. It is about 8 miles from here, and as by now I know every lane in Flanders, we were able to ride by nice quiet tracks instead of keeping to the dusty roads. Poor Dallas is feeling very sorry for himself. He has had two operations, and they have taken a small piece of shell out of the knee-joint. It was just a question of whether he would lose the use of his leg altogether, but the surgeon who is looking after him assured me that he would almost certainly get off with a stiff knee. At first there was a question that he might have to have his leg off, but that is over now. He was very depressed, but glad to see us. I had tea with the doctors afterwards and got their true opinion about his case, so shall write to his father and tell him all about it.

RENINGHELST, 8TH AUGUST, 1917

I felt too tired to do anything to-day, and have not been out of the wagon-lines all day. I have had a lot of visitors, including Fox, the staff captain, who brought a new French interpreter who is attached to this brigade, and who the general wishes to live with me. He is a very nice fellow and was a partner of Fox's in business before the war. Coates is going to Divisional Artillery to-morrow, having been appointed as A.D.C. It is very hard luck on me. In exchange for Dallas and Coates I get Lissant and Ryves. Now to-day my acting sergeant-major, Sergeant Porter, has been hit and gone away, which leaves me without a single responsible sergeant. I hear that the losses in the Divisional Artillery Group exceed five hundred officers and men in the last two weeks !

BLAUPOORT, 9TH AUGUST, 1917

It has been arranged for the personnel of my battery to come out of action for four days. But the rain was so heavy that a certain attack had to be put off ; consequently we had to remain in action. I had meant to meet them in the wagon-lines, but of course I have had to go back to the guns. I rode up before lunch and spent the whole afternoon and evening working out the barrage tables. It is a simple scheme with only seven lifts, and was not much trouble. Since dinner we have been very heavily shelled by a 5·9 howitzer. He has been dropping them regularly every minute for the last three-quarters of an hour just behind my No. 5 gun. The result is that my hand is rather shaky. I find that when I am being really heavily shelled in an exposed place my pulse goes up from its normal seventy-five to over a hundred a minute ; at the same time, I feel cold all over. It is a curious phenomenon. One would think that the faster the heart beat the warmer one would be. I have just asked for help and the heavies have started. If they are lucky, and engage the right battery, it often stops the hostile shelling; if not, it generally makes it worse.

RENINGHELST, 10TH AUGUST, 1917

The Hun evidently knew of our attack, as he shelled the whole country continuously all night and right up to zero this morning (4.35 a.m.). It was a much bigger attack than I expected, as the divisions on our right and left also went forward. I have not heard what the result was yet, but from rumours I am afraid it was something

of a failure. At noon I brought away my battery for
their hard-earned four days' rest in the wagon-lines.
I had one G.S. wagon up to the position for the kits and
office, and the rest of us walked as far as Voormezeele,
where I had ordered another G.S. wagon to wait with
the officers' horses. When we got there we found that
it had just been shelled, so we walked on another half-
mile and found the party waiting for us. I have spent a
lazy afternoon doing nothing, and had a glorious bath
before dinner.

Reninghelst, 11th August, 1917

To-day I had the sad news that poor Bath is dead.
He died in the 3rd Canadian General Hospital at Boulogne,
of broncho-pneumonia, caused by the blood he had swallowed. It is a terrible grief to me, as he did everything
for me, and had been with me night and day for two years.
It poured most of the night and has rained at intervals
all day, with the usual result that the whole place is one
sea of mud. I have had a very fine office built of corrugated iron and have spent the whole day in sorting out
my papers and getting my office going on some system.
The files are a great blessing, and as long as my clerks
really get into the system it will save much time and
trouble. We were bombed early this morning, but nothing
fell nearer than about four hundred yards off, where an
officer and some men of the A.S.C. were killed. It will
cause some comment when the notification comes out in
the papers ; I have never seen the name of an A.S.C.
officer in the list of killed before, but it may have happened.

Reninghelst, 12th August, 1917

Another twelfth of August out here. I wonder how many
more years it will last. There is no chance whatever of
it being over this year, and I really do not see why it
should come to an end next, especially now that the
Russians have thrown up the sponge. However, I suppose
America will counter-balance that. I had breakfast with

Daddy Talbot this morning. He really is a sporting old gentleman. He has commanded the D.A.C. now for two years out here, and must be nearly seventy.

RENINGHELST, 13TH AUGUST, 1917

Still raining at intervals. To-morrow we return to the line after our short rest. I have inspected all the gas-helmets, identity discs, field dressings, etc. We have to take the new gas-shells very seriously, there have been so many gas casualties lately. Baker, who succeeded Ryder, has gone home very bad, and Neaves, his captain, and one or two other subalterns are pretty bad. Lewis, who was in 107th Brigade, but came out with us in the 108th, has died of it. The horse lines are like thick porridge, and it is impossible to keep the horses in anything like decent condition. I have had to entirely redistribute the men in the six subsections, as I have so many new men that the battery was simply a mass of half-trained gunners. Fortunately, we have had very large drafts of men and horses, and so are nearly up to strength again. This being our last night in camp, we have had a dinner party— Mortimer, Hann, and de Tassigny, with some quite good champagne. Lissant is going on leave to-morrow and takes this part of my diary with him.

BLAUPOORT, 14TH AUGUST, 1917

After four nights' rest in the wagon-lines, we have returned to our position in the Valley of the Shadow. It gave us the usual reception—a salvo of gas-shells landing within 50 yards of us just as we reached the guns. I found the sergeant who had been left in charge of the guns in a horrid state of nerves. He says they have been shelled all the time and gassed every night for at least five hours at a time. There certainly are a lot of new and large holes everywhere ; however, that is what is to be expected in this charming spot. We arrived at 11.45, and I got everything going by 12 ; the guns were left here, and so were already on their S.O.S. lines. Now that there are only two batteries of 18-pounders in action at a time, we have to fire a correspondingly larger amount of ammunition ; my present allotment being 540 rounds a day, exclusive of registration or S.O.S. We have had a peaceful afternoon on the whole, and Rentell has gone to the O.P. for twenty-four hours. The colonel has sprung a bombshell on me to-night, by asking if I can give him an officer as assistant adjutant. I have had to send Harman, so with Lissant going on leave I shall be reduced to Rentell and Selwyn.

BLAUPOORT, 15TH AUGUST, 1917

We were badly gassed last night. About midnight the Hun started off and we had to wear our gas-helmets for four consecutive hours. He is not content with firing ·77 gas-shells, but is sending the gas over in 5·9 shells now. This is simply horrid, as the amount of gas liberated from one shell is so great that it is still highly concentrated at a considerable distance from where the shell burst. By bad luck the very first gas-shell that arrived last night burst just outside our dug-out. We were asleep at the time but woke at the crash and with the debris falling on the roof. In less than ten seconds the place was filled with concentrated phosgene. The first mouthful simply seized me by the throat like swallowing a spoonful of cayenne pepper. In the dark I was rather slow getting my gas-mask on, and could not get the nose-clip to go on right. The result was that I got quite a lot of the horrible stuff. Within ten minutes I was feeling pretty bad—great difficulty in breathing and a dreadful sinking pain in the heart ; the latter going rather fast and every now and then missing out a beat, which gave the sensation of sinking through the floor. This morning I am feeling very sick with a dull aching round the heart that is very uncomfortable. The bombardment is becoming intense again. I have to fire a thousand rounds to-day with my remaining five guns. We are carrying out what is known as " harassing fire " on the Boche approaches and dug-outs in rear.

(7 p.m.) I have had to fire an extra four hundred

rounds this evening at a German battery. I hope we annoyed him; this makes nearly a thousand rounds to-day. Orders have just come in for a big battle at dawn to-morrow. We are getting very ambitious and hope to capture the whole of the Polygon Wood, and right up to the railway crossing west of Zonnebeke. I wish we were up there. I should like to fight over the 1914 ground again.

BLAUPOORT, 16TH AUGUST, 1917

Another battle. I only got the barrage tables at 7 o'clock last night, and finished working them out by 11 o'clock. Just then we got the notification of zero, which was 4.45 a.m. It was simply luck if the thing could be completed, as, had we had gas, like every other night, I don't see how I could possibly have got the writing done in a gas-helmet. However, all is well that ends well, and everything was finished, including the duplicate copies for the No. 1, by 1 o'clock. It was lucky we finished early as at 2 o'clock we were very heavily shelled with 5·9's right into the battery. Selwyn and I, who sleep in the mess, put up with it for the first dozen rounds, but when we had four running within 20 yards, we decided to clear out, and ran across to No. 1 gun. We had just got there when a shell landed practically on us. I really think it was about the closest shave I have ever had. We had just time to lie down in the mud, right in the open, when the horrid thing burst, certainly not more than 10 yards off. I thought the debris would never stop falling; a huge clod of earth, twice as big as my head, fell on my back from Heaven only knows what height. It knocked all the wind out of me and this morning I am so stiff I can hardly move; my back and side are black and blue. We got back to bed soon after and had an hour's sleep before synchronising watches. We made the usual noise, with the addition of two more batteries who have come into action a hundred yards behind me, and who fire straight into our backs. I have been praying all the morning that they won't have any prematures, or we shall be blown off the face of the earth. Fritz did not reply till 8 o'clock, when a couple of naval guns opened up and gave us a bad time. Everything seems concentrated on my wretched mess ; it is a miracle it has not been hit yet.

(10 a.m.) We have just heard that the attack has gone very well up in the north, but the situation is still obscure on our immediate left. My own division is not attacking to-day, but we had to prolong the main barrage, so that the Hun should not know the limits of the real attack.

(10 p.m.) The men have had a hard day, as we have been barraging since 5 o'clock this morning without stopping, even though at a slow rate of fire. We have been shelled off and on the whole time. In addition one of our own 6-in. batteries has been dropping its shells on our heads ; fortunately they have not exploded. To complete the day several German aeroplanes have just been over us and dropped a dozen large bombs. They just missed the battery, falling a hundred yards in rear. I hate bombs, they make such a nasty sort of noise and the pieces fly very low. Now, as I am writing, he has just begun to give us gas-shells. I must put on my gas-helmet at once. What a life !

BLAUPOORT, 17TH AUGUST, 1917

It has not rained to-day and with a warm sun and a 20-foot-second wind the ground is drying up fast. Thank goodness the ammunition allotment has been cut down to-day and we only have to fire about three hundred and eighty rounds. The trench mortars have been registering Lower Star Post—the place that has now twice held us up, so I suppose we are going to attack it again. Still no news of yesterday's battle. On the Somme we used to get most interesting little situation sketches showing exactly what line we held, but in the Vth Army we are told nothing, merely being ordered when and where to shoot. It takes all interest out of the game. At 8 o'clock this morning I counted no less than twelve German " sausages," a quite unusual number ; at that time there were none of ours up at all. These last two evenings have been wonderfully clear, and the air has fairly hummed with 'planes, both ours and theirs. I notice there is much less close fighting between the aeroplanes than there was last year ; they seem content to fire their machine-guns at each other at a very long range and then break away at once. Lissant went on leave to-day, so I have sent Rentell to the wagon-lines, and am left alone with Selwyn and Ryves.

Blauport, 18th August, 1917

A calm night ; at least I slept all the time, so I presume nothing fell very close. Just at dusk I got a wireless call for help from one of our 'planes who was being shot at by a German " Archie." It did not take long to get the guns on to him. I took him on at gun-fire with high explosive and shrapnel mixed. It is still fine and the ground is drying up very rapidly ; in a few days it will be dusty. I never saw such a soil as Flanders.

Blaupoort, 19th August, 1917

There has been a great deal of trouble in the division about some gun that is shooting short. It has been going on for days and all attempts to locate it have failed so far. As there was no battle on to-day, I took the opportunity of calibrating my guns ; that is, testing them for range to find out exactly how much their shooting differs from normal. Needless to say, there was very little wrong with them. There was a certain Territorial battery ranging at the same time, and I have never seen a more pitiable sight or a more disgraceful exhibition in action. The battery commander actually did not know where his zero-line was, and was firing eight degrees off his proper line ; in other words, some five hundred yards too far to the left. I showed him the target and even then he did not know where it was on the map !

Blaupoort, 20th August, 1917

Selwyn is Liaison and Ryves has gone as Brigade O.P. officer, so I should have been left all alone if I had not sent for Rentell from the wagon-lines. We had a perfectly vile night. We were shelled for twelve hours on end and had to wear gas-masks for several hours. I was so tired that I succeeded in going to sleep with mine on. It shows how good the new respirators are that it should be possible to do so. I have spent most of the day in working out the calibrations of my guns ; it is a long and most intricate business, which eventually gives one the muzzle velocity of the gun. Having got this, one can find what allowance has to be made at any range for the loss of muzzle velocity due to wear and tear of the bore of the gun.

BLAUPOORT, 21ST AUGUST, 1917

To-day has been a red-letter day. This morning it was my day for calling on the battalion commander whom we cover. I went to the O.P. first and checked my registration, making certain that my guns were absolutely accurately on their zero point, and also finding out for certain what the corrector of the day was. From there I went into the tunnels and saw the colonel of the 12/Royal Fusiliers. I had lunch with him, and he told me that one of his subalterns had discovered a place from which a German battery could be seen. The battery was caught in the act of firing, and located as far as seeing it was concerned. They did not know in the least where it was on the map, but they showed me the exact spot from which it could be seen. I was rather horrified to hear that it was in the middle of Lower Star Post and only 20 yards from a German post. However, the subaltern who was told off to take me there assured me that they had a complete understanding with the Hun infantry, and that we should not be sniped. We went all through Shrewsbury Forest and I was able to really appreciate how badly we had crumped the back of the Hun position. Not a tree was left more than two feet high, and the whole place was just one mass of shell-holes touching each other. We quickly reached the place we were making for, and I was not a little astonished when my guide pointed out a tree

30 yards off, and said that the Hun sentry was there. It is really a most extraordinary situation, neither side has any sign of a trench—both are sitting in shell-holes a few yards apart, with no wire in between, and separated by nothing but a few yards of open ground. We stood in a shell-hole and looked down on the Hun back-country, a truly wonderful view, right back to Zandvoorde. My guide, by name Mears-Devenish, pointed out the place where he had seen the German guns firing this morning. For some time I could make nothing out, but after examining the place for some time through my Zeiss glasses, I saw one gun. It was right in the edge of a wood, covered over by branches. I could clearly see the shield of the gun and one wheel ; later I picked out two more guns. There used to be a German battery there in very large concrete pits, but our heavies have smashed these up, and the guns at present are in the intervals between the old pits. I fired my salvo of smoke-shells as I had arranged with Rentell. There was no doubt about them. They sent up a vast column of smoke like an 8-in. shell bursting. I at once gave a correction by guess, switching on to the hostile battery. After some time I got the guns definitely on to the gun that I could see. It was such a wonderful sight to see Huns walking about in the open. I next put a salvo of high explosive close to my target, and having located the place I at once gave them five rounds of gun-fire from all guns. The range was exact, and so was the height of the bursts. My twenty-five shells arrived almost simultaneously and simply plastered the Huns who were moving in the trees. After that I ranged a single gun with high explosive non-delay on to one of the German guns ; the range was 4,800 yards ; all the same the shooting and laying were excellent, round after round falling within a few yards of the target. One shell hit a wheel and brought the gun down on its axle ; shortly afterwards another shell fell right into the German ammunition dump beside the gun. It blew up with a tremendous explosion and wrecked the whole place. When the smoke cleared away I could see the gun lying on its side pointing the

opposite way to what it had before. I then tackled a second gun, and got two hits into its emplacement, but the camouflage of branches was so thick round it that I could not see the result. Before I could finish it off my wire went, and I had reluctantly to stop firing. On my way back I called at Brigade Headquarters and re-reported the result of my shoot, being much congratulated. The colonel rang up the general right away, and told him what had happened. Later I sent in a full report.

BLAUPOORT, 22ND AUGUST, 1917

Gassed most of the night. I was so tired that I slept with my gas-mask on my face. Early this morning we had another battle, supporting the division on our left, who attacked Glencorse Wood. I don't know what the result has been, but we have been firing the whole day. I had to wire to the wagon-lines to send me up another thousand rounds during the afternoon. I had a very handsome compliment from the general, who sent an official letter through the brigade major and our brigade. It ran :

" The C.R.A. wishes to congratulate Major Hamilton on successfully engaging a German battery with excellent effect. The result attained and the method of carrying it out were both excellent."

There is also a notice about it in *Corps Intelligence*, as follows :

" . . . In addition to the above A/106 successfully engaged a hostile 77 mm. battery in J.26, d. A direct hit was observed on one gun located at J.26, d, 60, 04, and a second at J.26, d, 78, 15 is believed to have been damaged. An ammunition dump was destroyed and casualties were inflicted on the detachments which were shelled during their retirement into the wood. A third gun is believed to be in position at J.32, b, 60, 97."

BLAUPOORT, 23RD AUGUST, 1917

The most exciting day I have had since I came out.
It brackets with the first time I shot a rhino in East Africa.
At dawn this morning I got a telegram from the colonel
of 12/Royal Fusiliers to say that there was another gun
firing from 50 yards north of the place I knocked out.
I wired back to say that it should have my personal
attention. At midnight at last a brand-new gun arrived
for my battery to replace one that had been condemned as
worn out. Rentell and I got it into its pit and there and
then I tested the sights for range. Having put them right,
I was able to fire with that gun half an hour after it arrived.
Directly after breakfast I went to the Mount Sorrel O.P.
and registered it. As things were fairly quiet there, I
took the opportunity of recalibrating all my guns, and was
delighted to find that, although the weather conditions
were quite different to two days ago, the guns calibrated
at precisely the same muzzle velocity. On my way there
I called on the colonel and extracted half a mile of double
wire from him, which I proceeded to lay from the O.P.
to Battalion Headquarters; from there on I had to use the
much-despised German enamel-covered wire, which is
nothing more than a single strand of very thin steel wire
coated with black enamel. It can be used only once, but
has the advantage that a reel of a mile can be put in one's
pocket. I had enough of this to reach to Lower Star Post,
where I found that my Fusilier friends had been replaced
by the 1/Leinsters. I got a guide from them who took
me on to the Company Headquarters of the battalion on
their left. Here I introduced myself to the company
commander—Captain Flack, 1/Royal Fusiliers, who said
that he knew every inch of the ground round there. I
told him I wanted to find a place from which I could see
down into the valley where I was shelling a trench junction
—Java Trench and Java Avenue. He took me to his
most advanced post at Het Papotje Farm, which is half-
way down Java Drive. When we got there I found I
still could not quite see over the crest. I asked him if

it was possible to go on a little way and look over the
edge, a distance of not more than 50 yards. He said
he knew for certain that the enemy were not within
150 yards of us, and that it would be quite safe to go on
a little farther. I must now describe the situation in
some detail in order to make intelligible what follows.
We hold this old German communication trench for a
certain distance and then have put up a " block " or
barricade across it. Behind this we have a post of a
sergeant and a dozen men. Beyond the barricade,
and some 100 yards or so on, the Hun has a similar
barricade. The trench is very wide, with sloping sides,
and turns to the right about 30 yards in front of our
barricade ; consequently, one can only see the above
distance down it. I thought that if I could get 30 yards
down the trench, I could look over the side and see all
I wanted. Flack felt so sure that the Boche was a long
way off that he said we might safely continue as far as
the bend. We drew our pistols and saw that they were
loaded and in good order, and then proceeded to climb
over the barricade. The latter is only 3 or 4 feet high,
but has strands of wire stretched across the trench above
it. Flack kept on the right and I on the left, so as to
allow the men behind the barricade to fire between us
if we were attacked. We crept along yard by yard, holding
our pistols in front of us. We got almost up to the bend
in the trench, that is, 30 yards from our barricade, when
I saw an old hurdle across the trench just at the bend.
Flack was about 5 yards behind me at the moment.
Suddenly without any warning a German, with a pork-
pie cap on, jumped up from behind the hurdle where he
had been lying, and without a word flung a bomb in our
faces. It went over my head and burst with a crack
between ¡Flack and me. As the German rose up I threw
myself forward on to my left hand, at the same time firing ;
at the moment I fired he had his hand above his head,
having just let go the bomb. My bullet caught him in
the throat ; he threw up his other arm and collapsed like
an ox that has been pole-axed. Before he reached the

ground my second bullet hit him in the chest. At the first shot his head went back, and I had time to distinctly see the bullet-hole in his throat just above the low collar. I turned my head to see where the bomb had fallen, and through the dust and smoke I saw Flack fall just in front of our barricade. His men pulled him over, but it was difficult to get him through the barbed wire. I fired shot after shot round the corner to keep back the rest of the German listening post, whom · I expected to see rush round every second. As soon as Flack had been got over, I turned and ran for it, scrambling over the barricade in record time. I knew I had been hit in the left knee, because I could feel the blood running down my leg, as I was wearing shorts; but I felt positively no pain at the time. I fired a parting shot just as I reached the barricade and immediately loaded a fresh magazine full of cartridges into my pistol. I was thankful I had an automatic and not an ordinary service revolver. Flack was lying in the bottom of the trench, simply covered with blood. I first of all saw that the men at the post were all ready and lining the barricade and sides of the trench. I told them that I should take command of the garrison of the trench till another infantry officer could be fetched, and ordered them to fix bayonets and have their bombs ready in their hands ; I thought the enemy might send a strong patrol after us, to see what it was all about. I then went to Flack, and saw that he was terribly wounded. His right arm was shattered above the elbow and was bleeding profusely ; a large piece of the bomb or possibly the bone was sticking through the flesh on the opposite side to where the wound was ; he also had a dreadful wound in the side. He was in great pain and would not let us touch him. His sergeant and I managed to cut away his tunic and shirt, and put a shell dressing on each wound, and eventually got him back to his own Company Headquarters which were in a large concrete dug-out near there. I remained with the post till a subaltern arrived to whom I handed over. I stayed with Flack until we got him away on a stretcher en route for the Aid Post, a mile in rear.

I then went back to Lower Star Post and continued my examination of the country from there. I saw that the gun-pit I had destroyed two days ago had been repaired and there was a wire screen in front of the opening. I was very anxious to engage it again, but could not get through to my battery for a long time. I could see numbers of the enemy walking about in the shade of the wood, so as soon as I got through I turned all my guns on to it at the fastest rate of fire. The result was excellent, the shells bursting all over the wood level with the tops of the trees. The wire went again soon after and I was not able to shoot any more. However, I studied the country until 6 o'clock with my excellent glasses, and picked up a mass of useful information. By this time my leg was very stiff and becoming distinctly painful, so I limped back to Battalion Headquarters, where I had a drink. They offered me food, but I could not touch anything with my hands, as they were simply caked with blood, as were my clothes and belts, etc. I went on to our Brigade Headquarters and reported the result of my day to the colonel, who was much horrified at my going out in front ; however, I pointed out to him that if valuable information is to be obtained a certain amount of risk must be taken. I went to see Mortimer at his Dressing Station on my way back, and he examined my knee, pronouncing it to be a clean wound with no pieces sticking in it. He says that the pain is more from the blow on the bone than from the cut, which is quite small. It ought to be well in a week.

BLAUPOORT, 24TH AUGUST, 1917

Had an excellent night and slept till 8 o'clock. They put a pip-squeak high explosive just at the door of our dug-out, but I knew nothing about it. We have had a heavy programme of firing for the last twenty-four hours, but as there are only Ryves and myself here I let the sergeants do part of the night work. The Germans have counter-attacked very heavily on our right this afternoon. and I fancy they have regained part of the ground we had

25

won. We have fired hard all day. Coates called to-day and said that Divisional Headquarters were all very pleased at my shoot three days ago. Rentell has gone on leave to-night, lucky man.

LARCH WOOD, 25TH AUGUST, 1917

Another tragedy. At 10 o'clock this morning Colonel Street was killed as he was standing outside his Headquarters. The adjutant telephoned to me and I at once went over and took command of the group. It is perfectly extraordinary how history repeats itself; this is now the third time my colonels have been killed and wounded. I at once telephoned to Divisional Headquarters and reported that I had taken command of both brigades, pending further orders from the general, and soon after the brigade major told me that the general had applied to the corps to have me permanently posted to command this brigade, so perhaps it will come off this time. I have been very busy all day picking up all the threads and making various arrangements. I am trying to establish a new O.P. right up in the front line where I was two days ago. I had tea with General Duggan, who lives close here and who commands the infantry that we are covering; afterwards I hobbled over to the Dressing Station and got my knee seen to. It has almost stopped bleeding now, but is still very stiff and it is rather painful to walk. Our tunnels were again shelled this evening, but no damage.

LARCH WOOD, 26TH AUGUST, 1917

We had an S.O.S. at daylight this morning, but it was on the front of the brigade on our left, so I only turned on three batteries, keeping the other batteries ready for anything that might turn up. It soon quieted down and 1 went to sleep again. This afternoon I visited all the batteries of the group, and my leg was pretty sore by the time I had finished.

LARCH WOOD, 27TH AUGUST, 1917

It has rained all day, and I have not been out, having

been very busy all day reorganising many things. The post where I got bombed the other day was captured by the Germans yesterday afternoon in broad daylight. I am very glad they did not attack it whilst I was there. Hobday has been up to the front again all day, and has registered several new places in the new area we can see. He came back wet to the skin, but has done a really good piece of work. I am sure the general will be pleased with the visibility map I have been able to send in. We attacked along the Menin Road again to-day, but I am afraid it was not a great success. At 8 p.m., just as we were going to start dinner, the S.O.S. went up, and I started all the batteries off. However, it proved to be a false alarm ; apparently the rockets began on our left and spread along the front ; these things are very catching. I live in an underground tunnel with about two inches of water on the floor. The temperature is about 80 degrees, and the atmosphere simply awful. I am sure we shall all be ill ; it is as bad as the railway dug-outs.

LARCH WOOD, 28TH AUGUST, 1917

Not much rain, but there has been a 90-foot-second wind, which makes accurate shooting an impossibility. The colonel of the Australians came to see me this morning. He seemed very efficient, and suggested that the shells which are continually being reported as short are coming from the south from a German battery. I am so annoyed at the thing that I have taken the extreme measure of convening a Court of Inquiry to examine into and report on the whole thing.

LARCH WOOD, 29TH AUGUST, 1917

During breakfast this morning the staff captain rang me up and said " Good morning, colonel." I asked him if he was pulling my leg, but he told me a wire had just come through appointing me to command the 106th Brigade

with the rank of lieut.-colonel; so I have reached that
exalted rank at last! Everyone has been ringing up to
congratulate me and I am delighted to get this brigade,
as I was very much afraid I should have been posted to
some strange brigade. My Court of Inquiry reported to-
day, and confirmed my own suspicions, namely, that
A/298 have their sights in such bad condition that it can
easily account for short shooting on their zone. I have
to-day changed over the 106th and 298th zones, and hope
we shall hear no more of this infernal short shooting.

LARCH WOOD, 30TH AUGUST, 1917

The Hun has shelled us all day. It is really quite harmless as long as one remains at the bottom of the tunnel,
but it is a nuisance if one wants to go out, and very dangerous for the orderlies coming in.

I have not yet got into the way of signing myself " Lieut.-
Colonel," and it sounds very strange to be spoken of as
" the colonel." I think it is a bigger jump than from
captain to major. My infantry general is very fidgety
and I have to go and hold his hand several times a day.
I am trying to get the tunnellers to do something to improve
this place. The atmosphere is simply fœtid and horrible ;
one wakes up in the morning with such a sore throat that
one can hardly speak. There are six inches of inky black
and stinking water under my bed, and everything is
dripping wet ; the difficulty is ever to get any towels
dried. Heaven forbid we should be here during the
winter !

LARCH WOOD, 31ST AUGUST, 1917

We have had the usual intermittent shelling all day.
It is rather a nuisance, as one never knows when to expect
it, or where it is coming from. Some of the infantry got
caught inside here, and several were killed—I think, about
twelve—with one shell. In the morning I went to see my
old battery, who are still commanded by Selwyn. The
railway people are taking a broad-gauge line right through

the battery and have made a dreadful mess. After dinner
I called on the infantry brigadier, who lives a couple of
hundred yards away down the tunnel.

LARCH WOOD, 1ST SEPTEMBER, 1917

Two years ago this morning the 24th Division landed in
France. It seems more like ten years. I was adding up
last night how many officers of the Divisional Artillery
are still with the division ; out of about a hundred and
twenty I can only think of twelve left. Some have been
transferred elsewhere, and some have gone home sick,
besides the killed and wounded.

(4 p.m.) Nectarine and Profligate have been heavily
shelled all the afternoon ; I have appealed for help to
the heavies.

LARCH WOOD, 2ND SEPTEMBER, 1917

We have been heavily shelled all day and so have the
batteries. All day I have been getting telephone messages of " Sherry " or " Port," which means either " We
are being shelled " or " We have had to withdraw." With
great difficulty I got the Heavies to help, but they
have evidently not got the right place, as it made no
difference.

LARCH WOOD, 3RD SEPTEMBER, 1917

A very dull day, which I have spent mostly underground, and have been going through old correspondence
in the Brigade Office. It does not take one very long to
find out about all the various subjects that have been
going on. Wilmot, the real adjutant of the brigade,
has come back from leave and Harman, who was acting
for him, has gone back to A Battery. I called on the
infantry general this evening (General Billingham, 118th
Brigade) and found him a very amiable person, as well he
might be, considering he is going on leave to-night. Dirty
and wet as the tunnel is, it is a great blessing when they are
shelling on top.

LARCH WOOD, 4TH SEPTEMBER, 1917

Selwyn was liaison officer with the infantry last night and reported here at 8 o'clock this morning on his way back. He had hardly left here ten minutes when B Battery rang up to say that he had been hit outside their battery as he was passing. Apparently an 8-inch shell practically landed on him and his orderly. Fortunately, Hobday saw the shell explode and saw the orderly get up out of the smoke and run towards him. He and Cooper ran out to help the man and saw Selwyn lying there. He was hit in the mouth and under the eye ; the wounds themselves are not bad, but I am afraid he is very bad with concussion of the brain. He was taken away at once and got down to the Field Ambulance at La Clytte, and sent on to the same place that Dallas went to. I have had a message this evening to say that he is still unconscious, so I am afraid that he is in a serious condition. I am very distressed about it, as he was such a nice boy and a most capable officer. I wired to General Headquarters at once, where he has a brother on the Staff.

LARCH WOOD, 5TH SEPTEMBER, 1917

Yesterday afternoon I had a very busy time, as I was sent for to meet our new general. His name is Nairne, and he has commanded the Lahore Divisional Artillery since the beginning of the war. I liked him very much—he is obviously a " sahib " and, everyone says, most capable. We went round most of the battery positions, and he made very shrewd remarks. If we have to lose General Sheppard it is a good thing to get another general that we shall like. I have been frantically busy all day, as our batteries are changing their positions in a day or so, and I have had to make most elaborate arrangements. The colonel taking over turns out to be a man I know—Butler.

LARCH WOOD TUNNELS, 6TH SEPTEMBER, 1917

All to-day I have been busy clearing up and getting

papers ready to hand over to the relieving brigade. One section of each battery of my brigade was relieved by another battery, and in its own turn went forward and relieved a section of Australian Artillery. At 7.30 we fired an S.O.S., but stopped in twenty minutes as it turned out to be a false alarm, the real attack being well off our zone to the north—I imagine about in the Polygon Wood. I dined with the infantry brigadier of the 118th Brigade, and had an excellent dinner. The Sherwood Foresters have sent me a copy of the amusing paper, the *Wipers' Times*. It is very funny if one knows the allusions. They are reprinting all the old numbers, so I shall buy a set.

LARCH WOOD, 7TH SEPTEMBER, 1917

We have finished the double relief to-night. My batteries have relieved two Australian batteries and two of the 298th, we, at the same time, being relieved in our old positions by four batteries of the 186th. At the present moment I am in the strange position of commanding none of my own brigade and the whole of the 186th. To-morrow I and my Headquarters go out of action for twenty-four hours, and retire to our wagon-lines. After that we come back to within 100 yards of where we are now, and I take command of another double group consisting of my own four batteries and four of Butler's. It is all very confusing, as one gets contradictory orders from no less than four divisions at a time. However, one muddles through somehow at great loss of energy. But where is Butler ?

RENINGHELST, 8TH SEPTEMBER, 1917

I was relieved this morning and handed over B Group to the 186th. Wilmot and I rode from Lock 8 to the wagon-lines. As our men had not arrived, I got Ryder to give me lunch. I changed into some clean and tidy clothes, and had tea with Divisional Artillery Headquarters. After that I had a long talk with our new C.R.A., General

Hoare-Nairne, about who shall be given the command of
D Battery.

LARCH WOOD, 9TH SEPTEMBER, 1917

I went to see the general at 9 o'clock. He lent me
his car to come back into action, but we broke a
spring and the car would not go any farther, so we had to
walk till we found a motor-lorry going our way. This
eventually landed us near Lock 8, whence we walked up
here, arriving very hot, at 12 o'clock. I have taken over
A Group from the 5th Australian Brigade (Colonel
Lloyd, C.M.G., D.S.O.); the latter is one of the best
officers I have met yet. His group office is simply a
model, being a very efficient military office run on modern
commercial lines, with files and card indexes all complete.
I have taken a lot of notes and hope to copy them. A
Group is about a record, it is the biggest one-man command
I have ever heard of, consisting of no less than nine batteries.
I have four batteries of my own 106th Brigade, three of
the 156th, and two of the 190th. I have not seen all the
battery commanders yet, but those I have so far met
seem very good. It is quite impossible to run a concern
like this with nothing but the staff of a single brigade. I
have therefore taken on Rentell as assistant adjutant.
My zone is further to the north than before, and I am now
covering the most vital part of our line in these parts,
namely, Hooge and Stirling Castle. I have over fifty
guns and howitzers, so I ought to be able to do some damage
if I have a " concentration " on some unfortunate spot.
I think I know of a German battery well within range ;
if I can get good enough information about it, I will
concentrate every gun on it and give it five minutes'
intense fire at five rounds per gun per minute. This will
mean about seven hundred and fifty shells on to the same
spot in five minutes. I have got a most comfortable
headquarters this time, plenty of rooms, electric light,
and nice and dry. It is all underground, but not deep
enough to keep out any big shell.

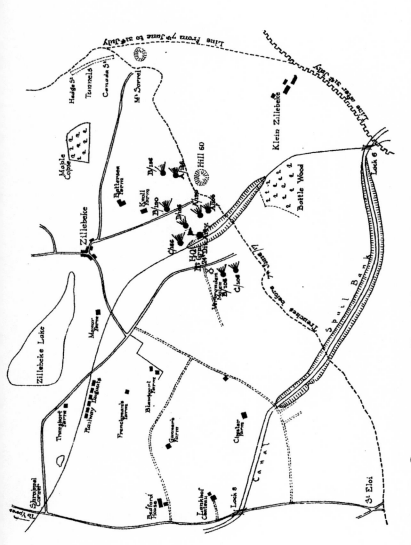

POSITION NEAR HILL 60, SHOWING LINE, AUG. 1917.

LARCH WOOD, 10TH SEPTEMBER, 1917

We are to be relieved in a few days and I have had a constant succession of visitors the whole day. The Corps C.R.A., General Reed, came about 11, followed by the colonel and all the battery commanders of the relieving brigade. In addition, nearly all my own B.C.s have called to see me on various subjects. I have a dozen things in hand—new O.P.s to be found and established, shoots to be arranged, matters to be arranged with the infantry, etc. My signal office is like a London exchange, three operators at the switch-board night and day, and my table covered with 'phones. Wilmot is doing the tactical work and Rentell the administrative. These two trot into my private office all day with files full of papers for my decision and signature. The excellent Richardson has found me a signal officer, who has taken charge of all my communications and is an immense help. I managed to get out for a couple of hours this afternoon and took the relieving colonel round some of the batteries, and also to my tactical O.P. on Hill 60. We had hardly got there when the Germans turned a storm of shrapnel on to us ; it lasted for about ten minutes, during which we had to lie flat against a concrete dug-out, whilst stones and earth flew all round. I met General Lushington, C.R.A. of the 41st Division, who was having a look round. He is a dear old gentleman with white hair, who has been out since the beginning of the war. He is taking over some of my positions. I had tea with Welch and Hobday, and told them exactly how I wanted the batteries turned out for our march, when Nairne is sure to inspect us.

LARCH WOOD, 11TH SEPTEMBER, 1917

I am writing this under great difficulty as we are being heavily bombarded with gas—both of the mustard variety and phosgene. Even the gas-curtains won't keep it out, and we have had to put on our respirators. We have been subjected to an intense bombardment all day, which has been very trying. B Battery have had four guns knocked out, but they hope to be able to repair two of them. Another battery has lost one gun. I am afraid the casualties have been heavy. I only know of one sergeant and one man killed, but there are a number wounded in the group. I retaliated to-night and concentrated all my nine batteries on one spot where there is a German battery—this is just behind Gheluvelt church, which I well remember from 1914. I ordered two minutes' intense fire from every gun and howitzer in the group. That is about fifty guns. As each gun would fire about six rounds a minute, that would make six hundred shells in the two minutes—all into one battery. It certainly ought to do some damage, both material and moral. My eyes are hurting so much from the mustard gas that I cannot see to write any more.

LARCH WOOD, 12TH SEPTEMBER, 1917

A perfectly horrible night. We were gassed half the time and crumped all night. The phosgene affected my heart and I could not sleep, as my pulse was racing, and I could not breathe properly. About 3 in the morning, the brigade major rang up to say that the batteries which had been gassing us had been located, whereupon I turned on some of my batteries to engage them. I think we stopped them, as no more gas came over after that, but naturally it was hours before the horrible stuff could be cleared out of our tunnels. Butler is relieving me, and I hand over to him at 6 p.m. to-morrow night. We have had a very busy day making all arrangements to hand over and also issuing my own march orders. The whole scheme was suddenly changed to-night, and we have been up most of the night getting fresh orders out. I have been very anxious about the relief of the first section of each battery, as if we had been gassed and shelled to-night as we were last night, it would have meant very heavy casualties in men and horses. Fortunately, everything was quiet just at the critical time when the horses came up. A new battalion has come into the tunnels alongside of us, one of the Rifle Brigade battalions. I have made friends with their colonel, who looks like a twin brother of Archie Douglas. The people he is relieving have not been here long, so he was glad of all the information that I was able to give him. As we have been in this place since May, we are by far the oldest inhabitants ; we have seen many generations of fresh divisions come and go. Our casualties have been very heavy for the last day or two, owing to the persistent shelling of this place ; it is largely due to the absurd way in which the infantry stand about in the open, quite irrespective of whether the Boche balloons or planes are up. In addition, numerous railways have been pushed up, both broad and narrow gauge.

RENINGHELST, 13TH SEPTEMBER, 1917

At last we are out of action. All day I have been handing over to Butler and explaining everything to him. I made out a very elaborate file of things to give him, so that he might have no difficulty in picking up all the threads. I officially handed over at 6 p.m., after which Wilmot, Rentell, the attached signal officer, and I walked down to Lock 8. The Hun could not resist saying good-bye to us, and was putting a terrific fire on an unfortunate battery that we passed. On arrival at Lock 8, we found our horses, and mounted under shrapnel fire, as he was hating the Lock at the time. The heavies were just beginning their evening strafe, and we were nearly deafened as we picked our way through them ; there seemed to be an 8-in. or a 9·2 in every hedge. Dinner was ready for us on arrival, and it was not long before we went to bed, as we had a very early start.

BOESCHEPE, 14TH SEPTEMBER, 1917

We marched off at 6 o'clock this morning, the general, Richardson, and Fox all turning out to see us go by. It was a kind attention on their part, but rather trying, as the guns and men had only got out of action at midnight and reveille was at 3 o'clock. Fortunately, the turn-out was as good as could be expected under the circumstances and the general was quite satisfied. There were various little things that I don't like, and I have sent them round to batteries this evening. I intend to have one sealed pattern for the whole brigade, and have it rigidly adhered to. As the march was only about 4 miles, we were all in by 7.30, and had a second breakfast. I know Boeschepe well, as my wagon-lines were here in October and November, 1915. It is a nice little place on the slopes of Mont-des-Cats, plenty of trees and green fields. The relief and change after being so long in action in that horrible Valley of Death is indescribable. Wilmot and I had a look at the horses of B and C Batteries in the afternoon and then rode on to Abeele to get money from the field cashier. The batteries are all in one large field and my Headquarters in a small house in the village. Personally, I have an excellent bedroom in the local château belonging to the maire. It is a large room with a beautiful view over 20 miles of country. Also a spring bed and snow-white sheets. What luxury!

BOESCHEPE, 15TH SEPTEMBER, 1917

Such a night! I felt as if I never wanted to get up again; all the stale tiredness is beginning to come out; in fact I am far more tired to-day than when in action. At the same time there is a glorious feeling of having nothing to do and nothing to worry about. Above all—no telephone. I went round all the batteries and inspected the horses of A and D. The sun was shining, and everything looked *couleur de rose*. After lunch I had the chestnut mare out—I have inherited her from Colonels Street and Balston. She is a very nice 15·3 creature with good paces, but inclined to pull; however, I think I can get her out of that. I rode all through the lanes, up the little hills, round by Mont-des-Cats, and went to see Selwyn, who is in the same bed that Dallas had in No. 41 C.C.S. at Godewaersvelde. I was surprised to find him looking very well and sitting up in bed. He says he has no pain, and the wounds in the face are nearly healed. I saw the doctor who is looking after him, and he said that all he wants now is some months' complete rest in his own home. I lost my way coming home and found myself on a narrow foot-path that got steeper and steeper—ending in a place like a staircase. It was so narrow that I could not even lead my horse, so I left her with the orderly and climbed up to the top ; then the orderly started the horses off one by one and they climbed and scrambled up and I caught them as they reached the top. Quite a case of mountaineering, and in flat Flanders !

BOESCHEPE, 16TH SEPTEMBER, 1917

To-day the whole brigade is entraining at Hopoutre, a siding just outside Poperinghe ; the batteries go at intervals of three hours all day up to just after midnight to-night. Our destination is Bapaume. It seems funny going there by train after spending most of last summer fighting 4 miles this side of it ; however, I believe the line is now well to the east of the place. My headquarters shares a train with part of No. 1 Section of the D.A.C., and we start at 10.45 p.m. I shall leave here about 6 and see C Battery go off, and then supervise the en-training of my own little party. It is not much of a com-mand, being under fifty men. They say the journey ought to take about twelve hours, so we shall arrive by daylight, which is always a blessing.

BAPAUME, 17TH SEPTEMBER, 1917

We arrived here at 5 o'clock this evening, after a very long and tiring journey. We were just twenty-four hours from camp to camp. Leaving Boeschepe at 6 p.m. yesterday, we ought to have entrained as soon as we got to Hopoutre, but two trains had run into each other near the station, and the line was blocked. We had to wait on the platform till 2 in the morning before our train came in, and it was not till 8 o'clock this morning that we crossed the frontier at Abeele. I am sure we all pray devoutly that we shall never, never see Flanders again. It has been a beautiful day, and I thoroughly enjoyed myself looking out of the window and seeing the green country with people and cows and such-like strange sights. We passed Haze-

brouck and St. Pol and entered the war zone again at
Arras. The latter is a large station, but practically
wrecked ; the trains run through it, but everything is
smashed by shell fire. After leaving Arras the railway
crosses the old " No Man's Land " almost at once and
heads for Achiet. As far as one can see, in every direction
is a great rolling grass plain without a house. The effect
is very similar to the country round Nairobi or the prairies
of North America. Hundreds of horses were grazing in
large herds ; as most of our horses come from Canada,
they must have thought they were back on their native
ranches. Towards evening we got to Bapaume, so famous
in March of this year, when the Germans retired. The
station is a hopeless wreck, but the Germans had kindly
provided excellent long platforms for entraining troops,
and we were only a few minutes getting our horses and
vehicles off the train. I watered the horses, and the men
had some tea, and then we marched off to our camp, which
was less than a mile. Three of the batteries had already
arrived and were comfortably settled down and the last
one got in at 11 p.m. The Headquarters have got a marquee
and several bell-tents, so we are very comfortable. Mortimer
has turned up after his fortnight's leave in London ; as
he was passing through Hazebrouck this morning, he
happened to see A Battery train going the other way,
so hastily changed trains and so saved himself going all
the way up to Ypres and back. He seems to have had a
very good time, and has ordered a really good gramophone.

BAPAUME, 18TH SEPTEMBER, 1917

We all breakfasted very late and could hardly believe
our eyes when we got up and found ourselves in this
beautiful and cheerful place. I rode to Divisional Artillery Headquarters to tell the general we had all arrived
safely, but found I had missed him and he had gone over
to see me. However, I found him later at my camp
and took him round. He is evidently very keen on horses
and is very particular about grooming and feeding ; he
seems to care less about the guns. Just the opposite to

General Sheppard, who hardly ever looked at the horses.
We have sent away every gun and howitzer in the brigade
to be overhauled in the workshops, so at present we are
unarmed. After lunch Ryder and I rode out to see the
country, going about 5 miles to the east. We passed
several villages in clumps of trees, and in no case was there
a single house standing. The place has not been shelled
at all, as the Germans retired as fast as possible and did
not put up a fight. But they blew up every house, church,
and cottage in the whole country. It is a wonderful
example of what can be done by systematic destruction.
We came on what had evidently been a very well-to-do
château, standing in good grounds, with a park wall all
round it. There was nothing left but the four walls, and
never a shell-hole in the neighbourhood. The house was
a modern and pretentious vulgarity, and no loss to anyone
except its owner, but I regretted the many fine trees that
had been wantonly cut down.

BAPAUME, 19TH SEPTEMBER, 1917

A heavenly day. Sun all the time, with just enough
breeze to keep one cool. I have spent the day doing
absolutely nothing. I wandered round the batteries during
" Stables " and made various criticisms, and found that
two hours passed very quickly. We have a great chance
of getting things pulled together and reorganising everything now. I had meant to have explored the ruins of
the town, but remained in camp as I heard the general
was probably coming to see me. It is extraordinarily
quiet here—I have not seen a German plane or heard a
gun since we have been here. My leave is about due now,
but I expect I shall have to wait till we are settled into our
new place in the Line.

BAPAUME, 20TH SEPTEMBER, 1917

Wilmot and I explored the ruins of the town this afternoon ; the Germans certainly made a good job of the
destruction. There is not a single house in the place
that has not been deliberately blown up. It is quite easy

to distinguish the destruction caused by our shell-fire from the damage done by dynamiting the houses. The usual procedure seems to have been for them to place heavy charges of explosives in the cellars ; as far as I can see the charges must have been attached to the iron girders supporting the roof of the cellars. The result in most cases was to blow out all the walls of the houses, so that the roofs fell in—in many cases the latter lying on top of the debris without being very much broken. Nothing seems to have escaped the kindly attention of the Hun. Even lamp-posts have been broken in half and the lower half rooted up. Most of the big trees beside the roads have been cut down, and the work so carefully done that they have all fallen parallel and at right angles to the road. Perhaps the finest example of Kultur is the church in the centre of Bapaume. It was evidently quite a big place and of a certain age. Most of the walls are still standing, but the Germans blew up all the heavy round columns supporting the roof and so brought the whole superstructure down. The columns are lying there now all in pieces. They had been built up in half-circles without mortar, and have simply fallen apart. The charges were put in the crypt, and as the latter must have been full of coffins the whole place is littered with skulls and bones. The church itself is filled up to a height of about 6 to 10 feet with fallen masonry and beams. We climbed all over it, but it was very difficult going. The curious thing is that practically no debris fell outside the walls on the grass. The German officers seem to have stabled their horses in the best houses. All the partition walls on the ground-floors were knocked out, and the space fitted up as very comfortable stables. The Town Hall has disappeared altogether. It had been very little damaged and the Germans were careful not to destroy it before leaving. They put an extra heavy explosive charge in the foundations with some clock-work arrangement which was timed not to go off for a long time. Unfortunately, our people fell into the trap, and a Brigade Headquarters established itself in the place. Ten days after the Germans had left Bapaume there was a tremendous explosion and the Town Hall blew up, the entire brigade staff going with it. Since then we have been very careful about entering places that are unusually well preserved.

BAPAUME, 21ST SEPTEMBER, 1917

The C.R.A. inspected all the horses of the brigade this morning, and was pleased with what he saw on the whole. Unlike General Sheppard, who specialised on the gunnery, General Nairne is chiefly interested in the horses. It was a sunny day, and the horses were looking their best. I made a number of notes of the things he seems to like, and shall see that the batteries carry them out. After lunch, Mortimer and I started off to see the battlefields of the Somme ; we reached Le Transloy in half an hour, and turned off the main road towards Les Bœufs. Both these places have been completely obliterated by shell fire, and the cheering thing to think about is that it was all done by British guns. Other places like Ypres and Arras were destroyed by the German guns, but now we were able to see that our own fire is quite as bad as theirs, and that the Germans holding these villages had quite as bad a time as they ever gave us. The road has been repaired, and we were able to ride along it at a walk. The moment the main road to Peronne is left behind, one enters the scene of utter desolation. One battle-field is like another, so it is not worth describing it, except that this differs from all others in being now completely covered by a dense tropical growth of weeds. Never have I seen anything like it. The whole area for miles and miles in every direction is covered with a uniform green growth, which is from 3 to 4 feet high. The shell-holes are still there, but they are all hidden, and woe betide the person who attempts to leave the road. It is impossible to walk one yard in any direction without falling into a deep pit. And mixed with the vegetation in inextricable confusion are masses of barbed wire. After leaving Les Bœufs, we passed close to the famous Quadrilateral, which held us up so long just a year ago, and near there came to what is left of Guinchy.

26

Every few yards there is a cemetery beside the road, varying from half a dozen to a hundred graves. In addition, one can see hundreds of white crosses sticking their heads out of the long grass. There must be thousands and thousands of these isolated graves all over the district. In many cases, the rifles stuck in the ground by the bayonet and with a steel helmet on top, are still standing beside the graves. These were put up at the time the men fell to mark where the body was lying. In addition to those who were buried months after the battle, there must be many thousands who were never found. Also, what has happened to the countless German dead, as I did not see any German graves ? From Guinchy we made our way down the famous sunken road, which was our final objective on the 3rd September to all that is left of Guillemont. Only someone who had been there in the battle could have found the place. There is literally nothing left at all, not even a brick. I found the awful sunken road in which my guns were, and even could distinguish the shell-hole we had dug out for the mess. Some of the empty cases were still lying there. I went along the sunken road till I came to the Quarry, but found it hard to believe it was the same dreadful place that I knew exactly a year ago. Gone were the thousands of empty shell-cases, and the many hundreds of dead—both British and German. Instead, there was a sea of rank vegetation waist deep, through which it was almost impossible to force one's way. The only familiar landmark that had not changed was a certain famous concrete machine-gun emplacement, which had defied the 9·2's and 8-in.

We left our horses at the old battery position and walked up to Arrow Head Copse, whence I looked through my glasses at the Quadrilateral, as I did on the 15th September when General Walthall sent hastily for me to take on the German counter-attack, which was developing after our unsuccessful assault in the morning. The whole experience was weird in the extreme. The absolute silence and absence of all movement and noise was uncanny, and at the same time one felt that thousands of ghosts were in the air, and that any moment the barrage might break out. I found myself instinctively keeping close to the trenches, ready to drop in if a shell came. There is now a large railway junction at the corner of Trônes Wood and a main road right across the battle-field.

What will the French do with the place after the war ? It does not seem possible that the ground can ever be cultivated again ; it would take years of work, and cost millions to restore it to a level surface, to say nothing of redraining everywhere. It certainly appears to be a rich soil, judging by the crop of weeds, and well it ought to be, considering that it has been watered by the blood of innumerable men ; at the lowest estimate, I suppose a million, French, English, and Germans, were killed or wounded on this particular track of land. The belt of utter desolation is from ten to fifteen miles across and must extend for thirty miles north and south, and then on the flanks it only joins up with other battle-fields—Arras, Vimy, and finally, the more awful place by far—Messines and Ypres.

BAPAUME, 22ND SEPTEMBER, 1917

The same glorious weather continues. I have done very little to-day, but after tea I had a game of polo with C Battery. One can hardly dignify it by the word " polo," as we were all riding chargers which had no idea of the game whatever. My black mare was simply mad with excitement, and it was impossible to keep her on the ground with one hand. However, it was good exercise and a welcome change.

BAPAUME, 23RD SEPTEMBER, 1917

(Sunday.) We had a large church parade of over five hundred, and managed to get hold of the divisional band. It also played in camp during midday stables. It is quite a good band, and the first time we have heard it.

BAPAUME, 24TH SEPTEMBER, 1917

The nights are getting quite cold, and as the moon is rising fairly early now, I expect we shall be bombed again soon. Perhaps, though, the Hun does not do such nasty tricks in this quiet little backwater. We march to Peronne to-morrow and go into camp there, I believe, for two nights. By a curious coincidence we relieve General Walthall in the line.

PERONNE, 25TH SEPTEMBER, 1917

We had a long and very hot march to-day. We started soon after 9 and were to be inspected by General Daly, our new general, one mile from the start. I had definite orders not to pass this point till the general arrived. We waited half an hour, and then an hour, and when the two generals did not turn up, I had a conference with Spiller, who commands the 107th Brigade, and we decided that we had better start, as we were blocking the road for 4 miles back. A brigade on the march is an endless procession and, including its normal intervals, stretches over a mile and a half of road. We passed through Le Transloy and an hour or so after reached Sailly-Saillisel, which was so famous last year—or rather, infamous. It was, of course, very heavily shelled by us all through the Somme battles, and was our front line last winter, when the Guards Division held this part of the line. It is just like poor old Guillemont, not a single birch left standing; in fact, if it was not for a large sign-board with the name painted on it, one would not know there had ever been a village there. About this point we met the new divisional commander and the C.R.A., both raging at having been kept waiting over an hour. However, I produced my orders, and it was all right. It seems that they forgot to send out an order last night saying that we should be inspected at a different place. The brigade was quite well turned out and, in fact, did themselves great credit. All the drag-ropes, etc., were pipe-clayed and the steel work burnished like silver. It was a great pity that the inspection did not take place at the beginning of the march, as a couple of hours on the chalky road had not made anything look any cleaner. The generals were very pleased with the whole turn-out, as well they might be, after all the trouble taken.

I halted for an hour to feed, half-way through the march, but there is no water in all that arid desert, so the unfortunate horses had to go without. In the afternoon we passed Bouchavesnes, and from there onwards passed hundreds of graves of French soldiers. They are marked with a large tricolour rosette pinned on the centre of the cross. There was one rather well-made white cross inscribed " Un soldat Français, mort pour sa patrie—erected by his British comrades." The road was very hilly and culminated when we reached the top of Mont St. Quentin, which overlooks and dominates the town of Peronne. The French could have entered the latter place at any time after they reached Clery, except for the fact that they knew they could not hold it.

Peronne, 26th September, 1917

At 9 o'clock this morning a lorry called at my camp and the battery commanders and others with myself embarked and proceeded to inspect our new sector in the line. It is a most interesting place, being the extreme right of the British Army. The French are on my immediate right and we work in liaison with them a great deal. The Chestnut Troop—A Battery R.H.A.—are in my group ; they are commanded by a Major Dudley, whom I used to know in England. The colonel of the group that I am relieving is on leave, so Dudley is handing over to me. The whole thing seems to be more like a field-day than a battle, it is all quite quiet and I did not hear a gun or a shell all day. We " de-bussed " at the Group Headquarters, where they had horses and guides waiting, and all my B.C.s and officers went off to see their own batteries. I had a long talk with Dudley, who showed me the maps and explained the Defence Scheme. Afterwards Wilmot and I rode round each of the battery positions, only getting back to Group Headquarters in time for a very late lunch. The Headquarters are very comfortable, but too far back; they must be nearly 4 miles from the batteries, which is quite impossible, so I shall move closer up as soon as I can. The batteries are in good places and do not seem to have been worried by the Hun at all yet, except the battery that my A Battery is relieving. They have been shelled out of existence and are now out in the open in a sunken road. I shall have to find somewhere for them as soon as possible. We had a very tedious and bumpy journey back. We tried to return by the same road that we had come, but of course, the traffic controls would not hear of it. All heavy traffic has to go one way only on a road, so we were made to come back by a road that took us miles up to the north, and eventually came into Peronne by the Bapaume road—just the opposite side from which we had started. The general called late in the evening and had a drink; I complained that I was short of officers, and he has promised to send me some more from the D.A.C.

PERONNE, 27TH SEPTEMBER, 1917

It rained last night, but only enough to lay the dust. The dew in the morning is so heavy that it does not matter much if it rains instead. I always wear gum-boots for breakfast and put on my nice polished boots and spurs when the grass is dry. I rode into Peronne to get money from the field cashier and had lunch at the Officers' Club. This is quite a big affair run by the Expeditionary Force Canteen. The food was vile, and the attendance worse, but it was a change, and I met many people whom I have not seen for a long time and heard all the news. Wilmot has gone up to the line this afternoon, so I am all alone for the moment.

MONTIGNY, 28TH SEPTEMBER, 1917

I sent Wilmot up to the Headquarters of the 152nd Brigade, whom we are relieving, and followed myself this afternoon. I took my groom with me on the black mare

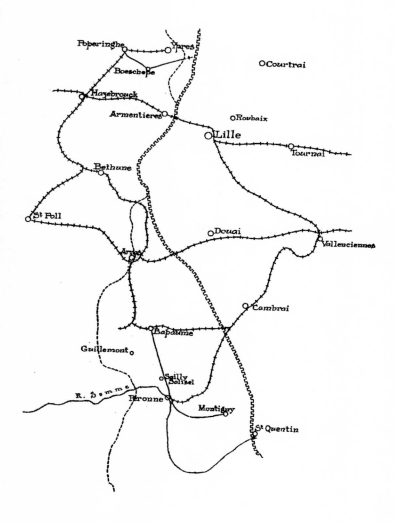

PERONNE-YPRES, SEPT. 1917.

and rode my chestnut. I had to follow the hard road till clear of the town and then soon struck south over a small river. I at once got out on to a rolling prairie of long coarse grass, mixed with a lot of good clover. As far as one can see in every direction there is nothing but grass, not a single house or hedge. It must have been an extraordinary country before the war, as it is not a case of the houses having been blown up, there simply aren't any. There are just a few villages several miles apart; these are, of course, completely ruined. The Hun has not left a single roof up.

With great care and continual reference to my map, I managed to find the particular clump of trees in which General Walthall has his Headquarters. He was not in, but had left a message for me to tell me to wait for him. In half an hour or so he and General Nairne turned up, and we had a very cheery tea, exchanging experiences since I left him at Carency in November. He again told me the story of how the Honours List of the 108th Brigade was lost by Divisional Headquarters last Christmas. He said he did all he could to get it resubmitted but without success. I reached my new Headquarters about 6, and found Dudley still in charge. I stay with him to-night as his guest as I do not take over the command of the Right Group till to-morrow night, when the relief is completed. We had an excellent dinner in their mess hut, which is quite a large place with real genuine glass windows—probably the only glass left in this part of France. Dudley and I are sharing a hut for to-night; I shall be in clover here, with a large Nissen hut for the office and a mess hut, also good, well-built huts for the officers—two officers to a hut, except mine, which I shall have all to myself.

MONTIGNY, 29TH SEPTEMBER, 1917

Fine, but very misty. This morning Dudley and I rode out to see the batteries. It is about four miles to the nearest, and we wasted so much time calling on the cavalry general who is holding this part of the line, with his squadrons dismounted, that we could not get round them all and only got home to a late lunch at 3 p.m. I sorted out papers most of the afternoon in the office and after tea walked down the hill to see my own wagon-lines and also A Battery's. The outgoing brigade have nearly finished building excellent stables, very nearly as good, and on the same pattern as all Government stables in India. We met Walthall and my own general and all went to see the stables ; Walthall was full of beans and simply oozed prosperity. He has got enormously fatter in the last year ; from all accounts he is a quite exceptionally good C.R.A. He certainly was the best brigade commander I have ever come across.

I have developed a perfectly appalling sore throat, probably the result of so much gas in the last four months.

MONTIGNY, 30TH SEPTEMBER, 1917

Another glorious day. I have never known such perfect weather anywhere—day after day of bright sunshine. It is extraordinary to wake up to find the sun streaming into my little hut, and all the doors and windows wide open. The nights are cold, but with my beloved fur bag, that does not affect me at all. To-day is Sunday, and at church this morning there were English, French, and American officers, quite a representative gathering. There is a camp of American troops about 100 yards or so from my Headquarters. They are a very fine-looking lot of men and very well turned out ; they wear the same poncho hat as the New Zealanders. Their officers are not up to much, but they probably know their job, which is all that matters. This particular lot are railway engineers, and they run all the narrow-gauge lines in this district. After lunch Dudley and I rode to all the batteries. It took us from 2 o'clock till 6, but it is a charming ride straight across country and one takes one's horses right up to the guns. In fact, we actually rode up to one of the O.P.s. Brother Boche seems very tame here, but he was crumping a French heavy battery all day on and off. I fancy there are limits to the liberties one can afford to take, and one day we shall get a salvo over without warning. We shall certainly not like going back to a fighting sector after this rest cure. Once more I have been asked for my full Christian names !

MONTIGNY, 1ST OCTOBER, 1917

My throat was so bad this morning that I thought I would rest it and not get hot. So I have spent the whole day in camp, working up my Defence Scheme for Divisional Artillery. I have been at it all day and have nothing like finished it as it is very complicated, with all the French barrages mixed up with our own. It is quite the most interesting place I have been in, and quite different to trench warfare. There are no trenches, to begin with. We each hold posts and are anything from 500 to 2,000 yards apart. I was very interested in seeing St. Quentin cathedral to-day. It is quite near here, and on a fine day it stands up like a landmark. Colonel Talbot came to tea ; he is really wonderful—nearly seventy.

MONTIGNY, 2ND OCTOBER, 1917

The Corps C.R.A. and General Nairne called this morning. After lunch, Mortimer, De Tassigny, and I rode over the river to pay our respects to Commandant Michel, who commands the Group of French Artillery immediately on our right. We found him living in a dug-out in a ruined street in Maissemy. Unfortunately the French batteries were being strafed at the time by 4·2's and we had to walk into the middle of it. Neither Mortimer nor I exactly enjoyed being shelled, but we had to walk along the street as though we had not noticed that there were any shells about. My friend the commandant was very business-like and explained the whole situation very carefully. We went over our mutual protective barrages and made some minor alterations. Heaven only knows how a colonel gets on at his work if he can't talk French as easily as English. It is very technical, and when once they get excited the Frogs talk very quickly. He took me to see a 75 battery firing ; it was very interesting after having heard and read so much about their wonderful gun. It is extraordinarily simple and wonderfully efficient. They can fire up to thirty rounds per minute with it, which is about double what we can with ours. They never have trouble with their buffer springs like we do ; I must say I do envy them. On my way home I called at 17th Infantry Brigade Headquarters to see General Stone and found Richardson there and rode part of the way home with him.

MONTIGNY, 3RD OCTOBER, 1917

I managed to do a little work in my office this morning, but have had to spend the rest of the day riding about the country. I get through two horses every day. I went over to see the general about various matters, and he insisted on taking me over to see General Stone whose brigade I am covering. I am very angry with our infantry to-day, as they allowed one of our patrols to be taken prisoner, and would not agree to my putting down a box barrage that had been carefully arranged for the capture of the Hun patrol. After lunch I again went over to Divisional Artillery and had another long talk with the general about brigade affairs. Afterwards I rode to the battery wagon-lines, which are at Caulaincourt—a very pretty place, but of course in ruins.

MONTIGNY, 4TH OCTOBER, 1917

To-day we have had all the horses of the brigade inspected. The D.D.R. of the Army, accompanied by the A.D.D.R. of the Corps, plus the A.D.V.S. of the division, and the more humble V.O. of the brigade, arrived in a train of motors. General Nairne and Fox accompanied them. The whole cortège proceeded from one wagon-line to another, and many words of wisdom fell from their lips. In the end they agreed that the horses might be worse, but were quite surprised that they were not as fat as the cavalry horses, who have been here doing nothing for the last three years. It is quite a long ride to Caulaincourt, but there is a soft track nearly all the way, so one can canter, which takes just thirty-five minutes.

Montigny, 5th October, 1917

I meant to have gone round the batteries to-day, but have been too busy with papers in the office. I am trying to complete my Defence Scheme, which is rather a business as it is the most complicated scheme I have ever seen, owing to the numerous French barrages. One of the French batteries has been heavily shelled to-day, and my friend the Commandant Michel seems very nervous. I have arranged for all my howitzers to cover the left of the French line to-night to assist them if anything happens. It is rapidly getting colder and we have to dine with our cloaks now. What a change from a fortnight ago ! I hope to go on leave the day after to-morrow.

Montigny, 6th October, 1917

Bitterly cold, and raining, with a hurricane blowing. We are very miserable in our paper summer-houses. The walls of all our headquarter huts are rough boards an inch or more apart, with tarred paper on the outside. They were built at the time of the German retirement last April, and have been delightful summer residences, but are hardly what one would choose for winter. I am going to move up a mile nearer the batteries soon, and have selected a place at the bottom of a deep railway cutting. The Germans blew up all the bridges and took away the rails, so we shall not be disturbed by trains for some time. I have settled my leave for the 11th so expect to start from here on the 10th.

Montigny, 7th October, 1917

I had invited Commandant Michel, who commands the French group of Field Artillery on my right, to lunch with me at 1 o'clock. At 10 the general rang up and said he wanted to go round all the batteries of my group, and would call for me. I explained that I had got a party of French officers lunching, so he promised to bring me back by 1. We went to see Dudley first, and then on to the others, with the natural result that I was late for lunch ; it did not matter, as Michel quite understood that I could not help it. We had a most jovial meal, which commenced at a little after 1, merged into tea, and finally came to an end at 6 o'clock. We have a case of very good champagne (Lanson-brut /09) of which we got through a number of bottles. Michel does not talk English, but most of my officers speak French as well as their own language, and one of the French officers spoke English at the other end of the table, so it was quite easy. They certainly enjoyed themselves very much, and I have to do a return lunch with them the day after to-morrow. I have seldom known such an awful day ; it has simply poured cats and dogs, and every moment I expected the roof to be torn off by the wind. As a result of five hours' talking at the top of my voice, with ten other people also shouting in the same little hut, I have got a violent headache. The noise of the rain beating on the tin roof is deafening.

MONTIGNY, 8TH OCTOBER, 1917

Still raining and blowing hurricanes. After breakfast I left the Child in charge of the office and took Wilmot and Harris and rode over to the cutting where I am going to establish my Headquarters. We planned it all out, and then reconnoitred for a new way to ride up to the batteries without coming into view of the enemy. It is possible to get into the valley in which all the batteries are without being seen, but it is a long way round and I want to find a short cut. My five batteries are spread over a front of over two miles, so it is a long job to visit them all on foot. Carmen, my black mare, has been clipped, and was very pleased with herself.

MONTIGNY, 9TH OCTOBER, 1917

A horrible night, and incessant downpour ; it looks as if it would never be fine again. What an awful crossing I shall have ! I hear the boats have been stopped two or three days, and that there is fearful congestion at Boulogne. I doubt if I shall be able to get a room to-morrow night. I was going over to see the French to-day, but my general wanted me to lunch with him as he goes on leave this afternoon. We had a cheerful meal, and talked shop afterwards. My chief trouble is that " Q " won't let me move my huts when I shift my Headquarters to the railway cutting, and I won't move till there is adequate accommodation at the other end. As I don't in the least want to move, it does not worry me very much.

HÔTEL DE LONDRES, BOULOGNE, 10TH OCTOBER, 1917

I borrowed a car from the Train and, with Mortimer, motored from my Headquarters to Amiens. It must be about forty miles, and it took us two hours. There was a very cold and wet wind blowing, so it was not altogether joy. Dudley and Welch came to breakfast with me at 9 o'clock. The former has taken command of the group in my absence, and the latter had to represent the C.R.A. at a small field-day the infantry are having behind the lines. Fancy having a sham fight within three miles of the real trenches ! On arrival at Amiens I deposited my kit at the station and ascertained what time the train started and then had lunch. We had a wonderful meal at the Hôtel du Rhin, which was a great joy after all the vile cooking of the last six months. Last time I was in this hotel was just before we went into the Battle of the Somme. At 1.80 I left Amiens by the French " Train des Permissionaires," and after a most comfortable journey in a first-class carriage, reached Boulogne at 6 o'clock. There were no cabs at the station, but I persuaded a man to carry my kit to this hotel. I have brought home a German shield, worn by the " storming troops," to protect them against shrapnel and rifle-fire. This is not a bad little hotel, and I got quite a decent dinner, with a bottle of first-class claret.

1, ST. JAMES's TERRACE, 11TH OCTOBER, 1917

The boat sailed at 11 o'clock, and as I was lucky enough to secure a cabin, I did not mind it being a bit rough. I was prepared for a really bad crossing, but was pleasantly surprised to find it was nothing very serious. I took the precaution to have a couple of very strong brandies and sodas before we left port. We got to Folkestone in exactly an hour and a half, and the train started as soon as enough officers had landed to fill it. I had to run, and jumped in as it was starting. Lunch in the Pullman, and home by tea-time. What a six months! I can honestly say I have earned my ten days' leave.

HÔTEL DE LONDRES, BOULOGNE, 22ND OCTOBER, 1917

I left London at 1 o'clock this afternoon after a delightful ten days' rest, the only event of interest being a Zeppelin raid on London, in which a bomb was dropped in Piccadilly. I went to see the place. It was curious seeing wrecked houses and holes in the streets of London. I landed at 6 o'clock this evening after quite a good crossing, and have got a room in this hotel again.

VENDELLES, 23RD OCTOBER, 1917

(Midnight.) I have just arrived at my Headquarters after a long and tiring day in the train. I had to start at 7 o'clock this morning and travel by the French civilian train to Amiens, which we only reached at midday. I left my five heavy parcels at the station, and had lunch at the Hôtel du Rhin. The first person I saw was Hunt, who was my captain in the 3rd Hussars in India. He has now become a colonel in the 8/King's Own in the 76th Infantry Brigade. He says he is really enjoying the war, and I believe he meant it. Unmarried and drawing Indian pay, he is having an excellent time; the more so as he is one of the few men who have no nerves. I went on by train at 4 p.m., and had to change in the dark at Chaulnes; I had a dreadful time as there was no one to carry my luggage, and I had to cart the heavy typewriter, duplicator, etc., etc., along about two hundred yards of railway track, making three trips. We eventually reached Peronne, where I was told there was no train on till 11 o'clock, so I went to the club in the town and had dinner. I reached railhead at Roisel at last and was delighted to be met by my trumpeter, who had brought my horses and the mess-

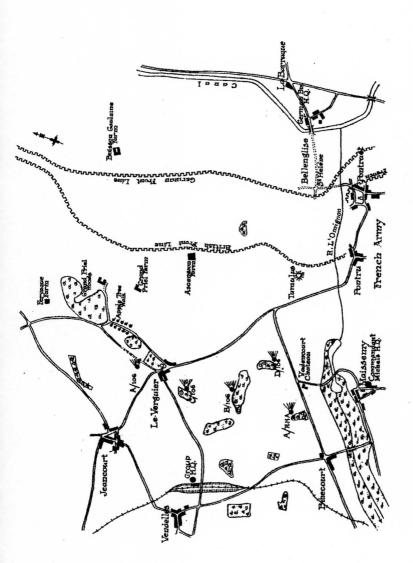

VENDELLES, OCT. 1917.

cart for my kit. I had a 5-mile ride to the new Headquarters, as they had moved up nearer the batteries during
my absence. We are now established in a deep railway
cutting, and shall be very comfortable when the new mess
and huts are built. Meanwhile it is bitterly cold at night
under canvas in this weather.

VENDELLES, 24TH OCTOBER, 1917

Hobday has been commanding the group whilst I have
been away, as Welch and his battery are lent to the
Centre Group. The latter has been commanding the
brigade, so it must have been rather complicated. There
has been a lot of changes on the Protective Barrages, etc.,
whilst I have been away, so I have spent the whole day
getting it all up and making out my Defence Scheme.
The duplicator is a great success, and we have done several
sheets of the scheme. The new mess was nearly finished
this evening, and we have been able to dine in it. It is
going to be very comfortable, as we have built a huge open
fireplace of brick, and the whole room is lined with green
canvas. Unfortunately, the fire smoked and we could
hardly keep our eyes open. To-morrow the chimney is
going to be raised.

VENDELLES, 26TH OCTOBER, 1917

It is blowing a hurricane to-day, but I struggled round
all the batteries and visited the battalion commanders in
the line. I had lunch with the 1/Royal Fusiliers, who are
one of the battalions that I am covering. I was quite
tired by the time I got back, as the ground is very slippery
after the rain.

VENDELLES, 27TH OCTOBER, 1917

This morning I rode to Caulaincourt to inspect the
horses of some of the batteries. I telephoned to Colonel
Chesney, who helps to look after all the wagon-lines of
the Divisional Artillery, and asked him to meet me. I
took a bee-line straight across country and found that it

was under 5 miles ; by cantering on the soft grass nearly all
the way I did it in half an hour,   I am getting accustomed
to galloping through the long grass there is everywhere
here, and no longer expect to fall into an old shell-hole
every stride.   As a matter of fact there are very few holes
in this country, except close round the sites of villages
where the Hun rearguard put up a fight sometimes.
Chesney and I looked at all the horses and agreed that
there was a distinct improvement in them, especially
C Battery.   General Nairne turned up before we had
finished and spent an hour and a half with D Battery.
He is a most lengthy person to look at horses with, as it
takes him hours and hours to inspect one battery.   By
the time he had finished it was raining hard, so I had a
disagreeable ride back, arriving very late for lunch.   It
is very nice to have a comfortable mess to come back to
when it is wet and cold.   Our great brick fireplace is a
great success, now it does not smoke.

VENDELLES, 28TH OCTOBER, 1917

De Tassigny and I rode to B's wagon-lines, where
I inspected their horses, huts, cookhouses, etc.   I think
they are quite the best ; probably A would be as good
if they had better accommodation, but they have had to
build stables and huts for their men themselves, whereas
the other batteries found most of the work done when
they arrived.

VENDELLES, 29TH OCTOBER, 1917

Having finished our Defence Scheme, Wilmot and I
took a day out and have been riding all over the country,
calling on different units, and finding out where they
live.   Colonel Chesney and the Divisional P.V.O. came to
A's wagon-lines, and picked out brood mares.   These are
to be specially branded, and used at the end of the war.
I suppose it depends on how long the war lasts.   From
there we went on to the left group, where we happened to
find a conference going on between Generals Nairne and
Sweeney, with Spiller and Richardson.   We discussed

new S.O.S. lines for an hour, and I stopped to lunch with Spiller. After lunch I called on the Heavy Artillery Group, but found their colonel out. We next went to the Sherwood Foresters and had a drink with them, and arranged for more copies of the *Wipers' Times* to be sent to the brigade. This is a very amusing paper that the battalion publishes at irregular intervals; they carry their own printing press about with them. Finally, we went to see the Balloon Section and talked to the " Sausage " officers. They offered to take me up, but as the wind was blowing towards the Huns I did not feel brave enough.

Vendelles, 30th October, 1917

As it was a fine day and clear, I went to my O.P. in Le Verguier and had a good look at the zone. It is not a bad O.P., but the zone being some 5,000 yards wide, it is impossible to see it all from any one place. Of course each battery has its own O.P., so between them they cover everything. It is quite a new kind of warfare for all of us, as No Man's Land is 2,000 yards wide in places, and we have detached posts in the front system, instead of the usual continuous trenches. I took my " Davon " telescope, and was able to make out the German line very well. I did not see anything very interesting, but there were plenty of isolated Huns walking about far beyond my range.

Vendelles, 31st October, 1917

I have two vacancies for captain in the brigade, and the general wanted me to have a man from the 107th, but from all I heard I do not think we should have liked him. Welch is very keen on having his own subaltern, Webster, promoted, so I wrote a personal letter to the general, making a great point of it. To-day I hear that Webster and Coates have become captains of C and D Batteries respectively, which I think will do very well. Hobday dined with me and brought his gramo-

27

phone, as ours had not yet arrived. I brought some new records from England—"Aïda" and "Chu Chin Chow," principally. They make a good combination; there is no doubt that the gramophone has done much to make war bearable.

VENDELLES, 1ST NOVEMBER, 1917

Colonel Nicholls, who commands the Heavy Group, asked if I would like to motor to the advanced map depot, and see if they had any new maps that would be useful to us. He called for me in his car and we had a delightful run to the place, which is some 6 miles off. I do envy him, having a motor of his own. All Group Headquarters ought to have one, especially in a place like this where distances are so great. The map place was quite like Stanford in London, all the various maps hanging on the wall, and one just went round and picked up what one wanted. The clerk in charge wrapped them up, and we walked away with them—and nothing to pay, which was very pleasing.

VENDELLES, 2ND NOVEMBER, 1917

The rearrangement of the S.O.S. lines is so complicated that Wilmot and I had to ride over to Divisional Headquarters and see the general. I did not want to duplicate my orders, and then have to alter them. We had tea there, and rode back in the dark, in time to meet all the battery commanders, to whom I explained the new arrangements. They all dined with me, and admired our new set of crockery which I had ordered from Goode in South Audley Street. It is a huge success, as I got the complete set of the green china ; it is much nicer than the horrible cups and saucers one buys in Amiens, and no more expensive, especially as the carriage costs nothing.

VENDELLES, 3RD NOVEMBER, 1917

I rode round all the batteries and both battalion headquarters this morning. As it was a misty day I risked riding over the sky-line, and went straight across country. As a matter of fact it was much clearer than I had thought, and I was in full view of the German position for 500 yards. I suppose he did not think it was worth while wasting shells on trying to hit two horses at a long range. However, I have no doubt it will appear in his Divisional Summary of Intelligence to-night : " Two horsemen were seen to cross the sky-line in —— square, and disappeared into the valley." Just as I rode up to B Battery I saw two staff officers coming along, and was surprised to find it was the corps commander—old General Snow ; it is not often one meets so exalted a person in the line. He said he would like to see B's gun position, so I took him over it. He was delighted with all the little paths they have in the wood and asked the men the usual questions about rations, etc.

VENDELLES, 4TH NOVEMBER, 1917

Orders have just come for me to go to a Higher Command Course at Shoeburyness, commencing next Sunday. It lasts a fortnight. I am very bored with the idea, as I have just returned from leave, and it is a beastly journey, and I don't see what they propose to teach me. The idea of forty colonels commanding brigades in France going to a school of Gunnery, and being taught a lot of theoretical stuff, by the " experts " who sit at home is rather ludicrous. At any rate I hope to get a day or two at home before coming back. This afternoon we all went to a Divisional Concert, in aid of the French Croix Rouge, the attraction being a Mlle something or other from the Comédie Française. She sang quite beautifully and gave us things from " Bohème " and " Faust." I must say I enjoyed myself immensely The most amusing moment was when a special signed programme was auctioned. The auctioneer was a very witty staff captain ; there were a number of officers of the 17th Lancers there, and when the bidding began to slow down the auctioneer turned to them and shouted : " Come on, you cavalry people ; you don't do much to help the war on." Rather unkind to the poor cavalry, but it produced a roar of laughter from the whole audience of a thousand men.

VENDELLES, 5TH NOVEMBER, 1917

I had to go and see the general this morning, to take up a man who wants a commission. General Nairne suddenly decided that he would go round all the battery positions of the division, so we started from Divisional Headquarters at 11, with the result that I did not get back to my own Headquarters till after 2 o'clock. I had only just finished my lunch when the French C.R.A. came to call on me. He brought my friend Commandant Michel, and for the next hour my mess resembled the parrot-house at the Zoo. Everyone talked as fast as they could, as loud as they could, and all together. However, the French know what they want, and by the end of the hour we had redistributed all the liaison barrages, and I had explained all my dispositions to them. Wilmot stood behind me and I translated whenever it was necessary for him to make notes. The French C.R.A. has asked me to lunch with him to-morrow.

VENDELLES, 6TH NOVEMBER, 1917

At 11 o'clock Michel called for me in a motor and took me off to see the Bois D'Holnon, not far from St. Quentin, and there we found the French Headquarters. We had quite an excellent lunch, wonderful cooking, by a real chef, not the wretched baked meat and pudding my own cook gives me. They dine in a very good dug-out in a clearing in the wood. Several group and battery commanders had been asked to meet me, and we went through the mutual defence scheme again. On my return I found Colonel Nicholls, of the Heavy Group, waiting to see me ; he had come about my request for him to blow down " Dog's Leg," a little copse near our front line, that the Hun often gets into and is tiresome for the infantry. I asked Hobday to come and dine, as I had many things to tell him before I go off to England to-morrow,

Boulogne, 7th November, 1917

The general lent me his car, and Dutton, who is major in the 107th, and I motored into Amiens, a little over 50 miles, in time for lunch. We caught the 1.20 p.m. train, and got here for dinner. I have gone to the same Hôtel de Londres where I was last month.

1, St. James's Terrace, 8th November, 1917

We had quite a good crossing, though the sea was a little choppy, and reached London at 2 o'clock. I had lunch at Lennox Gardens, and did some shopping before arriving home to tea. I go to Shoeburyness on Sunday for two weeks on this senior officers' course.

Westcliff-on-Sea, 11th November, 1917

I came down this afternoon and found that I am billeted at the Queen's Hotel. It is quite comfortable, but crowded with officers who are on gunnery courses.

1, St. James's Terrace, 16th November, 1917

I have finished the first half of the course, and go to Salisbury Plain on Sunday. G. came down for three days and we got rooms at a very nice private hotel at Westcliff. The course so far has not been very instructive, but a pleasant change, and the weather is perfect.

1, St. James's Terrace, 27th November, 1917

G. and I have spent the last week at Salisbury, where I did the second half of my course. We had charming thirteenth-century rooms at the Old George Hotel. Each day the party of us motored out to the Plain in a lorry, and, after walking many miles on the downs, saw a few shells fired. Nothing could have been more boring or less instructive to people who have been doing the real thing in France. We got back to London on Friday night, and I have had till to-day, Tuesday, to finish my shopping, etc.

Boulogne, 28th November, 1917

We had a bad crossing, as there was a stiff wind and a big sea running, but I just managed not to be ill. I am staying at the usual hotel, and go up by train very early in the morning.

Vendelles, 30th November, 1917

Yesterday was long and exhausting. I had to start soon after 7 from Boulogne and only reached Amiens at noon. I had a good lunch there and went to see the Cathedral with an excellent guide-book. I spent an hour there and discovered all sorts of interesting things that I did not know of before. My train left at 4 o'clock and, after changing at Chaulnes, got me to Peronne in time for dinner at the club. I was told there was a train on to Roisel at 10 o'clock, but had to wait on the platform till midnight, eventually reaching my station at a little before 1. My horses and mess-cart were waiting, and I rode out to Headquarters. It was very cold, but a brilliant moon— in fact, so bright that I decided to leave the road and go across country by tracks that I know well. I was much touched to find my officers sitting up for me with whisky and biscuits. They gave me all the news of what had happened since I left, the most important thing being that we are to be relieved in a few days, and presumably go into the great battle five miles north of us. It is a great blow as we are very comfortable here, and had hoped to spend Christmas in this peaceful place. The battle on our left is in full swing and sounds almost as bad as Ypres.

(11 p.m.) It has been a great day of excitement as we were woke up about 6 o'clock by a tremendous noise on our left, evidently an S.O.S. on a wide front. We got no news till the middle of the morning, when we heard that there was a serious attack on the division on our left, and that things were not going well for us. All day the heavy battery cannonade was kept up, and rumours were received of trenches lost and even batteries captured. Late this morning I got a situation report, and found

things were worse than we had realised. The Hun has penetrated our line to a depth of 8,000 yards in places, and some batteries have been lost, including A/107, which is sad, as it belongs to our division. It was lent to another division, so we cannot be blamed for the loss ; still, it is the first time we have lost any of our divisional artillery. Connor, who has just been promoted out of my C battery, was commanding at the time. He seems to have behaved very well. The gunners kept on firing till the Germans were within 400 yards, and then removed the sights and breech blocks and covered the operation with rifle-fire. The officer and men then withdrew to a trench in rear where they tried to keep the enemy off with rifles. Their casualties were not heavy—two killed and two wounded and one prisoner, the latter a badly wounded man, who was taken to a dressing-station, which was afterwards captured. From all accounts, Connor did all that could have been expected of him, and cannot be blamed for the loss of his guns.

VENDELLES, 1ST DECEMBER, 1917

Late last night I was warned that a fresh and heavy attack was expected again this morning, as a German Guards Division had arrived for the assault. In the light of what happened yesterday, I have been told to have all my gun-limbers close up to the battery positions by 5 o'clock in the morning, so as to try and save them in case the Germans get through on our front. The whole brigade " stood to " by 5 o'clock and I was ready in the mess with my maps, etc., by that time. However, nothing happened, and we all " stood down " by 9 o'clock. I called on General Stone, whom I am covering, this morning and found out exactly what he means to do if we have to retire. I don't anticipate it for a moment, but it is better to be ready for everything. I rode on and inspected the positions already chosen to which batteries withdraw if necessary. After that I went on to Divisional Headquarters and saw the general. He told me all the new fads that General Knapp, the Corps C.R.A., wants. My office is very cold in spite of an oil-stove I bought at Boulogne. That is the worst of living in a tin hut in winter. At 3 o'clock a furious bombardment broke out again to the north, but I have not yet heard if the Hun is attacking again or if we are counter-attacking.

VENDELLES, 2ND DECEMBER, 1917

Another day of excitement and rumours. The most intense fire has been raging day and night on our immediate left. We have counter-attacked and regained some of the lost ground ; the Hun has also attacked several times with varying success. I think we have the situation well in hand now, and reinforcements of all sorts have arrived, including the Life Guards who are close behind me, but I have not had time to go and see them. It is bitterly cold, and I can hardly bear myself in my office. Unfortunately we have not been able to get any carbide or oil for the lamps and stoves. This afternoon I rode round the batteries and found Welch who had just returned from his month's leave at Bordeaux. My chestnut mare was so excited that I could hardly manage her. I don't think she can have had much exercise whilst I was away. I also reconnoitred the positions we should take up if we have to retire. The Hun claims to have taken four thousand prisoners and many batteries. I hope it is one of his usual exaggerations, but I am afraid he must have got a good deal.

VENDELLES, 3RD DECEMBER, 1917

The coldest night I ever remember ; even my fur bag could not keep me warm. An intense bombardment began at 5 o'clock, but I don't know who is attacking. It is still raging now at midday. I have just heard that the Huns are attacking down Watling Street, which is on my front, so I have turned on my batteries. I hear that there are three French batteries close behind me and at my disposal in case of necessity. Also I believe that I can get hold of three batteries of English Horse Artillery. In the

afternoon I rode to Bernes to see if I could find the 2nd,
but was told that they were at Hervilly, so went on there.
I found the quartermaster, who reminded me that he had
still got my pack saddle which I left when I went home in
1915. He said the regiment was digging trenches up in
the line, but would probably be back to-morrow. As I
was so close I called in to see Spiller to condole on the
loss of his A Battery. I found Connor there, who was
in command of the battery at the time it was captured.
He was still very excited and I could not get much out of
him. He seems to have gone on firing for fifteen minutes
after the infantry had passed through him, and until the
Huns were only four hundred yards from his left flank,
when he turned two guns round and fired into them with
Fuse Zero. He got all his men away with his breech-
blocks and sights, so he did all that could have been asked
of him. The disaster seems to have been much worse than
we have been told. I understand we lost 150 guns, including an army brigade complete with its horses, wagons,
and all. They were surrounded by machine-guns just as
they were limbering up. There is no doubt this is the worst
reverse the British Army has ever had in France. I
believe we lost about 4,000 prisoners, but it is impossible
to get any reliable information. The cold is something
dreadful, thick ice everywhere—I can hardly hold my pen
to write.

Vendelles, 4th December, 1917

Another bitter night, but I was able to sleep as I had
taken the precaution to put my fur coat over my bed.
The battle has been roaring hard night and day, but we
have not had much information about it. Only rumours,
and these are always unreliable. I am afraid there is no
doubt it has been a regrettable incident. With all this
noise going on, I do not like going far away from H.Q.,
so I only went out for a short time this afternoon to see
the reserve positions. Heavy French reinforcements
have arrived behind us, and they have been practising
an attack round here all this afternoon.

VENDELLES, 5TH DECEMBER, 1917

General Daly came to see me to-day; he was much interested in my fighting map with coloured silks and pins all over it. After lunch Wilmot and I rode over to see the 2nd Life Guards and found Archie Sinclair and Fenwick Palmer; they are coming to lunch with me to-morrow. We inspected the horses of A Battery and our own H.Q. wagon-lines. The cold is getting worse than ever, and we shiver all day, as it is impossible to keep the huts warm as they have nothing on the roof but a single sheet of corrugated iron. Harris went to sleep in the mess after dinner, so the doctor blacked his face all over with burnt cork. He only discovered it this morning.

VENDELLES, 6TH DECEMBER, 1917

There is going to be a demonstration on my front to-night, and I have had to arrange all the artillery co-operation for it, both my own batteries and the French. Commandant Michel has very kindly lent me two of his batteries for the occasion. The news from the battle is very bad; we seem to have lost almost all the ground we had gained in the original attack. If we got more news the thing would look more hopeful, as we get lots of telegrams if we are winning and nothing if we are getting the worst of it. The London joy-bells were certainly premature, and make us look very foolish.

VENDELLES, 7TH DECEMBER, 1917

Last night we had a complicated sort of raid on my front. Both battalions sent out parties across No Man's Land to blow up the Hun wire with " Bengal torpedoes." I had to create a diversion to cover them. I picked out all the company headquarters on my front, and put my available guns and howitzers on to them at zero hour. I also arranged with Commandant Michel to fire two of his batteries on my front. We all sat up till it was over about 1 a.m. this morning. It made quite a noise, and

the Hun probably thought he was going to be attacked ;
we managed to collar one prisoner, and so got identification
of the people who are holding the line opposite to us.
They appear to be the 5th Guards Division. At midday
General Nairne told me on the 'phone that we are shortly
going to be relieved, and soon after Colonel Wainwright,
who is C.R.A. of the 3rd Cavalry Division, arrived to
arrange about taking over from me. The whole thing is
hopelessly complicated, and as far as I can see we are
likely to have two, if not three, Bde. H.Q.s crowded in to
my place for the time being.

VENDELLES, 8TH DECEMBER, 1917

Events have been moving fast. We had a two-hour
conference to-day with General Nairne and several brigade
commanders. Batteries are being rushed up in shoals
in anticipation of a great attack on this front by the enemy,
who is reported to be massing troops opposite us. Brigade
after brigade of Horse Artillery is arriving, and we shall
soon be as thick as we were at Ypres last summer. Most
of my own batteries are moving farther to the north to
reinforce Spiller, and we shall eventually form the two
brigades into one group under Spiller and me alternately.
I have handed over my group as it was constituted up to
to-day, and am going out of action with my Headquarters
for a few days till my own batteries have changed their
positions. Meanwhile, I am staying on till the day after
to-morrow, as Wainwright, who has just arrived on this
front, knows nothing about the place or the dispositions
for the defence of the line. There is no news from the
Cambrai Battle, but there has been no heavy firing. The
weather has broken, and it is raining.

VENDELLES, 9TH DECEMBER, 1917

Wainwright and I went to Div. H.Q. in the C.R.A.'s
car at 9 o'clock this morning, where we found Spiller and
a Cavalry Corps Officer R.A. We had a long conference.
Things are getting more and more complicated ; there are

now seventy-two guns covering the same zone as I had to hold for two months with two 18-pounders. Everyone has got the wind up badly, in fact there is a hurricane blowing. My unfortunate B and C Batteries have got to turn out of their comfortable warm positions into the open mud. Their places are being handed over to the Horse Artillery. It is very hard on them, as they have been working for two months to improve the positions. It is not as if they were being relieved and going to a new area; they are only moving a mile and will be firing on the same spot. This sort of thing is bound to cause great ill-feeling. Unfortunately we are now under the Cavalry Corps, so we are not likely to get much consideration when it is a matter of choosing between the Horse Artillery and us. The general told me about where he wanted me to put my two batteries, so Spiller and I met at Jeancourt and hunted for positions. We found a bad one for B and quite a good one in a copse for C. I lunched with Spiller, and had a good look at the place I am likely to take over when Spiller goes on leave. General Seligmann—who commands the artillery of the Cavalry Corps, came to tea to-day. He confirmed what we all thought, namely, that the " Army " have got the wind up badly—in fact, a hurricane is blowing. There are all sorts of rumours about the Hun making a huge attack on us ; if he does I think it will be on the northern part of the divisional front, not on my part.

CAULAINCOURT, 10TH DECEMBER, 1917

I finally handed over to Wainwright this morning, and transferred myself and my headquarter officers to D Battery's wagon-lines, where we are sharing a Nissen hut with Coates, who is now captain of that battery. It is very uncomfortable and horribly cold—in fact, I don't think I have ever felt the cold so much. My feet have not been warm since I arrived. There is a stove of sorts, but it only smokes us out, and gives absolutely no heat at all. I have been inspecting the horses all day, of the three batteries whose wagon-lines are here. I also called on a French battery commander who is camped close to us. I went for a walk round the lake and grounds of the Château de Caulaincourt in the park of which we are camped. It has been quite a large place, and belongs to the duc de Valenciennes, who bred race-horses here, including three Derby winners. The Kaiser and the Crown Prince are supposed to have stayed here. It has been so thoroughly wrecked that it is now hard to identify anything.

CAULAINCOURT, 11TH DECEMBER, 1917

Last night I dined with General Daly, who now commands our division. He sent the D.A. car for me, but as I live in a sea of mud, the car could not get within a quarter of a mile of my hut, and I had to wade to it in my long gum-boots, and carry my ordinary brown boots. The general has got the best mess I have seen out here, and excellent furniture. His A.D.C.—Maclaine of Lochbuie, who is a most amusing person—played the piano after dinner. I enjoyed myself very much, and got back to my hut about 11 o'clock. Coates and I sat up till 5 in the morning talking, when we went round his horses. I lost a gum-boot in the mud, and had to walk back barefooted.

CAULAINCOURT, 12TH DECEMBER, 1917

The cold is worse than ever. I don't think I have ever suffered from it so much. We had the wretched stove taken to pieces to-day by D Battery's fitter, who found that it was more than half choked up with soot and water, so now it may behave better. I inspected B Battery's wagon-lines before lunch and was very pleased with all I saw. There is no doubt they are the best. Hobday is an old soldier and knows how to run a battery. It is rare to find a ranker who turns into such an excellent battery commander. In the afternoon we had a revolver competition ; needless to say, my automatic won. It is a beautiful weapon and now, fortunately, the Government issues ammunition for it.

CAULAINCOURT, 13TH DECEMBER, 1917

We woke up at 5.30 this morning to hear the most tremendous bombardment roaring, close on our left. I have seldom heard a heavier one. It was one continuous roar, real " drum fire." It lasted without a break for three hours. I could not find out what it was all about, and was about to order all the wagon-lines to " stand to " when I heard from D.A. that the firing was not on our divisional front. To-day I inspected C Battery and was very pleased with the improvement in their horses and gunpark. Welch came to lunch, and as usual we had an animated discussion on intricate problems of gunnery. I hear the attack this morning was just to the north of us. Result unknown.

CAULAINCOURT, 14TH DECEMBER, 1917

The weather is much warmer, and now that the stove has been mended it is possible to keep the temperature of the hut up to a reasonable heat. After lunch I rode over to Vraignes to call on Daddy Talbot, but he was out. I therefore looked in at the Train who generally have all the latest rumours, if not news. Vraignes is the only village for miles that has not been destroyed. When the Hun retired he collected all the natives of the countryside and marched them into Vraignes, gave them two days' food, and left them for us to find when we advanced. The sight of houses, complete even to glass windows, is quite uncanny.

CAULAINCOURT, 15TH DECEMBER, 1917

There has been heavy firing at intervals all day, but we have no news about it. I have had a lazy day, only going for a walk and seeing the horses. The doctor and Harris returned from thirty-six hours' leave to Amiens, and have brought back vast quantities of new records. All sorts of good things like " Bohème," " Tosca," etc.

CAULAINCOURT, 16TH DECEMBER, 1917

I invited the officers of a French battery to lunch to-day. We managed to give them a good feed and sat down twelve, which was rather a strain on our slender resources. I like the battery commander very much, and his senior subaltern—Lieutenant Constant—was a typical French gentleman of one's own world. After lunch we had a two-hours' Grand Opera Concert, which was a great success. War must have been very dull before the days of gramophones. The French colonel came to tea, and has asked me to dine with him to-morrow night.

CAULAINCOURT, 17TH DECEMBER, 1917

Wilmot, M.O., de Tassigny, Harris, and I all went to lunch with the French battery. They did us very well, except that after drinking excellent claret all through lunch, we had to finish up with sweet champagne. They took us to see their :75's, and even took the whole thing to pieces to show us the mechanism. It was very interesting, as I examined their sights as well. The gun is far in advance of ours, much lighter, far simpler and stronger. I have never been able to understand why we did not adopt it at the beginning of the war. We had to make thousands of new guns, in any case, and our own 18-pounders could have been used up in Mesopotamia, Egypt, etc. At 6.80 I started off on foot to dine with the French colonel. I lost my way in the deep snow, and floundered about up to my knees. I was quite exhausted by the time I got there. I found they had asked nearly all the officers of the regiment to meet me, and we sat down over twenty. It was a regular feast that lasted for two hours. Their cook was a chef in a French restaurant before the war, so the cooking was excellent. The colonel made a fifteen-minutes' speech, including proposing the health of the King, the British Army, etc. I followed with about ten minutes in the same strain ; it was the first real speech I had made in a foreign language, but under the influence of a little good red wine I found it very easy. On my return to my Headquarters I found that the papers had arrived and that *The Times* gives my name as being Mentioned in Despatches. Five of my officers are also mentioned ; so we have not done so badly after all.

CAULAINCOURT, 18TH DECEMBER, 1917

I am to take over the command of the Centre Group from Spiller. This includes the whole divisional artillery. I had intended to ride over to see Spiller to-day, and make all the arrangements for the taking over, but there has been such an intense frost that the roads are one sheet of ice. Bevis and two of his howitzers came out of action last night, so we were very crowded in our little hut. To-day he and Coates went to see their new position, right up to the north. They did not get the order till after lunch, and as they decided that the roads were impassable for horses, they walked all the way there and back. They did not get back till 1 o'clock in the morning, after walking nearly 20 miles. I have arranged to start after breakfast to-morrow.

HERVILLY, 19TH DECEMBER, 1917

We have had a difficult day. It was the coldest night we have ever had, and when I started to shave I found that my sponge was frozen as hard as a cricket-ball. I nearly died of cold whilst I was dressing. I was very doubtful if it would be possible for the wagons to get along the road, but they turned up all right at 10 o'clock. I rode on ahead with my trumpeter, and had a most unpleasant journey. It was out of the question to ride on the road ; my black mare could not keep her feet, and it was very difficult to lead her even, as we both kept slipping. Eventually I decided to leave the road and strike across country. It was not very pleasant as the snow was up to the mare's knees in places, and all the shell-holes, trenches, wire, etc., were hidden. However, we arrived after three hours, and I had lunch with Spiller before he packed his mess kit. I expected our wagons to arrive about 2 o'clock, but we heard nothing of them till tea-time, when the mess corporal came in and gave me the cheerful news that the G.S. wagon had taken the wrong road, got into a snow-drift, and been completely smashed up. It seems they tried to take a short cut across country, and that the horses bolted down a steep ravine, smashing the wagon. We were very nervous, as all our new glass and crockery were in it. Fortunately, the things had been well packed, and hardly anything was found to be broken. Spiller handed over to me and departed about 5 o'clock. He is off to England to-night for a month's leave, including Christmas. I have kept on one of his officers for twenty-four hours to show me round to-morrow. This group consists of six English batteries, four batteries of French heavy artillery, and all the trench mortars of the division. The French commandant came to call on me in the evening, a very pleasant fellow.

Hervilly, 20th December, 1917

Still the same bitter cold and a thick mist. I had intended to go to the O.P.s to-day and begin to learn the zone, but it would have been quite useless in this fog. So I contented myself with riding to four of the battery positions. It took a long time to get round, as we had to leave our horses some way from the batteries, so as not to make tracks in the snow up to them. B/107th have made a wonderful place in a steep bank ; the whole position is underground, with nothing but the muzzles of the guns pointing out of their pits. They have yards and yards of wooden galleries 40 feet into the bank, with cook-houses, officers' mess, quarters for the men, ammunition dumps, etc., all complete in the hill. They can fight a whole battle without a man coming above ground. Besides my own interpreter, I have also got a French liaison officer attached to me, so my staff is growing. In the afternoon I studied the numerous papers bequeathed to me by Spiller, such as Defence Schemes, etc. It is a very complicated sector to hold, as there have been so many alterations owing to the cavalry coming into the

28

line dismounted, and also owing to the recent disaster south of Cambrai. I have asked Major Lance of the Native Cavalry to dinner to-night.

HERVILLY, 21ST DECEMBER, 1917

We had a very amusing dinner last night. I had asked Lance of the Indian Cavalry and three of his subalterns to dinner. It turned out that we had met in India. He has been two years a brigade general in Salonica, but for some reason has reverted to major, and is now engaged in digging second-line trenches near here with his squadron. I had again meant to go to the O.P.s, but found there was such a thick fog as to be useless. The brigade major and staff captain came in the afternoon, and gave me the cheering news that my Headquarters is being moved again, just as we were settling down.

HERVILLY, 22ND DECEMBER, 1917

It is colder than ever, but the sun came out for a few hours. I have had orders to select reserve positions for all my batteries in case of a retirement ; I worked out the scheme on the layered map this morning, and then sent for some of the battery commanders and rode over the ground, finally deciding on the exact spot. Just as we had finished lunch, we heard fairly heavy shelling and C/107 rang up to ask for help. I at once got into communication with the French heavy group, and asked them to fire on a German battalion headquarters ; I also turned on several of my own batteries. The hostile fire ceased at once.

HERVILLY, 23RD DECEMBER, 1917

Last night we had a great dinner party. I asked the Commandant Rebuffet and his adjutant to dinner. They stayed till 2 in the morning and enjoyed themselves very much. We have certainly done a good deal to improve the relations between the two armies. It is even colder than before, but as the sun was shining and the light was not

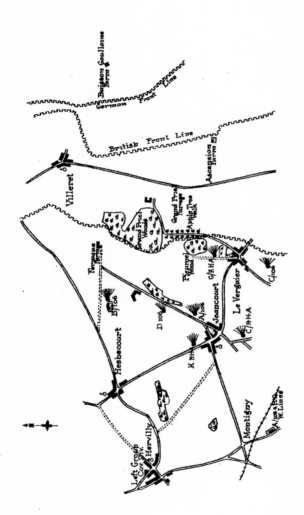

HERVILLY, DEC. 1917.

too bad, Wilmot and I decided to go round the front-line trenches. It is a very long walk, as one cannot go direct to Battalion H.Q., without passing through Villeret, which is a small village with an evil reputation for shelling. We first of all visited one of my day O.P.s called " Eve." There we found a French subaltern who was registering his battery on the corner of Malakhof Wood. I was interested to see that they had a most excellent director of the same kind as the German artillery use. It is the same sort of instrument as I saw being used at Darmstadt. Why is it that, after three years of war, we are the only nation that has not got good modern instruments for artillery work ? We called on the Infantry H.Q. in the line, and then went on to the front-line trenches. We are almost 150 yards from the Germans at that place, which is too close to be safe without a periscope. I put my head up a few times, but got sniped at from just in front. I went on and saw Colonel Fane of the 12th Lancers, who is commanding a battalion made up of men from the 12th Lancers, 20th Hussars, and Royals. I arranged to put an F.O.O. in direct communication with him, so he will be quite happy there. We had a long walk back to B Battery, through deep snow, and passed my night O.P. " Lucienne " on the way. We found our horses at B Battery. They had left Hervilly at the same time as we left Battalion H.Q. Late this evening there was a great deal of noise up north, but I have not yet heard what it was. It is colder than ever, I think.

Hervilly, 24th December, 1917

All the battalions and brigades have been sending us Christmas-cards. We had not thought of it, so feel rather left. So I spent the morning printing off a hundred little double sheets on the duplicator, with 106th Brigade Royal Field Artillery on one side and " With best wishes for Xmas and the New Year from Lt.-Col. The Master of Belhaven and Officers 106th Brigade, R.F.A." To-night I dined with General Campbell, late 16th Lancers, who commands the 2nd Dismounted Division. We had a great dinner and I have offered to take him down to the trenches and knock out a sniper for him to see how it is done. I found three men there who knew East Africa well.

HERVILLY, CHRISTMAS DAY, 1917

Our fourth War Christmas, and a typical Christmas Day, snow everywhere, though it is beginning to thaw now. I have been round to the French group and said all the right things and invited them to tea. Unfortunately they are all going away to-morrow, so our liaison will be over. The men on my H.Q. had a tremendous dinner with six turkeys and a bottle of stout a man, which I provided. I visited them whilst they were eating and wished a Merry Christmas, etc.—rather sarcastic under the circumstances, but the usual thing to say. We had a cold lunch, so as to let the servants off, and had our feast in the evening. General Nairne called in the afternoon; he is acting as G.O.C. of the Division for the time, as General Daly is on leave. Commandant Rebuffet and his staff had tea with us to say good-bye as they leave us to-night. We had a tremendous dinner with five French officers; it was really overpowering, as I had only four of my own, and Campbell-Johnston was not well and had to go to bed. Wilmot's French is limited, so the doctor and I had to do all the talking. I was glad when they went off at midnight and I was able to go to bed. It had been thawing all day and I was afraid we should have to move, but after dark it began to snow, and there was an extra 6 inches before midnight.

HERVILLY, 26TH DECEMBER, 1917

I sent for the battery commanders of A and C Batteries this morning, and took them up to Templeux to see their new positions. These are at present occupied by H, I, and Y Batteries, R.H.A. We first of all went to see our new H.Q., and found that it consists of one Nissen hut only for the officers, and a little sandbag hutch for the office, into which it will be impossible to put my clerks or their typewriters. The whole thing is absolutely inadequate, and may suit a Horse Artillery Brigade in what they call " Cap Formation," i.e. with nothing but what they can carry on their horses. It will be no good to me, and as usual we shall have to build. We walked on to the batteries' positions and got the battery commanders to show us round. There is practically nothing there at all ; the guns are under camouflage, and the men have small shelters in the ruins. I do not propose to use these positions, but to make complete new ones near. As we were walking from one position to another a nasty 4·2 shell arrived and landed not more than 20 yards off. It is the first shell that I have met at really close quarters since Ypres, so I can't complain ; they only sent over three shells, and they all fell in much the same place. Richardson and Fox came to see me after lunch and we argued out this move. It looks as if I shall be turned out into the snow.

HERVILLY, 27TH DECEMBER, 1917

It thawed during the afternoon, and I thought the frost was over, but to-night it is freezing as hard as ever. So far as we are concerned I hope the frost will last for weeks, as my brigade cannot move up to Templeux as long as the snow is on the ground, for fear of giving away the gun positions by making tracks in the snow. We are all very comfortable where we are and are not looking forward to moving into the Horse Artillery positions farther north. The latter have been there several weeks, and have done very little to improve their positions, and the headquarters are quite inadequate, as their staff is less than half the size of mine.

HERVILLY, 28TH DECEMBER, 1917

To-morrow the double group splits up, and Galloway comes in here to command the 107th. I go out of action for twenty-four hours and then take command of the left group of the Cavalry Divisional Artillery, which will consist of the 106th Brigade and a Horse Artillery Brigade commanded by Scarlett (G, K, and C batteries). The latter brigade will be a sub-group under me. New

Headquarters are being built for me about 100 yards from here, but so far nothing has been done, and I see myself sitting in the snow. Four Nissen huts are being put up, but the R.E. seems to have lost most of the necessary parts.

HERVILLY, 29TH DECEMBER, 1917

Galloway and the H.Q. of the 107th took over from me at 11 o'clock, and we removed our belongings into a snow-covered field near by. As I had expected, the huts were not ready, and we could not get in till after dark. I have never felt anything like the cold, and my feet were just a block of ice till I went to bed. We managed to get a stove going, but even so there was an inch of snow on the floor of the hut all night, the roof having only been put on in the afternoon. I lunched with Young, who is commanding Scarlett's Group, whilst the latter is on leave. The servants were wonderful, and produced quite a good dinner somehow.

HERVILLY, 30TH DECEMBER, 1917

I woke up warmer than I expected, and found that the stove had done some good after all, as the snow on the floor of the hut had turned into black mud. At 10 o'clock I began to " function," as they say out here. I took command of the new double group, and issued all sorts of orders about liaison and O.P. duties, etc. I am now detached from my own division and am lent to the Cavalry Dismounted Division. I saw General Campbell and the new general, who is relieving him—Pitman—and explained my dispositions for covering them. We have got hold of some canvas and divided up the hut into sections, which is better and warmer.

HERVILLY, 31ST DECEMBER, 1917

I rode over to A Battery this morning and found them very comfortable in a quite excellently camouflaged position. They have wire stretched over all the trenches leading from one gun-pit to another and bits of white calico tied on to harmonise with the snow. Lissant is in command whilst Farrar is away ; he is very keen on getting the Flying Corps to take a photo of the position to see what it looks like from the air. Our hut is now more than comfortable ; we have divided it up with canvas partitions in three parts and a passage—the mess and a bedroom each for the adjutant and me.

HERVILLY, 1ST JANUARY, 1918

To-day we start the fifth year of war, and I am convinced it will still be going on next New Year. The question is how many of us will be alive to see it ? Some, at any rate, will survive. We saw the New Year in properly and at exactly midnight by the signal officer's watch I gave the toast : " Success to ourselves and damnation to the —— Hun." Lance brought his subalterns in after dinner, and we had a very cheerful time. The subalterns all danced ragtimes to the gramophone, and afterwards played polo on chairs with a tobacco-tin. We sat up till 1 o'clock to see if the Hun would attempt any bombardment.

HERVILLY, 2ND JANUARY, 1918

It has thawed all day, and if it lasts a little longer the snow will be gone, and then we shall have to move up to Templeux and begin building more Headquarters. The C.R.A. of the Dismounted Cavalry Division came to see me, and showed me some secret papers which were very interesting. Hobday goes on a month's leave to-night ; I envy him very much, though he will have a dreadful journey down to Havre in this weather. The general came in after dinner and listened to the gramophone. Fortunately, most of my officers like good music, so I don't have to put up with much ragtime and suchlike rubbish. The Hun has done another attack up north.

HERVILLY, 3RD JANUARY, 1918

Fortunately it snowed a little last night, so the ground is still white. I took Harris on a long reconnaissance of the Intermediate Line and selected four good O.P.s for its defence. I have typed out a long report from the C.R.A. I am thankful that I brought my machine out with me ; it is so much better than writing everything in a notebook with pencil and carbon paper. We went to see C Battery and were stopped near there by an excited cavalryman, who implored us not to go that way as the Hun had been shelling the battery a few minutes before. I suppose the man was not accustomed to shells in the back areas.

HERVILLY, 4TH JANUARY, 1918

This afternoon Wilmot and I walked to Montigny to hear a lecture by Professor Vaughan-Cornish on Military Geography. It was quite interesting, but contained nothing that most of us did not already know. The most interesting thing he said was that he thought that the landslips which have so often blocked the Panama Canal would cease in about two years, as by that time the ground would have consolidated round the cutting and that tropical vegetation was beginning to bind the surface of the steep slopes. It was bitterly cold in the large hut in which the lecturer spoke, and as we were walking we had not taken coats with us.

HERVILLY, 5TH JANUARY, 1918

Colder than ever. To-day we got *The Times* with the New Year Honours. Not a single thing for this brigade. It is very disheartening, after all the hard fighting of the last year. I had put several officers in for the Military Cross, all of whom had richly earned some reward. As usual, the Staff got the rewards. Coates came to lunch ; he is commanding D Battery, whilst Bevis is on his course in England. I dined with General Pitman, late of the 11th Hussars. He commands the Cavalry Division

I am covering. He gave me a simple but very good dinner with excellent port. One of my wretched clerks managed to break my typewriter, and Harris and I spent hours trying to mend it. We found out at last what was the matter.

HERVILLY, 6TH JANUARY, 1918

When I got up this morning I found my sponge frozen into a solid ball, and my shaving-brush the same. I had to soak them in hot water before I could get on with my dressing. We were woken up this morning at 5 o'clock with a tremendous crash, and heard a plane evidently flying very low close over us. He dropped five more bombs, one of which was a very big one. I thought they must have been quite close ; but when I went to Roisel this morning I found that they had all dropped there. Very little damage was done, except that about twenty artillery horses were killed. By a curious coincidence I am covering the 3rd Hussars ; they had one man killed and two wounded yesterday.

HERVILLY, 7TH JANUARY, 1918

At 9 o'clock last night a sudden change came over the weather, and after having frozen hard all day, a west wind sprang up and it poured with rain all night. All the snow has gone now, but the ground is too hard to allow the water to sink in, and as it is still frozen underneath, the whole country is one great sheet of ice. It is impossible to get about, except on rubber tyres. I have spent a very busy day in working out the new and most complicated defence of the Intermediate Line. We had a cheering telegram to say that 25,000 German soldiers had entrenched themselves on the Russian front and refused to fight any more. I doubt it.

HERVILLY, 8TH JANUARY, 1918

The German guns have been shelling our back areas a good deal the last four days, especially round by my night O.P.s and the Intermediate Line. They have no doubt seen the large working parties that are digging and wiring the new trenches. General Pitman asked me to take him round the batteries, so we went to-day. The ground was very slippery, and we both fell on our backs several times. In the course of the morning a blizzard began and in three hours there was over three inches of snow lying over everything. I congratulated Sergeant-Major Elliott of A Battery on getting his D.C.M. I am very pleased about it, and tried hard to get him rewarded.

HERVILLY, 9TH JANUARY, 1918

It has been blowing a hurricane with fine driving snow and the thermometer well below freezing point. I have had a great piece of luck to-day. A new draft has arrived, probably most of them conscripts, but among them is a professional draughtsman—a middle-aged man who has been in an architect's office all his life. I have always wanted to have one to make me beautiful maps on blue linen. The only people who have draughtsmen are Corps and Divisional H.Q., so I shall feel very superior when I can produce blue linen maps in many colours like the R.E. There were also several clerks and typists, including a shorthand writer.

HERVILLY, 10TH JANUARY, 1918'

The same thing has happened again. Late last night it suddenly started to thaw and has rained ever since. All the snow has gone, and I am afraid it means we shall soon have to move. My new toy—the draughtsman—is a great success, and is making me a magnificent plan of the trenches in my zone on the scale of 1/5,000, just double the ordinary scale of the maps. He has put our trenches in red and the Huns in blue. To my intense disgust I have had orders to move my wagon-lines to a place five miles in rear ; it will be very awkward for me, as I never know when I want my horses and trumpeter.

HERVILLY, 11TH JANUARY, 1918

It has poured all day, and the place is becoming mud instead of iron. I have had a brick path laid alongside

the huts. It is better than wooden " duckboards," as
they were very slippery in muddy weather. I found a
Corps Intelligence Officer at the Cavalry Division H.Q.
this morning, and brought him back to lunch. He was
very interesting, and said that there was nothing to lead
us to suppose that the Hun meant to attack for the present,
though doubtless he will before the spring. I have got
a collection of aeroplane photos of our front, that have just
been taken. Campbell-Johnston and I have been very
busy cutting them up and making a map out of them.

HERVILLY, 12TH JANUARY, 1918

The Hun has been very active to-day on our front
line and against Le Verguier. All day long I have been
receiving reports of heavy artillery fire. Now that the
snow is off the ground I am able to shoot back, and I
have fairly drenched the Hun trenches. I put ten rounds
of gun-fire from every gun in the double group into a
German Company H.Q. in retaliation for his shelling our
Company H.Q. The whole three hundred and sixty were
in the air practically at the same time ; certainly they
arrived within two minutes. The Hun shot down one of
our planes, which fell in the German lines. Our observers
reported that there were at least a hundred Huns crowded
round it, examining it. Fortunately, two of my batteries
could reach the plane, so I gave a zero-time, synchronised
watches and ordered ten rounds of gun-fire, i.e. the most
rapid rate of fire possible. The observers reported that
the shells burst right on the crowd, which fled in all directions. With any luck we must have got a good bag. I
am always sorry for our airmen on these occasions, but
we have strict orders to bombard any of our planes that
we can reach if they fall in the Boche lines. If the
airman is not wounded, he probably has time to get
away before we begin. In the evening we had a combined shoot with the 9·2's and 6-in., so I hope the Hun
liked it.

HERVILLY, 13TH JANUARY, 1918

Wilmot and I rode to our new wagon-lines at Boucly this afternoon, and I was disgusted to find what a filthy state they are in. The much-vaunted horse artillery do not seem to live up to their former reputation. I have never seen anything like the state of the place, except perhaps the wagon-lines I took over from the 17th Division at Ypres in January 1916. I went on to see General Nairne about it and complained bitterly. He is giving me assistance from our D.A.C. to get the place habitable. The ground is very sodden and riding across country difficult, but at any rate it is no longer slippery.

HERVILLY, 14TH JANUARY, 1918

The carabineers are going to do a raid on my front shortly, and I have been very busy working out the artillery plans. I have just had a consultation with the cavalry general, and found out exactly what his party are going to do. I then studied the map and aeroplane photos for hours, and decided exactly what I would cover with each of my batteries. Finding that I could hardly reach the northern part of the zone with our own batteries, I borrowed three batteries from the horse artillery brigade in the division on our left. I have also got all the trench mortars put under me, so that for this raid I have an enormous amount of artillery at my disposal. I shall have my own seven batteries, three northern horse artillery batteries, which makes ten, and the medium and light trench mortars. I am very anxious the thing should go off well for everyone's sake, and particularly as it is the first little battle that I have entirely arranged by myself. The C.R.A. has nothing to do with it, beyond having approved my dispositions. Wilmot, the infant child, and I were working till 2 in the morning. The duplicators are a great help, and with the clay tray we are able to take off coloured maps. As a matter of fact, I generally touch up the colouring with a paint-brush, but it does not take long. There is a terrific storm blowing, and I expect the roof to come off.

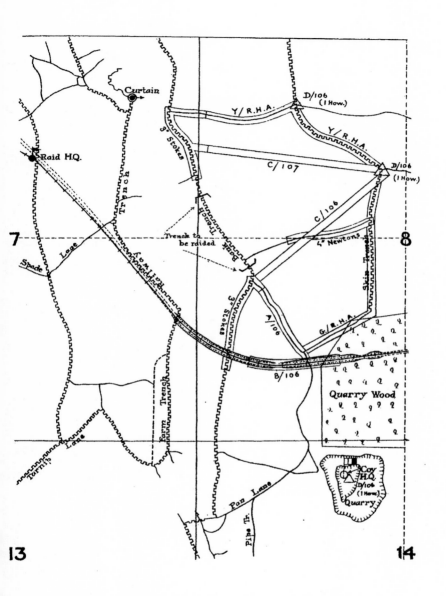

RAID NEAR HERVILLY, JAN. 1918.

HERVILLY, 15TH JANUARY, 1918

I have never had the tooth finished off that was so troublesome at Ypres, so I went to the Casualty Clearing Station this morning at Tincourt. The 73rd Field Ambulance very kindly lent me a motor ambulance which took me there and back. It is as well that I had it done, as although the nerve was quite dead, it had not been taken out, and was in a horrid state. On my way back I called at the map shop, i.e. the advanced map depot, and got half a dozen of the new maps of this district. I spent most of the day finishing details for the raid. It ought to be a success, considering all the trouble we have taken to get our part of it perfect.

Secret.   Copy No. 1.

OPERATION ORDER NO. 122

By LIEUT.-COLONEL THE HON. R. G. A. HAMILTON, R.F.A., COMMANDING LEFT GROUP CAVALRY DIVISIONAL ARTILLERY

Ref. HARGICOURT,
Special Sheet 1a 1/10,000.

1. The Second Cavalry Dismounted Division intend to carry out a raid on the German trenches on the night of the 16/17 January, 1918. The trench to be raided is that between the following points :—G, 8, c, 3070 and G, 8, a, 1020.

2. Zero hour will be notified later.

3. The raid will be carried out without assistance from the artillery if possible, but batteries will be prepared to fire as under if a special rocket is sent up.

4. The rocket calling for artillery fire will be " gold and silver rain." In the first instance the rockets will be sent up from our trenches opposite the trench to be raided and will be repeated by LUCIENNE O.P. (L, 16, d, 2090).

5. All batteries concerned will " stand to " ten minutes before Zero and will continue to do so till they receive the word " FINISHED " by 'phone.

6. Any registration necessary will be carried out on the 15th or morning of the 16th.

7. The Left Group of the 24th Div. Arty. have agreed to assist and will cover the northern portions of area to be raided with one battery of 18-pdrs., one battery of 18-pdrs., and one section of howitzers.

8. Barrages are allotted as follows, also see attached sketch :—

1 Battery 24th D.A. G, 8, a, 0362 along C.T. to G, 8, a, 8045.

1 Battery 24th D.A. G, 8, a, 1245 to G, 8, a, 8540.

1 How. 24th D.A. T.J. at G, 8, a, 5065.

1 How. 24th D.A. T.J. at G, 8, a, 8545.

1 Battery Scarlett's Group. G, 8, a, 8020 along SKIN TRENCH to G, 8, c, 5045.

A/106. G, 8, c, 3558 along trench to G, 8, c, 5045.

B/106. G, 8, c, 2535 along railway to G, 8, c, 7033.

C/106. G, 8, a, 9040 to G, 8, c, 4060.

D/106. (1 How.) Company H.Q. at G, 14, a, 7075.

9. The 6-in. Newton Trench Mortars will co-operate by firing on the new C.T. from G, 8, c, 5095 to G, 8, a, 8000.

10. The 3-in. Stokes Mortars will also co-operate by firing on the German front line from G, 7, b, 9065 to G, 8, a, 0530, searching C.T. from G, 7, b, 9065 to G, 8, a, 0565 and from G, 8, a, 0045 to 1545. They will also fire on the German front line from G, 8, c, 3065 to G, 8, c, 1530, including from G, 8, c, 3065 to G, 8, c, 3858.

11. A Special Liaison officer will report to O.C. Raid at Coy. H.Q., one hour before Zero. This duty will be found by C/106.

12. The Special Liaison officer will remain with the O.C. Raid and will keep the Group Commander informed as to the situation from time to time.

13. The Signal Officer Left Group will arrange for communication between the " EGG "—" CURTAIN " line and Coy. H.Q. The above officer will also arrange for batteries of the Left Group 24th D.A. to register from " CURTAIN " O.P. by 10 a.m. 15th.

14. Batteries will open fire on seeing the special rocket or if ordered to do so by 'phone from Group H.Q.

15. Rates of fire will be :—

18-pdrs. and 13-pdrs. : 4 rounds per gun per min. for 5 mins., after which 2 rounds per gun per min. for 5 mins., then stop. Howitzers : half the above rates.

If after ceasing fire the rocket is again sent up the above will be repeated.

16. ACKNOWLEDGE.

(Signed)   R. WILMOT,

15/1/18.   *Captain and Adjutant,*

Left Group, Cav. Div. Artillery.

Copy No. 1 to Bde. Maj. 24th D. Art.
             2 to Bde. Maj. Cav. Div. Art.
             3 to 2nd Dis. Div.
             4 to Left Bde. Cav. Div.
             5 to Rt. Bn. 24th Div.
             6 to Inf. Bde. 24th Div.
             7 to Group Commander.
             8 to D.T.M.O. 24th Div.
             9 to D.D.T.M.O. Cav. Div.
          10 to Right Group, 24th D.A.
          11 to Left Group, 24 D.A.
          12 to   do.   do.
          13 to   do.   do.
          14 to   do.   do.
          15 to   do.   do.
          16 to Scarlett's Group.
          17 to   do.   do.
          18 to   do.   do.
          19 to   do.   do.
          20 to A/106.
          21 to B/106.
          22 to C/106.
          23 to D/106.
          24 to File.
          25 to Spare.

Issued at 7 a.m. by hand.

HERVILLY, 16TH JANUARY, 1918

The thaw has come with a vengeance now, and the country is in an awful state. The roads are three inches deep in liquid mud, and the grass is like a bog. After lunch I went to B Battery and met the special liaison officer for the raid—Walsh—from C Battery. I gave him his final orders in writing and forbade him to go over the top with the raiders. I can't afford to have good officers killed in joy riding. The raid is to-night and I have sent a special officer to the O.P. with duplicate rockets. The rocket signal will be repeated from the O.P. in case artillery help is required. The Carabineers hope to do the job without any help from us.

HERVILLY, 17TH JANUARY, 1818

Last night's raid went off very successfully. We got one live Hun, who turns out to be a Bavarian, a Bavarian Erzatz Division having just arrived. I have not yet had details of his examination, but imagine they have lately arrived from Russia. One party of our raiders got into the trench without being seen and found a deep dug-out. They flashed a light into it and saw a Hun standing just inside. The officer said " Kamerad " to him and the man put up his hands at once and was led out. He was in such a hurry to get safely over to our lines that he showed our man the easiest and quickest way to get through the German wire. The other party were fired on before they reached the German trench and had a more difficult time. However, they got back without any losses. General Pitman came to my Headquarters at 8.80 and remained with me till it was all over. The raid was supposed to take forty minutes, but they were out an hour and forty minutes, so we began to wonder if they had all been captured. In the middle of it we got a wire from Corps to say that a German message had just been intercepted by the corps on our right, to say that the Germans had ordered their people to be ready at 5 o'clock, i.e 4 a.m.

by our time. I "stood to" with all batteries till 6 o'clock, but nothing happened.

By a curious coincidence I discovered that Dr. Mitchell —G.'s Harley Street doctor—is in this division. He has been with the 78rd Field Ambulance for six months, without either of us knowing it. I saw him the week I was at Havre as we both came together from Southampton. Mortimer and I lunched with him at Bernes to-day, after which I went to 24th D.A., and settled all the details of the coming change of positions with the brigade major. I shall be very glad when we get back into our own division, as the present cavalry people muddle everything and are always giving me contradictory orders. I rode my chestnut mare ; she was almost unmanageable for want of exercise.

HERVILLY, 18TH JANUARY, 1918

It has rained and stormed all day, so as I have a cold I have not gone out. I spent all the evening with the adjutant going through the N.C.O.s' promotion roll. We have been so busy that we have not kept it up properly. I am going to keep the roll by card index in future. I already have the whole brigade in one card index, some eight hundred cards in all. Our move up to Templeux has again been postponed, for which I am very glad in this weather. The mud is now something quite dreadful and half the tracks have disappeared. I hear both we and the Huns are brazenly walking about on the top of the parapets, as it is impossible to get along the trenches.

HERVILLY, 19TH JANUARY, 1918

This morning I paid a final visit to the dentist. He is a quite excellent man and has stopped three teeth for me without hurting me to any appreciable extent. This is the one standard I have for judging dentists. The general sent an American artillery officer to me to-day to learn what he could of our methods. I sent Harris round with

29

him. They seem to have enjoyed themselves very much. They saw an 18-pdr. battery, a 4·5, an 8-in., and the 9·2. All the battery commanders did shoots for him, and on his return I gave him a little lecture on some of our methods. He was a most charming fellow and seemed very capable. Let us hope all the American artillery will be like him.

HERVILLY, 20TH JANUARY, 1918

I have turned into a Babu—I spend my whole time writing reports and organising things. It seems to get worse and worse. I have increased my office staff, and still we hardly get through the paper that comes by one despatch rider before another arrives. To-day the Rifle Brigade did a raid, in which two of my batteries took part. They got two live Huns and killed several, but one of our parties was cut off, and an officer and eleven men are missing. Two were killed by our own Bengal torpedo in blowing up the Hun wire. The wretched men lit the fuse and then tried to get clear before the explosion, but the mud was so bad that they stuck, and were blown up by their own charge. The general came to see me this after-noon and wasted an hour and a half of my time explaining in minute detail how to drain the roads through the mud of the wagon-lines, as if I had not had to compete with the mud of Flanders for years. He is a dear old man, but I wish we had Sheppard still with us, or Walthall. The latter said what he wanted done, and then left it to his subordinates to carry out the work their own way. We move now in two days, so I shall have all the old game over again of building yet another new Headquarters; needless to say, the great Horse Artillery have done abso-lutely nothing to improve the place whilst they have been there for a whole six weeks.

HERVILLY, 21ST JANUARY, 1918

Mortimer came back from his two days' leave to Amiens that I gave him. He has brought more records for the gramophone, including a magnificent one from Prince

Igor, which I am quite delighted with. I hear they are getting up a pack of hounds at Divisional H.Q., and going to hunt the numerous hares there are about here. I am afraid I am too busy to go out.

HERVILLY, 22ND JANUARY, 1918

The cavalry tried to do a raid to-night without any artillery assistance. It seems to have been a fiasco. The Hun saw them and opened fire, and they had several casualties. One unfortunate man was badly wounded, and had to be dragged two hundred yards back by his collar.

TEMPLEUX-LE-GUERARD, 23RD JANUARY, 1918

This afternoon we moved out of our old Headquarters and have installed ourselves here. Our present accommodation is quite inadequate as we have only one Nissen hut for all the officers. Some of them are living in little sandbag hutches and I have boarded out two of them in the wagon-lines. It was a very complicated move, as I took over this group at the same moment as I handed over the old one. Colonel W. Clarke of the 7th Horse Artillery Brigade took over from me. His batteries and mine are changing places, half last night and the remainder to-night. Clarke and I lunched with General Pitman, after which I formally handed over and then galloped here, and took charge on arrival. We managed to get settled in by dark.

TEMPLEUX, 24TH JANUARY, 1918

Richardson came to see me and he, Welch, and I inspected the new C Battery position that they are starting on to-day. The Corps R.E. have started a deep mined dug-out for this battery and also for A, but they have been working in the open without any camouflage, and made huge heaps of white chalk; the result is that

Welch won't put his guns near the place, as it is bound to be shelled as soon as any battle begins. It is a great pity we are not consulted about it, as we should have had the dug-out put in a wood quite close, and where the mess would not have mattered. After lunch Campbell-Johnston and I walked to near Ronssoy, where we have to make positions for two anti-tank guns. The Horse Artillery were supposed to have done it before they left. The place chosen for the anti-tank gun has a wonderful view up all the valleys near here, and the gunners will have the time of their lives if the German tanks come this way. Whilst we were there the Hun gave some heavy battery fair hell with a 5·9 battery ; they pumped shells in at the rate of a dozen a minute and kept it up for an hour. I could not see the result, as it was just behind a crest from me. He has lately shelled that whole area very heavily, as all the ground is covered with shell-holes. We came back by C and A, whom I welcomed to their new homes. I am afraid the officers are not very comfortable, as their predecessors seemed to be quite content to pig it. By the time I got there I was quite pleasantly tired, having walked 5 miles on very sticky clay and mostly up and down steep valleys. I am going to make our own mess more comfortable to-morrow, by dividing it up with canvas partitions, and have managed to get the stuff out of the R.E. The next thing will be to build a decent-sized office for my clerks.

TEMPLEUX, 25TH JANUARY, 1918

This morning it was reported that the Hun is doing new work in the middle of No Man's Land, and is perhaps thinking of making a strong point near our lines. I put a battery of howitzers on the spot, and as soon as they opened fire I let loose two 18-pounder batteries. Things turned out just as I had expected, and the battery commander, who was observing, at once reported that some Germans ran away from the howitzer shell towards their own lines and were caught by the shrapnel of the field-

TEMPLEUX, JAN. 1918.

guns. It will teach brother Hun to be more careful how he works in No Man's Land in future. The howitzers then went on and smashed up his nice new work.

TEMPLEUX, 26TH JANUARY, 1918

Richardson came to see me this morning, and we rode up to the front to finally select an anti-tank gun position for a gun of C. It was so misty that it was impossible to see more than 100 yards, so we were unable to select any positions. We called on the left battalion Headquarters, and had the greatest difficulty in finding the place, as we had been given the wrong map location and the fog made it impossible to get our bearings. We rode to Pimple Post, but the road there had been so heavily shelled that we sent our horses back and went on, on foot. We lost our way and took an hour to find the place, which turned out to be within 200 yards of where we had sent our horses to. Welch and Lissant are working hard on their positions near me, and ought to be ready to move back to them in three or four days. I arranged a little battle for to-night with the Middlesex ; they wanted to send out a strong patrol to reconnoitre the new outpost the Bosche has established in the middle of No Man's Land. I put eight guns on to this work and four more on to a couple of machine-guns that fire that way. After two minutes' intense fire, the infantry went forward and examined the place, but found nothing ; I suppose the first bombardment had frightened him out. We kept fire on the machine-guns till the patrol got back. The infantry have just rung me up to say that our shooting was excellent, the patrol lay up under a bank within 100 yards of our shells and said that they all burst on a line that might have been drawn in chalk. No short shooting, as was to be expected with batteries of so much experience ; still, we have had a great many casualties in the last six months, and it was very satisfactory to hear that shooting had not fallen off at all. The young officer who led the patrol has telephoned to say that he has brought in a rifle for me. I suppose one of the Huns was wounded and dropped his rifle, or else they were in such a hurry to get away that they left their rifles behind.

TEMPLEUX, 27TH JANUARY, 1918

It was very misty, so I cancelled my orders for my horses. I had intended to take all the battery commanders and look at the positions for the defence of the second line. I have been very busy getting all my various barrage maps made up for this new position. I have put coloured silks, and special coloured pins for all the different batteries. Each battery of brigade has a different colour allotted to it for all purposes, including my card index of N.C.O.s. Red for A, Blue for B, Green for C, and Yellow for D. I put in a coloured pin in the battery position and others of the same colour for the S.O.S. lines and connect them with silks of the same colour.

TEMPLEUX, 28TH JANUARY, 1918

Yesterday was the German Emperor's birthday (the Kaiser Geburstag), so the division celebrated it by giving salvos from every gun and machine-gun late last night on the Hun trenches and tracks. This morning, the general and Richardson went with me to finally choose the positions for the two anti-tank guns that I am putting out. It was a long walk of some 5 miles, and I did not get back till 2 o'clock. After a quarter of an hour for lunch, I galloped into Roisel, where all the battery commanders were waiting for me, and we selected positions for the defence of the second line. I do not like them very much, as they are too near the town itself, which would be shelled during a battle.

TEMPLEUX, 29TH JANUARY, 1918

Late last night I was asked by the infantry to shoot up a machine-gun that was troubling them. As I did not want to have to fire on it at intervals all night, I thought I would settle him once and for all, so I put two six-gun batteries on to it and fired a hundred H.E.

shells at gun-fire right away. He has not been heard of
since, and the infantry are delighted. There is nothing
like sledge-hammer tactics with the Hun ; it is the sort
of argument that he understands. The 'planes were
very active last night, and there was a full moon. They
were dropping eggs all over the place. He very nearly
got my A Battery wagon-lines—as a matter of fact,
he hit the divisional theatre and killed four of the per-
formers. To-day, General Nairne lectured to all the
drivers in the wagon-lines on what we are fighting for.
It was quite a good speech, and he explained that really
we are not fighting for any abstract treaties, but because
there is not room in the world for us and the Huns. One
or other of us must be top dog, and he explained how very
unpleasant it would be for the working man if the Bosche
happened to win. After that the general inspected the
various wagon-lines which we have greatly improved
in the fortnight since we have been here. I sent my head
clerk to a battery yesterday to learn something about
gunnery ; by all ill-luck he managed to get wounded to-
day. B Battery were shelled this morning by 4·2's.
It was not very serious, but their position has been
found, so I am moving them.

TEMPLEUX, 30TH JANUARY, 1918

I rode up to Ronssoy this morning and met Lissant and
Webster in order to show them exactly where I want
their anti-tank guns. These guns are to be manned by
a picked detachment of men who volunteer for the job and
have orders to fight their guns to the last. They have a
wonderful view down two valleys and ought to have a
very sporting shoot if the Hun tanks break through our
lines. It ought not to be difficult to hit a great thing
like a tank as it moves so slowly. After doing that I
left my horses in a sunken road and walked up to Hussar
Post where I have an O.P. One gets a good view from
there into the Hun lines ; in fact we look right down on
to them. There is the wreckage of one of our 'planes
lying in the open just behind the German trenches. There

is a white cross facing us with is supposed to be the grave of the English airman. So far we have managed not to hit it. Wilmot is going on leave in a day or two, so I sent for Harman to do acting adjutant whilst he is away. The general is going on leave in a day or two, so I sent for Harman to do acting adjutant whilst he is away. The general is going on a month's leave on 3rd February, and has promised to try and get me a month when he comes back. A and C's new positions are nearly finished, and I hope to move them back in a day or two. It has begun to freeze again and is bitterly cold. We have a very indifferent fireplace, with the result that it has not been possible to keep warm lately.

TEMPLEUX, 31ST JANUARY, 1918

The ground is frozen quite hard and it is impossible to keep one's feet warm. General Daly, the divisional commander, has sent me the following letter:

HEADQUARTERS, 24TH DIVISION,
25th January, 1918.

" DEAR HAMILTON,

" It is a great pleasure to me to see that your good service and devotion to duty have been recognised in the New Year's Honours Gazette by the award of a Mention in Despatches, which you have well merited. Please accept my personal congratulations.

" Yours sincerely,
" A. C. DALY."

I don't know what the new policy is with regard to officers, but I am being simply inundated with them. Three more subalterns arrived this morning, which now makes me up to forty-four. I don't know what we shall do with them all.

TEMPLEUX, 1ST FEBRUARY, 1918

The general sent for Spiller and me at 10 a.m. to have a final conference before he goes on a month's leave. The general has promised to try and get a month's leave for me when he comes back. I wonder if he will be successful! I was very late starting, so did a non-stop gallop from here to Divisional Headquarters—5 miles of grass. My A and C Batteries are moving into new positions close to my H.Q. A moved three guns back last night, but were not able to register them to-day owing to a thick white fog. I have stopped the others moving to-night as I dare not have any more guns unregistered. The Authorities seem to expect we shall be attacked at any time.

TEMPLEUX, 2ND FEBRUARY, 1918

After two days of fog, to-day has been gloriously fine with a bright sun. After lunch Harris and I went to reconnoitre new O.P.s for the defence of the Second Line, and climbed to the top of Templeux Hill just behind my H.Q. One has a magnificent view of all the country between the Intermediate Line, and the Second Line, so I shall certainly establish an O.P. there. We went on to my night O.P. above Templeux village, and found that from there we can get visual communications with the front and all the batteries. I also called on Buchanan, who is in charge of my detached section of howitzers. The unfortunate child has been living alone for three months, but goes on leave to-day. At tea-time I got a message from my O.P. officer to say that the Hun had attacked and taken a place in front of our line, under cover of a barrage. It seems that a party of an officer and about twenty men left their trenches and rushed across No Man's Land in broad daylight—a most imprudent thing to do. I immediately rang up all my batteries and ordered a hurricane bombardment in ten minutes—gun-fire with H.E. from the 18-pounders and also the howitzers. My F.O.O. reported that the Germans were still there when it began. In two minutes it was all over and not a single man got back to his trenches. It was simply murder to send them out like that, as they had no cover whatever, right out in the open.

Templeux, 3rd February, 1918

I rode to Hervilly in the morning to see Galloway, who is commanding the 107th whilst the general is on leave. I wanted to make it quite clear that his liaison officer with the centre battalion must report to me if anything happens on my part of his front. There was a great waste of time yesterday owing to his ringing up his own brigade first. I also went to see the divisional trench mortar officer, to find out where he keeps his " flying pigs " and 6-in. Newton Pippins. All the trench mortars on my front have now been placed under me, so I must know where they are and what they can do. After lunch Spiller came to see me, and was much impressed by my maps, coloured pins, etc. We had great excitement just before lunch, as there was an air fight over the Hun lines ; one of our 'planes was brought down and landed within a few hundred yards of our mess. The airman was shot through the foot and his machine riddled with bullet-holes. His tank had been hit, so all the petrol had run out. He was brought into the mess, and as the medical officer was out, I dressed his wound, which was not at all serious. A bullet had gone through his big toe. We ran the 'plane down into a hollow and covered it with camouflage so that it could not be seen from the air. I told A Battery to mount an armed guard over it, according to orders.

Templeux, 4th February, 1918

I have been ringing up the wounded airman's squadron for twenty-four hours, but have only just got them to send for him. It is somewhat brutal to leave a wounded young officer so long without getting him away. Eventually I threatened to send him to hospital. Emmet, the D.T.M.O., came to lunch and brought me a map showing the dispositions of all his trench mortars. At 10 o'clock the S.O.S. went up on the right of my zone. I therefore turned on B Battery who cover that part. It was with the greatest difficulty that I could find out where the trouble really was. However, in the end it was located just off my zone, whereupon I slowed B down to a slow rate of fire, but kept all the rest " standing to " for an hour till all the noise was over. Even so, B got through three hundred rounds.

Templeux, 5th February, 1918

As far as I can make out this morning, nothing really happened, except that both sides lost their heads. The Germans started the excitement by seeing spooks. They bombed their own wire and put up their S.O.S., whereupon our people thought they were going to be attacked and sent up our S.O.S. Both artilleries promptly replied, and for the next half-hour there was hell in the front lines. I fancy it was fairly expensive for both sides, as I imagine there were a lot of casualties.

Templeux, 6th February, 1918

The air was wonderfully clear to-day, so Harris and I climbed up to the top of the Quarries to see what we thought of the place as an O.P. I was rather disappointed, as although it is the highest point for miles round, there is a long ridge in front of practically the same height. We went on to " Dick " O.P., which is another thousand yards forward. I have an F.O.O. there all day, and as it was so fine I asked " B " Battery to fire a round of battery fire on their S.O.S. lines. His two first shots dropped right into the Hun front trench, and the others burst nicely over it. On my return I found Hobday waiting. He is just back from his thirty days' leave. The infantry brigade major also came to see me.

Templeux, 7th February, 1918

I have spent six solid hours to-day on the typewriter. I have made out a complete scheme for withdrawal to the Second and Third Lines, with detailed orders for the various O.P. officers. It was a most complicated business, but with all the " wind " there is blowing, we cannot afford to leave anything to chance. I am going to have a dress rehearsal of the whole thing soon, and see if everyone knows what they have to do. We have had a tragedy—the gramophone is broken. I don't know how we shall exist till it is mended. I have tried to borrow a car to send someone into Amiens to try and get a new spring; but cars are hard to get unless one is on the Staff.

Templeux, 8th February, 1918

It has been a windy and wet day. I have finished up a lot of outstanding papers in the office. I took Welch after lunch to the top of a little hill behind the batteries where I propose to establish two battery O.P.s in case of retirement to the brown line. We found quite good places. There is a horrible rumour that all leave is going to be stopped after this month. I shall be disgusted if it is true, as all the other senior officers of the division have had their thirty days, and I am sure I deserve it as much as anyone else. I am very busy arranging for visual communication between all O.P.s and batteries in case the wires are cut in a bombardment.

Templeux, 9th February, 1918

I had my black mare up this morning and inspected the two anti-tank guns. I also called at the Left Battalion H.Q. and had a talk with their colonel. Afterwards I went on to St. Emilie and made the acquaintance of the right group of the next division. They have very comfortable quarters, but are quite unprotected in a much-shelled area. I prefer my own little quarry. It is small and very uncomfortable, but a good deal safer. We have seen a lot of German working parties the last few days—we always engage them and they run for their lives ; I cannot think why they are so careless on fine days, when they can easily be seen by our observers.

TEMPLEUX, 10TH FEBRUARY, 1918

I have been out all day. I arranged to meet the staff captain at my wagon-lines at 11.30. We had a look at them all, including A, who arrived there yesterday from Montigny Farm. I have at last got the whole of the brigade wagon-lines concentrated at one place, which is a great convenience. We have all the horses under cover and on brick standings ; also all the men have good bunks to sleep in. Most of the batteries are in Nissen huts, but some have the big French " Adrian " huts, which hold a hundred and fifty men. I went on to Divisional Headquarters to see the brigade major and stayed to lunch. After that I galloped straight across country to Jeancourt and on to D Battery. Bevis was away at his O.P., but Stephenson was there and showed me round. They have made an excellent position, and as usual are very clean and tidy. They have whitewashed the inside of the pits and pipe-clayed the drag-ropes. All " eye-wash," but they get much kudos from inspecting generals, etc. I met Hobday there and walked across the hill to his battery with him, sending my horses round by the road. I had a look at his guns also, and although there was nothing to complain of, they were not so tidy and well polished up as D's. I rode home at a sharp canter, and got there just before it was beginning to be dark. I had hardly sat down to tea when the brigade major rang up and said that the S.O.S. had gone up on the 107th's front, and asking if all was quiet with me. The next moment " Hussar " O.P. reported an intense barrage on them and the S.O.S. on our left. This meant a general S.O.S. on the whole divisional front. I at once ordered all batteries to open fire and reported to D.A. For once all my lines held and I was in constant communication with the infantry and my O.P.s. It soon became evident that there was no hostile attack, only the German bombardment on our trenches. I therefore slowed the batteries down to one round per gun per minute, and on hearing that all was quiet at the end of half an hour, I stopped altogether. I am afraid it was another case of " wind."

TEMPLEUX, 11TH FEBRUARY, 1918

I have been trying to find out what really happened last night. It seems that the Germans began by bombarding our front-line trenches, and then sent up —— and ——rockets, which happens also to be our S.O.S. signal. The Germans have a rocket signal which means " Lengthen your range " to their own artillery. They have fired into their own trenches several times lately, and I think it is very likely that that is what happened last night. The Battalion H.Q. look-out man saw these rockets and mistook them for our own, whereupon they sent up the real S.O.S. We, of course, were bound to fire, as it was impossible to assume there was no attack, although I felt quite certain the Hun would not try and come over in broad daylight. Anyway, we wasted over seventeen hundred shells, and the Hun now knows where our barrage comes down.

. . . .

It all depends whether the Hun has photographed the place during the last week. If he has, there is no doubt it will be discovered and sooner or later shot up.

TEMPLEUX, 12TH FEBRUARY, 1918

The sky has been dull and overcast to-day with a thick ground mist. Excellent weather for working on the positions as no 'planes can go up. Coates has got to work, and there is a distinct difference already. He has started to dig trenches to connect up his pits underground. We have just completed a new system of telephone lines from the O.P.s to the batteries. Up till now each battery has had its own line, but now all O.P. lines go up to a central exchange which is in a 30-foot dug-out ; from there, lines run to all the batteries. The result is that any battery can now use any O.P. on the corps front and be switched straight through. Each group has one of these exchanged, and they are all connected to each other. The idea is good, but the danger is that if the neighbourhood of the exchange is shelled, all the lines may be cut simultaneously. For the moment I have got through all the work I have on hand, as regards my own part of the business, but I expect there will be some alterations soon, which will keep me occupied.

TEMPLEUX, 13TH FEBRUARY, 1918

I arranged to meet Welch this morning at his anti-tank gun position, and put up the boards I have got the R.E. to make. There was nothing to show the tank guns how far off the tanks were, so I have had three kinds of 4-foot square boards made, with large white squares, circles, and triangles. I have put all the squares at a certain distance from the gun in a semicircle round it ; then all the triangles on an arc of a few hundred yards less, and so on. The N.C.O. in charge of the gun will know that as soon as a tank has passed through one ring of boards, the range is less than so much, and until it reaches the next lot the range must be more than so much. Consequently, he ought to have a good chance of hitting it. The men were so stupid about where to put the boards that I galloped about placing them myself. It was quite safe, as there was too much fog for the Hun to see me, but we were close up to the trenches and my mare had to be continually jumping shell-holes. The chief trouble is that there is so much barbed wire everywhere, and one can only cross the belts at gaps, which are few and far between. It rained hard the whole time, but my waterproof kept me dry. I have got a sort of apron which keeps my knees and legs dry.

TEMPLEUX, 14TH FEBRUARY, 1918

Another foggy day, which is nice for us to work, but is dangerous, as the Hun has now had three days to do what he likes without our 'planes having any chance of spotting him. Two more officers have arrived, which brings me up to forty-three in all. As our proper establishment is only twenty-eight, we are not doing badly. It is a great thing to have them up now when things are quiet, as we can train them, instead of like last year, when they arrived quite raw in the middle of a great battle. Marco has come up to live with us now that we have built an extra house for him ; he helps to keep us all cheerful with his continual jokes. He is quite irrepressible.

TEMPLEUX, 15TH FEBRUARY, 1918

A nice bright day, but very cold ; in fact, I think there was frost last night. Harris went on leave this afternoon, and Wilmot is due back to-morrow. I hear he went to tea with G. and took my diary. It is always a relief when I hear that a volume has got safely home. The Bosche has been very noisy to-day ; probably he has been saving up ammunition during the last three days of fog. He has been amusing himself shooting up my O.P.s, and I have retaliated on all his most tender places, including the officers' club at Bellicourt. I have put about fifty howitzer shells into the latter place. There are plenty of rumours going about as to our future move, but I never believe in rumours.

TEMPLEUX, 16TH FEBRUARY, 1918

Harris, my signal officer, went on leave to-day, and I have taken on a boy called Mattox, who has a signalling certificate. It has been very fine and there has been much activity in the air. A mysterious machine has been flying about all over the batteries for the last two evenings. It appears just after dark and flies so low that I thought it would hit the trees. One cannot see it and no one knows whether it is ours or the enemy's. I must find out from the Flying Corps if they own it ; if not, I shall open rifle-fire on it next time. Even on a moonlight night it is impossible to see a 'plane, but he can see the features of the ground.

Templeux, 17th February, 1918

Bevis came to lunch to-day and we selected a position for one of his sections which is coming into action alongside my H.Q. We have already got A and C batteries within 300 yards, so if we have howitzers as well I imagine it will not be long before we get some attention on the part of the Hun. I walked over to Welch's detached section with him in the afternoon. He lent me a gun and we put up quite a lot of partridges. The birds are very wild now, and we did not get any. However, it was great fun. The Hun, who is no sportsman, amused himself by putting out shrapnel not far off, but they were too high to be at all dangerous.

Templeux, 18th February, 1918

The Hun 'planes were very active last night. There were never less than half a dozen over at a time. There was a quarter moon, so not very light. They seemed to have great difficulty in locating themselves. They dropped a lot of bombs in back areas, but I don't think they did much harm. General Duggan, Spiller, and Richardson came to see me, and discussed our arrangements for mutual support for two hours. Duggan is now commanding the infantry brigade that I support, and is rather worried lest we should be cut off from each other by shells breaking the wires. I am putting out two extra lines to him. Wilmot arrived back from London to-day. He tells me he had tea with G. one day.

30

TEMPLEUX, 19TH FEBRUARY, 1918

It is colder than ever. Sharp frost at nights and just a degree above freezing by day. I am feeling the cold more now than during all the real snowy weather in January. I have had a succession of visitors this morning, including the corps commander—Sir J. Kavanagh. I reminded him that we last met at Zonnebeke in 1914, when I was sent by General Lawford to bring up reinforcements at all costs. He had hardly gone when General Seligmann, the Corps C.R.A., arrived and inspected A and C Batteries. He is the first inspecting general I have met who does not seem to have any special fad, or ask some pet question. I said at lunch that I wondered why so many of the Staff should come round the same day, and the irreverent intelligence child said he supposed the bright spring-like weather was bringing them all out. I hear the bombing has been serious in the back areas ; I am told that seven officers were killed at Corps H.Q. last night, including the legal adviser, which seems bad luck. Having once got a job like that, one might expect to live a quiet and safe life. Fox rang me up to say he had put in my leave for the first of next month, but I am very doubtful about it as I fancy we shall be going to rest soon. Commanding officers are not supposed to take their leave whilst in rest, as " rest " is always spelt " intensive training." What the men really want is to sit still and get themselves clean.

TEMPLEUX, 20TH FEBRUARY, 1918

There was a battle this afternoon. Ruby Wood overlooks all our lines and for a long time we have suspected that the Hun does most of his observation from there. A big concentration was ordered for 4 o'clock, in which the 6-in. howitzers took part, as well as all our own batteries. It made quite a noise. Brother Boche took it very quietly at the time, but as soon as it was dark he had his revenge and put down a very heavy barrage on our front line. Our people thought they were being attacked and sent up the S.O.S. with the usual result. We have not been bombed again this evening, which I put down to the fact that there has been a ground mist.

TEMPLEUX, 21ST FEBRUARY, 1918

At 4.50 this morning I was wakened up by a tremendous hostile barrage which seemed to be on my front. At the same time very heavy machine-gun and rifle fire broke out, almost the heaviest I have ever heard. Immediately after, Hobday rang me up to say he had seen the S.O.S. rocket on the left of our zone. I sent out S.O.S. at once and reported to division. For the next quarter of an hour I was talking on the 'phone incessantly, by which time it seemed clear that the attack was off my zone to the left. I slowed down to half-rates in order to cover the flank of the next division if they were being attacked. Things began to quieten down by 5.30, and we ceased fire. I have not been able to find out yet what happened, but I understand that the Hun raided us. It must have been a big raid judging by the amount of shelling the Hun did. It is extraordinary how difficult it is to get any information out of the infantry on these occasions. They never seem to know anything, and depend on the gunners. Wilmot and I rode over to the wagon-lines and lunched there with Bevis. I inspected most of the horses and was glad to find them looking very well after all the cold and mud. Hart of D/108 was there on a visit to Hobday. He gave me all the news of my old brigade. There are only three of the officers left who were with me a year ago, out of nearly thirty!

TEMPLEUX, 22ND FEBRUARY, 1918

My birthday again. I believe I have now reached the age of thirty-five, which is quite respectable, though still quite young for a colonel. It has been a misty and wet day, and I have spent the day in studying aeroplane photos. I have just received a photo of these headquarters and A and C batteries' positions. I am sorry to find that C shows up rather badly in spite of all the trouble that has-been taken to camouflage the pits. I have come to the conclusion-that it is impossible to hide gun-pits if they are sited right out in the open. A, who are dug into a bank, really are quite invisible. The gramophone spring has broken again.

TEMPLEUX, 23RD FEBRUARY, 1918

Richardson brought the C.R.A. of the relieving division to see me this morning. I took them round all my batteries and also most of the 107th as well, as we had to pass them. D/107 have made a really wonderful gun-pit ; the whole thing is lined with wood and fitted up like a house. The serjeant in charge of that gun is a carpenter by trade and amuses himself by decorating the interior of his gun-pit. It was really a wonderful piece of work, but I could not help thinking that he might have been employed on something more useful. I hear the commander-in-chief and a large staff have been riding about. I got no lunch, and was quite tired by the time I got back, just before tea.

TEMPLEUX, 24TH FEBRUARY, 1918

Wilmot and I have been sorting out old maps and papers and getting ready to hand over. We have been so long in this area that we have accumulated a terrible lot of stuff, and I am very much afraid we shall have some difficulty in moving. We have lately acquired another G.S. wagon by some means which will not bear investigation, but until I can also " find " a team of mules to draw it we shall not be too well off. I went up to Farm O.P. this afternoon and got a bunch of snowdrops for G., which one of my young officers is going to take on leave to-night. I wonder if they will be fresh on the 1st.

(11 p.m.) We have been listening to the gramophone since dinner and feeling very content with the world. We were in the middle of the Dance of the Moorish Slaves from " Aïda " when the first shell arrived. It landed right in my quarry, about 10 yards from our tin hut ; within the next two minutes we got some thirty of them, all right on top of us. The lamp was blown out and,

being acetylene, made a horrid smell till someone found a match and lit it. I made everyone lie down alongside the inner wall, whilst the lumps of chalk hit our tin roof. It *was* a nasty surprise ! All the weeks that this place has been used as headquarters there has never been a single shell, nor has he ever registered anything near here. To give the devil his due, it was wonderful shooting. Every shell landed within fifty yards of our hut, and most of them right into the quarry. I have been wondering ever since how he has found us out. The air photos give very little indication, and there has been hardly any movement round here lately. I can only imagine that he has had a spy through our lines, which would not be difficult here, or else he has captured a prisoner who has given the show away. Anyway, our sense of complete security is gone, as he may do it again now at any moment of the day or night. This evening they were only pip-squeak H.E. shells, but he often follows that up with 5·9's or more probably the next thing will be gas-shell. I made everyone get their gas-helmets.

TEMPLEUX, 25TH FEBRUARY, 1918

As soon as I had breakfast this morning I went out to see where last night's shells had landed. The nearest was in the quarry, about 6 feet from the doctor's hut, and some 20 feet from our tin hut where we all were. That was doubtless the one that put out the lamp. There were two just over the quarry and a dozen 30 or 40 yards short of it. Truly wonderful shooting considering the brute had not registered the place. I was very much surprised to find that they were not pip-squeaks, as I had supposed, but either a 4·2 howitzer or a 4·1 long gun. We dug the fuse out of the holes and found it was quite a new sort, very heavy and made of rough cast-iron. I walked over to see Welch in the afternoon and watched the Hun trying to barrage the Templeux-Roisel road. He also had a hate on the Farm O.P., where I picked the snowdrops for G. yesterday afternoon. It is lucky I did not leave it till to-day, as I imagine he has pretty well ploughed up the place and the snowdrops would have been destroyed. They looked so pretty that I only picked about half of them ; if I had known the brute would shoot it up I would have taken them all. It is possible he saw me yesterday, as he opened on the place just at the same time to-day. Perhaps he thought someone went there at the same time every day. There were some G.S. wagons on the road that were very nearly caught.

TEMPLEUX, 26TH FEBRUARY, 1918

The brigade commander of the relieving brigade turned up at 11 o'clock and I took him round all the batteries. We rode all the way and managed to do it in a little over two hours, including Bevis and his howitzers who are lent to the division on our right. I had a very near escape coming out of Templeux—there was a German 'plane over us and our Archies were firing at it. A dud shell came down and buried itself in the ground 6 feet in front of my horse's nose. Fortunately it did not explode. My black mare paid no attention to it whatever. We were very late by the time we got to B Battery, so I decided to take the short cut over the hill, which is in full view of the Hun for about three hundred yards. We galloped across and he did not have a shot at us. He would have to be very quick, as it does not take long to get across the open and under cover again. I went through the defence scheme with the new man, but he was not very intelligent and I don't think he understands very much about it. The people relieving us are third-line Territorials, and have not been out very long. I had a letter from General Sheppard to-day, thanking me for the print of Guillemont. He says it is very good, and reminds him of the horrid place. It certainly is the only realistic war picture that I have seen yet. I am wondering if it will sell well.

TEMPLEUX, 27TH FEBRUARY, 1918

I had just gone to bed at midnight last night when the S.O.S. went up. The night O.P. repeated the rocket and rang me up. The guns got going very quickly. There was very heavy rifle and machine-gun fire. The rockets were repeated all along my front and I began to think it was a real attack. As usual the infantry could give no information, but we eventually established that the Hun had tried to raid our trenches just off my zone on the right. This morning I hear that he did not get through our wire as he was met by heavy rifle fire and bombs. A new doctor called Kennedy has arrived to take Mortimer's place till he comes back from leave.

TEMPLEUX, 28TH FEBRUARY, 1918

A day of excitements. After lunch I got a message from the infantry brigadier asking me if I had heard from my brigade major. I told him nothing special, but soon after the staff lieutenant arrived with a message to say that we have just captured a German airman, who says that the great German offensive is fixed for the 2nd March. He is reported to have said that it will be north of our division, but will extend as far south as my zone. I went round the batteries and warned them. I have ordered up extra ammunition to bring them up to five hundred rounds per gun in the battery positions. Also I have said that the emergency rations are to be distributed to-night, and extra water to be got up. All gas respirators are being inspected to-day and everyone warned to be on the alert from now onwards. I have said that all ranks will " stand to " an hour before dawn, starting to-morrow. I don't think there is anything else that can be done as we have had everything ready for some time now. I have sent a special warning to the anti-tank guns to be ready. The Hun has been crumping an open field 400 yards away from my H.Q. with 8-in. ever since 3 o'clock, at the rate of about one a minute ; now, at 10 p.m., it is still going on. Heaven knows what he thinks he is shooting at, as there is nothing there. It makes a nasty noise.

TEMPLEUX, 1ST MARCH, 1918

My wedding day, and a very anxious one this time. We are expecting to be attacked at dawn to-morrow and have taken every possible precaution. It is anxious work waiting, but I have every confidence that the Hun will be stopped before he gets as far as the guns. News has just been received that the enemy has attempted to raid the whole of the French front from Switzerland to where they join up ; the report says he has not had much success. At 10.49 p.m. the S.O.S. was reported all along our front ; of course we opened up at once. Spiller on my right was firing hard also ; we kept it up for half an hour, till the Boche fire died down and then stopped. I very much doubt if there was any attack.

TEMPLEUX, 2ND MARCH, 1918

General Duggan rang me up early this morning and said that the Huns did raid us after all last night. Under cover of the barrage they came over and got into our trenches about the centre of my zone. My S.O.S. lines do not cover the whole of the zone, but have to be switched about according to where they were. Fortunately we were able to locate where the trouble was in time, and I dropped a heavy barrage just behind the raiders. The infantry disposed of three Huns who were left dead in our trenches, two more were captured alive, and the rest were caught in my barrage on their way home. The result is that there are four bodies lying out in No Man's Land this morning, besides the three killed in our trench and the two captured. An expensive raid for the Hun, as we only had one man killed and he failed to get a prisoner for identification. The orderly officer of the relieving brigade has arrived to stay till his own people come. It is rumoured that our rest near Amiens is cancelled and that we remain in this area. As there are no spare billets, it will mean bivouacking in the mud probably. The staff captain talks of getting us two hundred sheets of corrugated iron ; that won't be much use for eight hundred men and eight hundred horses in a snow blizzard. It is snowing, and the snow is lying an inch deep everywhere. It is also blowing two hurricanes.

Templeux, 3rd March, 1918

More of the relieving people have arrived, and to-night one section per battery and the anti-tank guns are relieved. We are not going back to rest near Amiens after all, and the whole division is to remain in support just behind. The staff captain and Wilmot went to see the place and report that there is no accommodation at all, and we shall have to bivouac in the open mud and sleet. It does not sound very promising. It seems that there are plenty of huts round there, but the infantry, etc., who have already been relieved, have spread themselves over the whole place, and the divisional artillery will have to go without.

Boucly, 4th March, 1918

Out of action at last. It has been a horrid day, high wind, and driving rain. Visibility was so bad that it was impossible to register the new guns properly. However, they managed to get a rough registration, which showed that there was nothing serious the matter with the line ; for range they must trust to sight testing. The new Brigade H.Q. arrived after lunch and the reliefs were all completed by 7 o'clock. Wilmot and I walked to Roisel, and got on our horses there. I have seldom known so dark a night—it was impossible to see the road at one's feet. We had a narrow escape, as the enemy fired four large shells from a naval gun into the town a few minutes after we left it. Our horses and grooms had a still nearer escape, as one of the shells burst in the stable where we have kept the officers' horses for the last six weeks. I hear that one of the new brigade's officer's servants was killed, and I imagine they must have lost all their chargers. We had mounted our horses there not ten minutes before. We had a slow and cold ride to the wagon-lines here, as it was too dark to trot much. Dinner was ready when we arrived, and although it was only cold tinned salmon and bread and cheese, we were very glad of it, not having had much to eat all day. I went over to B Battery's mess after dinner and found most of the brigade there, eventually getting to bed at two.

MONTECOURT, 5TH MARCH, 1918

My leave has at last come through. Thirty days, starting on the 8th, which means leaving here the day after to-morrow. I am trying to get off a telegram to G. We marched off from the old wagon-lines at 10 o'clock. It was quite a small column, only sixteen guns and no wagons, as all the latter went yesterday under Welch. I saw those all pass and took them as far as Hancourt, after which Wilmot and I trotted on. The whole division is concentrated here, being in corps reserve and liable to march at one hour's notice. There is practically no accommodation, and most of the men are in tents. We have got an old Nissen hut, without lining and with torn windows—therefore very cold.

MONTECOURT, 6TH MARCH, 1918

I rode round all batteries this morning. B and D are a mile and a half away at Monchy-Lagache. They are all fairly comfortable except A, who are all in tents. I saw some N.C.O.s of the Household Cavalry in the village, who told me their regiments were quite close. I rode out three or four miles in the direction they told me, but could not find them. It has been a glorious day, bright sun, no wind, and the grass just right for galloping. The general came back from leave to-day, so Spiller and I went to tea with him. We spent two hours going through the June Honours List ; as usual I think the only D.S.O. will go to the 107th. I am trying to get it for Hobday.

HÔTEL DE LONDRES, BOULOGNE, 7TH MARCH, 1918

Ridell, who is our new A.A. and D.A.Q.M.G., motored me into Amiens. We started at 8.45 and reached Amiens at 10 o'clock, nearly 50 miles. Our train went at 11.15, so we tried all the shops for the 1914 ribbon. Apparently it is not allowed to be sold in England, but the enterprising French are making it and selling it to the troops out here.

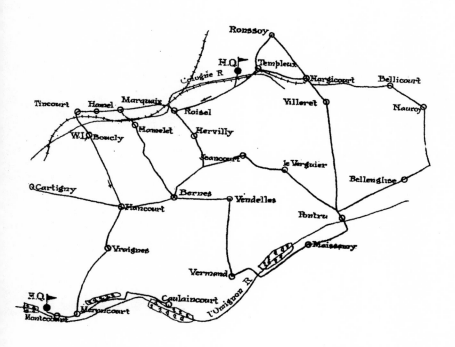

MONTECOURT—RONSSOY, MARCH 1918.

We found a restaurant car on the train and had lunch, before getting to Boulogne at 3 o'clock. We took rooms at my pet little hotel, and had a quite excellent dinner with a bottle of champagne at a little place that Harris told me of, almost next door to Cox.

1, St. James's Terrace, 8th March, 1918

I crossed this morning at 10 and found Tabor on board, who commanded a squadron of the 3rd Hussars at Sialkot. There was a bright sun and no wind, but a good deal of swell ; however, I did not feel sick. I got to Victoria at 8 o'clock and went to 41 as soon as I had got some money and called at my tailor's. They were not expecting me, as my telegram had not arrived, although sent off two days ago. It is scandalous the way telegrams are always detained at Boulogne for forty-eight hours. It may be necessary in the case of civilians, but certainly ought not to be done when they are signed by a responsible senior officer.

In Action, 27th March, 1918 (5 p.m.)

Dearest G.,

Just arrived.

I was on the battle-field twenty-four hours after I left you ! A dreadful journey, as I had to walk a long way. Things are not as bad as they might be. I have half my guns left ; not many officers lost. I have lost *everything* I possessed ! Kit, pistol, glasses, fur-bag, type-writers, and everything ! Don't send out anything yet, as I should never get anything under the present conditions. Real open warfare at last, lovely country, and undamaged houses. The Div. is still going strong and fighting with their tails up.

Yours,
Ralph.

Send on to 41.

This Div. has now met and defeated 7 German Divisions. Send some of my blue paper and envelopes, quick.

In Action, 29th March, 1918

Dearest Grizel,

I arrived at my brigade all right twenty-four hours after I left you. I had a perfectly horrible journey, as there were no proper trains running. We were nine in a second-class carriage all night, and took eleven hours from B—— to A——. The train did not reach the latter place, as it was being very heavily bombed, so I got out and walked into the town. I tried to get some breakfast at our usual hotel, but found it deserted, with pools of blood on the pavement and heaps of broken glass and bricks strewn everywhere. The population was flying in all directions, like during the great retreat in '14. I got a car belonging to a Canadian Press Correspondent to take me to Army H.Q., where I found out where my Corps H.Q. was. I got another lift in a staff car there, and was told where my division H.Q. was, and reached that by motor-lorry by midday. The general lent me a horse, and I rode out to my brigade. My batteries have been very lucky, as we still have half our guns; the rest were lost or destroyed by us the first day, except two of my old battery, which were captured by a surprise attack the morning I arrived. Few casualties to officers. One battalion commander was wounded and two or three more. Unfortunately my best subaltern was killed yesterday. We had a quiet night, and except that I was very cold sleeping on the ground with nothing but my cloak, not too uncomfortable. Nothing happened till about 8 a.m. yesterday, when we were heavily attacked. I cannot describe the whole day; it was too confused, but it was a wonderful experience I would not have missed for anything. We took up four different positions, I retiring one battery at a time when things became too hot. We were firing " open sights " part of the time, and Major Hobday caught a German battery coming into action at a gallop. Our infantry were splendid, fighting every yard of the way back. The Hun did not press us very hard, but came on very steadily, regardless of terrific losses ; our machine-guns mowed him down in hundreds. Our great difficulty was that he was always trying to work round our flanks ; at 10 o'clock he got on my left and rushed up a field battery which caught me with my A and C Batteries before they could limber up. It was a painful five minutes, but I got off better than might have been expected. The batteries went back from position to position as steadily as on a field-day. At one time two of the batteries were caught on a road under a tremendous barrage, which did great execution to the people in front of me. I galloped to the head of the brigade and led them off the road into the open fields and formed line at a trot. The drill was exceedingly good, and we trotted through the barrage into safety, with the loss of only three men and three horses wounded ! By nightfall I found myself with three guns of A and 8 of B still firing in the grounds of a large and fine château, but with only 800 rounds left. At 9 o'clock I got orders to withdraw across a river, which meant a six-mile night march across country in the dark and rain over ground which none of us knew. I found some infantry of my division and joined them, and we made our way over ploughed fields up and down hill, reaching the river at midnight. It was very nervous work, as I knew there were German cavalry patrols not far off, and guns are helpless in the dark and on the march. I got an escort of a company of Fusiliers to protect my rear. My general met me at the river and told me to come into action at once to protect the crossing. I reconnoitred by a good moon and got my remaining guns into action by 4 a.m., after which I went to sleep on a bed of wet leaves under a tree, and slept till 7 this morning, when I continued my reconnaissance.

I have no time to write another letter, so show this to my father and mother, and tell them that it was *exactly* like an old-fashioned field-day at Aldershot, except that the country is black with batteries. Quite the most interesting day I have had out here.

I have lost *everything* I possess, so please send me at once by post a scarf, a pair of lined leather gloves. Please order 2 shirts and 3 pairs of thin white socks to be sent at once. My new waterproof was ripped to pieces by a splinter, so try and get me another. The one I want is called a " Mattamack " : it lives upstairs in Conduit Street, about six doors from Bond Street on the south side. Height 5·9 ; chest 42 ; *small* neck (i.e. collar). Cavalry pattern. By post, please. Also a pair of ordinary riding gloves. Please order Hawkes to send at once a lining for steel helmet. Show him my black bowler hat as pattern. Also 2 quarter-pound tins of tobacco from Dunhill, No. 850, *not* in cartridges. We can buy nothing now. Also 1 Jaeger blanket medium weight and very wide, and a small pillow. I am afraid this is an awful list, but I am destitute !

Will you go to Aquascutum, 100 Regent Street, and order me a valise like a quilt that they make ? But not to be sent yet. I am afraid this will make your head go round, but do try and disentangle it. I am in a cottage to-night with a fire and very sleepy.

Your affectionate husband,
RALPH.

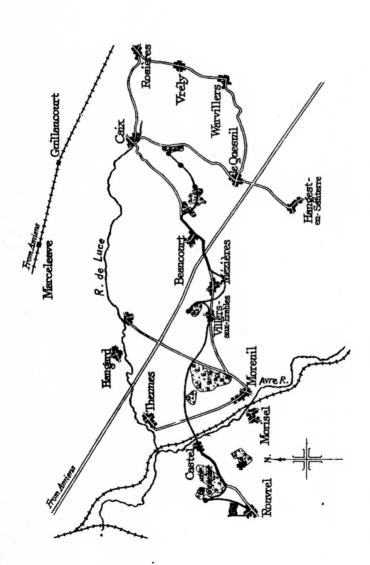

THE LAST ACTION, MARCH 1918.

O.H.M.S., ROYAL DOCKYARD, WOOLWICH, 7TH APRIL, 1918
LADY GRIZEL HAMILTON,
     1, St. James's Terrace, Regent's Park, N.W.

7/4. Regret to inform you that Lieut.-Colonel Hon. R. G. A. Hamilton, 106th Brigade, R.F.A., was killed in action 31st March. Lord Derby expresses his sympathy.

Artillery Office Records, Stanhope, Charlton, S.E.7.

1st April, 1918.

DEAR LADY GRIZEL HAMILTON,
     I have a sad letter to write to you, for it is to tell you that your husband was killed in action about midday yesterday.

He was riding round the batteries with his trumpeter when the enemy suddenly started shelling heavily, and a large shell burst right under his horse, killing him instantly.

We recovered the body yesterday afternoon and buried him late last night in the cemetery at Rouvrel, south-east of Amiens. A cross, with a durable inscription, has been placed on the grave, and the Authorities have been notified of the exact spot.

I don't know how to express my sorrow at the loss of my colonel and above all of my sympathy for you, and his whole family, in having to bear so sad a blow. It was so terribly sudden that even now I can scarcely realise its truth. Only two hours before he had left us exceptionally bright and cheerful in spite of the hard and uncomfortable time we had all been having.

It is poor comfort, I will admit, but I am thankful to be able to assure you that death was absolutely instantaneous.

The only personal belongings that we have been able to recover so far are a small prayer-book, a pocket-book, and a bunch of keys. These I will send on to you. In the confusion and stampede of horses caused by the shelling, his rosary, and possibly other things, may have been picked up by someone else before any of our officers reached the spot. If so, they will be sent on immediately. Father McCann made a thorough search all round the spot this morning, but has so far been unsuccessful.

As his adjutant for the last seven months, I have been constantly with him in all sorts of circumstances, and I have never ceased to realise how much I owe to him for his kindness, his help, and his support, and to admire and respect him as my commanding officer.

Everyone was full of admiration for the spirit he showed in returning long before his leave was up, and in forcing his way back to his own brigade at once, in spite of orders to report at the base.

The grave, I can assure you, will be well cared for so long as we are in the neighbourhood.

If there is anything else that I can tell you, or anything you would like me to do for him, I will gladly do so at any time.

Yours very sincerely,

RAYMOND WILMOT.

Printed in the United Kingdom
by Lightning Source UK Ltd.
118351UK00001B/31